KNIGHT RIDER

30 YEARS OF A LONE CRUSADER AND HIS

TALKING CAR

Joe Huth IV

David Bronstein

This book has not been approved, licensed, or sponsored by any entity involved in creating or producing *Knight Rider*, the television series, or any of its incarnations.

ISBN: 9781478221470

Printed in the United States of America

Table of Contents

Acknowledgements

The authors would like to graciously thank the following people, who were instrumental in bringing this book together:

AJ Palmgren

Martin Grant

Paul Nuthall

Mark Puette

From David Bronstein:

Thank you to everyone who helped and encouraged me: Trevor Fincham, Nathim Warmington, Monica Bronstein, Diggy, Sabine Coiffard. Special thanks to Jack Gill. This book is for Jacques and Alice.

Also, the authors would also like to extend a special thanks to the people who shared their memories of working on *Knight Rider:*

Burton Armus (Writer/Producer, Episodes 44-84)

Daphne Ashbrook (Katherine Granger, "A Knight in Shining Armor")

Guerin Barry (Photographer, "Custom Made Killer")

Lance Burton (Austin Templeton, "Deadly Knightshade")

Paul Carafotes (Velez, "Knight Song")

Eloy Casados (Raul, "Knight Flight to Freedom")

Dave Cass (Alex Webster, "Not a Drop to Drink"; Louis, "Knight By a Nose")

Catherine Clinch (Writer, "Just My Bill")

Phillip Coccioletti (Mario Lutenzo, "Slammin' Sammy's Stunt Show Spectacular")

Nicolas Coster (Paul Manley, "Return to Cadiz")

David Cowgill (Scott, "A Knight in Shining Armor")

Ed Crick (Eddie Dexter, "K.I.T.T. vs. K.A.R.R.")

Brian Cutler (Bar Manager, "Pilot"; Dobie, "Custom K.I.T.T.")

Alex Daniels (Lonny Spencer, "Good Day at White Rock")

Paul Diamond (Writer, "Knight Racer")

Alan Feinstein (Mark Taylor, "Knights of the Fast Lane")

Julie Friedgen (Writer, "Big Iron")

Richard Fullerton (Frank, "Knight of the Juggernaut")

Dick Gautier (The Chameleon, "Knight of the Chameleon")

Andy Gill (Stuntman, Episodes 3-84)

Jack Gill (Stunt Coordinator, Episodes 1-84)

Bruce Golin (Associate Producer, Episodes 46-84)

Bruce Gray (Russell Forbes, "Just My Bill")

Gino Grimaldi (Producer, Episodes 44-84)

Tyler Ham (Property Owner, "Knight of the Drones")

Richard Herd (Lyle Jastrow, "Knight Strike")

Rebecca Holden (April Curtis, Episodes 22-43)

John Hostetter (Police Man, "Trust Doesn't Rust")

Fitzhugh G. Houston (Speaker, "Just My Bill"; Brewster, "Brother's Keeper")

Aharon Ipale (Durante/Kurt Rolands, "The Scent of Roses")

Harvey Jason (Marco Berio, "Killer K.I.T.T.")

Marvin Karon (Marty Keen, "The Final Verdict")

Lenore Kasdorf (Lori Wainwright, "Lost Knight"; Karen Bennett, "Fright Knight")

Sandra Kronemeyer (Monica Brown, "Knight in Retreat")

Harvey Laidman (Director, "Nobody Does It Better", "Soul Survivor", "Knight in Disgrace", "Custom Made Killer", "Circus Knights", "Out of the Woods")

Judy Landers (Mikki, "Forget Me Not"; Sheila, "Knight Strike")

Janet Julian Lansbury (Jody Tompkins, "The Ice Bandits")

Stephen Liska (Casey, "Silent Knight")

Leigh Lombardi (Croupier, "Knight By a Nose")

Robert Lyons (Jeffery Cavanaugh, "K.I.T.T.nap")

Mario Marcelino (Julio Rodriguez, "Race for Life")

Mary Kate McGeehan (Jennifer Knight, "Knight of the Juggernaut")

Stephen Meadows (Matt Erikson, "Knight Behind Bars")

Alan Myerson (Director, "The Topaz Connection", "Return to Cadiz", "Merchants of Death")

Bruce Neckels (Lew Jonas, "Knight of a Thousand Devils")

Taafe O'Connell (Denise Grant, "Halloween Knight")

Jack O'Halloran (Rawleigh, "Knight Strike")

Jeff Osterhage (John Stanton, "K.I.T.T. vs. K.A.R.R.")

Peter Parros (RC3, Episodes 64-84)

Allen Payne (Hair/Make-up Department Head, Episodes 22-84)

Babette Props (Sally Flynn, "Ten Wheel Trouble")

Rudy Ramos (Roberto Laguna, "Hearts of Stone")

Peter Mark Richman (Klaus Bergstrom, "Goliath Returns"; Kleiss, "Many Happy Returns")

Michael D. Roberts (Jackson, "Pilot")

Joel Rogosin (Supervising Producer, Season 1-2)

William Sanderson (The Rev, "Trust Doesn't Rust")

Gerald Sanford (Producer, Season 3)

Wendy Schaal (Jamie Downs, "The Nineteenth Hole")

Marty Schiff (Cab Driver, "Knightmares")

John Alan Schwartz (Writer, "Slammin' Sammy's Stunt Show Spectacular";

"The Final Verdict")

Hannah L. Shearer (Producer, Season 1)

Ann Turkel (Adrianne Margeaux, "Soul Survivor", "Goliath Returns"; Bianca

Morgan, "Knight in Retreat")

In Their Own Words:

Rebecca Holden ("April Curtis")

(Actress, *Knight Rider* Season 2)

I cherish my memories of my time on *Knight Rider*. It was an honor to work on a show that has been so embraced by the fans and that has had such longevity---not only nationally, but internationally. It is truly profound that a television show has resonated in viewers' hearts in such a remarkable way, and that it could still to this day be serving as a catalyst to bring people together, allowing them to connect and forge friendships through their common love for it.

Glen Larson, in his brilliance, created a morality play that clearly delineated good and evil; it truly entertained, but it was more than mere escapism, because it served to teach values to young people and encouraged them to make better life choices. It inspired them to believe that one individual truly could "make a difference".

Any television series is a creative endeavor that requires immense collaborative effort, and we were so blessed to have such an extraordinary team. David, of course, WAS "The *Knight Rider*"; he embodied our hero with perfection and with heart. Edward was a true gentleman.... and indeed a gentle man. Bill Daniels gave K.I.T.T. his personality and soul. Our producers, writers, directors, crew, stunt guys, music composers, car designers and builders---every integral component contributed to the show's specialness.

For me, it was a true joy to play my character; April was smart, resourceful, creative and yet had a sense of humor and never took herself too seriously. She was an honorable person of considerable integrity, tremendous loyalty for her colleagues, and a steadfast commitment to fighting crime alongside them. I was privileged to play a character who was and continues to be a terrific role model for young women.

Photo courtesy of Rebecca Holden

The show's popularity has opened so many doors and allowed me to tour all over the world with my music, bringing fascinating places, rich experiences and lasting friendships into my life in abundance. As I continue to meet fans at the *Knight Rider* festivals and conventions around the globe and receive correspondence from them, I remain humbled and awed to have been a part of an entity that could touch lives in such a meaningful way.

Rebecca Holden

August 4, 2011

In Their Own Words:

Burton Armus

(Producer/Writer, *Knight Rider* Seasons 3-4)

LIFE BEFORE *KNIGHT RIDER*

Before I went to Hollywood, I was a police officer. I loved my job and I have wonderful memories of my time with the New York Police Department. When I started out, I was 22 and physically fit and looking back I do miss those days. I got into television because I was an advisor that people would use when they were shooting police dramas. I started out writing screenplays of my own and then *Kojak* started. Writing scripts was all I knew in Hollywood. I was new to the whole process. I also wrote an episode for *The Streets of San Francisco*. People could see that I was able to meet deadlines and get scripts in on time. My career went from strength to strength.

I worked on *Street Hawk* immediately before *Knight Rider*, but that show got canceled after just one season. The bike was a lot like K.I.T.T. in terms of the story you were seeing but the show did not take off. So, I became available because *Street Hawk* was over. It could have been someone different - it just happened to be me.

THE FIRST EPISODE/ HARVEY LAIDMAN

I had seen *Knight Rider* before I worked on it. It was good clean fun, and it was good for me to work on this because I had done action shows before. I knew the characters and how they worked before I started on the show. I remember my first episode of *Knight Rider* that I worked on. I was the producer and I wrote the episode called "Custom Made Killer". I was brought in to deliver the show on time and within budget. That particular script that I wrote was known as a speed script. We shot it over 7 days. We didn't want to go over because that was money. Once I was on the show, we didn't go over. My job was to balance the sheets and make the show work. Harvey Laidman directed that episode and he was very confident and a good man. We were good friends and I know that he directed quite a few episodes of the show, along with directing the first episode I was involved in. I always wish him very well.

PRESSURES AND INTERNAL PROBLEMS

When I took over, the show was shutting down and I was brought in to help. There were quite a few people on the crew that needed weeded out. They were getting too comfortable and the show needed refreshed behind the scenes. There were some arguments and disagreements and some of the crew were there because David Hasselhoff wanted them to be there. Some had to go because it wasn't a pleasant time. So, there was a lot of trouble at first. There were many conflicts and a lot of tension. There was a lot of pressure to get the show in on time and it was costing them a lot of money. At that time, the crew did not help because everyone wanted to run the show and people were not working together, so the pressure was there.

BUDGETS

The budget of each episode is a whole study in and of itself. I was responsible to get each episode in for between $1 and 1.2 million dollars. Now, that didn't all go on what you saw on the screen. That budget was everything - locations, set dressings, salaries, etc. The real figure of what went on screen was around $600,000. It was my job to stay within that budget. This was no different for Season 4. We still had exactly the same budget - it was not lowered.

REUSING OLD FOOTAGE

We did reuse footage, especially for the last season, but this was not because of budget restraints. We owned that footage, we had paid for that footage the first time, and if you have a speeding car panning down the road, it is easy just to reuse that footage instead of going out on location and shooting it again. Bottom line is that the footage was the property of Universal Studios and we were going to reuse it again.

PROCESS OF WRITING FOR TELEVISION

For the process of writing television, you had five steps. As the producer, I could come right in and stop the process after the first step, which was the outline. I could take a decision right there to carry it on or have it changed. The time process of writing a story for *Knight Rider* was based on the confidence of the writer and how good he/she was. If we had an old pro you would be looking at having a new story in two weeks or just under. If it was a new writer, you may have a time of two months, that's how it worked. Ideally, we liked to try and stay 3 scripts in front of the episode that had just aired, but that was usually very difficult to do.

THE CAST

David Hasselhoff and I did not see eye to eye. I didn't get on with him and we had quite a few disagreements. I thought that the show went to his head a little. It seemed that he believed he was Michael Knight. He was not the star of the show though, the car was.

Edward Mulhare was from a different school of acting from the rest of the cast. He was from the stage. He was a wonderful actor and a pleasant man. Because he was getting old at the time, sometimes he would have trouble with his lines, but he would always be able to bring it together when he needed to.

Peter Parros was brought in and he was excellent. He was very good because he did what he was told and got on with it in a professional manner.

I called Patricia McPherson the 'Rain Set' because most of her scenes were interior shots in the mansion or in the truck. So every time it rained, she was inside a rain set. She did help guest stars with their lines in between takes. I remember she had such an excellent memory for remembering lines, so people really appreciated that from her. As for her acting, if I am being honest she was not the best. I think she thought she was but her role could have been filled by 100 different actresses. She was a sweet person.

William Daniels was very professional and a pleasure to share company with. He had the best job in Hollywood. He would come in to the studio for a few days every two weeks and read for K.I.T.T.'s part, just him and the microphone. He would usually read two episodes worth and return in a fortnight. If you broke it down, he probably worked twenty minutes a day. I remember sometimes he would bring his wife or some friends to the reading. He was the star of the show.

PAST PRODUCERS

Robert Cinader was a very confident man, a class act. He knew his stuff, but unfortunately he died soon after *Knight Rider* started to air. Joel Rogosin was very good - another confident guy, but he left after two years.

Robert Foster had no idea how to produce for television. He had a contract so his name would appear on screen for credit only. We ended up writing together for the season 4 opener "Knight of the Juggernaut".

DIRECTORS

Georg Fenady - A wonderful man that has sadly passed away. He was very good at what he did and we became good friends. Even today, I will visit his family and usually I spend Thanksgiving at his house.

Sidney Hayers - The Englishman. Sidney knew what he was doing and was another regular we had on the show. He was a great guy. I worked with him many times. I remember we had some memorable shoots down in Mexico on other shows after *Knight Rider*.

Winrich Kolbe - Winrich was technically very gifted. He was very capable behind the lens. I believe he had just started in the business and was more used to being an assistant director at the time. You would watch him work on the set and he was very well organized. When you look at the episodes he directed, you can see he had done a great job. He could get cranky sometimes and I remember him being shy and nervous at other times. A great guy.

When I look back, *Knight Rider* was a one hour slice of entertainment from a much more innocent time in both television and in society in general.

Burton Armus

December 10, 2011

In Their Own Words:

Alan Myerson

(Director, "The Topaz Connection", "Return to Cadiz" & "Merchants of Death")

My favorite off screen moment of any of the episodes was early in the first season shortly after the 1st episode aired. We were shooting some tow shots in an outlying area of L.A. (maybe West Covina?) where we were towing K.I.T.T. and David Hasselhoff in a suburban strip mall area and shooting them from the towing camera car. We needed to go around the block several times to get the shot with all the dialog that was scripted. As far as we knew, *Knight Rider* was virtually unknown to the American TV public but by the second time around the block the word was out that *Knight Rider* (and David) were there. Suddenly, the curbs and streets were crowded with people, many of them running up to the car to try to get David's autograph. Of course, this made it impossible to shoot the scene but my fondest memory was seeing David's face as he realized he was now a star! I've worked with many stars and had the occasional opportunity to see them made but I've never known anyone to delight and glory in the moment and experience with the sheer joy that David did.

David and Edward were obviously from different schools of acting but both felt strongly that they were there to do a job -- and they did it. There seemed to be, on the surface at least, a mutual respect for the work and each other.

Alan Myerson

August 4, 2011

In Their Own Words:

Allen Payne

(Hair/Make-up Department Head, Episodes 22-84)

I did every *Knight Rider* episode after the first season, the first being the one with Anne Lockhart called "Return to Cadiz". I was David's haircutter, as well as the haircutter for everyone else on the show. I then did some movies of the week with David, followed by ten years of *Baywatch*. After *Baywatch*, I traveled with David all over the world as his personal liaison, just as I had during the *Knight Rider* days.

David and *Knight Rider*

David was one of the best stars on the Universal lot as far as meeting and greeting people. He was a fantastic guy - and he still is today. If we were on the lot shooting, we always had one of our hero cars standing by. David would grab me and we would jump in that car and he'd say, "Let's go raid the tram". He would get in the car and drive by the tram and light up the tires in a 180 The people in the tram thought it was a stunt driver. David would stop the car and the tram would stop. When he would get out of the car, the people would just start applauding. We used to have these cards we would give out to the people on the tram that would have his name on it. Another time, we took the car and we got it stuck in the icicle tunnel. We couldn't get out because the tunnel rotated. Finally, the guy had to come and shut the thing down to get us out of there.

David has the quickest wit of anyone I know. He always has an answer. As an example, he was being interviewed during the *Knight Rider* days and the reporter asked him how it felt to play second fiddle to a car. He quickly replied, "Let me tell you something about that car. That car is the focal point of our show. It's given heart and soul and comedy and it's voiced by a very talented actor, William Daniels. I don't consider it playing second fiddle to a fine actor like William Daniels." That was just such a great answer. I'm sure David remembers it, but it's not something he would bring up again. But for me, it just stuck because he really just nailed the answer.

The Stuntmen

A lot of times, I had wigs on the stunt guys like Matt McColm so they would resemble David. Well, Matt did a jump for us, and when he landed, his head went right into the steering column. There was a big gash in his forehead and the blood was going everywhere. I had a wig on him and I ran up to the car because they were going to take him to the hospital and I had to get the wig off. I did and jumped out of the way so the other guys could take care of him. I didn't think he would want to go to the hospital with that wig on. Thankfully, Matt was fine.

I have a picture of David and Jack Gill from 1986 when they told us that there wouldn't be another season. Jack Gill is sitting on a table looking very, very glum and David was talking to him saying, "It will be okay", because Jack did so much of our driving and was really an integral part of the show.

David Hasselhoff

David is like a brother to me. In 1983, we won the best hairstylist award. It was the same year that David won the People's Choice Award and he was very excited. Having a friend like David is like having Tom Brady on your team. You always get the best rooms and the best table in the restaurant. Regarding that, David once told me, "That's the good thing. The bad thing is that everybody watches you eat".

David and I were in a New Year's Day parade in 1984. At the time, David was promoting these little rag balls. They were like a baseball only soft. I was riding in the parade with him and I was in the back seat of the car down low. All of a sudden, David said, "Throw out the rag balls". So, I started throwing them out and all these kids started surrounding our car saying, "The *Knight Rider*! *The Knight Rider*!". The guy who was running the parade comes over to us and yells at David, "Don't throw anything else out of this car!" David says, "OK". About 50 feet down the road, David turns around to me and says, "Throw out the rag balls". The parade coordinator just snubbed David after that.

A lot of people don't know this about David, but every time we went to a city, we would always go to a Children's Hospital and we would bring all of our cards and pictures. David knew that those kids were all *Knight Rider* fans. David never really got publicity about it. I don't think he cared about it. He always felt that having a show like *Knight Rider* was always about the kids and that's why he did that.

Allen Payne

February 20, 2012

KNIGHT RIDER

SEASON ONE (1982-1983)

Starring:

David Hasselhoff as Michael Knight

Edward Mulhare as Devon Miles

Patricia McPherson as Bonnie Barstow

William Daniels as the voice of K.I.T.T.

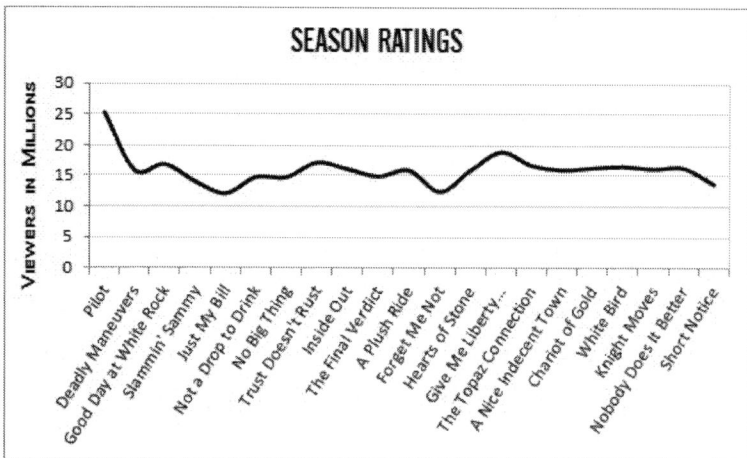

SEASON RATINGS

PROD. # 57309

Syndicated Two Part PROD. #57375 / 57376

Script History:

March 18, 1982 (Spec. Run)

April 7, 1982 (Spec. Run)

June 25, 1982 (F.R.)

July 2, 1982 (F.R.)

July 8, 1982 (F.R.)

July 13, 1982 (F.R.)

July 13, 1982 - 2nd rev. (F.R.)

July 15, 1982 (F.R.)

July 16, 1982 (F.R.)

PILOT (TWO HOUR SERIES PREMIERE)

Also known as: "Knight of the Phoenix"

Written By: Glen A. Larson

Directed By: Daniel Haller

Original Airdate: September 26, 1982 (Sunday, 8:00 PM) (30.3%; 25,240,000)

NBC Rerun #1: January 7, 1983 (Friday, 8:00 PM) (26.7%; 22,240,000)

NBC Rerun #2: May 13, 1983 (Friday, 8:00 PM) (24.6%; 20,490,000)

Filming Dates: July 8-26, August 18-19, 26, 1982

"One man can make a difference, Michael."

-Wilton Knight

Crew: William Martin (Film Editor), David Howe (Film Editor), Seymour Klate (Art Director), Charles R. Davis (Art Director), Frank P. Beascoechea (Director of Photography), Harker Wade (Producer), Stu Phillips (Music), Richard Friedman (Set Decorations), Hal Gausman (Set Decorations), John R. McDonald (Sound), Alan Bernard (Sound), Mark Malis (Casting), Ron Stephenson (Casting), Frank Crawford (Unit Production Manager), James A. Westman (Unit Production Manager), Ron Martinez (1st Assistant Director), Don Edward Wilkerson (2nd Assistant Director), Herb Adelman (2nd Assistant Director), Walt Jenevein (Sound Effects Editor), Jerry Cohen (Music Editor), Jean-Pierre Dorleac (Costume Designer), Don Snyder (Costume Supervisor), Robert Ellsworth (Costume Supervisor), Jeremy Swan (Make-up), Dick Dawson (Make-up), Ora Tillman Green (Hairstylist), Tim Jones (Hairstylist), Robert Bralver (Stunt Coordinator), Jerry Summers (Stunt Coordinator)

Guest Cast: Phyllis Davis (Tanya Walker), Pamela Susan Shoop (Maggie), Lance LeGault (Security Officer Craig Gray), Noel Conlon (William Benjamin), Michael D. Roberts (Jackson), Bert Rosario (Browne), Richard Anderson (Dr. Ralph Wesley), Vince Edwards (Fred Wilson), Richard Basehart (Wilton Knight), Edmund Gilbert (Charles Acton), Shawn Southwick (Lonnie), Brian Cutler (Bar Manager), Barret Oliver (Buddy), Robert Phillips (Symes), Alma L. Beltran (Luce), Ed Hooks (Guard), Tyler Murray (Sally), Victoria Harned (Doris), Larry Anderson (Michael Long), Charles Napier (Carney), Herb Jefferson, Jr. (Muntzy), John Quade (Dolan), Harold "Hal" Frizzell (Comtron Security Guard), Jack Gill (Demolition Derby Driver)

Dying billionaire Wilton Knight recruits an injured police officer to help fight criminals who are above the reach of the law, with help from a talking, computerized supercar named K.I.T.T.

A Look Back:

Michael D. Roberts starred as Jackson in *Knight Rider's* very first adventure, playing a petty thief who was hell bent on taking K.I.T.T. for a joyride with his partner in crime, Browne (Bert Rosario). "I remember the audition and, interestingly, Bert Rosario auditioned at the same time. We had a tremendous connection and chemistry during the audition."

Roberts confirms that the show's creator was there to oversee the production. "Glen Larson was at the audition, which is something that doesn't usually happen. I had just starred in *The Fall Guy* along with Richard Burton and, based upon that success, Mr. Larson auditioned me directly." That episode of *The Fall Guy* was titled "The Reluctant Travelling Companion" and, coincidentally, Roberts' character was also named Jackson.

Roberts has fond memories of working with Bert Rosario. "Bert was really fun to work with as we both seemed to understand the comedic nature of what we were doing," enthuses Roberts. Roberts is a huge admirer of Glen Larson. "On the set, I was driving Glen Larson's son's hot-rod Firebird, which was really HOT. As a result, I kept getting admonished for burning rubber every time I pulled out. Then there was K.I.T.T. One is always amazed at the incredible genius and imagination of Glen Larson."

Jackson looked very hip in his leather jacket, pullover and boots and Roberts admits that despite the heat when filming the pilot episode, he got to choose what he wanted to wear. "Unfortunately, the wardrobe department of Universal no longer exists today, but back in those days, one could go into the wardrobe department and find clothing that spanned all the years of the studio. As a result, I felt like a little kid in a candy store. The heat during filming meant nothing to me as I got to choose every piece of wardrobe myself. That included the cowboy boots worn by at least 500 cowboys throughout the 1950's. The words 'broken in' were an understatement. I felt like I was walking on a cloud and who hasn't dreamed of hitting their marks in cowboy boots, blue jeans and a well-worn leather jacket? Marlon Brando, thank you so much," jokes Roberts.

Welcome aboard the Knight 2000 (Photo courtesy of Christopher Orlando)

Throughout the course of the series, fans have witnessed petty thieves to millionaire crooks attempting to break into K.I.T.T., but Roberts was the very first one to successfully do so. "That's very interesting, because in the first episode of *Barretta*, I'm driving down the street in the 'pimp mobile'. So driving K.I.T.T., one could say I had 'come a long way, baby'. Dealing with all the activities of K.I.T.T. was challenging and fun."

After stealing K.I.T.T., it isn't long before everyone's favorite Trans Am puts the crooks in their places, chauffeuring them directly to the local police station by way of the auto cruise and some ejection seats. "As much as I fought to do the stunt myself, in the end out of sheer cowardice and fear I decided to step aside and allow the stunt men to risk their lives. A magnanimous gesture, if I do say so myself."

Because of the show, Roberts was able to make many friendships, including Glen Larson. "We had a wrap party for the pilot at Universal where David (Hasselhoff) and I became good friends for many years. David was very warm and very caring and a hardworking man. You really got that he deserved his success. I have established other friendships that I hold to this day - Glen Larson being one of them."

Roberts had little doubt that *Knight Rider* would end up becoming popular. "I saw the pilot and I did think that the show had longevity. It had all the sweetness the American audience would enjoy. Also, Glen Larson's Midas touch guaranteed success."

Roberts believes that starting from the mid 1970's, American television left its comfort zone and that is when action shows became incredibly popular. "It was a pretty exciting time. TV was in a period of vigor and strength. I was working on the series *Barretta* that basically brought a level of 'street' to television screens and into the homes of everyday people. I played Rooster, a comedic street pimp that would have without question been out of place in the days of *Lucy and Desi*. Shows like *Kojak* and *Starsky and Hutch* took a turn away from fantasy and perfect families to a more realistic level of entertainment."

Brian Cutler was one of the lucky few who guest starred in multiple episodes of *Knight Rider*, starting with the Pilot. He played the bartender at the "House of the Rising Sun" restaurant. However, Cutler came close to being even more well-known in the *Knight Rider* universe. "Prior to David (Hasselhoff) being cast, there was a group of 6 or 8 of us up for the lead role as Michael Knight".

Cutler's scene would act as a macguffin as Michael Knight started his pursuit of Tanya Walker, the lady who had shot him in the face earlier in the episode. "That was a real bar. It was in Reseda in the San Fernando Valley".

Cutler starred alongside both Hasselhoff and Pamela Susan Shoop, the episode's leading lady. "David was very professional. He had just finished a long run in *The Young and the Restless* and was probably relieved to be shooting a series rather than a soap opera. Pamela was very easy to work with and was very nice".

The Pilot was directed by Daniel Haller and Cutler remembers that the director was very confident shooting a new series. "He had his storyboards and shot lists ready and knew what and how he wanted to shoot. He was a very good director, and a very nice man. He always made sure he covered a sequence - close up, wide shot, master, two shot. So however long it takes to get the coverage is what it takes. My scene took four hours to shoot".

Knight Rider creator Glen Larson was on location throughout the majority of the first episode's filming. "Glen was there and fortunately for me, I was lucky (as was Pamela Susan Shoop), because Glen liked our work. He used me in other shows. I consider Glen a good friend".

At that time, nobody could quite predict how successful *Knight Rider* would go on to be, producing an additional 83 episodes over four seasons, a TV movie, two spin off series and scores of memorabilia. "You never know how a show will be received. I starred in *Isis* and I still get emails from around the world because of the positive effect the show had on kids growing up in the 70's. Now, all of these kids have purchased the DVD box sets to share with *their* kids."

Knight Knotes:

- The original airing of the Pilot began with a thirty second teaser:

NBC announcer:

"Tonight, *Knight Rider* The Two Hour Movie Spectacular crashes into your living room!"

Michael:

"I don't believe this."

NBC announcer:

"Well, you better believe it! A lone crusader for justice drives his crime crasher."

Michael:

"The world's most fantastic car."

NBC announcer:

"Together they can do just about anything."

K.I.T.T.:

"After all, we're only human."

Michael:

"Don't press your luck.

NBC announcer:

"Now buckle up for action for the fastest new show on television, *Knight Rider: The Movie!*"

- Michael D. Roberts would go on to play another character named Jackson a few months later in an episode of *The Fall Guy* titled "Reluctant Traveling Companion". Oddly enough, Bert Rosario (Browne) guest starred on the very next episode.

- The scene in which Michael Long is shot by Tanya Walker is reused multiple times in this episode, as well as in "A Good Knight's Work" and "Junk Yard Dog".

- The first two aired episodes do not feature a voiceover in the opening narration.

- *Knight Rider* crew member Harold "Hal" Frizzell appears briefly in this episode as a Comtron security guard. He makes similar brief appearances in "The Final Verdict", "White Bird", "Brother's Keeper", "Ring of Fire", "Knight of the Drones", "Knight Strike", "Knight Behind Bars" and "Fright Knight".

- The tractor trailers used as Comtron trucks can be seen in the background of many future *Knight Rider* episodes throughout the rest of the series. These trucks, painted with red and orange stripes, were part of Universal Studios equipment fleet and were used on many other productions, including *B.J. and the Bear.*

- The helicopter used by Gray and Wilson during the climax of the episode is a Bell 206B Jet Ranger III, registration number N250CA, serial number 2615. This same helicopter can also be seen in *Blue Thunder, Dreamscape, Cobra, Alien Nation, 3 Ninjas* and *Speed.* It is still in service today.

- The airplane that "explodes" at the end of this episode is a 1968 Learjet 24A, registration number N664CL, serial number 167. It re-appears in "Just My Bill" and "The Topaz Connection". Even though the climax of this episode is re-used in season three's "Dead of

Knight", they did manage to acquire this plane one last time to shoot extra scenes! It can also be seen in *Remington Steele* and *The Rockford Files*. Today, it is privately owned by an individual in Idaho.

- This episode was nominated for a 1983 Primetime Emmy for "Outstanding Film Sound Editing for a Series".

Script to Screen:

- Comtron was originally named Caltron Technologies. Watch when Michael takes Maggie back to her apartment - she is saying Caltron but her voice is dubbed to say Comtron.
- Early drafts had Lonnie, not Muntzy, as Michael's partner. Immediately after Michael is shot, Lonnie is killed by Wilson.
- Michael's doctor is named Dr. Miles; Devon's last name is Shire.
- K.I.T.T. was originally presented to Michael by Wilton pulling off a silk sheet off the car.
- Devon toggles a switch to turn K.I.T.T. from normal mode to super mode in which the dash lit up and car roared to life.
- F.L.A.G. was initially called the Knight Foundation for Law and Justice.
- K.I.T.T.'s KNIGHT license plate was from Nevada, not California.

Déjà Vu:

- Stuntman Jack Gill has more small roles in "Inside Out", "Return to Cadiz", "Ring of Fire", "Buy Out", "Knight Strike" and "Knight of the Juggernaut".
- Brian Cutler returns in "Custom K.I.T.T."; Lance LeGault returns in "A Knight in Shining Armor"; Pamela Susan Shoop can be seen in "Knight of the Juggernaut"; and Shawn Southwick plays Rita Wilcox in "Goliath".

Featured Songs:

"Proud Mary (Rollin' on the River)" by Credence Clearwater Revival

"Harden My Heart" by Quarterflash

"Take It Easy" by The Eagles

"Carolina in My Mind" by James Taylor

"Peaceful, Easy Feeling" by The Eagles

"Don't Stop" by Fleetwood Mac

"Third Rate Romance" by Amazing Rhythm Aces

"Hit Me With Your Best Shot" by Pat Benetar

K.I.T.T.'s Capabilities:

- Auto Collision Avoidance, Auto Cruise, Auto-Roof Left, Auto-Roof Right, Eject Left, Eject Right, Medical Scan, Microwave Mobile Line, Oil, Pursuit, Ski Mode, Smoke Release, Turbo Boost

PROD. #57305

$$\left[\begin{array}{c} \text{EPISODE} \\ 2 \end{array}\right]$$

Script History:

August 6, 1982 (F.R.)

August 10, 1982 (F.R.)

August 19, 1982 (F.R.)

August 20, 1982 (F.R.)

August 23, 1982 (F.R.)

DEADLY MANEUVERS

Written By: William Schmidt and Bob Shayne

Directed By: Paul Stanley

Original Airdate: October 1, 1982 (Friday, 9:00 PM) (19.0%; 15,830,000)

NBC Rerun #1: July 15, 1983 (Friday, 9:00 PM) (18.9%; 15,740,000)

Filming Dates: August 20-30, 1982

"Michael, I believe as usual you may have attracted the attention of some very homicidal personalities."

-K.I.T.T.

Crew: R.A. Cinader (Co-Executive Producer), Steven E. de Souza (Producer), Hannah Shearer (Producer), Gilbert Bettman (Associate Producer), Bernadette Joyce (Associate Producer), Morton Stevens (Music), H. John Penner (Director of Photography), Seymour Klate (Art Director), R. Lynn Smartt (Set Decoration), April Webster (Casting), Edwin F. England (Film Editor), John R. McDonald (Sound), Frank Crawford (Unit Production Manager), Phil Bowles (1st Assistant Director), Don Edward Wilkerson (2nd Assistant Director), Walt Jenevein (Sound Effects Editor), Jerry Cohen (Music Editor), George R. Whittaker (Costume Designer), Don Snyder (Costume Supervisor), Robert Bralver (2nd Unit Director-Stunt Coordinator)

Guest Cast: Devon Ericson (Lieutenant Robin Mirian Ladd), Alan Oppenheimer (General Frederick Duncton), Allen Williams (Major Doug Sanderson), Ron Kuhlman (Sergeant Ray Perkins), Andre' Harvey (Lieutenant Hugh Rainey), Thomas Gilleran (Colonel Ernest T. Ladd), Dennis Kerwin (Corporal Cotler), Danil Torppe (Corporal James), James Lough (Military Policeman #2), Peter Harrell (Military Policeman #1), Judy Johns (Corporal Webb), Jeff Silverman (Sanj), Greg Norberg (Soldier), Charles Bazaldua (Fat Soldier)

Michael investigates the mysterious death of an army colonel at the Engleheart Weapons Center.

A Look Back:

Writer Bob Shayne had the distinct honor of being involved in penning the first regular episode of the series, "Deadly Maneuvers". Shayne recalls, "It was the very first episode aired and the second filmed. Glen had moved from Universal to Fox before the series went into production, so he had little or nothing to do with it after the pilot. A new executive producer,

Bob Cinader, had taken over the series. He was a veteran in the business, working on *Emergency!* and possibly *Adam-12*. He had also worked for Jack Webb. The studio brought in Steve de Souza, who, like me, was one of the younger writers under overall deals, to be executive story editor. Steve wrote the first episode script ["Inside Out"] and the studio pleaded with me to write the second.

While "Deadly Maneuvers" was the second episode to air, the first one written after the pilot was de Souza's "Inside Out", which didn't air until later in the season. Shayne recalls, "There was some production trouble with Steve's episode, so they switched the order and ran this one first. I know the story had to do with Robin's father having been killed and I guess the bad guys were after her. I've never watched it. While I thought I was above that kind of material, I soon went to work for and with Glen Larson at Fox. I wrote two pilots for or with him and produced a series for him that was called *Cover Up*. Now, of course, talking cars don't seem quite as ridiculous. In fact, I drive one that drives me crazy with directions when I can't figure out how to turn the voice off."

Knight Knotes:

- Patricia McPherson joins the team as K.I.T.T.'s mechanic, Bonnie Barstow. Also making its first appearance is the Foundation mobile unit, a black 1982 GMC General with a white Dorsey trailer.
- K.I.T.T.'s alpha circuit is damaged here. K.A.R.R. experiences the same malfunction in "K.I.T.T. vs. K.A.R.R."
- The opening scenes of this episode appear again as flashbacks in *Knight Rider 2000*.
- This episode, along with "Good Day at White Rock" and "Halloween Knight", do not utilize the *Knight Rider* theme in the teaser.

- Stuntman Jack Gill: "The car caught on fire during the big climax, then I drove into a field and the field caught on fire!"

Script to Screen:

- Originally, it was K.I.T.T.'s saline converter, not alpha circuit, that was damaged by towing Robin's car. Michael makes a comment that it will be alright as long as they don't go underwater. When Bonnie discovers the damage, Michael tells Bonnie that it's probably a factory defect.

- Devon requests Michael's presence when two lawyers are being attacked by a man named Clay Feltzer over a legal matter. As Michael is explaining K.I.T.T.'s damaged saline converter, a "thud" can be heard when Feltzer throws one of the lawyers against the side of the semi.

- K.I.T.T. is nearly covered in garbage when two officers, Kosko and Weiss, pull a lever on their garbage truck by accident. K.I.T.T. backs up and around a corner, but the two officers think that the car is buried and start to dig it out!

- One of the funniest lines from this episode never made it to screen. Michael calls K.I.T.T. on his comlink from a closet. He tells K.I.T.T. that he needs a status check. K.I.T.T. replies, "Certainly, Michael. You are in a broom closet".

Déjà Vu:

- Thomas Gilleran returns in "Mouth of the Snake"; Alan Oppenheimer can be seen in "Custom Made Killer"; and Allen Williams guest stars in "Knights of the Fast Lane".

Featured Songs:

"Ricky Don't Lose That Number" by Steely Dan

K.I.T.T.'s Capabilities:

- Auto Cruise, Pursuit, Radar, Rocket Booster, Surveillance Mode

PROD. #57303

$$\left[\begin{array}{c} \text{EPISODE} \\ 3 \end{array}\right]$$

Script History:

July 27, 1982 (F.R.)

August 3, 1982 (F.R.)

GOOD DAY AT WHITE ROCK

Written By: Deborah Davis

Directed By: Daniel Haller

Original Airdate: October 8, 1982 (Friday, 9:00 PM) (20.2%; 16,830,000)

NBC Rerun #1: December 31, 1982 (Friday, 9:00 PM) (15.4%; 12,830,000)

NBC Rerun #2: June 17, 1983 (Friday, 9:00 PM) (22.7%; 18,910,000)

Filming Dates: August 9-17, 1982

"Let me have a double cheeseburger with some onions, french fries and a coke. Oh, if you can't handle that, there's a take-out joint across the street."

-Michael

Crew: R.A. Cinader (Co-Executive Producer), Steven E. de Souza (Producer), Hannah Shearer (Producer), Gilbert Bettman (Associate Producer), Bernadette Joyce (Associate Producer), Stu Phillips (Music), H. John Penner (Director of Photography), Seymour Klate (Art Director), R. Lynn Smartt (Set Decoration), April Webster (Casting), Lawrence J. Gleason (Film Editor), John R. McDonald (Sound), Edward D. Markley (Unit Production Manager), Ron Martinez (1st Assistant Director), Don Edward Wilkerson (2nd Assistant Director), Walt Jenevein (Sound Effects Editor), Richard Lapham (Music Editor), George R. Whittaker (Costume Designer), Don Snyder (Costume Supervisor), Robert Bralver (2nd Unit Director-Stunt Coordinator)

Guest Cast: Anne Lockhart (Sherry Benson), Don Stroud (Hilly), James Callahan (Sheriff Bruckner), Keith Mitchell (Davey Benson), Michael Champion (Monk), Robert Dryer (The Priest), Gregory Clemens (Sneaker), Alex Daniels (Big Lonny Spencer), George Fisher (Boss), Kyle Oliver (Big Donny Spencer)

While on vacation in White Rock, Michael helps rid the town of a group of bikers planning a turf war.

A Look Back:

Veteran actor and stuntman Alex Daniels played local White Rock resident Big Lonny Spencer in this instalment. "I remember the episode very well. It was my first guest star role on TV," remembers Daniels. "I was cast by casting director April Webster and to this day I run into her because she still works in TV and film projects."

Actor Don Stroud and others made up the motorcycle gang, but Daniels remembers that regular stunt men also filled in. "I know that Jack Gill, Lane Leavitt, Paul Lane and the other stunt guys were riding the motorcycles because I have worked with them a lot since filming the episode."

Daniels character is best known for the love of his yellow van, which Daniels remembers well, especially when it gets destroyed by the biker gang. "I feel quite sure that the van that my character owned was purchased or rented for the show because it had to be altered and supported so the motorcycles could ride on top and destroy it."

The sheriff was played by James Callahan and Daniels explains an incident that occurred during the climax of the episode when the pair team up to trip the bikers re-entering White Rock. "I remember James Callahan very well because I was quite nervous. I remember towards the end of the episode that I got his fingers caught in the prop rope that we were using to unseat the bad guys from their motorcycles."

Daniels shared screen time with David Hasselhoff and not only would they work together in the future but they would become the best of friends. "Years later, I became David's stunt double on the last six seasons of *Baywatch*. David and I became the best of friends and remain so to this day. Due to our friendship and trust, I have travelled with David many times on film and TV projects. He made sure I was always hired as stunt coordinator as well as his stunt double. I became a full time stuntman during those times working on *Baywatch* and also working on the motion pictures *Batman Forever* and *Batman and Robin*."

So is it true that David Hasselhoff owns half of Daniels home in Hawaii? "Even though it's not true, David claims to own a part of my house in Hawaii that I bought while filming the first season of *Baywatch Hawaii*. In a way, I guess it is true because if not for David Hasselhoff, I would not have been in Hawaii."

"At that time, my buddy 'The Hoff' pulled out clips from the old episodes of *Knight Rider* and said 'we should write you into *Baywatch* as an old Navy Seal buddy gone bad'. David and I have had a lot of adventures including scuba diving trips, skydiving, river rafting, movie jobs and Hoff concerts. The trips are always filled with laughter, pranks and discovery. You definitely have to stay on your game while hanging with 'The Hoff'. He might start quoting goofy dialogue from *Knight Rider*. My goofy dialogue," jokes Daniels. Daniels adds, "I know we will always be in each other's corner." Daniels concludes, "I will always fondly remember the *Knight Rider* experience."

Andy Gill, the younger brother of stunt coordinator Jack Gill, was brought on to the series to do stunts. Gill recalls his first days on the job that would lead to a series long job. "My first day working as a real stuntman in the business was this show. I was bartending at night up at Universal Studios at a restaurant called Victoria Station. In the day, I would go out to the sets with Jack and help him set up stunts, watch how the stunt was performed and then break the stunt equipment down at the end. I would train with Jack on off days or weekends when he wasn't working. We would put together fight scenes some days, practice wheeling and sliding motorcycles other days. I did this for about a year. Then one day, Jack took me out and we practiced what is called a "cable-off" stunt. We took the motorcycles, along with some rope and went out in to a riding area and found a spot with a soft sand landing area. Jack set up the motorcycle by tying the rope to the triple clamps of the motorcycle. The rope then went down through a ring he put on the front wheel axel. He laid down about 30' of rope then tied the end off to a rock. He told me to ride the bike to the end of the rope. He told me to put it in 2nd gear and go about 20mph, get my feet up high on the engine and push when I get to the end of the rope. I must have practiced that stunt about 20 times until I was very comfortable performing it. At the end of the day is when he told me I was working on *Knight Rider* the next day and performing that very stunt. The stunt was my first stunt I ever performed in the business. Jack and I were on 2 different motorcycles and each one was rigged for a "cable-off". We rode the bikes toward the car and the cables stopped the motorcycles right before they hit the side of the *Knight Rider* car. They pitched us over the car and down a sand hill behind. The cables stopped the motorcycles from damaging the K.I.T.T. car because everyone knows that K.I.T.T. is indestructible! I don't remember having the rubber skin on top of K.I.T.T. for this stunt. I think we did this stunt 2 times. I am the one in the air over K.I.T.T. He passes us and slides in front and that is why we run into him. Jack did the 90 degree slide up to the down telephone pole in K.I.T.T. I think another stuntman, Mike Tillman, may have been riding as Jack's character for the lead in shots when Jack was driving K.I.T.T. This was all filmed out at Indian Dunes. I also performed another stunt that day. I did a second cable-off stunt on my motorcycle. This time into a pond as K.I.T.T. went by. I played a different character for the pond stunt. The rest of the day was nothing but fun, fun, fun, chasing and getting chased by K.I.T.T. through the dirt and back streets. I was in heaven and knew I loved this business.

At the time I had no idea how big of an impact *Knight Rider* would have on my future career. I spent the next 4 years learning and working on *Knight Rider* as a stuntman and then stunt coordinator under Jack when he started directing 2nd unit action sequences. I drove K.I.T.T. as Michael Knight and had to wear the curly wig that everyone who doubled Michael had to wear. I can remember how hot it was filming in summer, sitting in K.I.T.T., waiting for the action call. I would be wearing all black with a black leather jacket inside an all black car...with all windows up and running the heater to help cool the motor. Oh yeah, and a curly wig on your head just to make your head sweat and have the drips run down into your eyes! We would take it off at the end of the day and give it back to Alan Payne (make-up department) and tell him he can have the 'wet rat' back. I always wondered how many times that wig actually got washed."

Knight Knotes:

- Keith Mitchell, who played Davey, won a 1983 Young Artist Award (Best Young Actor, Guest on a Series) for his performance in this episode. *Knight Rider* was also nominated for "Best New Family Television Series", but didn't win.

- Don Stroud played a character nearly identical to Hilly in an episode of *The Fall Guy* called "Colt's Angels".

- The episode's title is a play on the title of the 1955 movie *Bad Day at Black Rock.*

- Michael makes a passing reference to another Trans Am heavy production, *Smokey and the Bandit.*

- The biker war that was to take place in White Rock consisted of two rival gangs – The Scorpians and The Road Dogs.

Script to Screen:

- The opening of the episode has Michael stopping some robbers at an unemployment office as opposed to the drug traffickers seen on screen.

- Davey is described as a ten year old contemporary Huck Finn.

- Big Lonny's van was originally conceived as a pickup truck.

- When K.I.T.T. self-activates to rescue Michael from jail, the script says that his "microprocessor switches from normal to impact" and then he moves the car in front of, and behind him.

- After Michael infiltrates the gang's camp and learns of their plans, he goes to Sherry's house. Still dressed in his gang outfit, Michael startles Sherry and she pulls a shotgun on him.

Déjà Vu:

- Anne Lockhart guest stars in season two's "Return to Cadiz"; Michael Champion can be seen in "Speed Demons"; and James Callahan returns in "Circus Knights".

Featured Songs:

"Born to Be Wild" by Steppenwolf

"After Midnight" by Eric Clapton

"Can I See You Tonight" by Tanya Tucker

K.I.T.T.'s Capabilities:

- Anharmonic Synthesizer, Auto Cruise, Auto-Roof Left, Pursuit, Turbo Boost

PROD. #57315

⎡ EPISODE ⎤
⎣   4   ⎦

Script History:

September 1, 1982 (F.R.)

September 9, 1982 (F.R.)

September 13, 1982 (F.R.)

September 14, 1982 (F.R.)

September 15, 1982 (F.R.)

SLAMMIN' SAMMY'S STUNT SHOW

SPECTACULAR

Written By: E. Paul Edwards and John Alan Schwartz

Directed By: Bruce Bilson

Original Airdate: October 22, 1982 (Friday, 9:00 PM) (16.8%; 13,990,000)

NBC Rerun #1: March 25, 1983 (Friday, 9:00 PM) (19.6%; 16,330,000)

NBC Rerun #2: July 15, 1984 (Sunday, 8:00 PM) (16.6%; 13,910,000)

Filming Dates: September 13-21, 1982

"Keep pasting, Michael. Please, keep pasting."

-K.I.T.T.

Crew: R.A. Cinader (Co-Executive Producer), Steven E. de Souza (Producer), Hannah Shearer (Producer), Gilbert Bettman (Associate Producer), Bernadette Joyce (Associate Producer), David Braff (Story Editor), Stu Phillips (Music), H. John Penner (Director of Photography), Seymour Klate (Art Director), R. Lynn Smartt (Set Decoration), April Webster (Casting), Stanley Wohlberg (Film Editor), John R. McDonald (Sound), Ron Martinez (Unit Production Manager), Fred L. Miller (1st Assistant Director), Don Edward Wilkerson (2nd Assistant Director), Walt Jenevein (Sound Effects Editor), Richard Lapham (Music Editor), George R. Whittaker (Costume Designer), Don Snyder (Costume Supervisor), Robert Bralver (2nd Unit Director-Stunt Coordinator)

Guest Cast: Susan Kase (Lisa Phillips), Lin McCarthy (Lawrence Blake), Eddie Firestone (Sammy Phillips), Jimmy Weldon (Announcer), Adam Postil (Mark Phillips), Phil Cocciolatti (Mario Lutenzo), Mark Alaimo (Bill Gordon), Michael Santiago (Highway Patrolman)

Michael joins a local stunt show after the main attraction's car was sabotaged, leaving the driver with a broken leg.

A Look Back:

Philip Coccioletti played the devious Mario Lutenzo who worked with Bill Gordon in an attempt to shut down Sammy Phillips' stunt show. Coccioletti recalls how he got the part of Mario and how he nearly became the *Knight Rider* himself. "I was signed as a guest star to play the bad guy. I remember that we were shooting a scene and in between takes, David Hasselhoff came up to me and said 'Wow, you could have been the lead in the series!' I found this ironic as I was originally one of the eight actors brought to the network for the lead role of Michael Knight. I told him and we laughed about that. It was nice of him to say that though."

Coccioletti made it through multiple auditions with the network before the role of Michael Knight went to Hasselhoff. "It ended up being a series of meetings...maybe three in all. I met the casting people in round one, the producers in round two and the producer/director of the pilot in round three. I believe they brought in 8 to 10 actors to meet everyone from the network. All the financial deals had to be agreed to before this final casting. Going before the network was the final step. I don't recall who else auditioned other than (I believe) Joseph Bottoms. You just all go and meet in one room, sit there until they call your name and then you read for everyone...including the head of the entire network – usually 6 to 12 people.

It has been rumored that Don Johnson was among those called for a final audition. To that, Coccioletti remarks, "I didn't see Don Johnson there, but there were always well known actors making deals as we were reading for the role. I have also been on auditions where no one was picked and out of the blue they name some famous actor. It happens all the time. It's not the most scrupulous business and you better have thick skin. I just always gave my best and if I felt good about what I did at the audition then I knew it was out of my hands."

Bruce Bilson was behind the camera for "Slammin' Sammy's Stunt Show Spectacular", a well respected director who had overseen everything from *The Six Million Dollar Man* to *Wonder Woman*. "Bruce was the kind of guy that would always let you spread your wings," remembers Coccioletti. "You really could try out anything. He was open 24/7, even though it was an action show- so he was great to work with."

Coccioletti has equally fond memories of the cast. "David Hasselhoff was very cool. He was professional and a real pleasure to work with. He always had a positive attitude. I loved my time working with the rest of the cast. All of the actors were experienced and very giving as performers. I loved my time on the shoot."

Coccioletti remembers the scene in which he is trying to plant a device under K.I.T.T. "One of the toughest scenes for me was reacting to K.I.T.T. I took a creeper and tried to get under K.I.T.T. to plant an explosive. The car would actually move and a voice would talk to me. I remember having a hard time as an actor with that one."

But the episode shooting would become even harder for Coccioletti when a stunt went wrong that left both him and stunt coordinator Jack Gill injured. "There were a lot of people in the stands - some were racetrack fans, extras and friends of the crew. One of my scenes required me to run 60 yards to my escape as K.I.T.T. came flying in at 50 mph to cut me off. I had to make it look as close as possible as K.I.T.T. hit the brakes inches from me. Unfortunately, the sun heated the asphalt and when K.I.T.T. hit the brakes, the car slid and knocked me twenty feet through the air and I slid on the asphalt, tearing my race jumpsuit. I had a nice giant strawberry burn on the side of my right thigh. As they took me to get cleaned up, stuntman Jack Gill was drafted in to replace me in my scene. Jack was also hit by K.I.T.T. and he went through the windshield! Jack had to have 18 stitches in his arm from all the broken glass."

With the scene failing two times, the action was not over for Coccioletti and Gill. "Now I was on the hood of K.I.T.T. - the still broken glass version of K.I.T.T. On action, I had to jump off the hood and sprint for my life. K.I.T.T. was chasing me down at 60 mph. I didn't, as I recall, have that warm fuzzy feeling running for my life in the middle of nowhere, hearing that supped up Pontiac barreling down on me from behind. The stunt driver had to come within inches along side of me. Needless to say, I was very concerned as the car was almost touching me. Jack Gill, fresh with his 18 stitches in his arm and brown wig to match my look, came back to replace me. At this point, two stuntmen are now in the car, one driving and the second on the floor holding the wheel to keep the car perfectly straight as the driver reaches out with both hands to grab Jack, holding and dragging him as the car comes to a stop. I remember Jack came inches from being run over by the back wheels!" Coccioletti was then almost run over by David Hasselhoff himself. "At the climax of the episode, David pulls me into the frame and screams, 'Where did you plant the bomb?'. I reply, 'Third row, Section E', and he spins off burning rubber as the car fishtails and again almost runs me over! I am happy to work...but I was relieved to get through that day!"

Towards the end of the episode, there was one action scene where Michael Knight asks track owner Sammy Phillips if he can complete the 'show stopper stunt' to pull in the crowds. Much to Coccioletti's relief, he was not involved in that scene, but instead watched from the video replay. "I remember seeing the playback of the jump they set up and the cut didn't work at all. I was really glad I wasn't the driver. I believe he got the crap knocked out of him. What happened is that K.I.T.T. was going around the track at a very high rate of speed so that he could fly up a ramp that was hooked to the back of a big truck as it was moving. K.I.T.T. went up over the truck and due to the weight of the front end, the car took a rapid nosedive and hit the tarmac. I remember Bruce Bilson wanted it to fly horizontally - it just dived nose first. Afterwards, the car looked like a shark nose as it was all bent upward. That scene just didn't match the cut at all. They also had a fiberglass shield that they covered the car with to protect it crashing through a wall. But the glass kept breaking. I heard that Pontiac gave the production a bunch of cars. I believe they crashed five during the pilot."

Coccioletti jokes that he wouldn't have minded having one item from the episode shoot. "They should have given me the trackside suit - the one with the torn out hip. We didn't get anything like that, but I do have the fondest memories of working on the show."

David Hasselhoff, 1983 (Photo courtesy of Christopher Orlando)

John Alan Schwartz co-wrote "Slammin' Sammy's Stunt Show Spectacular" with E. Paul Edwards. Schwartz explains that he had *Knight Rider's* leading man to thank for the job. "David Hasselhoff was my roommate at CAL Arts and we were close friends," confirms Schwartz. "At the time, I was working on a script with Paul when David set us up for a pitch meeting with Bob Cinader and Steven De Souza. They read our script and liked the writing. We pitched them what would become 'Slammin' Sammy's Stunt Show Spectacular' and they loved our story and we were off to the races." Regarding his collaboration with Edwards, Schwartz recalls, "Writing with a partner is always a challenge. We worked well together."

As is common with television scripts, the original draft for the episode included some elements that didn't make it to film. "I remember that I had Michael playing football with K.I.T.T. Also, I gave K.I.T.T. the ability to sketch pictures from verbal commands." That second feature showed up in Schwartz's other writing credit in the series, "The Final Verdict".

Schwartz recalls the differences between television and film writing and the process of writing for *Knight Rider*. "Writing for television is totally different from film. Each is its own beast. The faster you can churn out good material, the faster your value goes up. For this story, we would break it in several days and once that was accepted we would deliver a draft in ten days. Then rewrites would follow and that would take a couple of days."

Knight Knotes:

- At the start of the episode, Michael reads the Knight 2000 owner's manual, which is actually the 1982 Pontiac Firebird owner's manual with the words "Knight 2000" on the front.

- "Slammin' Sammy" was named after a real life employee of Universal Studios who was assigned to drive the water trucks. In fact, the real Sammy's water truck can be seen in this episode as the water truck used by the Phillips family!

- This installment marks the first time that the name of the episode is spoken by one of the actors, but not the last. Other episodes include "Inside Out", "Hearts of Stone", "Chariot of Gold", "White Bird",

"Goliath", "Ring of Fire", "A Knight in Shining Armor", "Speed Demons", "Mouth of the Snake", "Let It Be Me", "Big Iron", "Buy Out", "The Nineteenth Hole", "Burial Ground", "The Wrong Crowd", "Many Happy Returns" and "The Scent of Roses".

Script to Screen:

- Sammy's stunt where he drives on two wheels is known as a "ski jump".
- Michael goes undercover as a handyman in Lawrence Blake's office, where he learns of his plan to rig an accident with Sammy's car. With the accident planned for less than 30 minutes, Michael races K.I.T.T. back to the stunt show, engaging the Booster button for extra speed.
- Sammy pats the side of his helmet twice for good luck before performing a stunt.
- Lawrence Blake's first name was originally Robert.
- After Michael gets the job with Sammy, he returns to the semi where Devon says the following: "a) Kitt is not to be used in any profit making venture, b) you are supposed to be undercover not center ring in a circus, and c) you are attempting to destroy an indestructible car."
- K.I.T.T.'s oxygen vents originally deploy from the floorboards, not the roof.
- Blake pulls a gun on Michael when he tries to arrest him.

K.I.T.T.'s Capabilities:

- Auto Cruise, Horizontal Turbo Boost, Oxygen Vent, Pursuit, Radar, Ski Mode, Turbo Boost

PROD. #57311

[EPISODE 5]

Script History:

September 13, 1982 (F.R.)

September 20, 1982 (F.R.)

September 21, 1982 (F.R.)

JUST MY BILL

Teleplay By: Deborah Davis and David Braff

Story By: Catherine Bacos

Contributing Writer: Steven E. de Souza

Directed By: Sidney Hayers

Original Airdate: October 29, 1982 (Friday, 9:00 PM) (14.5%; 12,080,000)

NBC Rerun #1: February 11, 1983 (Friday, 9:00 PM) (15.2%; 12,660,000)

NBC Rerun #2: July 1, 1983 (Friday, 9:00 PM) (17.6%; 14,660,000)

Filming Dates: September 22-30, 1982

"Kit? It's a kit car?"

-Maggie Flynn

Crew: R.A. Cinader (Co-Executive Producer), Steven E. de Souza (Producer), Hannah Shearer (Producer), Gilbert Bettman (Associate Producer), Bernadette Joyce (Associate Producer), David Braff (Story Editor), Stu Phillips (Music), H. John Penner (Director of Photography), Seymour Klate (Art Director), R. Lynn Smartt (Set Decoration), April Webster (Casting), Lawrence J. Gleason (Film Editor), John R. McDonald (Sound), Ron Martinez (Unit Production Manager), Charles Watson Sanford, Jr. (1st Assistant Director), Don Edward Wilkerson (2nd Assistant Director), Walt Jenevein (Sound Effects Editor), Richard Lapham (Music Editor), George R. Whittaker (Costume Designer), Don Snyder (Costume Supervisor), Robert Bralver (2nd Unit Director-Stunt Coordinator)

Guest Cast: Carole Cook (Senator Maggie Flynn), Robert Sampson (J. Hanford Dixon), Bruce Gray (Senator Russell Forbes), Nancy Grahn (Jane Adams), David Haskell (Brian Owendorf), Alex Kubik (Luger), June Christopher (Miriam), Barry Cutler (Garage Guard), London Donfield (Al), Fitzhugh G. Houston (Assembly Speaker), Roger Til (Professor LeCalir), Kenneth Men'ard (Charlie Kemp), Jeri Gaile (Kate), Steve Alterman (Valet Attendant)

Michael acts as a body guard to a state senator whose views on a controversial power bill make her a target.

A Look Back:

Catherine Bacos Clinch wrote the stories for many hit TV shows during the 1980's, starting with *Hart to Hart*. In fact, *Knight Rider* would only be her second job in the profession. "I didn't really plan on being a writer," confesses Clinch. "I actually wanted to be a director, but the unfortunate reality that existed in the 1970's meant that I was repeatedly told, 'You can't direct. You're a girl, and girls don't direct'. Writing was not a consideration until I enrolled at Columbia University in a graduate screenwriting course. The class was taught by Samson Raphaelson, who had written *The Jazz Singer*. Sam insisted that I was meant to be a writer and became my mentor. In retrospect, I cannot imagine what my life would have been like if I had ignored his advice."

Keep your scanners peeled (Photo courtesy of Christopher Orlando)

Clinch has Steven E. de Souza to thank for giving her the opportunity to work on a *Knight Rider* story. "I had written my first two television scripts for Steven E. de Souza when he was the executive story editor on *Foul Play*. When that show was canceled, ABC put me on *Hart to Hart* when he was hired onto this series as well. Steven liked my writing well enough to bring me on to *Knight Rider*. I had heard of the series and it fit the kind of writing I was doing at the time."

"Just My Bill" is fondly remembered for Carole Cook's eccentric performance as Maggie Flynn, the senator who had time for everyone.

"When I grew up in New York City in the sixties, one of my heroes was Bella Abzug. She was an attorney and an activist who was ultimately elected to the US House of Representatives. The part of her life that really inspired me was her role as one of the founding mothers of the women's movement. I would watch her on television and think that I want to be that confident. I want to stand up against those who do terrible things for personal gain - I want to help right the wrongs of the world. The character of Maggie Flynn was very much inspired by my exalted impression of Bella Abzug."

Clinch has her own opinions of the character that she brought to life. "Maggie Flynn is emblematic of the older women who, by 1982, had made significant progress toward women's equality. She was feisty and opinionated, yet maternal. She gives a damn and is willing to stand up for what she believes, even when it's challenging to do so. Maggie is charming but can't be charmed. She's an instinctive leader who would never think of following anybody else's lead. She is either an equal partner or she stands alone. Maggie believes that one (wo)man can make a difference. The concept that her vote has so much power is essential to the plot because it is essential to how women were self-actualizing at that point in history."

Clinch recalls that most of what she wrote made it to the final cut for the actual filming of the episode. "Every time I write an episode of television, I begin with a simple challenge: if I get to talk to 20 million people, what do I really believe is important enough to say to them? For an episode of *Jake and the Fatman*, I asked, 'Who does the abused wife turn to when the abusive husband is a hero cop who took a bullet for his partner?' In one of the episodes I wrote for *Hunter*, I asked, 'When a cop delivers a baby and participates in the most intimate moment of a stranger's life, what kind of emotional bond does the cop feel toward the mother and child?' In this episode of *Knight Rider*, I wanted to explore the simple issue we all grapple with throughout our lives - how much of a difference can one person's voice make to the greater good of all mankind? The actual bones of the story I wrote weren't very different from what ultimately appeared on screen. Flexibility isn't an option – it's expected. The character of Maggie was softened a bit and the political debates were eliminated."

Clinch's intention was to give K.I.T.T. a political voice, but that never materialized on screen. "The 80's were a time when everybody was speculating on how 'human' computers would be, so I thought it would be fun if K.I.T.T., who was already extremely humanized, were to have strong political opinions. Then, I took it a step further. K.I.T.T. was supposed to have opinions that differed drastically from those of the Senator he had to protect. In essence, Maggie was a Democrat and K.I.T.T. was a Republican. Maggie's passion would be balanced by K.I.T.T.'s objectivity. I had intended for them to have an ongoing debate while the action scenes unfolded. In 1982, I don't believe this kind of scene had been done yet."

"Just My Bill" was directed by Sidney Hayers and, though it was par for the course that writers did not meet with directors, Hayers and Clinch were good friends before the show. "Sidney Hayers was a friend of mine at the time. Sidney was a gregarious man whose charm and intellect offered a great compliment to his work as a director. He was from the UK and I was a New Yorker – and neither of us had yet come to terms with the fact that Hollywood seemed to operate without a sense of business propriety. We would often sit on his patio in Little Holmby Hills and laugh about how much Hollywood seemed to be a foreign world that you had to navigate without any translation book on how to speak to the natives or interpret their cultural idiosyncrasies. A couple of years later, we worked on a horror film that never made it out of development and into production. We lost touch over the years."

Ultimately, Clinch was satisfied with the transfer of her original ideas onto television. "By the time the episode went to script, I had moved on to another project. At that point, my story and characters were in the hands of a writing team. I am confident that they contributed their best efforts to the work. As I watch it now, I think the episode holds up quite well."

The Puerto Rican born actor Bruce Gray played the role of Senator Forbes. "I don't remember too much about the episode. It was a shock to see the show again - I had never seen my episode before, contrary to what you might imagine!"

Gray does remember the flamboyant Carole Cook, who starred as his opponent, Maggie Flynn. "Carole brought an energy and an exuberance to the role of the US Senator. Her character was always on the run...in every shot. She gave the senator a star quality that lifted the part above its usual interpretations. She also lent the role a comedic edge. She had plenty of sass and energy during filming. I believe she had the same manager as me at the time. After the shoot was over, we met socially several times. She was sweet - a real trooper...and she is married to Tom Troupe - so a double Trouper," jokes Gray.

Gray concludes that the series' philosophy was perfect for Cook. "I think *Knight Rider* as a series always had a tongue in cheek attitude about it, so she fit right into that."

Fitz Houston is one of those lucky actors who was able to appear in *Knight Rider* more than once. His first appearance was as an assembly speaker in "Just My Bill". "I remember that April Webster was the casting director at the time. I auditioned for this role and she cast me," recalls Houston.

Even though his scenes were brief, it still required a significant amount of time. "Even though my scene in 'Just My Bill' was short, it actually took us half the day to film because of the number of people in the court assembly room. The camera angle that Sidney Hayers, the director, wanted was complex but that set up an atmosphere for the scene in the room."

In fact, Sidney Hayers would also direct Houston in his second *Knight Rider* appearance the following season in "Brother's Keeper". "Sidney was very professional," remembers Houston. "He had a nice way of working with actors to keep the whole set relaxed. And he got what he wanted out of a scene without making it too stressful."

Though Houston was in the same assembly room as David Hasselhoff in the episode's climax, he did not meet the leading man of the show. "I didn't get to meet David. I remember the scene during the exchange and we were literally 20 yards apart. The hall was huge and then you had the actress [Carole Cooke] interrupting the session and projecting her lines from the back of the hall."

"Just My Bill" was filming during the same week that the Pilot premiered on NBC, so Houston had not seen the show prior. Still, he felt that having a super car like K.I.T.T. on board could make the show a success. "We didn't know the show would catch on, but we did know that the public loved cars. Having the car have its own personality was the icing on the cake."

Knight Knotes:

- "Just My Bill" was the lowest rated all-new episode of the entire series, with a little over 12 million viewers watching.
- The helicopter seen in the climax of this episode is a Bell 206B Jet Ranger III, registration number N764CL, serial number 2811. This same helicopter reappears in "Hearts of Stone", "Mouth of the Snake", "Knight in Disgrace" and "Knight Strike". It can also be seen in the 1985 movie *Malibu Express*. It is still in service today and owned by a private company in Van Nuys, CA.
- This is the only episode where Devon rides in the back seat.
- K.I.T.T. tells Maggie that part of his circuitry was developed at Stanford University.

Script to Screen:

- When Michael tells K.I.T.T. to not look too conspicuous, K.I.T.T. makes two flags pop out from his hood.

- After Michael begins chasing the car that tried to hit him and Maggie in the parking garage, it wasn't a truck that forced them to stop, but a school bus at an intersection.

- Professor LeCalir was originally named Professor Owani.

- As Michael leaves the retreat with Maggie, he employs K.I.T.T.'s ski mode to sneak between two of Luger's vehicles. Then, Luger's men force a tree to fall in Michael's path. He presses a button marked "Power Boost" that sends K.I.T.T. under the falling tree with a burst of speed.

- The final scene doesn't take place in K.I.T.T., but rather at a restaurant called the Dew Drop Inn. Maggie is present and challenges Devon to a game of Darts. Devon states that he won the East Coast Championships when he was at Yale.

- The first scene in the teaser where Jane says "Do you know what I'd really like to do?" and Michael responds "Nope, but I got a feeling you are going to tell me" is not in the actual episode. However, it does appear in the script. Jane responds that she wants to talk to K.I.T.T.

Déjà Vu:

- June Christopher can be seen in "The Final Verdict"; Fitzhugh G. Houston returns in "Brother's Keeper"; Alex Kubik is in "Big Iron" and "Junk Yard Dog".

K.I.T.T.'s Capabilities:

- Auto Cruise, Auto-Roof Left, Instant Replay, Pursuit, Radar, Rocket Thrusters, Surveillance Mode, Zoom-In, Turbo Boost, Peng (Smoke Release)

PROD. #57304

<table>
<tr><td>

⎡ EPISODE ⎤
⎣ 6 ⎦

</td><td>

Script History:

September 23, 1982 (F.R.)

September 28, 1982 (F.R.)

</td></tr>
</table>

NOT A DROP TO DRINK

Written By: Hannah L. Shearer

Directed By: Virgil W. Vogel

Original Airdate: November 5, 1982 (Friday, 9:00 PM) (17.7%; 14,740,000)

NBC Rerun #1: April 1, 1983 (Friday, 9:00 PM) (18.6%; 15,490,000)

Filming Dates: October 1-11, 1982

"You were very offensive last night, earthling."

-K.I.T.T.

Crew: R.A. Cinader (Co-Executive Producer), Steven E. de Souza (Producer), Hannah Shearer (Producer), Gilbert Bettman (Associate Producer), Bernadette Joyce (Associate Producer), David Braff (Story Editor), Stu Phillips (Music), H. John Penner (Director of Photography), Seymour Klate (Art Director), R. Lynn Smartt (Set Decoration), April Webster (Casting), Edwin F. England (Film Editor), John R. McDonald (Sound), Ron Martinez (Unit Production Manager), Fred L. Miller (1st Assistant Director), Don Edward Wilkerson (2nd Assistant Director), Walt Jenevein (Sound Effects Editor), Richard Lapham (Music Editor), George R. Whittaker (Costume Designer), Don Snyder (Costume Supervisor), Robert Bralver (2nd Unit Director-Stunt Coordinator)

Guest Cast: Sondra Currie (Francesca Morgan), Jason Evers (Herb Bremen), Harry Carey, Jr. (Josh Morgan), Lynn Hamilton (Susan Wade), Bumper Yothers (The Bull), Dave Cass (Alex Webster), Joe Burnett (Kirk Webster), Tom Lester (Ted Moore), Lyndel Stuart (Myra Moore), Jan Rabson (Dewey)

Michael helps a feisty widow protect her land rights against a ruthless rancher intent on stealing her water.

A Look Back:

Dave Cass starred as one of Herb Bremen's henchmen in "Not a Drop to Drink", and he owes his starring role to the director of the episode. "I first met Virgil Vogel in 1969 when I was working as a stuntman and actor on a series called *Here Come the Brides*. He took me under his wing. He became one of my mentors and was a legend in his own right. Virgil wanted me for this part. He could be a little gruff but also had a keen sense of humor."

Cass starred in *Knight Rider* twice, reappearing in season three's "Knight By a Nose", and each time he played the bad guy. "I always liked the bad guy roles. There are few leading men, but they all need a bad guy to play off of and the roles were fun. I did get the girl once in a while, but then the good guy would come along and save her," jokes Cass.

There is one scene where Cass is required to capture Francesca Morgan (played by Sondra Currie) from escaping. "I remember that scene well," confirms Cass. "Sondra was, and still is, a doll and I enjoyed throwing her over my shoulder. I remember that Virgil got a laugh out of it."

Cass remembers that the filming locations were not too far from the Universal studio lot. "We were about 30 miles from the studio. We filmed the farm locations at Hidden Valley, California, just past West Lake Village. It's a beautiful valley with a winding two lane road and ranches."

Cass got along well with David Hasselhoff. "David was a great guy to work with. I knew David since Glen Larson put the presentation tape together to sell *Knight Rider* to the studios. The last time I worked with David was on *Knight Rider 2000*, and he had not changed one lick."

Knight Knotes:

- The scene where K.I.T.T. uses his rockets to blow up a dam is re-used footage from the 1978 *Superman* movie.
- Bonnie installs K.I.T.T.'s grappling hook in this episode.

Script to Screen:

- Kirk Webster was originally not intended to be Alex Webster's brother, but instead a man named Richard Kirk.
- As Bonnie adds K.I.T.T.'s grappling hook, Michael takes a nap while watching a ball game.
- Kevin's mare is named Terra instead of Kid, and Bumper the Bull is named Frank.

- K.I.T.T. originally skis forward between the bulldozers, not backwards from a standstill.
- Devon and Susan Wade do not meet with Michael in the semi to brief him on the mission; instead, Devon summons Michael to Shasta City and they meet in a café to discuss the mission.
- Kirk and Alex attack Michael in a bar. Josh Morgan puts a gun to Alex's back to break up the fight. Later, Alex is watching K.I.T.T. Michael catches him and warns Alex that his "car has some very weird capabilities that I don't think you want to find out about." This segment replaces the "Alien K.I.T.T." segment seen in the episode.

Déjà Vu:

- Dave Cass can be seen in "Knight By a Nose" and *Knight Rider 2000*; Jason Evers returns in "Halloween Knight".

K.I.T.T.'s Capabilities:

- Auto Cruise, Grappling Hook, Pursuit, Retro Rockets, Rocket Fire, Ski Mode, Surveillance Mode, Turbo Boost

PROD. #57313

$$\left[\begin{array}{c} \text{EPISODE} \\ 7 \end{array}\right]$$

Script History:

October 7, 1982 (F.R.)

October 13, 1982 (F.R.)

NO BIG THING

Written By: Judy Burns

Directed By: Bernard L. Kowalski

Original Airdate: November 12, 1982 (Friday, 9:00 PM) (17.7%; 14,740,000)

NBC Rerun #1: April 8, 1983 (Friday, 9:00 PM) (21.1%; 17,580,000)

Filming Dates: October 13-22, 1982

"I wouldn't miss the chance to bail out our illustrious leader for all the pasta in

Italy."

-Michael

Crew: R.A. Cinader (Co-Executive Producer), Steven E. de Souza (Producer), Hannah Shearer (Producer), Gilbert Bettman (Associate Producer), Bernadette Joyce (Associate Producer), David Braff (Story Editor), Stu Phillips (Music), H. John Penner (Director of Photography), Seymour Klate (Art Director), R. Lynn Smartt (Set Decoration), April Webster (Casting), William Martin (Film Editor), John R. McDonald (Sound), Ron Martinez (Unit Production Manager), Charles Watson Sanford, Jr. (1st Assistant Director), Don Edward Wilkerson (2nd Assistant Director), Walt Jenevein (Sound Effects Editor), Richard Lapham (Music Editor), George R. Whittaker (Costume Designer), Don Snyder (Costume Supervisor), Robert Bralver (2nd Unit Director-Stunt Coordinator)

Guest Cast: Ted Markland (Sergeant Ted Wallace), Mary Margaret Humes (Carol Reston), Grainger Hines (Officer Rex Saunders), Jim Haynie (Frank Reston), Logan Ramsey (Judge Roland S. Paxton), Paul Harper (Man), Jimmy Murphy (Pink), Earl Billings (Shep), Duke Stroud (Captain Dave Butler), Robert Carnegie (Officer Van Dyke), Louie Elias (Pauly), Vance Davis (Guard), Patrick Puccinelli (Officer Charly Smith), Bruce Neckels (Pete), Elmarie Wendel (Woman), Jay T. Will (Brute)

Devon is arrested on phony charges and gets caught up in a scandal involving the local judge and the entire police force.

A Look Back:

Jack Gill on powering all of K.I.T.T.'s accessories: "The cars did have a secondary battery to run the scanner and the electronics. When we first started the show, we ran it off the original battery and we found out that to get the actors dialogue clean. you had to turn off the car and just run it on auxiliary mode so you could get the scanner and all the interior lights to work.

But that would run the battery down really, really fast, so they stuck another battery in there and sometimes two batteries so we could switch them out quick. If the car was sitting still and there was dialogue in the car and they want the scanner to work and the inside lights to work, it would really drain the battery quickly."

Knight Knotes:

- Devon escapes from prison by jumping a white pick-up truck over a fence using a ramp made of bags of concrete. In a 1981 episode of *The Fall Guy* called "That's Right, We're Bad", Colt and Howie escape from a chain gang by – you guessed it – stealing a white pick-up truck and jumping over a fence using a ramp made of bags of concrete!

- The police car that pulls Devon over for running the stop sign and a sedan at the prison both carry the same license plate number – CA 13553.

Script to Screen:

- The episode originally starts with K.I.T.T. alerting Michael that he is low on gas, not Devon getting arrested.

- K.I.T.T. requests only 5 gallons of gasoline so that he doesn't have to get his tanks purged. When the gas attendant asks why only 5 gallons, Michael tells him that he's doing a mileage test.

- Michael pumps the gasoline into K.I.T.T.'s tailpipe.

- According to the script, Devon is playing Bach's "Tocatta and Fugue in D Minor" when he is pulled over and arrested.

- A scene in the semi finds Michael coding his first program for K.I.T.T. Bonnie inserts the disk in the computer where the lights blink on and off. Bonnie comments that she loves the way K.I.T.T. consumes his information, and Michael replies that there's something sensual about it, referring to Bonnie. She quickly corrects him. While viewers don't see this scene, the results of his first programming experience are seen in the episode – he programs K.I.T.T. with sports statistics.

Déjà Vu:

- Louis Elias is back in "Junk Yard Dog" and "Knight of the Juggernaut"; Grainger Hines returns in season four's "Knight Racer"; Bruce Neckels is in "Ten Wheel Trouble" and "Knight of a Thousand Devils"; Jimmy Murphy is in "Custom Made Killer"; and Logan Ramsey can be seen in "Knight Strike".

Featured Songs:

- "Eine Kleine Nachtmusik" by Wolfgang Amadeus Mozart
- "Love's Been a Little Bit Hard On Me" by Juice Newton
- "You Were Always On My Mind" by Willie Nelson

K.I.T.T.'s Capabilities:

- Auto Cruise, Auto-Roof Right, Eject Right, Pursuit, Radar, Security Alert, Turbo Boost

PROD. #57307

⎡ EPISODE ⎤
⎣ 8 ⎦

Script History:

October 15, 1982 (F.R.)

October 20, 1982 (F.R.)

October 22, 1982 (F.R.)

October 25, 1982 (F.R.)

October 26, 1982 (F.R.)

October 27, 1982 (F.R.)

October 28, 1982 (F.R.)

October 29, 1982 (F.R.)

November 1, 1982 (F.R.)

TRUST DOESN'T RUST

Written By: Steven E. de Souza

Directed By: Paul Stanley

Original Airdate: November 19, 1982 (Friday, 9:00 PM) (20.6%; 17,160,000)

NBC Rerun #1: March 18, 1983 (Friday, 9:00 PM) (17.9%, 14,910,000)

NBC Rerun #2: August 19, 1983 (Friday, 9:00 PM) (19.6%, 16,330,000)

Filming Dates: October 27- November 4, 1982

"I am the prototype of the car of the future."

-K.A.R.R.

Crew: R.A. Cinader (Co-Executive Producer), Steven E. de Souza (Producer), Hannah Shearer (Producer), Gilbert Bettman (Associate Producer), Bernadette Joyce (Associate Producer), David Braff (Story Editor), Stu Phillips (Music), H. John Penner (Director of Photography), Russell Smith (Art Director), R. Lynn Smartt (Set Decoration), April Webster (Casting), Stanley Wohlberg (Film Editor), John R. McDonald (Sound), Ron Martinez (Unit Production Manager), Fred L. Miller (1st Assistant Director), Don Edward Wilkerson (2nd Assistant Director), Walt Jenevein (Sound Effects Editor), Richard Lapham (Music Editor), Richard Hopper (Costume Designer), Don Snyder (Costume Supervisor), Robert Bralver (2nd Unit Director-Stunt Coordinator)

Guest Cast: Michael MacRae (Tony Coscarelli), William Sanderson (The "Rev" Jeremiah Beaudine), John Brandon (Police Captain), John Hostetter (Police Officer), Gary A. McMillan (Security Guard), Ivan E. Roth (Jerry Clarke), Peter Cullen (Voice of K.A.R.R.)

The Knight Automated Roving Robot, or K.A.R.R., is reactivated by a pair of bums and Michael must stop it before anyone is injured.

A Look Back:

Actor William Sanderson ("The Rev") recalls an amusing incident that occurred during the filming of this episode: "There was a female extra on the set. I remember thinking that she had pretty boots on. I was dressed in character, which included a bottle of whiskey in a paper bag. I was relaxed and preparing to play the role of a drunk. Months later, a buddy of mine met this same girl in the Hard Rock Café. When she found out that I was a friend of his, she commented to my friend, 'I worked with him once – at 10 AM in the morning, he was dead drunk!' The funny thing was that I didn't even drink!"

Sanderson has nothing but fond memories from his time on set. "It was great fun and everyone was very welcoming. Michael MacRae (Tony) was a very fine actor. I remember that our characters had to get into a scuffle during one scene. We had to re-shoot that scene many times, and by the time we reached the last take, Michael really unloaded on me and pushed me down hard on the table. David Hasselhoff was great to work with. He gave me a glossy photo that I kept for many years".

John Hostetter briefly appears in this episode as a police officer. He recalls his time on the set. "This was during my first year of working in Hollywood, so I didn't know anybody and nobody knew me. My agent was sending me out on these auditions for small roles to see if I could snag something. April Webster was casting and I was thrilled to get a day's work. She remained a helpful person to know over my twenty year career as an actor in LA. The part of playing a police officer was a staple for the unknown character actor. It still is. As actors, we usually feel that our versatility is being overlooked, but the reality was that the parts being written for guys like me were cops and office workers and bus drivers - almost invisible cogs in the machine of the plot. I remember the term 'five and under' - which meant the number of lines that we would have."

Hostetter's part in "Trust Doesn't Rust" takes place in the Foundation semi, where he tries to advise Devon Miles on disguising K.I.T.T. "I tell them that they should probably paint their car a different color to avoid confusion (with K.A.R.R.) – personally, I don't think they took my advice seriously!" he jokes.

While Hostetter's scene is brief, he did share camera time with all the regular cast, "Everyone was cordial and welcoming. The part was early in my work history, so I was still a bit in awe of the whole situation. I probably lacked the confidence to be too chatty. Filming took place in the morning and it took a few hours. That's not all shooting time - that includes make up, wardrobe, hanging around..."

Peter Cullen was the man behind the voice of K.A.R.R. – a man Hostetter would run into later. "I only met the folks I worked with. I got to know Peter Cullen after filming. He was with the same voiceover agent that I had and I met him several times. We both worked on cartoons and would meet up at *G.I. Joe* conventions."

Now out of the spotlight, Hostetter fondly remembers his time in Hollywood. "I had a recurring role on *Murphy Brown* as John the stage manager for ten years. I had roles on *Simon & Simon*, *Remington Steele*, *CHiPS* and *T.J. Hooker* to name a few. I shared time and creativity with Candice Bergen, Clint Eastwood, Wes Craven and Kermit the Frog. Overall, I enjoyed the journey."

Knight Knotes:
- K.A.R.R. returns in season three's "K.I.T.T. vs. K.A.R.R."
- The police cruiser that chases K.A.R.R. has the same license plate as a cruiser seen in the Pilot – CA 91919.
- Peter Cullen, who voices K.A.R.R. in this episode, is perhaps best known for his role as the voice of Optimus Prime in *Transformers*. While he did not voice K.A.R.R. during his second appearance on the series, he returns as the voice of K.A.R.R. in the 2008 reboot of *Knight Rider* in the episode "A Knight to King's Pawn".

Script to Screen:
- "The Rev" got his nickname because he used to be a preacher, but his alcohol problems forced him to leave the church.
- The Three Rings Restaurant was originally called The Crunchy Clown.

- K.I.T.T. and K.A.R.R. exchange dialog when they come face to face. K.A.R.R. originally tells K.I.T.T. that while being one of a kind is special, so is being two of a kind.
- As a way of reducing weight, K.A.R.R. activates a button called "Load Jettison" which opened the trunk and expelled the jewels. When Tony protested this move, it was then that K.A.R.R. ejected him out as well.
- When the laser hits K.A.R.R. while he is skiing, it blows out a headlight. An audible "metallic scream" can be heard.
- Instead of Michael and K.I.T.T. going back and forth with who has control of the car, Michael simply presses an override button that forces K.I.T.T. back to manual.
- The final scene of the episode has K.I.T.T. replaying his conversation with K.A.R.R. outside the warehouse, where K.A.R.R. tells him how special they are.

Déjà Vu:

- Gary McMillan returns in "Knight of a Thousand Devils".

K.I.T.T.'s Capabilities:

- **By K.I.T.T.:** Auto Cruise, Manual Override, Police/Radio Frequency, Resonating Laser, Turbo Boost
- **By K.A.R.R.:** Auto Cruise, Auto-Roof Right, Eject Right, Ski Mode, Tinted Windows, Turbo Boost

PROD. #57302

{ EPISODE
9 }

Script History:

July 19, 1982 (F.R.)

INSIDE OUT

Written By: Steven E. de Souza

Directed By: Peter Crane

Original Airdate: November 26, 1982 (Friday, 9:00 PM) (19.3%; 16,080,000)

NBC Rerun #1: April 22, 1983 (Friday, 9:00 PM) (15.0%; 12,500,000)

Filming Dates: July 29- August 6, 1982

"With my rocket powered thrusters, I could do this on four cylinders."

-K.I.T.T.

Crew: R.A. Cinader (Co-Executive Producer), Steven E. de Souza (Producer), Hannah Shearer (Producer), Gilbert Bettman (Associate Producer), Bernadette Joyce (Associate Producer), David Braff (Story Editor), Stu Phillips (Music), H. John Penner (Director of Photography), Seymour Klate (Art Director), R. Lynn Smartt (Set Decoration), Ron Stephenson (Casting), Stanley Wohlberg (Film Editor), John R. McDonald (Sound), Frank Crawford (Unit Production Manager), Phil Bowles (1st Assistant Director), Don Edward Wilkerson (2nd Assistant Director), Walt Jenevein (Sound Effects Editor), Richard Lapham (Music Editor), George R. Whittaker (Costume Designer), Don Snyder (Costume Supervisor), Robert Bralver (2nd Unit Director-Stunt Coordinator)

Guest Cast: Lawrence Dobkin (Colonel Alvin B. Kincaid), Judith Chapman (Linda Elliot), Erik Stern (Thompson), Jack Gill (Dugan), Morgan Jones (Warden), Michael O'Guinne (Officer Wally), Bill Cross (Officer Lester), Jim Boeke (Baker), Lee Duncan (Clark), Stephen Pershing (O'Brian), Talmage Scott (Front Jeep Driver), Greg Finley (Prison Guard), Kay Worthington (Woman Driver)

Michael and K.I.T.T. infiltrate a compound where a group of skilled soldiers are planning a daring gold robbery.

Knight Knotes:

- K.I.T.T. shows up his newest feature in this episode – Micro Jam.
- The convoy for the gold shipment consists of the following code names: Midas, Golden Goose, Front Door, Back Door and Watchdog.

Script to Screen:

- When Michael ejects Dugan from the car, he originally lands in a swamp, not in a tree.

- After Michael locks Dugan in an abandoned building (not a camper, as seen in the episode), instead of driving to the semi, the semi arrives at the abandoned building. A man in a Knight Industries cap is driving and Devon is in the passenger seat.

- The description of the first time viewers see the inside of the semi and Bonnie: "We see that the rear of the semi has been outfitted as a state-of-the-art electronics lab and garage. Towards the front are some chairs and other human touches...even a coffee maker. Also inside is Bonnie Barstow, a young engineer who makes her Knight Industries overalls look like a Bob Mackie original."

- Michael confiscates one half of a thousand dollar bill from Dugan. He meets a contact in the forest who has the other half. Once the halves are joined, Michael is told to follow the motorcycle rider where they proceed to Kincaid's estate. As they pull away, the rider splashes mud all over K.I.T.T. Once they arrive at the estate, the motorcycle rider is revealed to be Linda Elliot.

- Kincaid's team includes a midget named Forrest.

- Michael's (as Dugan) excuse for being late: "I was being tailed by this guy, Michael Knight, who happens to work for the Foundation for Law and Justice." It's during this speech that Michael says a line that appears in the episode's teaser, but not in the episode itself: "They're gunning for you, Colonel. You're the Muhammad Ali of crime".

- When Michael presses the button on K.I.T.T.'s comlink that allows him to communicate, the word ENGAGE appears on the face.

- In early drafts of the story, Jack Gill's character, Dugan, is known simply as "The Delivery Man".

- The script has Kincaid's first name as Thomas.
- Michael threatens to tell the world about K.I.T.T. unless he helps Linda by supplying her with an attorney. Devon responds, "Michael, listen to me. Wilton Knight never intended for the Knight 2000 to become public knowledge until after a long test in the field." He then reluctantly agrees, and tells Linda that she can choose between two Foundation lawyers – F. Lee Bailey or Mervin Belli.

Déjà Vu:
- Bill Cross can be seen in "Lost Knight".

Featured Songs:
"Do You Wanna Make Love?" by Peter McCann

"Long, Long Time" by Linda Ronstadt

"You Were Always on My Mind" by Willie Nelson

K.I.T.T.'s Capabilities:
- Auto Cruise, Auto Phone, Auto-Roof Left, Auto-Roof Right, Eject Right, Micro Jam, Turbo Boost

PROD. #57316

⎡ EPISODE ⎤
⎣ 10 ⎦

Script History:

October 28, 1982 (F.R.)

November 2, 1982 (F.R.)

November 5, 1982 (F.R.)

November 8, 1982 (F.R.)

November 8, 1982 – 2nd rev. (F.R.)

November 9, 1982 (F.R.)

THE FINAL VERDICT

Working Title: "A Shred of Evidence"

Teleplay By: John Alan Schwartz and E. Paul Edwards

Story By: Tom Greene, John Alan Schwartz, and Paul Edwards

Directed By: Bernard Kowalski

Original Airdate: December 3, 1982 (Friday, 9:00 PM) (17.9%; 14,910,000)

NBC Rerun #1: April 15, 1983 (Friday, 9:00 PM) (19.0%; 15,830,000)

Filming Dates: November 5-15, 1982

"Try and stay sober until I get back."

-Michael

Crew: R.A. Cinader (Co-Executive Producer), Steven E. de Souza (Producer), Hannah Shearer (Producer), Gilbert Bettman (Associate Producer), Bernadette Joyce (Associate Producer), David Braff (Story Editor), Stu Phillips (Music), H. John Penner (Director of Photography), Russell Smith (Art Director), R. Lynn Smartt (Set Decoration), April Webster (Casting), Lawrence J. Gleason (Film Editor), Beryl Gelfond (Film Editor), Jim Alexander (Sound), Ron Martinez (Unit Production Manager), Charles Watson Sanford, Jr. (1st Assistant Director), Don Edward Wilkerson (2nd Assistant Director), Walt Jenevein (Sound Effects Editor), Richard Lapham (Music Editor), Richard Hopper (Costume Designer), Don Snyder (Costume Supervisor), Robert Bralver (2nd Unit Director-Stunt Coordinator)

Guest Cast: Marvin Karon (Marty Keen), Don Gordon (Lieutenant Dickerson), Ramon Bieri (Al Farlan), Penny Peyser (Cheryl Burns), Rick Fitts (Brad), Tim Rossovich (Butch), Bob Schott (Dink), June Christopher (Kim the Bartender), Cynthia Ream (Tracy), Michael Masters (Garbage Man), Harold "Hal" Frizzell (Security Guard)

When Michael's good friend is wrongly accused of murder, it's up to him to find the only alibi that can clear her name.

A Look Back:

Marvin Karon played the much remembered lead role of Marty in "The Final Verdict". Karon recalls how he got the part. "I was a young Canadian actor, just a few years out of the National Theatre School of Canada, and had visited Los Angeles for the first time in August of 1982. My Toronto agent had established a connection with Hal Stalmaster, one of the principals of an agency called The Artists' Group. He offered to represent me if I were to come to California. In September of 1982, I drove down to LA.

Soon after, I had an interview with Steven Kolzak, who was behind the comedy series *Cheers*. He introduced me to April Webster, the casting director on *Knight Rider*. She called me into her office on the Universal lot for a pre-read and it was there that I met Bernard Kowalski, the director of the episode and one of the series' producers. As I recall, there were just four of us who were brought in to read for the role. A few days later, my agent called me with the good news".

While the producers were confident in their decision to hire Karon, a paperwork snafu nearly led to the role being recast before filming began. "Being Canadian, my agent asked me if I had my H-1 work permit," recalls Karon. "I had to confess that I did not but that I could get it. There was less than a week until filming began and the standard waiting period for an H-1 in 1982 was three months. Jerry Serviss got my working papers in three days. I also needed a testimonial letter of support from a client on the Artists' Group which they represented. Lorne Greene gave me the required signature. Greene had starred as Pa Cartwright in *Bonanza* for fourteen years and was also known as 'The Voice of Doom' for his broadcasts during World War II. To this day, I cannot thank April Webster enough for sticking by me even though time was running out with Universal's willingness to hold the part for me. For a period of time after the *Knight Rider* incident, whenever my agent got me in to read for a role, the first thing any casting director would say to me was not 'I saw your work in *Knight Rider*....thought you were very good', but rather, 'Marvin Karon? Hey...aren't you the guy who got his working papers in three days? What was that lawyer's name?'"

Karon spent the majority of his time on set with David Hasselhoff and remembers the first time they met. "I have only the fondest memories of working with David. He couldn't have been more generous, welcoming, warm or supportive. On the first day of the shoot, there was a knock on my door. I scrambled to get into my pants and opened it up to find David on the steps leading up to my Honeywagon. He took my hand, shook it, introduced himself and told me that, while the show might not be Shakespeare, we'd have a lot of fun. And we did. One night, we were shooting very late...well past midnight. He saw me sitting on set in a chair. 'What are you doing here?' he asked me. 'It will be hours before they need you. Go to my trailer...help yourself to anything you want in the fridge...drinks, food. Go ahead and watch TV in there'.   That's the kind of guy he was...a big, sweet, thoughtful, incredibly generous and unpretentious star."

Karon recalls a humorous moment during the filming of one of his scenes. "On the second or third night of shooting, we were stopped and the crew was setting up a shot. A crowd of kids recognized David and came running over to get his autograph. They were quite literally reaching over me in the passenger seat to get to him with their scraps of paper to sign. As the assistant director shooed them away so we could start the shoot, I told them that as much as I would love to be as generous as David, I really had to get back to work and would have to offer my signatures to them some other time. They didn't have a clue as to what I was talking about, of course!"

In between takes, Karon and Hasselhoff would entertain themselves by singing. "In the scene where we're coming out of the office with the books that will convict my boss, we had to enter from a warehouse door. While waiting for the signal to go in between adjustments to lighting and blocking, he and I would harmonize on Beatles tunes – 'Eight Days A Week' was one I vividly remember the two of us singing".

"The Final Verdict" was directed by Bernard L. Kowalski, who would go on to become a regular on the series. "Bernie Kowalski was one of the dearest, most generous, thoughtful and wonderful men I have ever met since graduating from theatre school almost thirty-five years ago. In a stage production, a director's job is to help you with any acting problems you might have but on a film or television set, of course, they are more concerned with the composition of the picture for the camera, what lens they want to use for a shot, how many set ups they are behind at any given point in the day, whether they are losing the light, etc. Rare is the director who can help you with your performance but Bernie was definitely one of those directors. We became friends and I was always invited to the Kowalski home for both Thanksgiving and for Christmas dinner".

Karon's character Marty was involved in some hair-raising stunts in K.I.T.T., including a turbo boost. However, Karon was not allowed to do any of the stunts himself. "Bernie Kowalski's son, Peter, was my stunt double. Any shots that even hinted of any danger were scenes where Peter was involved".

Because of the success of *Knight Rider*, everyone from his niece to his local newspaper noted his role as Marty. "Starring in *Knight Rider* had a bit of an impact on my career for a while. My hometown newspaper, <u>The Hamilton Spectator</u>, interviewed me and that may have made my parents proud of me. My niece was two when the show aired and for months after she apparently wailed my signature line in the episode: 'Who's driving the car?'"

Knight Knotes:

- This episode is in dedicated to producer R.A. Cinader - "He was an original".
- Writer Tom Greene named the character of Cheryl Burns after an ex-girlfriend that "burned" him.
- Michael quotes Wilton Knight's dying words ("One man making a difference") here, something he does again in "Knight of the Juggernaut" and *Knight Rider 2000*.
- Michael's comlink is destroyed here, as well as in "Knightmares", "Killer K.I.T.T.", and "Voo Doo Knight".
- K.I.T.T. receives a Graphic Analyzer here.

Script to Screen:

- The script's description of the opening scene of the episode, where Michael and K.I.T.T. are driving: "K.I.T.T. and Michael surge down the open road accompanied by the pulsating rhythms of the hot theme music."

Déjà Vu:

- Ramon Bieri guest stars in "Junk Yard Dog"; Don Gordon is in "Knight By a Nose"; Michael Masters can be seen in "Knight Strike" and "Knight Song"; Tim Rossovich is back in "Knights of the Fast Lane".

Featured Songs:

"Highways Run Forever" by Johnny Lee

"Love Will Turn You Around" by Kenny Rogers

"It Ain't Easy Being Easy" by Janie Fricke

K.I.T.T.'s Capabilities:

- Auto Cruise, Auto-Roof Left, Composite Identification Mode, Eject Left, Micro Jam, Phone Tap, Radar, Surveillance Mode, Tinted Windows, Turbo Boost

PROD. #57306

[EPISODE
11]

Script History:

July 28, 1982 (F.R.)

August 3, 1982 (F.R.)

August 16, 1982 (F.R.)

A PLUSH RIDE

Written By: Gregory S. Dinallo

Directed By: Sidney Hayers

Original Airdate: December 10, 1982 (Friday, 9:00 PM) (19.1%; 15,910,000)

NBC Rerun #1: July 22, 1983 (Friday, 9:00 PM) (19.0%; 15,830,000)

Filming Dates: August 31- September 10, 1982

"Michael, where are your pants?"

-K.I.T.T.

Crew: R.A. Cinader (Co-Executive Producer), Steven E. de Souza (Producer), Hannah Shearer (Producer), Gilbert Bettman (Associate Producer), Bernadette Joyce (Associate Producer), David Braff (Story Editor), Stu Phillips (Music), H. John Penner (Director of Photography), Seymour Klate (Art Director), R. Lynn Smartt (Set Decoration), April Webster (Casting), William Martin (Film Editor), John R. McDonald (Sound), Ron Martinez (Unit Production Manager), Charles Watson Sanford, Jr. (1st Assistant Director), Don Edward Wilkerson (2nd Assistant Director), Walt Jenevein (Sound Effects Editor), Richard Lapham (Music Editor), George R. Whittaker (Costume Designer), Don Snyder (Costume Supervisor), Robert Bralver (2nd Unit Director-Stunt Coordinator)

Guest Cast: William Lucking (Marc Redmond), Wendy Fulton (Margot Wells), Hector Elias (Roberto Lopez), Michael Carven (M.W. Jacobs), M.C. Gainey (Jason Kellar), Don Mantooth (Corey)

Michael goes undercover at a driving school to uncover who is planning the assassination of a group of world leaders.

A Look Back:

Fans of the series who have seen pictures of K.I.T.T.'s engine will note that, along with some other modifications, the factory air cleaners were always replaced with an aftermarket version. Jack Gill explains, "The reason that we put an aftermarket air cleaner on the cars was because the original one was way too big and you couldn't really get to the carburetor quickly to try and fix anything that was wrong. So we were always trying to put a small air cleaner on there so Willie Stabile, our car mechanic, could pop the hood and get in there quite quickly and try and fix whatever I needed fixing. Most of the cars were carbonated. I don't remember any fuel injection models. There might have been but I don't remember any. I never really got under the hood, I just told them what was wrong with it. In general, they all ran great."

Knight Knotes:

- One of the assault limos that K.I.T.T. jumps over has a license plate of CA 1E59885 – the same plate as Devon's Mercedes in "Chariot of Gold".

- Michael meets Devon and Bonnie at the Buckaroo Club, which was frequented by Colt Seavers in Glen Larson's *The Fall Guy*. Incidentally, an early 1982 episode of *The Fall Guy* called "Soldiers of Misfortune" finds Seavers infiltrating a survivalists camp similar to the school here. The episode ends with Seavers climbing out of a truck on to a helicopter skid to subdue the villain, a la "Just My Bill".

Script to Screen:

- In the opening scene, Devon comments to Michael that he wishes they were using the "Knight 2000 for this errand" instead of the limo. It's interesting that he doesn't call him K.I.T.T.

- Redmond's first name is Marc.

- Immediately after Redmond and Michael meet, there is a scene where Bonnie adjusts K.I.T.T.'s video equipment with a joystick to give him the ability to see 180 degrees. K.I.T.T. then complains to Bonnie that Michael was driving around in "an inferior assembly line clone", meaning the limo. This jealousy continues throughout the script.

- Early scripts portrayed Redmond as more of a cowboy "good ol' boy".

- The original list of drivers was: Jason Keller, M.W. Jacobs, Roberto Lopez, Joanna Cory, Tip Maguire and Margot Wells. Note that the character of Corey was originally to be a woman.
- Redmond's Victory Academy was originally known as the Vanguard School.
- K.I.T.T. recalls the time when Michael had him pose as a junked car in a salvage yard for two weeks. A tattooed man kept trying to crush him, but K.I.T.T. resisted. K.I.T.T. thought that "his plugs would never fire again".
- Margot Wells was originally envisioned as a blonde.
- The unseen character Tip Maguire was to be fighting Keller when Michael first arrives at the academy. The episode depicts the fight between Corey and Lopez.
- Besides Redmond, another figure enters Michael's bungalow. K.I.T.T. recorded the break-in, but the person was wearing a helmet with Redmond's Vanguard school logo on it. Michael examines the logo and sees that it has a "V" shaped scratch in it. It turns out to be Margot. She broke into Michael's bungalow, not the other way around. Margot also knows that Michael works for the Knight Foundation.
- Instead of taking the Third World Leaders out to a bar, Devon instead suggests they do some sightseeing. Michael suggests, among other things, the Universal Studios tour.

Déjà Vu:

- M.C. Gainey returns in "Out of the Woods".

Featured Songs:

"Pickin' Up Strangers" by Johnny Lee

"Home on the Range" sung by the cast

K.I.T.T.'s Capabilities:

- Auto Cruise, Oxygen Vent, Pursuit Mode, Rotated Turbo Booster, Turbo Boost, X-Ray Mode

PROD. #57312

⎧ EPISODE ⎫
⎩ 12 ⎭

Script History:

November 8, 1982 (F.R.)

November 15, 1982 (F.R.)

November 19, 1982 – EN (F.R.)

November 19, 1982 – 2nd rev. (F.R.)

November 23, 1982 (F.R.)

FORGET ME NOT

Teleplay By: Richard Christian Matheson, Thomas Szollosi, Karen Harris, and Deborah Davis

Story By: Chris Lucky, Richard Christian Matheson, and Thomas Szollosi

Directed By: Gil Bettman

Original Airdate: December 17, 1982 (Friday, 9:00 PM) (14.9%; 12,410,000)

NBC Rerun #1: July 8, 1983 (Friday, 9:00 PM) (19.3%; 16,080,000)

Filming Dates: November 22- December 1, 1982

"Michael, could your 1956 Chevrolet go into Surveillance Mode?"

-K.I.T.T.

Crew: R.A. Cinader (Co-Executive Producer), Steven E. de Souza (Producer), Hannah Shearer (Producer), Karen Harris (Co-Producer), Gilbert Bettman (Associate Producer), Bernadette Joyce (Associate Producer), David Braff (Story Editor), Stu Phillips (Music), H. John Penner (Director of Photography), Russell Smith (Art Director), R. Lynn Smartt (Set Decoration), April Webster (Casting), Edwin F. England (Film Editor), Beryl Gelfond (Film Editor), Stan Gordon (Sound), Ron Martinez (Unit Production Manager), Charles Watson Sanford, Jr. (1st Assistant Director), Don Edward Wilkerson (2nd Assistant Director), Walt Jenevein (Sound Effects Editor), Richard Lapham (Music Editor), Richard Hopper (Costume Designer), Don Snyder (Costume Supervisor), Robert Bralver (2nd Unit Director-Stunt Coordinator)

Guest Cast: Alejandro Rey (Rudy DelJuago), Judy Landers (Micki Bradburn), Maria Conchita (Marie Elena Casafranca), Reid L. Shelton (David Burns/The Eagle), Victor Millan (Eduardo Casafranca), Michael Lane (Jerry), Fred Lerner (Ray), David Olivier (The Frenchman), Katia Christine (Margo), Michael Horsley (Valet Attendant), Michael Lamont (Male Guest), Helen Duffy (Actress)

Michael is assigned to protect the daughter of Latin American president while on a visit to the United States.

A Look Back:

Judy Landers was one of the most recognizable faces on American television in the 1980's, but it was a talent for gymnastics that gave her the belief to be an actress. "As a child, I was very shy and introverted," confesses Landers. "I found I had a talent for gymnastics and before long, I became an award winning gymnast. This accomplishment gave me the confidence to admit that I wanted to be an actress. I began studying acting at the American

Academy of Dramatic Arts and actually landed the very first acting job that I auditioned for in Hollywood. Aside from a few hardships along the way, my career fulfilled just about everything I had hoped for."

Landers starred as Micki Bradburn in "Forget me Not" and recalls how she got the part. "When I auditioned for the role of Micki, there were about 40 other beautiful actresses auditioning at the same time," remembers Landers. "It was a little intimidating as most of them had already been successful in their careers. I remember telling myself to relax and be myself. That is advice that has always been beneficial to me because no one can be 'you' better than you can."

In the episode, Micki loses her memory and Landers remembers that she had to do some research prior to filming. "After I found out that I would be playing Micki, I researched different types of amnesia and memory loss to find out how it affects people's behavior so I could be authentic in the role."

Landers recalls that she liked the location of the shoot, which included a house by the sea. "We shot the episode on location in a beautiful beach house in Malibu. It was a lovely and romantic place to be filming."

"Forget Me Not" was directed by Gil Bettman. "I believe this episode was one of Gil's first directing jobs. He was a great director. He was very creative and organized. He had a vision of exactly what he wanted in each scene."

Landers worked alongside Maria Conchita Alonso, who would also enjoy a career in television and movies. "It was wonderful working with Maria Conchita. She was a sweet girl and always professional. I remember during the filming that she broke a tooth!"

Landers also shared screen time with David Hasselhoff. "David and I always had great chemistry. We were both in relationships at the time, but there was always a little flirting going on between us. We did a lot of personal appearances together and became good friends. I think I always had a little crush on him," confesses Landers.

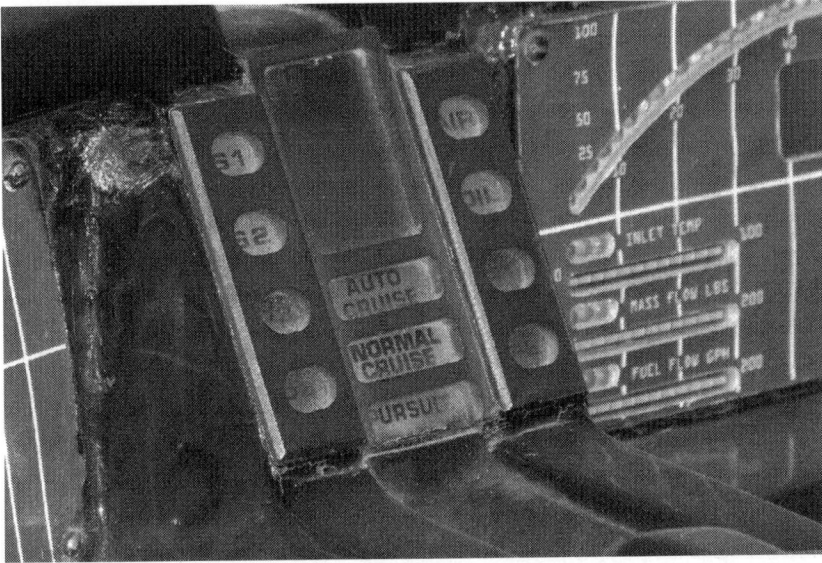

An original voice box bezel

At the climax of the episode, Micki and Michael are involved in a chase scene an at equestrian show. "That chase scene was very exciting and very intense. There was always an element of danger because of the high speed car stunts. Also, I always find it very challenging to run in spike heels," jokes Landers.

Knight Knotes:

- The episode re-uses footage from the 1977 movie *The Car* during the scene where K.I.T.T. drives off the cliff. It was also used when K.A.R.R. careened off a cliff at the end of "Trust Doesn't Rust".
- In the scene where K.I.T.T. pushes the Mercedes out of his way in order to pick up Michael, one of the cars has a license plate of CA 863 OGF. This same plate is seen on Elliott Steven's Mazda in "Nobody Does It Better".

Script to Screen:

- The script refers to the move that K.I.T.T. makes when he cuts off Ray and Jerry's car (after Micki jumps out) as a "brodie".

- As K.I.T.T. auto-starts before leaping off the cliff, the script notes that he shift from "Drive" into "4-Wheel".

- Michael jokingly asks K.I.T.T., "Sometimes I wonder if you're my wheels or I'm your feet."

Déjà Vu:

- Michael Horsley is in season three's "Knight in Disgrace"; Judy Landers returns in "Knight Strike"; and Fred Lerner guest stars in "Brother's Keeper".

Featured Songs:

"Get Closer" by Linda Ronstadt

K.I.T.T.'s Capabilities:

- Auto Cruise, Auto-Roof Left, Grappling Hook, Surveillance Mode, Turbo Boost, Winch

PROD. #57322

[
EPISODE
13
]

Script History:

December 1, 1982 (F.R.)

December 7, 1982 (F.R.)

December 10, 1982 (F.R.)

December 13, 1982 (F.R.)

HEARTS OF STONE

Working Title: "High Noon in Houston"

Written By: Robert Foster

Directed By: Jeffrey Hayden

Original Airdate: January 14, 1983 (Friday, 9:00 PM) (19.1%; 15,910,000)

NBC Rerun #1: September 11, 1983 (Sunday, 8:00 PM) (24.2%; 20,280,000)

Filming Dates: December 13-21, 1982

"I don't have a strange dash. I'm proud of my dash."

-K.I.T.T.

Crew: Robert Foster (Executive Producer), Joel Rogosin (Supervising Producer), Steven E. de Souza (Producer), Gilbert Bettman (Associate Producer), Bernadette Joyce (Associate Producer), David Braff (Story Editor), Don Peake (Music), H. John Penner (Director of Photography), Russell Smith (Art Director), R. Lynn Smartt (Set Decoration), April Webster (Casting), William Martin (Film Editor), Stan Gordon (Sound), Ron Martinez (Unit Production Manager), Charles Watson Sanford, Jr. (1st Assistant Director), Don Edward Wilkerson (2nd Assistant Director), Walt Jenevein (Sound Effects Editor), Richard Lapham (Music Editor), Richard Hopper (Costume Designer), Don Snyder (Costume Supervisor), Robert Bralver (2nd Unit Director-Stunt Coordinator)

Guest Cast: Mary McCusker (Angeline Beth Martin), Rudy Ramos (Roberto Laguna), Jeff Cooper (Ricky Stone), Sam Vlahos (Father Carlos Laguna), Zitto Kazann (Emile Pavlon), Arell Blanton (Danny Dwight), Constance Ball (Nurse), Connie Downing (Girl at Party), Larry Bame (Bartender)

Michael attempts to stop the sale of illegal handguns along the Texas border by posing as a potential buyer.

A Look Back:

Rudy Ramos starred as Roberto Laguna, the younger brother of Father Carlos Laguna. "I don't think I read for the part in *Knight Rider*," recalls Ramos. "I believe they called my agent and asked for me."

Ramos is a veteran actor who was a regular on US television, but he may have had a different career. "I got into acting by accident. I was working in a shoe store on La Cienaga Boulevard in Los Angeles. I met a casting assistant who took me to a casting director at MGM studios. From there, I was guided to Sherman Marks, who was to become my mentor for the first 8 years of my career. He and Lee Strasberg are the only true genius's I have ever known. When Sherman passed away, I studied under Lee."

In Ramos' first scene in "Hearts of Stone", his brother tells Michael Knight that Roberto is the "youngest and the craziest one" and Ramos can see similarities with his character. "I have always been slightly off center and passionate. So it is true that Roberto and myself were very much alike."

Ramos remembers the cast with affection. "Sam (Vlahos - who played Roberto's brother) is a very good actor and we had a good working relationship during the shoot. Mary McCusker (Roberto's girlfriend) was a sweetheart. She was fun to work with and be around. Mary should have worked more than she did because she was/is a wonderful actress."

One person Ramos did find difficult during the shooting of "Hearts of Stone" was director Jefferey Hayden. "Jefferey Hayden was a great director but not a nice person. He lacked in people skills and manners," recalls Ramos.

Ramos says that David Hasselhoff ticked all the boxes as the main star of *Knight Rider*.

"I loved working with David. He was very professional and approachable. He's also a very good actor, and just a really nice person. And yes he really is that handsome, even in person."

Ramos believes that television has changed radically since he first started acting in the 1970's. "I've worked in TV since 1971. My first job was as a regular on *The High Chaparral* during its fourth season. I then moved on to stage and feature films. The TV and film making business was very similar in the 70's and 80's but it all started to change in the 90's. Now it is not the business that I originally fell in love with. Still, I love the creative process and I have made adjustments to the way things are now. I don't work as much now, but I don't need to. I still work when called and enjoy and love my life when I'm not working."

As for working on *Knight Rider*, Ramos had a good time. "I always enjoy every role I play. I love the creative process. I had great fun and a great time working on *Knight Rider*."

Knight Knotes:

- The semi receives its familiar black and gold paint job in this episode. Producer Gerald Sanford recalls, "When Foster took over, he said, 'Change everything to black. Make the truck black and put David in black to match the car'."
- This episode, along with "Give Me Liberty...or Give Me Death", utilize different fonts styles for the beginning episode credits.
- The helicopter used in this episode is the same one used in "Just My Bill", "Knight Strike", and "Knight in Disgrace".
- The assault rifle that Devon shows Michael is called the Nunn X-19.

Script to Screen:

- Early drafts made no mention of K.I.T.T.'s voice box change or the semi's new paint job. It does, however, describe K.I.T.T. pulling into the semi while it's moving, a first for the series: "The semi's hydraulic loading ramp descends and the Trans Am drives up and in. The semi continues down the highway."
- The episode's teaser features a scene with Devon saying that the Nunn X-19 is to combat rifles "what K.I.T.T. is to conventional cars". The scene doesn't appear in the episode, but according to the script, takes place during Michael's testing of the gun.
- Bonnie comments to Michael that she's a vegetarian.
- When Michael first meets Roberto, he says, "To be Catholic is hard enough, but to have a brother who's a priest -- Que Dios tenga

misericordia." Translated, the last sentence means, "God have mercy".

Déjà Vu:

- Arell Blanton guest stars in "Mouth of the Snake"; Sam Vlahos returns in "Blind Spot".

Featured Songs:

"Skin Game" by John Hiatt and Ry Cooder

"Lonesome, On'ry and Mean by Waylon Jennings

"Don't You Think This Outlaw Bit Has Done Got Out of Hand" by Waylon Jennings

K.I.T.T.'s Capabilities:

- Auto Cruise, Auto Phone, Auto-Roof Left, Ground-to-Air Surveillance, Horizontal Turbo Boost, Micro Jam, Pursuit, Retro Rockets, Surveillance Mode, Turbo Boost, Tear Gas

PROD. #57323

$$\begin{bmatrix} \text{EPISODE} \\ 14 \end{bmatrix}$$

Script History:

December 17, 1982 (F.R.)

December 20, 1982 (F.R.)

December 20, 1982 – 2nd rev. (F.R.)

December 21, 1982 (F.R.)

December 23, 1982 (F.R.)

GIVE ME LIBERTY...OR GIVE ME DEATH

Written By: David Braff

Directed By: Bernard L. Kowalski

Original Airdate: January 21, 1983 (Friday, 9:00 PM) (22.7%; 18,910,000)

NBC Rerun #1: September 4, 1983 (Sunday, 8:00 PM) (18.4%; 15,420,000)

NBC Rerun #2: July 1, 1984 (Sunday, 8:00 PM) (12.6%; 10,560,000)

Filming Dates: December 23, 1982- January 4, 1983

"Michael, the car of the future is already here - me."

-K.I.T.T.

Crew: Robert Foster (Executive Producer), Joel Rogosin (Supervising Producer), Steven E. de Souza (Producer), Gilbert Bettman (Associate Producer), Bernadette Joyce (Associate Producer), David Braff (Story Editor), Don Peake (Music), H. John Penner (Director of Photography), Russell Smith (Art Director), R. Lynn Smartt (Set Decoration), April Webster (Casting), Lawrence J. Gleason (Film Editor), Stan Gordon (Sound), Ron Martinez (Unit Production Manager), Fred L. Miller (1st Assistant Director), Don Edward Wilkerson (2nd Assistant Director), Walt Jenevein (Sound Effects Editor), Richard Lapham (Music Editor), Richard Hopper (Costume Designer), Don Snyder (Costume Supervisor), Robert Bralver (2nd Unit Director-Stunt Coordinator)

Guest Cast: Robin Dearden (Liberty Cox), Brett Halsey (Clark Sellers), Alan Fudge (Ed Shaw), Francine Lembi (Dorothy Ackridge), Kai Wulff (Helmutt Grus), Kenneth Tigar (Dr. Norman Kempler), Sab Shimono (Hito Osaka), Richard Young (Sonny Prince), Adam Ageli (Hashi Al Qatar), Gary Houston Phillips (Lester Prince), Frank Pesce (Director), Robert Balderson (P.A. Announcer)

After an alternative energy race is sabotaged, Michael and K.I.T.T. enter as competitors to flush out the person responsible.

Knight Knotes:

- K.I.T.T. receives a number of improvements in this episode – an infrared tracking scope, liquid hydrogen fuel and tinted windows.

Script to Screen:

- In earlier versions of the scripts, Dr. Kempler's first name was Gordon, Dorothy Ackridge's last name was Arnold, and there was a seventh driver named Andy Russel.

- The Prince brothers in the orange Dodge Charger had a conversation that was cut from the final script. They make a reference to *The Dukes of Hazzard*: "Are you kidding? After we win this race and get all that publicity, we're goin' to Hollywood. Gonna get us our own TV show." At the mention of the word they emit rebel yells.

Déjà Vu:

- Kai Wulff plays the bad guy in "Custom Made Killer"; Robin Dearden guest stars in "Buy Out".

Featured Songs:

"Hold Me" by Fleetwood Mac

"Hurts So Good" by John Cougar Mellencamp

K.I.T.T.'s Capabilities:

- Auto Cruise, Chemical Detectors, Grappling Hook, Infrared Tracking Scope, Pursuit, Radar, Tinted Windows, Turbo Boost, Winch

PROD. #57321

EPISODE
15

Script History:

December 30, 1982 (F.R.)

January 3, 1983 (F.R.)

January 5, 1983 (F.R.)

January 5, 1983 – 2nd rev. (F.R.)

January 11, 1983 (F.R.)

THE TOPAZ CONNECTION

Working Title: "The Topaz File"

Written By: Stephen Katz

Directed By: Alan Myerson

Original Airdate: January 28, 1983 (Friday, 9:00 PM) (20.1%; 16,740,000)

NBC Rerun #1: May 20, 1983 (Friday, 9:00 PM) (20.7%; 17,240,000)

NBC Rerun #2: August 12, 1983 (Friday, 9:00 PM) (20.0%; 16,660,000)

Filming Dates: January 5-13, 1983

"Please remove the staple from my fender."

-K.I.T.T.

Crew: Robert Foster (Executive Producer), Joel Rogosin (Supervising Producer), Steven E. de Souza (Producer), Gian R. Grimaldi (Coordinating Producer), Gilbert Bettman (Associate Producer), Bernadette Joyce (Associate Producer), David Braff (Story Editor), Don Peake (Music), H. John Penner (Director of Photography), Russell Smith (Art Director), R. Lynn Smartt (Set Decoration), April Webster (Casting), Beryl Gelfond (Film Editor), Stan Gordon (Sound), Ron Martinez (Unit Production Manager), Charles Watson Sanford, Jr. (1st Assistant Director), Don Edward Wilkerson (2nd Assistant Director), Walt Jenevein (Sound Effects Editor), Richard Lapham (Music Editor), Richard Hopper (Costume Designer), Don Snyder (Costume Supervisor), Robert Bralver (2nd Unit Director-Stunt Coordinator)

Guest Cast: Michael Durrell (Paul DeBrett), Jeanna Michaels (Lauren Royce), Jack Starrett (Hagen), Michael Alldredge (Bob Kroiger), John Ericson (Philip Royce), Tina Louise (Anne Tyler), George Caldwell (George Olin), Pendleton Brown (Photographer), Richardson Morse (Doctor Carlyle), Joy Hyler (Janet), Natalie Carroll (Model), Charles Walker (Franks the Pilot), Herb L. Mitchell (Butler), Eve McVeagh (Slot Granny)

Michael works with the daughter of a magazine editor to find out who is responsible for her father's death.

A Look Back:

The most famous (and most reused) *Knight Rider* car jump came in season one's "The Topaz Connection", where a driverless K.I.T.T. leaps a ravine. That jump would be reused in "Nobody Does It Better", "Lost Knight", "Junk Yard Dog", and "Knight Flight to Freedom". Jack Gill recalls, "The jump across the ravine was one we did at Lang Ranch Parkway. At the time of filming, it wasn't developed, but now it has houses, a golf course and everything else. It's in Thousand Oaks, California. I picked the spot and had a guy with a bulldozer cut the road in, but it was about 85 or 90 feet across the ravine just to get to the far side.

David Hasselhoff and "Topaz" guest star Natalie Carroll at a 1983 car show
(Photo courtesy of Christopher Orlando)

About halfway through the jump, viewers can see what appears to be a black jacket fluttering out the window. Gill recalls this very well. "That's because I got all harnessed up and had my jump harness and my helmet on, and then the wardrobe guy came running over and said that I didn't have the black *Knight Rider* jacket on. I told him that I also had a helmet on and a black jump harness so there's no real way I could put it on. So the wardrobe guy kind of draped this Michael Knight black coat around me and when I got up to speed, it tried to work its way out of the window."

Viewers can also spot a strange cable protruding from K.I.T.T.'s passenger side fender. Gill stated, "We always mount a camera inside a crash box on the right side of the car for a point-of-view feeling. We ran cables from the box into the car and then I would turn the camera on when I approached the ramp. It would only run for about a minute. When I hit the ramp, it broke the cable loose and sent it flying through the air. When I hit on the other side, the camera came loose and started tumbling, but the footage survived."

While the K.I.T.T. portrayed on television was indestructible, the Trans Ams used to play him weren't – especially the jump cars. They needed to be specially modified to protect both the integrity of the car and, more importantly, the safety of the driver inside. Addressing the safety enhancements, Gill commented, "I was harnessed from the ceiling on a bungee cord. I had a jump harness - it's like a rib cage corset that goes around your rib cage and then has loops on the top. I had plastic nylon webbing straps over my shoulder with clips and you could clip it into the roof on a bungee cord. This would enable you to push yourself down into the 5 point harness so your actual torso is suspended upwards and downwards for the impact. It meant that when I hit I wouldn't be slamming my butt into the seat. I would be getting pulled underneath my arms, which tends to stretch your spinal cord a bit, but it does keep you from breaking your back."

The modifications done to the cars were equally as elaborate. "All of the cars had cages in them, especially the jump cars. They also had skid pads at the bottom of them. This meant we were not ripping anything and nothing was getting caught up on a landing. They went all the way from the front nose to a foot or two past the front wheels and the cars were all weighted. We didn't use concrete - we usually just used sand or lead and a steel weight box on the back which was welded to the actual cage frame so it couldn't get loose. Other than that - the seats were all the same, but we did take the gas tanks out and replaced them with fuel cells. All of the cars were modified with heavy duty shocks and it all worked out pretty well."

Knight Knotes:

- Director Alan Myerson on the scene where Michael falls from the tail of an airplane: "I remember that the stunt double was very good and he had much experience with Jack Gill, who was blind-driving K.I.T.T. and worked with the double. It was a good and effective stunt, well executed, and all were happy with it."

- Myerson on the ravine jump: "I remember this jump also taking forever to set up and, as I recall, we may have wrecked one car before we got the shot with a second stunt vehicle."

- A keen eye can spot a 1982 Trans Am promotional artwork piece behind Lauren in the Escape mansion.

- This episode features the first use of K.I.T.T.'s Computer Printout feature.

- The Pontiac Firebird spokes model, Natalie Carroll, appears briefly as the model that poses on K.I.T.T.'s hood. Myerson noted, "One would think a lascivious fellow like me would have very powerful memories of a beautiful model like Ms. Carroll, but the truth is I remember nothing of her, her casting, or her acting."

- We meet the Foundation's Dr. Carlyle in this episode. He is mentioned, but not seen, in season two's "Goliath".

Script to Screen:

- In earlier incarnations of the script, the character of Paul DeBrett was known first as Paul DeNicolo and then Paul DeWitt.
- Escape magazine was originally called Escapade.
- When Michael leaves the Royce mansion, he finds two models sitting on K.I.T.T. getting their picture taken. When Michael asks K.I.T.T. about it, he replies that they were "comparing bodywork".
- A scene takes place in the semi before Michael chases Lauren to Las Vegas. There, Michael tells Bonnie to "check his fuel cells" and "give his logic circuits a pep talk". Bonnie replies for K.I.T.T. to "say ahh'".
- Bob Krioger is originally known as Bob Kruger.
- Once Michael realizes that the key to "Topaz" is Anne Tyler's measurements, he has K.I.T.T. run the first issue of Escapade in order to find them. The script notes, "INSERT - K.I.T.T.'S MONITOR - FEMALE OUTLINE - STOCK FROM "INSIDE OUT". Anne Tyler's measurements appear."
- When Paul escapes in the 4 wheeler at the climax of the episode, he leaves Lauren behind at the house. Michael stops them and throws Paul in K.I.T.T.'s trunk, along with Hagen.

Déjà Vu:

- Jack Starrett guest stars again in "K.I.T.T. the Cat" and "Sky Knight".

Featured Songs:

"Hold Me" by Fleetwood Mac

"Down Under" by Men at Work

"Love's Been a Little Bit Hard On Me" by Juice Newton

K.I.T.T.'s Capabilities:

- Auto Cruise, Auto-Roof Left, Printer, Pursuit, Surveillance Mode, Turbo Boost

PROD. #57317

⎧ EPISODE ⎫
⎩   16   ⎭

Script History:

January 19, 1983 (F.R.)

January 22, 1983 (F.R.)

A NICE, INDECENT LITTLE TOWN

Written By: Frank Telford

Directed By: Gil Bettman

Original Airdate: February 18, 1983 (Friday, 9:00 PM) (19.2%; 15,990,000)

NBC Rerun #1: June 3, 1983 (Friday, 9:00 PM) (19.2%; 15,990,000)

Filming Dates: January 25- February 2, 1983

"My dear I'm a car, not a plane."

-K.I.T.T.

Crew: Robert Foster (Executive Producer), Joel Rogosin (Supervising Producer), Steven E. de Souza (Producer), Gian R. Grimaldi (Coordinating Producer), Gilbert Bettman (Associate Producer), Bernadette Joyce (Associate Producer), Robert Ewing (Associate Producer), David Braff (Executive Script Consultant), William Schmidt (Story Editor), Don Peake (Music), H. John Penner (Director of Photography), Russell Smith (Art Director), R. Lynn Smartt (Set Decoration), April Webster (Casting), Lawrence J. Vallario (Film Editor), Stan Gordon (Sound), Ron Martinez (Unit Production Manager), Charles Watson Sanford, Jr. (1st Assistant Director), Don Edward Wilkerson (2nd Assistant Director), Walt Jenevein (Sound Effects Editor), Richard Lapham (Music Editor), Nancy McArdle (Costume Designer), Gil Loe (Costume Supervisor), Robert Bralver (2nd Unit Director-Stunt Coordinator)

Guest Cast: Norman Burton (Charles Barnswell), John Crawford (Sheriff Moore), Jean Bruce Scott (Jobina Bruce), Eric Server (Agent Peter Larkin), Amzie Strickland (Martha Haberstraw), Luke Askew (Ron Austin), Charles Bartlett (Deputy Hanks), Stacy MacGregor (Deputy Cole), Charles Picerni (Produce Driver)

Ron Austin, a known counterfeiter, stops in a sleepy town in an attempt to evade capture by Michael and K.I.T.T.

Knight Knotes:
- Sheriff Moore, seen in this episode, and Lt. George Barth from "K.I.T.T. the Cat", share the same license plate on their cruisers – CA 55989.
- The building that Devon stands in front of while presenting the Lowest Crime Rate Award to Alpine Crest is the same building used as the Courthouse in the *Back to the Future* trilogy. The town square

where the building is located is on the Universal Studios' back lot and was used in many future *Knight Rider* episodes, including "Sky Knight" and "Fright Knight".

- Charles Picerni, the man who drives the pickup that K.I.T.T. jumps over near the end of the episode, is a member of *Knight Rider's* stunt team. He appears in a bigger role as William Donner in "White Bird".
- Throughout most of the climax of this episode, K.I.T.T. is missing his turn signal blackouts on either side of the scanner.

Script to Screen:

- In the script, Bonnie tells Michael that K.I.T.T.'s rotors are overheating (which can be heard in the episode) and asks if he has been overusing Turbo Boost.
- As Michael exits K.I.T.T. to pursue Austin at the start of the episode, he tells K.I.T.T. to go into "Stand-by" mode, at which time various lights on the dash turn on.
- In addition to K.I.T.T., Devon also comments during his speech that Alpine Crest is a "nice, decent town".
- Michael notes that Deputy Cole is tailing him while leaving town. Michael presses the Turbo Boost and jets out of Cole's sight.

Déjà Vu:

- Norman Burton guest stars in "Redemption of a Champion"; John Crawford returns in "Knight Racer".

Featured Songs:

"I've Got a Rock N Roll Heart" by Eric Clapton

"Shame on the Moon" by Bob Seger

K.I.T.T.'s Capabilities:

- Auto Cruise, Auto Phone, Horizontal Turbo Boost, Printer, Pursuit, Radar, Ski Mode, Surveillance Mode, Turbo Boost, Video Playback, Voice Projection

PROD. #57326

Script History:

January 10, 1983 (F.R.)

January 12, 1983 (F.R.)

January 13, 1983 (F.R.)

January 14, 1983 (F.R.)

January 17, 1983 (F.R.)

January 17, 1983 – 2nd rev. (F.R.)

January 18, 1983 (F.R.)

January 20, 1983 (F.R.)

EPISODE 17

CHARIOT OF GOLD

Working Title: "Survival of the Fittest"

Written By: William Schmidt

Directed By: Bernard L. Kowalski

Original Airdate: February 25, 1983 (Friday, 9:00 PM) (19.6%; 16,330,000)

NBC Rerun #1: June 10, 1983 (Friday, 9:00 PM) (18.8%; 15,660,000)

Filming Dates: January 14-24, 1983

"You are the Knight Industries Two Thousand. You are my car. You belong to me."

-Michael

Crew: Robert Foster (Executive Producer), Joel Rogosin (Supervising Producer), Steven E. de Souza (Producer), Gian R. Grimaldi (Coordinating Producer), Gilbert Bettman (Associate Producer), Bernadette Joyce (Associate Producer), Robert W. Ewing II (Associate Producer), David Braff (Story Editor), William Schmidt (Story Editor), Don Peake (Music), H. John Penner (Director of Photography), Russell Smith (Art Director), R. Lynn Smartt (Set Decoration), April Webster (Casting), Stanley Wohlberg (Film Editor), Stan Gordon (Sound), Ron Martinez (Unit Production Manager), Fred L. Miller (1st Assistant Director), Don Edward Wilkerson (2nd Assistant Director), Walt Jenevein (Sound Effects Editor), Richard Lapham (Music Editor), Richard Hopper (Costume Designer), Don Snyder (Costume Supervisor), Robert Bralver (2nd Unit Director-Stunt Coordinator)

Guest Cast: Theodore Bikel (Graham Deauville), George McDaniel (Peter Stark), Lynne Topping (Charlene Hanover), Sandy Helberg (Irving Farber), Garnett Smith (Jim Litton), Lorinne Vozoff (Ellen Sullivan)

Bonnie is brainwashed by the head of an elite society and reprograms K.I.T.T. to assist in a robbery.

Knight Knotes:

- Patricia McPherson once commented that this was her favorite episode.
- The footage of K.I.T.T. seen by the Helios members consists of clips from the pilot episode, "Deadly Maneuvers", "Good Day at White Rock", "The Final Verdict", and "Hearts of Stone".
- K.I.T.T.'s blood pressure machine is only featured in this episode, but can be spotted under the car's dash in "Knight Moves".

Script to Screen:

- When Dr. Litton slams his Jeep against K.I.T.T., his right front wheel is damaged. Michael forces him into a ditch before the wheel falls off.

- The scene with Ellen showing the other Helios members footage of K.I.T.T. originally came immediately after Michael stopped Dr. Litton's Jeep near the beginning of the episode.

- Viewers are initially introduced to Peter Stark during the Jeep chase at the archeological dig site at the episode's beginning.

- Graham Deauville encourages Michael to take the Helios examination himself. When told he could use every resource at his disposal, Michael calls upon K.I.T.T. for the answers!

- Sparks fly under K.I.T.T.'s hood as Bonnie modifies his programming.

- K.I.T.T. micro jams the museum's door locks to trap the Helios members inside before taking off after Deauville.

K.I.T.T.'s Capabilities:

- Auto Cruise, Auto-Roof Left, Auto-Roof Right, Blood Analyzer, Chemical Analyzer/Dating System, Computer Override, Eject Left, Micro Jam, Printer, Ski Mode, Turbo Boost

PROD. #57330

Script History:

February 2, 1983 (F.R.)

February 5, 1983 (F.R.)

February 7, 1983 (F.R.)

February 14, 1983 (F.R.)

[
EPISODE
18
]

WHITE BIRD

Working Title: "The Long Way Home"

Written By: Virginia Aldridge

Directed By: Winrich Kolbe

Original Airdate: March 4, 1983 (Friday, 9:00 PM) (19.9%; 16,580,000)

NBC Rerun #1: September 18, 1983 (Sunday, 8:00 PM) (17.7%; 14,830,000)

NBC Rerun #2: July 22, 1984 (Sunday, 8:00 PM) (14.3%; 11,980,000)

Filming Dates: February 3-11, 1983

"I read about a bird once, a long time ago. A white bird. It eats. Sleeps. Spends its entire life in flight. It never lands. That's its purpose. Its destiny. To fly forever."

-Stevie Mason

Crew: Robert Foster (Executive Producer), Joel Rogosin (Supervising Producer), Gian R. Grimaldi (Coordinating Producer), Gilbert Bettman (Associate Producer), Bernadette Joyce (Associate Producer), Robert Ewing (Associate Producer), David Braff (Executive Script Consultant), William Schmidt (Story Editor), Don Peake (Music), H. John Penner (Director of Photography), Russell Smith (Art Director), R. Lynn Smartt (Set Decoration), April Webster (Casting), Stanley Wohlberg (Film Editor), Domenic G. DiMascio (Film Editor), Stan Gordon (Sound), Ron Martinez (Unit Production Manager), Robert Villar (1st Assistant Director), Bruce Humphrey (2nd Assistant Director), Walt Jenevein (Sound Effects Editor), Richard Lapham (Music Editor), Nancy McArdle (Costume Designer), Gil Loe (Costume Supervisor), Robert Bralver (2nd Unit Director-Stunt Coordinator)

Guest Cast: Catherine Hickland (Stefanie "Stevie" Mason), Bert Freed (Anthony Solan), Don Galloway (Gilbert Cole), Richard Caine (Federal Agent Carson James), Charles Picerni (William Donner), Eddy Donno (Blake), Harold "Hal" Frizzell (Security Guard)

Michael's former fiancée needs protection when she is wrongly implicated in a conspiracy involving her boss.

Knight Knotes:

- The new F.L.A.G. headquarters debuts here. This is one of four *Knight Rider* episodes in which scenes are shot at that mansion. The other three are "Brother's Keeper", "A Knight in Shining Armor", and "Goliath Returns".
- This is Executive Producer Robert Foster's favorite episode.

Script to Screen:

- Gilbert Cole's first name was originally Edward.

- The feature that links K.I.T.T. to the Foundation via his monitor is known as the "car-com".

- As soon as Michael sees the newspaper with Stevie on the front, he calls Devon at the Foundation. Bonnie answers as Devon is on a flight to Quebec.

- Gilbert Cole arrives at the police station to post Stevie's $500,000 bail, but is stunned to learn that someone else bailed her out.

- The car that chases Michael and Stevie is registered to a company called Amtec, Inc.

- K.I.T.T.'s turbo boost through the billboard sign was initially a jump over a ravine.

- Dr. Carlysle appears in the script and explains that Stevie is in a coma due to the fall she took after being shot. In the episode, he's only mentioned by name.

- A scene takes place with Michael and K.I.T.T. at the Foundation retreat after Stevie was shot. Michael goes out there to decide if he should reveal his true identity. K.I.T.T. senses Michael's distress and suggests that Bonnie give him a "tune-up".

- The original plan was for Bonnie to pose as Stevie during the big climax at the retreat. Bonnie even enters wearing a blonde wig, but Stevie decides to go herself.

- The story that Stevie tells Michael at the end of the episode differed slightly than what was seen on screen. Instead of a "white bird", it was a "swift".

Déjà Vu:

- Catherine Hickland returns in season two's "Let It Be Me" and season four's "The Scent of Roses"; Don Galloway is in "Knight in Retreat".

Featured Songs:

"Heart of the Night" by Juice Newton

"White Bird" by It's a Beautiful Day

K.I.T.T.'s Capabilities:

- Auto Cruise, Medical Scan, Phone Tap, Pursuit, Turbo Boost

PROD. #57332

$$\left[\begin{array}{c} \text{EPISODE} \\ 19 \end{array}\right]$$

Script History:

February 9, 1983 (F.R.)

February 12, 1983 (F.R.)

February 14, 1983 (F.R.)

KNIGHT MOVES

Working Title: "Wheels of Fear"

Written By: William Schmidt

Directed By: Christian I. Nyby II

Original Airdate: March 11, 1983 (Friday, 9:00 PM)19.4%; 16,160,000)

NBC Rerun #1: June 24, 1983 (Friday, 9:00 PM) (15.7%; 13,080,000)

Filming Dates: February 14-22, 1983

"Michael, I've been monitoring CB channels and Terri is right. 'K.I.T.T.' is
rather dull. How about 'Hot Knight'?"

-K.I.T.T.

Crew: Robert Foster (Executive Producer), Joel Rogosin (Supervising Producer), Gian R. Grimaldi (Coordinating Producer), Gilbert Bettman (Associate Producer), Bernadette Joyce (Associate Producer), Robert Ewing (Associate Producer), David Braff (Executive Script Consultant), William Schmidt (Story Editor), Don Peake (Music), H. John Penner (Director of Photography), Russell Smith (Art Director), R. Lynn Smartt (Set Decoration), April Webster (Casting), Beryl Gelfond (Film Editor), Lawrence J. Vallario (Film Editor), Stan Gordon (Sound), Ron Martinez (Unit Production Manager), Charles Watson Sanford, Jr. (1st Assistant Director), Don Edward Wilkerson (2nd Assistant Director), Walt Jenevein (Sound Effects Editor), Richard Lapham (Music Editor), Gil Loe (Costume Supervisor), Nancy McArdle (Costume Supervisor), Robert Bralver (2nd Unit Director-Stunt Coordinator)

Guest Cast: Morgan Woodward (Sheriff Hank Winston), James Whitmore, Jr. (Rick Calley), Guy Stockwell (Gil Riggins), Lonny Chapman (Sam Volker), Taylor Lacher (Kurt Brusker), Burton Gilliam (Gene Alley), Yvonne McCord (Terri Calley), Kathryn Butterfield (Norma Pell), Michael Potter (Ozzie Layton)

Rick and Terri Calley ask for the Foundation's help after a number of their semi trucks are hijacked while en route to deliver goods to market.

Knight Knotes:
- K.I.T.T. receives a long range tracking scope here.
- A Comtron shipping box can be spotted in the scene where Michael first meets Gil Riggins – a nod to the Pilot.
- Michael makes references to *The Virginian* and *The Alamo* while driving Terri to her hotel.

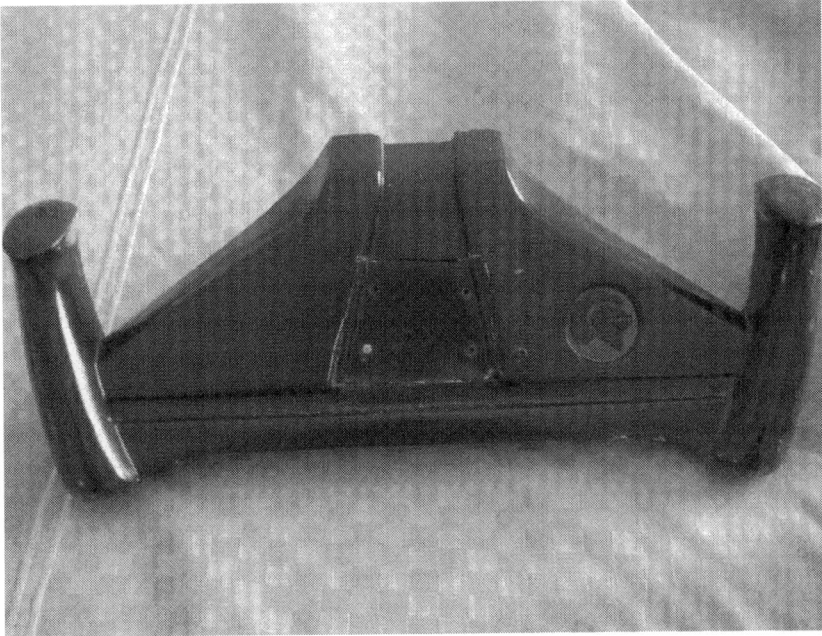

A screen used steering wheel.

Script to Screen:

- The first scene of the episode has Michael playing a space game on K.I.T.T.'s monitors. The scene plays out much the same as the video game scene in "Deadly Maneuvers", with the viewer assuming something bad is happening to Michael until the camera shows otherwise.

- Norma Pell, the waitress, is described in the script as "an overly made-up waitress in her mid-thirties. At one time -- in high school -- Norma was a knockout. Now, she has the tired look of a woman frustrated by fate."

- A scene near the start of the episode has Michael looking for Rick Calley in the Chief Joe Café, where Kurt, Gene and Ozzie are eating. Norma directs Michael to the trucking garage down the street.

- Michael calls Bonnie in the middle of the night at the Foundation to have her pull some data for him on the A.I.T.
- Norma asks Bonnie about what she envisions her "Mr. Right" to be like. Bonnie replies, "I'd like him to like classical music, but he should be open to all kinds of different styles. He's definitely got to love books and plays. I think he should have a good sense of humor, witty, you know, kind of sophisticated. It'd be nice if he were athletic, but I don't want him to be a jock. I like a guy who's full of surprises and...." She trails off.

Déjà Vu:

- Guy Stockwell also guest stars in "Return to Cadiz".

Featured Songs:

"Nobody" by Sylvia

K.I.T.T.'s Capabilities:

- Auto Cruise, Auto-Roof Left, Auto-Roof Right, CB Monitor, Long-Range Tracking Scope, Pursuit, Radar, Surveillance Mode, Turbo Boost

PROD. #57331

$$\left[\ \begin{array}{c} \text{EPISODE} \\ 20 \end{array}\ \right]$$

Script History:

February 17, 1983 (F.R.)

February 22, 1983 (F.R.)

NOBODY DOES IT BETTER

Written By: David Braff

Directed By: Harvey Laidman

Original Airdate: April 29, 1983 (Friday, 9:00 PM) (19.6%; 16,330,000)

NBC Rerun #1: August 5, 1983 (Friday, 9:00 PM) (19.2%; 15,990,000)

Filming Dates: February 23- March 4, 1983

"You better do what he says. That car means business."

-Flannery Roe

Crew: Robert Foster (Executive Producer), Joel Rogosin (Supervising Producer), Gian R. Grimaldi (Coordinating Producer), Gilbert Bettman (Associate Producer), Bernadette Joyce (Associate Producer), Robert Ewing (Associate Producer), David Braff (Executive Script Consultant), William Schmidt (Story Editor), Don Peake (Music), H. John Penner (Director of Photography), Russell Smith (Art Director), R. Lynn Smartt (Set Decoration), April Webster (Casting), Lawrence J. Gleason (Film Editor), Stanley Wohlberg (Film Editor), Stan Gordon (Sound), Ron Martinez (Unit Production Manager), Robert Villar (1st Assistant Director), Don Edward Wilkerson (2nd Assistant Director), Sam Shaw (Sound Effects Editor), Richard Lapham (Music Editor), Gil Loe (Costume Supervisor), Nancy McArdle (Costume Supervisor), Robert Bralver (2nd Unit Director-Stunt Coordinator), Jack Gill, Jr. (Co-Stunt Coordinator)

Guest Cast: Gail Edwards (Flannery Roe), Tony Dow (Julian Groves), Robert Ginty (Elliott Stevens), Angel Tompkins (Connie Chasen), Jimmy Bridges (Rollerskater), Marshall Teague (Armand), Laurie O'Brien (Linda Groves)

Michael works to uncover the person responsible for stealing development secrets from a fledgling computer company.

A Look Back:

Harvey Laidman, the veteran television director who had previously worked on such shows as *Hawaii Five-O*, *The Waltons* and the short lived series *Blue Knight*, directed this episode, the second to the last for the season. Laidman recalls how he ended up directing six episodes of *Knight Rider*. "When I was growing up in Cleveland, Ohio, television was new and exciting. I decided when I was 17 that I wanted to become a television director. I convinced my father to allow me to attend the University of

Southern California, majoring in cinema. After graduating from USC, I was employed by Channel 11 in Los Angeles. Three years later, I was accepted into the Directors Guild Producer Training Program, working as an assistant director and unit production manager. The job allowed me to work at all the major studios. I was then given the opportunity to direct an episode of *The Waltons* at Lorimar Productions. I was somewhat in demand and worked according to my availability. My agent would call and give me my schedule for the entire season ahead. Someone at *Knight Rider* knew me. It might have been Gino Grimaldi."

The opening scene of "Nobody Does It Better" depicts a character jumping a wall and breaking into a building. This is revealed to be a training exercise and the masked man is revealed as Michael Knight. Laidman explains the stunts needed for the scene. "Joel Kramer looked so much like David Hasselhoff that he could be mistaken for him at medium range. I remember Joel as a really good stunt man who could handle just about anything. Jack Gill and Bob Bralver were our stunt coordinators. That scene took place on the Universal lot. It was full of unit managers, assistant directors, production chiefs, accountants, etc. You could say we were truly 'under surveillance'."

The episode featured long sequences of David Hasselhoff driving K.I.T.T. and Laidman explained how the cameras were set up for the shots. "We didn't do process (rear projection). K.I.T.T. was towed behind a special camera vehicle called an insert car. We had at least two cameras mounted on the back pointed at K.I.T.T. - a wide shot and a tight close-up of David. Behind the two camera operators and their assistants were two electricians manning two big arc lights, John Penner, the cameraman, script supervisor and me. Sound sat in the passenger seat, and I had an intercom to the insert car driver and a radio to talk to David."

One of the key locations used in this episode is a tennis club, where Michael first meets Flannery Roe. Laidman recalls the troubles with moving the production outside of the Universal Studios lot. "Parts of the club were shut down during the week while we were filming. The club was very exclusive - The Toluca Lake Tennis Club. Universal Studios wanted to get away from what they perceived as a 'back lot look', so we spilled out onto the streets of LA proper. There were always problems shooting on location but money talks!"

Although most scenes in *Knight Rider* were filmed on sunny southern California days, the weather didn't always cooperate with the crew. "Nobody Does It Better" marked a rare time when it rained during the shoot. "It was terrible working in the rain," says Laidman. "It spoiled wardrobe, hair and makeup and we moved very slowly. The crew tried to limit exposure of themselves and equipment".

Working on *Knight Rider*, Laidman has fond memories of the main stars of the show. "This was a case of a very agreeable cast - easy to work with and good natured. Edward Mulhare was having back troubles at the time of shooting. David Hasselhoff was very professional and good natured as was Patricia McPherson. David always seemed to play Michael Knight 'larger than life'. My impression of him was that he was much quieter and introspective in real life. I didn't think that they made good use of Patricia's talents but she never complained." Tony Dow, famous for his role in *Leave It to Beaver,* also starred in this episode. "Tony and I are friends. I see him every week or so. We share an interest in woodworking and he is now a director himself."

Overall the *Knight Rider* experience and his first directorial effort on the show brought good memories to Laidman. "I really enjoyed working on *Knight Rider*. I made a lot of friends on the show. I remember that we were towing K.I.T.T. around Toluca Lake and we just pulled in to Baskin Robbins Ice Cream store and all got cones. I always liked having fun because I think it shows on the screen. I always watched the first TV runs of the episodes and since was a bit awed that the episodes came together in the end. They had a group of really great editors who regularly crossed over from feature films to television. I have always learned a lot watching editors work on my film."

Tony Dow is most recognizable as Wally in the late 1950's show *Leave it to Beaver*, but fans of the show remember him for another character. "David Hasselhoff and I would run into one another on the Universal back lot. At that time, I was at the studio filming *The New Leave it to Beaver*. My agent called me one day and said I had an appointment with the *Knight Rider* people and I got the role."

Dow's character, Julian Groves, comes across as a nervous and shy person, but in real life, Dow is the complete opposite. "I sure hope there is no similarity between Julian and myself. Julian was portrayed as jittery, a wimp and a loser. Back then, I played a pretty fair game of tennis, but in the scene at the tennis club, Julian is seen as not athletic."

Dow admits that the locations of the episode meant that he could stroll to work on occasion. "We lived in Venice at the time and the location shoot was nearby, on the Venice Beach boardwalk (where Julian Groves lived). It was the first time in my life that I could walk to work," jokes Dow.

The villain of the episode was played by the beautiful Angel Tompkins, who got her big break when she was discovered by Woody Allen. "Angel was great and fun to work with," remembers Dow. Also remembered fondly was the episode's director, Harvey Laidman. "I know Harvey very well, he's a great guy. Nowadays we hang out at the dog park. He has a wonderful dog as do I. We are good friends and I enjoy our conversations together."

Dow got along well with David Hasselhoff and explains the climax where he got hit by a door that Hasselhoff had barged into. "David and I didn't interact much, but he was fun to be around. I don't remember getting hit by a door - it must have been all planned."

Dow has had quite a career in television. "*Knight Rider* was just one episode, twenty eight years ago. My acting career began in 1956, when I played a wildlife photographer's son. Through the years, my roles ranged from Wally in *Leave it to Beaver* to a suspected rapist in *Death Scream*. I have played a multitude of characters, all of which I have enjoyed portraying. For twenty years, I had the opportunity to direct dozens of TV shows which was particularly gratifying, as I studied film at UCLA and had been interested in directing since my late teens. Dow is now a very successful sculptor in his own right.

Knight Knotes:

- Actor Robert Ginty on this episode: "I was good friends with the director, Harvey Laidman, and he called and asked me if I would be interested in guest starring on the series. It was a very good experience. The show was very clever and ahead of its time."
- Ginty on an experience at Universal Studios: "We would steal golf carts a lot and have races with them. I grabbed Alfred Hitchcock's cart and took off. I got pulled over and was told that I couldn't take Hitchcock's cart because he had trouble walking and needed it!"
- Although he worked on the show since the Pilot, Jack Gill doesn't receive on-screen credit until this episode.

Script to Screen:

- The guard that catches Michael at the start of the episode is named Sikes.
- The Hillsdale Tennis Club is originally known as the Match Point Tennis Club.
- Flannery's car of choice is a Mustang convertible, not the Red AMC Gremlin seen on screen.

- The police officer that arrests Michael is named Officer Kirby.

Déjà Vu:

- Angel Tompkins last name is misspelled in the opening credits of this episode (it appears as "Tomkins"). She returns in "Custom K.I.T.T."

Featured Songs:

"Get Closer" by Linda Rondstat

K.I.T.T.'s Capabilities:

- Auto Cruise, Infrared Tracking Scope, Pursuit, Surveillance Mode, Turbo Boost, Tinted Windows, Voice Projection, X-Ray Mode

PROD. #57336

$$\left[\begin{array}{c} \text{EPISODE} \\ 21 \end{array} \right]$$

Script History:

February 28, 1983 (F.R.)

March 1, 1983 (F.R.)

March 4, 1983 (F.R.)

SHORT NOTICE

Written By: Robert Foster

Directed By: Robert Foster

Original Airdate: May 6, 1983 (Friday, 9:00 PM) (16.4%; 13,660,000)

NBC Rerun #1: August 28, 1983 (Sunday, 8:00 PM) (16.1%; 13,410,000)

Filming Dates: March 8-16, 1983

"I try not to talk in front of adults. Sometimes, they don't understand."

-K.I.T.T.

Crew: Robert Foster (Executive Producer), Joel Rogosin (Supervising Producer), Gian R. Grimaldi (Coordinating Producer), Gilbert Bettman (Associate Producer), Bernadette Joyce (Associate Producer), Robert Ewing (Associate Producer), David Braff (Executive Script Consultant), William Schmidt (Story Editor), Don Peake (Music), H. John Penner (Director of Photography), Russell Smith (Art Director), R. Lynn Smartt (Set Decoration), April Webster (Casting), Beryl Gelfond (Film Editor), Lawrence J. Vallario (Film Editor), Stan Gordon (Sound), Ron Martinez (Unit Production Manager), Charles Watson Sanford, Jr. (1st Assistant Director), Don Edward Wilkerson (2nd Assistant Director), Sam Shaw (Sound Effects Editor), Richard Lapham (Music Editor), Gil Loe (Costume Supervisor), Nancy McArdle (Costume Supervisor), Robert Bralver (2nd Unit Director-Stunt Coordinator), Jack Gill (Co-Stunt Coordinator)

Guest Cast: Robin Curtis (Nicole Turner), William Smith (Harold T. Turner), Sandy McPeak (Arthur Wexley), Dennis Burkley (Tiny), Jordan Clarke (James "Jungle Jim" Ferris), Brittany Wilson (Natalie Turner), Joe Conley (Manager #1), David Hess (Donny), Linda L. Rand (Manager #2), Gail Fisher (Thelma)

After Michael is implicated in the murder of a biker, it's up to him to find a hitchhiker who can provide an alibi and keep Michael out of jail.

A Look Back:

As Michael Knight is trying to escape Harold T. Turner's gated compound, he employs K.I.T.T.'s ejection seat to rid the car of the bad guy sitting in the passenger's seat. What many fans don't realize is that the ejection seat was not a Hollywood magic trick, but a real, working ejection seat. The ejection seat mechanism was designed by stunt coordinator Jack Gill. "It was an air ram. Usually, air rams would propel you forward. What we did was have them design an air ram that went straight vertically. This meant that instead of pushing you forward, it pushed you straight up and then we had the stunt guy come in there and sit on the actual seat with his feet in these little areas where we knew his knees couldn't get caught. After that was done, all we did was push the button and throw him out of the car. There were times when we wanted him to go in a different angle and we would have him sit sideways on the seat or sit him completely forward. I remember we did a bunch of testing with me driving down a padded street. We would put pads down and would drive over the top of these two inch pads and then sling the guy out and see how it worked. We used it a few times and it worked pretty well.

Despite what many fans may think, they never used wires to pull the stunt men out. "We would never use wires to pull the guy out," says Gill. "It was always done with the air ram, which is really like a gymnastics beat board. It had two opposing hydraulic cylinders and they would let off air pressure. You would then sit on this plate and the plate would go up in the air. I think it was a foot and a half to two feet and it went very quickly, really fast pitching you in the air, so that's how we did it. We incorporated the scene with it because we had to see the seat come up as the guy got ejected. We also used it for when we did a high fall. I did a high fall off of an 8th story building ["A Good Knight's Work"] and I had to land in K.I.T.T., so we used that same ejection seat operation. This meant that when I went past the car, the seat went back down as if it had caught me."

Knight Knotes:
- Patricia McPherson makes her last appearance until season three's "Knight of the Drones".
- Nicole's Mercedes wears a license plate number of CA 1WY0977. This plate is seen again on Sam Dennis' car in "Custom Made Killer".

- Composer Don Peake can be seen lip-synching to "Sweet Home Alabama" in the bar scene.
- The cast and crew were informed during the filming of "Short Notice" that the series was renewed. Don Peake recalls, "Richard Lindheim came out and said, 'Guys, you've been renewed'. I thought, 'How nice of him to come out to this funky little night club to tell us.' He was quite pleased."
- Bonnie makes a reference to the 1969 movie *Easy Rider.*
- Robert Foster: "'Short Notice' was my first time out as director and the last show of the first year. Robin Curtis was a real trooper."

Script to Screen:

- Nicole's daughter Natalie is originally named Dana.
- When they arrive at the motel, Michael asks Nicole to get him a steak and a glass of wine. Nicole returns with a six pack of beer instead, claiming that it was the best she could do on short notice.
- The Satan Stompers motorcycle club was known as the Devil's Disciples.
- Michael asks if K.I.T.T. was shocked that Nicole used him. K.I.T.T. replies, "After a year on the road with you, Michael, nothing shocks me."

Featured Songs:

"Skin Game" by John Hiatt and Ry Cooder

"Sweet Home Alabama" by Lynyrd Skynyrd

"Night Moves" by Bob Seger

K.I.T.T.'s Capabilities:

- Auto Cruise, Auto-Roof Right, Eject Right, Pursuit, Surveillance Mode, Turbo Boost

Behind the KNIGHT: The License Plate

One of the most recognizable parts of K.I.T.T. is the California KNIGHT vanity license plate. Tony Hoffarth and his father were the men responsible for keeping the series supplied with these plates. Here, Tony recalls the construction of the plates and how you can tell a real one from a fake.

"In the mid '70's, my Dad started working for a small company called The Earl Hayes Press (EHP). EHP was an outfit that made 'inserts' for the motion pictures. Inserts could be anything from beer can labels, newspapers, I.D. cards, wanted posters, etc, including license plates. If the scene required multiple background vehicles to bear plates, the prop master would choose the cheaper printed cardboard plates. For the lead cars or close-ups, the raised metal plates were needed. Because of the extensive work needed to fabricate these raised plates, my Dad brought them home to work on in the evenings and would pay me to help with the work. All the letters, big and small, were cut out of a sheet of thick self-adhesive material. The letters and blank plates were shot with Krylon spray paint using the closest colors that we could match. California's colors were True Blue and Marigold Yellow. The numbers and letters were then applied to the painted plate and then shot with a dozen coats of clear, giving the final plate a raised look. We started making the plates in 1977. I worked on these plates with my Dad until I moved out in 1985 and my Dad continued making them for another five years or so, until the company started using a cheaper and faster vacuform plastic process. The prop master would order the plates from Earl Hayes through my Dad, then he would bring the orders home for me to work on. Given the time frame of the show, I could say that we made the sets needed for the full run of the series."

"It's hard to guess at how many sets of plates we made during the run of the series, but similar to the TANNA plates of *Vega$,* many were given away or lost. During one filming season, I would guess that we made about a dozen sets. Hind sight is always 20/20, so I never thought to make one for myself. I did take a lot of photos, but that was usually for documentation of non-California or vintage styles for further reference."

The following series of photographs document how the KNIGHT license plates were made for the series.

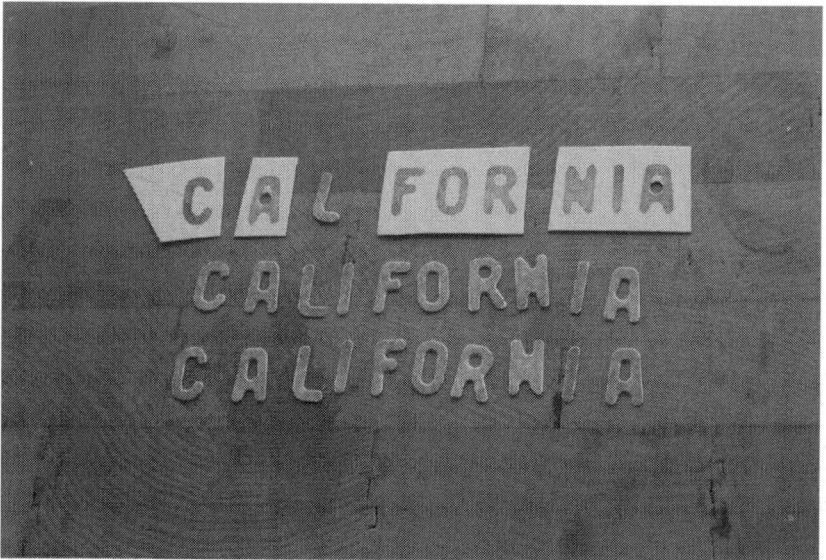

Step 1: The C-A-L-I-F-O-R-N-I-A letters are cut out.

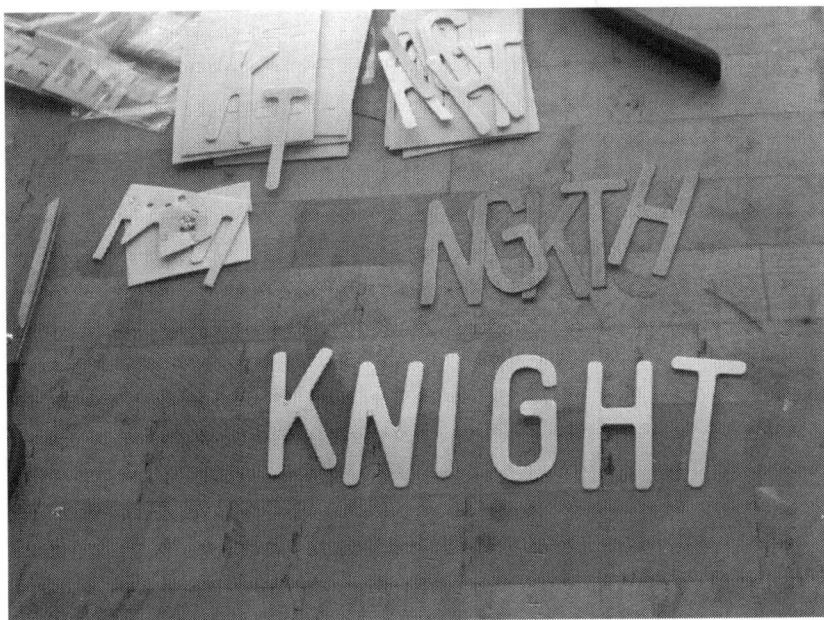

Step 2: The K-N-I-G-H-T letters are cut out next.

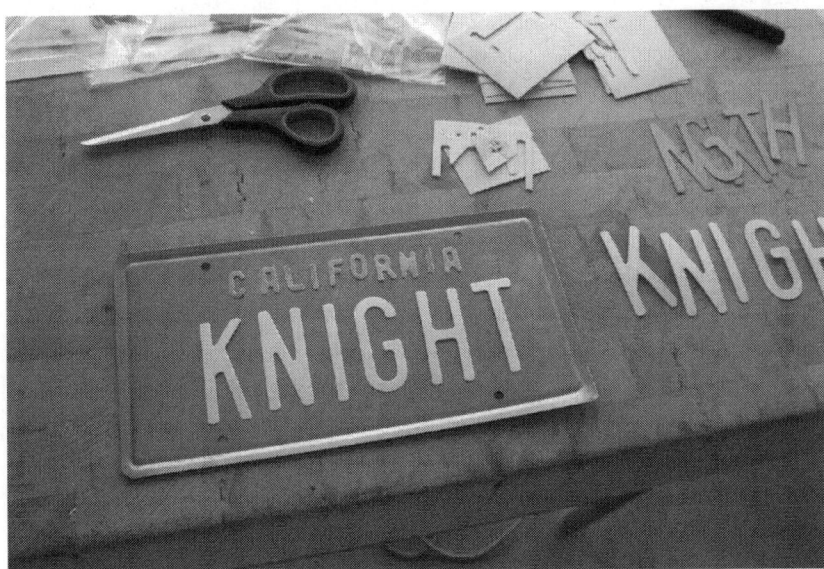

Step 3: The letters are temporarily laid in place to check fitment. The plate blank is steel and is slightly thicker than a normal license plate.

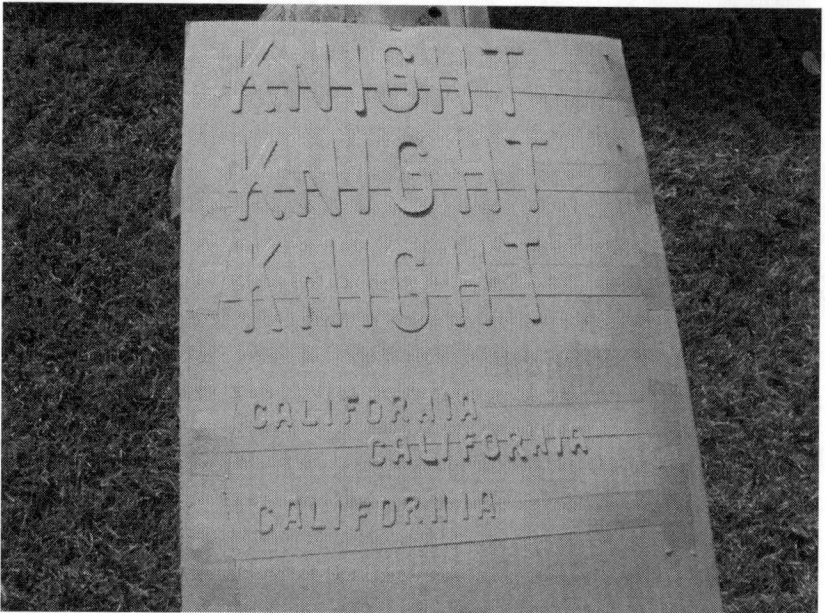

Step 4: The letters are laid out and spray painted their correct yellow color.

Step 5: The plate blanks are sprayed blue.

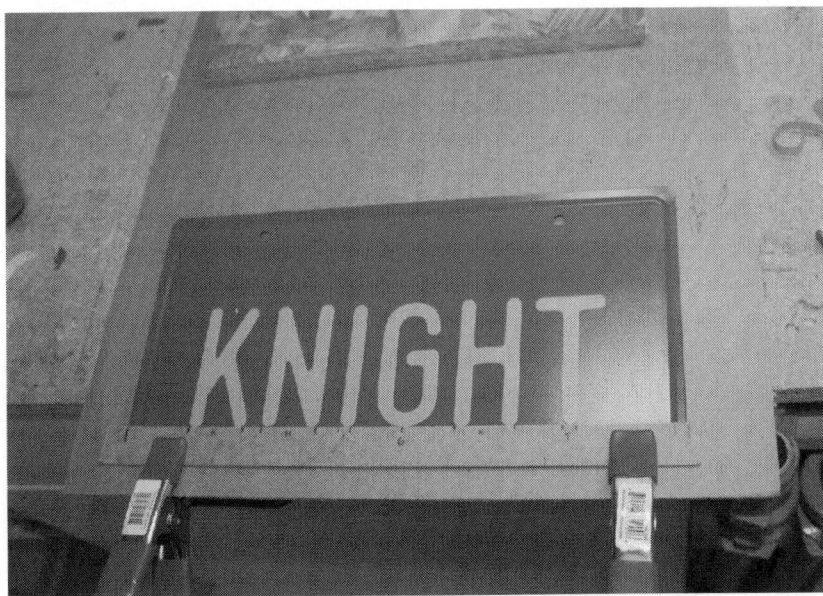

Step 6: Using a guide, the letters are affixed to the plate blank.

Step 7: The plate is sprayed with clear coat and ready for showtime!

Behind the KNIGHT: Auditions

Michael Knight	*Bonnie Barstow*	*Reginald Cornelius III*	*Voice of K.I.T.T.*
David Hasselhoff	Patricia McPherson	Peter Parros	William Daniels
Steve Bauer	Mary Margaret Humes	Blair Underwood	Guerin Barry
Don Johnson			
Phil Coccioletti			
Brian Cutler			
Jeffrey Osterhage			

KNIGHT RIDER

SEASON TWO (1983-1984)

Starring:

David Hasselhoff as Michael Knight

Edward Mulhare as Devon Miles

Rebecca Holden as April Curtis

William Daniels as the voice of K.I.T.T.

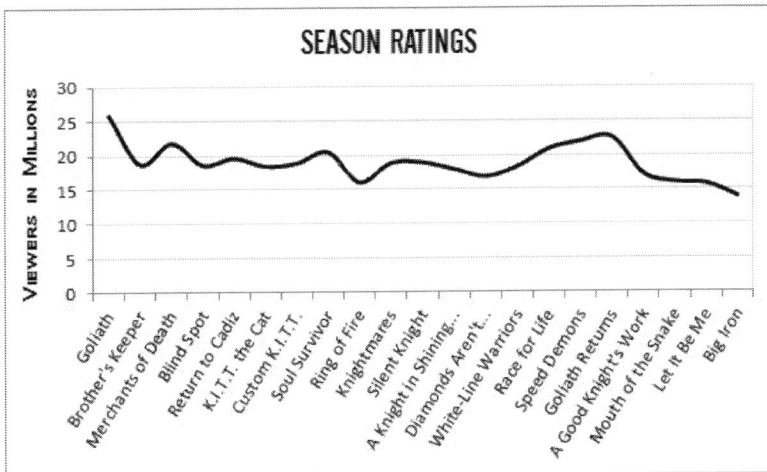

PROD. #57823

$$\begin{bmatrix} \text{EPISODE} \\ 22 \end{bmatrix}$$

Script History:

July 22, 1983 (F.R.)

July 27, 1983 (F.R.)

GOLIATH (TWO HOURS)

Working Title: "Mirror Image"

Written By: Robert Foster and Robert W. Gilmer

Directed By: Winrich Kolbe

Original Airdate: October 2, 1983 (Sunday, 8:00 PM) (30.9%; 25,890,000)

NBC Rerun #1: January 22, 1984 (Sunday, 8:00 PM) (24.0%; 20,110,000)

Filming Dates: August 8-25, 1983

"Michael Knight is a living, breathing insult to my existence."

-Garthe Knight

Crew: Robert Foster (Executive Producer), Joel Rogosin (Supervising Producer), Robert W. Gilmer (Co-Producer), Gian R. Grimaldi (Coordinating Producer), Stephen Downing (Co-Producer), Tom Greene (Co-Producer), Bernadette Joyce (Associate Producer), Robert Ewing (Associate Producer), George Crosby (Associate Producer), Janis Hendler (Executive Story Consultant), William Schmidt (Story Editor), Don Peake (Music), H. John Penner (Director of Photography), Russell Smith (Art Director), R. Lynn Smartt (Set Decoration), April Webster (Casting), Lawrence J. Gleason (Film Editor), Lawrence J. Vallario (Film Editor), Stanley Wohlberg (Film Editor), Beryl Gelfond (Film Editor), Howard B. Anderson (Film Editor), Grant Hoag (Film Editor), Ron Martinez (Unit Production Manager), Robert Villar (1st Assistant Director), Charles Watson Sanford, Jr. (1st Assistant Director), Gary Grillo (1st Assistant Director), Bruce Humphrey (2nd Assistant Director), Jack Breschard (2nd Assistant Director), Stan Gordon (Sound), Pat Somerset (Sound), John Shouse (Sound Effects Editor), Sam Gemette (Sound Effects Editor), Richard Lapham (Music Editor), Barry Downing (Costume Supervisor), Judie Champion (Costume Supervisor), Robert Bralver (Stunt Coordinator), Jack Gill (Stunt Coordinator), Jeremy Swan (Make-Up), Allen Payne (Hairstylist), Jean-Pierre Dorleac (Costume Designer)

Guest Cast: Barbara Rush (Elizabeth Knight), Zakes Mokae (Tsombe Kuna), Paul Lambert (General Thaddeus Maximillian Maddux), Shawn Southwick (Rita Wilcox), Pepper Davis (Gambler), Petrus Antonius (Hotel Clerk), Ivan Naranjo (Chief), Murray Westgate (Technician)

Michael returns to Las Vegas to investigate the disappearance of a blackjack dealer's brother, but is shocked to find out that the man responsible is a member of the Knight family.

A Look Back:

The second season premiere introduced the viewers to a beautiful new mechanic, April Curtis. April replaced Bonnie Barstow, who viewers would later learn left the Foundation to further her education. April was played by Rebecca Holden, who recalls filming in Las Vegas. "As a young girl, I used to go to Vegas quite frequently on weekends to see live shows; I adored all the great Vegas entertainers, and I always stayed at Caesar's Palace. So years later, to be actually filming a television series there seemed incredibly surreal. I remember when we did the scene at the front entrance, I reminisced on all the times I had come into the front of the lobby and would have never thought then of even becoming an actress, much less shooting a scene in that very place."

Rebecca Holden was added to the cast to replace Patricia McPherson, who left the series after the first year. "NBC came to us and asked if I would consider doing *Knight Rider* and said they were creating a new character and that the show was picked up for 22 more episodes," says Holden. "I told my agent that I thought it was a great show. We have a very good new time slot in the fall. The show has developed such a following. It has a TVQ in the top 10; it's number 6. It's above *Magnum P.I.* and *60 Minutes*. It's very rare that you can walk into a show that's already a hit like that. Usually you have to go through making the pilot, waiting to see if it sells."

In "Goliath", Michael and K.I.T.T. face their most dangerous nemesis yet, Garthe Knight, and his behemoth truck, Goliath. Holden recalls, "Goliath was indeed massive and built for destruction! But, of course, brawn and brute force were no match for the Knight Industries Two Thousand team! April used her brains and resourcefulness to invent the infrared feature for K.I.T.T. I thought of this episode as an analogy to the Bible story of David and

Goliath--good will always prevail over evil. And of course, Michael, K.I.T.T., Devon and I were on the side of truth, justice, and the American way!"

One of the most dramatic scenes in this episode comes when K.I.T.T. is nearly destroyed by Goliath at a rendezvous in the desert. Stunt Coordinator Jack Gill adds, "We shot this scene in Vegas. I had a special K.I.T.T. car there that was geared differently and I could do about 130 mph. We also had a makeshift K.I.T.T. car, which I believe not many people knew about. It was a manual transmission K.I.T.T. car which didn't really last long. I think I jumped it and it got broken in half. Al Jones was driving Goliath towards me and I was driving K.I.T.T. and we just had to make sure that we were both going left at the same time. We rehearsed the scene in slow speed and then fast speed. For the actual shoot, I was doing 100 mph. I remember that day as it was really hot, and this was the episode where we had a bunch of people from the set that wanted to watch. A couple of people dropped because it was so hot."

In another difficult stunt, Garthe Knight escapes his captivity in the F.L.A.G. semi by jumping from the back of it into a red Cadillac. That man jumping was Gill. "Al Jones was driving the *Knight Rider* truck and my brother was driving the Cadillac with his Burt Reynolds mustache that he thought was so cool, but it didn't look too cool. We finally got him to shave the damn thing off. Once you jumped off the side of the truck, it was kind of tough to hang on because it was such a slick surface. So, I had to make sure Andy was underneath it, because I didn't have very far to push."

One scene in "Goliath" has Devon and April heading to Rio de Janeiro to investigate the whereabouts of Kyle Elliott, one of the three men entrusted with the secret formula for K.I.T.T.'s molecular bonded shell. Once in Rio, they are greeted by a hotel manager, played by Peter Antonius. Antonius recalls, "I got a call from my agent to audition for the part of a Brazilian character. Since I spoke fluent Portuguese, I went to the casting director's office. Her name was April Webster. At the second audition, I read for the producers and the director (Winrich Kolbe). Winrich was very nice, friendly and approachable".

Antonius does remember one scene where he tried to correct the director's Portuguese, but lost the battle. "There was a bit of a disagreement on my part when my character was on the phone and Winrich insisted that I say the words 'operadora por favor' – which is not correct. I told him that if it is used the right way, it would be 'telefonista por favor'. Winrich thought 'operadora' sounded better and, right or wrong, the director has the final word".

Although the majority of "Goliath" was filmed on location, Antonius remembers that his scenes were shot at the studio. "The set for the hotel and room was built and shot at Universal Studios. I remember that one of my scenes was cut from the final editing".

Due to other commitments, Antonius missed the TV debut of "Goliath" and also missed the cast party, which was held due to it being the first episode of the much anticipated second season. "After shooting concluded, there was a cast party at Universal. Unfortunately, I was working out of town on another project and was unable to attend. My wife attended the party as my representative and found the cast and crew to be very friendly. I recorded the episode on the original air date on my VCR due to the fact that I was performing in a production at a local theatre in Hollywood".

Starring in "Goliath" would ultimately help Antonius in future acting projects. "Every time an actor works on a TV series, it helps build a strong resume and forms relationships with the studios. Suddenly, more doors were opened and opportunities developed for more work in the industry".

Knight Knotes:

- "Goliath" just barely beat out the Pilot as the highest rated all-new episode of the entire series, with almost 26 million viewers watching.

- Garthe reviews a video of K.I.T.T. that includes scenes from "Hearts of Stone", "Deadly Maneuvers", and a cut scene from "Chariot of Gold".

- Shawn Southwick, who played Rita Wilcox in this episode, was dating one of the *Knight Rider* producers during filming.

- Goliath was constructed from a 1973 Peterbilt 352 Pacemaker.

- The name of K.I.T.T.'s indestructible alloy is finally revealed – the Molecular Bonded Shell.

- As Michael is trying to repair K.I.T.T., he removes a factory Crossfire air cleaner.

- The airplane used to transport Devon and April to Rio de Janeiro is a 1980 Hughes Gate Learjet 35A, registration number N981TH, serial number 364. This plane is still in service today, although it has a new tail number – N353EF.

- Garthe's Mercedes has a license plate of Nevada 289GGG. This same plate can be seen on a Jeep at the Dune Drifter Hotel in "Knight Strike".

- K.I.T.T. gains a laser in this episode.

- NBC promoted this two-hour premiere by running a commercial where viewers could send away for a special document. The commercial read, "On Sunday, October 2nd, K.I.T.T. and I face our greatest challenge in a spectacular two-hour movie. We're hoping we can win with the secrets found in this, the K.I.T.T. Kit. To get your free copy, send a self-addressed, stamped envelope to 'K.I.T.T. Kit', Box 80, Hollywood. Get your K.I.T.T. Kit, and be there."

Script to Screen:

- The opening scene of the episode originally takes place at night. Garthe sits in a limo while a giant cargo jet lands. Dozens of combat troops ascend into the plane and a few moments later, Goliath drives out. From the script: "Shooting up into the darkness of the huge cargo hold as powerful diesel engines come to life. Then headlights. Then an enormous blunt snout emerges, chrome and black lacquer, and the oversized, specially modified truck and trailer descend. It is the centerpiece of a major undertaking. It's known simply as Goliath." A bit later in the script, another description emerges: "It occupies half the warehouse space, it's so large. This is our first full daylight view of it, and it's a behemoth, a huge grizzly bear of a truck, all lacquered black and spotless chrome. It's four times the length of K.I.T.T., and two stories high. It weighs fourteen tons."

- The description of the first time the viewers see Garthe: "Standing ten feet away, facing him, is the man from the limousine. He is tall and lean, wears a tuxedo and carries a black diamond-studded cane. He also wears a discreet diamond stud in his left ear. He moves with the grace of a panther, but also with a slight limp, the reason for which will be forthcoming. Except for minor cosmetic differences, the man is a dead-ringer for Michael Knight. The reason isn't coincidental. He is the late Wilton Knight's only son, Garthe."

- Rita doesn't work at Caesar's Palace, but rather The Royal Flush casino.

- Garthe comes off as more of a mystery man in the original script. When Michael asks his name, Rita replies, "Garthe. With an 'e.' He's very particular about the 'e.' And despite the fact he's buying up half the town, and everybody knows it, you never see his picture in the paper. You never see him on TV. It's like he's this incredible mystery man."

- Elizabeth Knight poisons Devon with a powder sprinkled on his food, not a vial of liquid in his drink.

- Dr. Alpert is officially described as "the Foundation doctor".

- When Michael first see Garthe in the casino, he asks a bystander what all the commotion is about. The bystander tells Michael that his name is Garthe Knight, and "There's rumors he's the bad-seed son of Wilton Knight, the industrialist.".

- In early drafts of the script, K.I.T.T.'s Molecular Bonded Shell was referred to simply as his "skin".

- Devon and April also fly to Africa to meet with a government official to learn about how Garthe was sentenced to three consecutive life sentences.. The official states, "Garthe Knight entered this country in October of 1977. He bought up rights and options on a vast quantity of diamond mines which had been declared inoperable for reasons of safety. He then proceeded to hire slave labor from a neighboring country to work the mines. Less than a month after commencing work, one of the mines collapsed and buried forty-nine men alive. None survived."

- Michael is followed to the bus depot by two men named Briggs and Stratton. He is held at gunpoint and ordered to hand over Ron's tapes. A chase ensues between their car and K.I.T.T. After K.I.T.T. activates ski mode, the thieves crash their car and escape on foot. Michael saves the tapes from the burning car before it explodes.

- K.I.T.T. uses his Rapid Thought Analyzer to analyze Ron's tapes to find similarities between them.

- The description of K.I.T.T.'s destruction: "At the last moment Michael swerves the wheel, hoping if all else fails to deflect Goliath's impact, but the huge bumper and fender catch K.I.T.T.'s left front fender. There's a horrible ripping sound, metal on metal. K.I.T.T.'S left side disintegrates, fender flying in one direction, hood and various other parts thrown a hundred feet in the air. He's thrown off the road, rolls half a dozen times before coming to a stop. Goliath has taken its toll on Kit: the windshield is shattered, one side of the car is badly crumpled, the trunk is sprung open, and the driver's side door hangs loosely on its hinges."

- Instead of rigging a ramjet to escape the desert, Michael uses a clothes hanger and is able to get K.I.T.T.'s engine running long enough to drive slowly out of the desert.
- The call that General Maddux receives as Devon leaves his office is from Elizabeth Knight.

Déjà Vu:

- Ivan Naranjo returns in "Burial Ground".

Featured Songs:

"Gimme Shelter" by The Rolling Stones

K.I.T.T.'s Capabilities:

- Audio Playback, Auto Cruise, Comprehensive Configuration Analyzer, Infrared, Laser, Map Search, Microlock, Micro Jam, Odds Calculator, Pursuit, Tinted Windows, Ultra Frequency Modulator, X-Ray

PROD. #57805

$\left[\begin{array}{c} \text{EPISODE} \\ 23 \end{array}\right]$

Script History:

June 13, 1983 (F.R.)

June 17, 1983 (F.R.)

June 20, 1983 (F.R.)

June 21, 1983 (F.R.)

June 22, 1983 (F.R.)

June 23, 1983 (F.R.)

BROTHER'S KEEPER

Written By: E.F. Wallengren

Directed By: Sidney Hayers

Original Airdate: October 9, 1983 (Sunday, 8:00 PM) (22.4%; 18,770,000)

NBC Rerun #1: December 25, 1983 (Sunday, 8:00 PM) (12.7%; 10,640,000)

NBC Rerun #2: June 24, 1984 (Sunday, 8:00 PM) (10.4%; 8,720,000)

Filming Dates: June 22-30, 1983

"Kindly un-hand me, you hard rock con!"

-K.I.T.T.

Crew: Robert Foster (Executive Producer), Joel Rogosin (Supervising Producer), Robert W. Gilmer (Co-Producer), Gian R. Grimaldi (Co-Producer), Bernadette Joyce (Associate Producer), Robert Ewing (Associate Producer), Janis Hendler (Executive Script Consultant), William Schmidt (Story Editor), Don Peake (Music), H. John Penner (Director of Photography), Russell Smith (Art Director), Lawrence J. Gleason (Film Editor), Ron Martinez (Unit Production Manager), Robert Villar (1st Assistant Director), Bruce Humphrey (2nd Assistant Director), R. Lynn Smartt (Set Decorator), Stan Gordon (Sound), April Webster (Casting), John Shouse (Sound Effects Editor), Richard Lapham (Music Editor), Barry Downing (Costume Supervisor), Judie Champion (Costume Supervisor), Robert Bralver (Stunt Coordinator), Jack Gill (Co-Stunt Coordinator), Jeremy Swan (Make-up), Allen Payne (Hairstylist)

Guest Cast: Gerald Gordon (Peter McCord), Catherine Mary Stewart (Lisa Martinson), Michael Fairman (Eric Fenton), Tim O'Connor (Phillip Hunt), Robert Bralver (Alex Payne), Fred Lerner (Sal Talman), Fitzhugh G. Houston (Brewster), Marland Proctor (Officer Jeffries), Dean Wein (Highway Patrolman #1), Michael J. Cutt (Highway Patrolman #2), Vince McKewin (Officer Rogers), Harold "Hal" Frizzell (Plainclothesman #2)

Michael and K.I.T.T. break a convicted murderer out of prison in order to use him to stop a madman from detonating a bomb in the city.

A Look Back:

Fitz Houston returned to *Knight Rider* after a brief appearance in season one's "Just My Bill". Here, Houston played a parole board member named Brewster at the beginning of the episode. "I remember that April Webster liked my work on 'Just My Bill'. I got the call and auditioned for 'Brother's Keeper' and she cast me again."

Much like his previous appearance, Houston starred in one scene which meant that, once again, he did not get the opportunity to meet the other cast members. "I didn't get to know any of the other actors, even the ones I worked with in my scene. When you film for one day, it makes it hard to get to know anyone." For those that are curious as to where the scene was filmed, Houston confirms, "The parole board scene was shot on the Universal lot."

Houston has had a rich career in television that has spanned over 30 years and he still continues to act in Hollywood to this day. "I think my most special time was on *Matlock* as I got to work with Andy Griffith. The most fun time I had was on *The Michael Richards Show*.

Looking back, Houston was proud of his time in *Knight Rider*. "I'm glad I could be a part of it. I loved being on a show that would later become such a hit."

"Brother's Keeper" returns the cast and crew to the mansion used for F.L.A.G. headquarters, Arden Villa in Pasadena, CA. Series regular Rebecca Holden fondly remembers her time filming there. "This episode was one of the few times that we actually filmed on location in Pasadena. We had been working on the Foundation set for a number of shows [on Stage 1 at Universal Studios] before we ever filmed on location in Pasadena, so it was nice to be there at the actual house and get a genuine feel of the environment. The house itself was gorgeous and was a beautiful 'home' for us, but I have to give credit to our production people--set designers, props, etc. Even though we were at the studio most of the time, our "on set" F.L.A.G. headquarters felt like the 'real deal'."

Knight Knotes:

- Philip Hunt's car wears the license plate CA NNU 322. During the scene where Peter McCord jumps over a parking lot wall, a car parked there also sports this plate.

- Supervising Producer Joel Rogosin on the semi's re-vamp: "We made an effort to redesign the truck by adding a sleeping compartment, We also redid the interior so it had a little bit more of an office feel to it. It warmed it up a bit."
- April installs a "Bomb Sniffer".
- Robert Bralver, who played Alex Payne, was the show's original stunt coordinator before Jack Gill took over.
- This episode marks the first time that the show utilized the "desert" commercial breaks, which would become a staple of the series.

Script to Screen:

- The other man sitting at the table at Peter McCord's parole hearing is named Rogers.
- K.I.T.T. voices concern to Michael that he doesn't have enough of an approach to clear the prison wall. Michael has no choice and tells K.I.T.T. to go for it. K.I.T.T. does and barely clears the wall.
- K.I.T.T. continues his analogies of famous partners in crime. He likens himself and Michael to Butch Cassidy and the Sundance Kid. Michael then jokes to K.I.T.T. about finding the closest bank to rob, to which K.I.T.T. replies that they can always utilize his special license plates feature again.

Featured Songs:

"She Works Hard for the Money" by Donna Summer

K.I.T.T.'s Capabilities:

- Auto Cruise, Electronic Detection Module, License Plates (KNIGHT to KNI 667), Map Search, Police/Radio Frequency, Pursuit, Radar, Surveillance Mode, Turbo Boost, Voice Analyzer

David Cowgill, David Hasselhoff and Thomas F. Wilson on the set of "A Knight in Shining Armor" (Photo courtesy of David Cowgill)

PROD. #57807

$$\left[\begin{array}{c} \text{EPISODE} \\ 24 \end{array}\right]$$

Script History:

May 19, 1983 (F.R.)

May 24, 1983 (F.R.)

EN May 28, 1983 (F.R.)

MERCHANTS OF DEATH

Written By: William Schmidt

Directed By: Alan Myerson

Original Airdate: October 16, 1983 (Sunday, 8:00 PM) (26.0%; 21,790,000)

NBC Rerun #1: March 18, 1984 (Sunday, 8:00 PM) (21.2%; 17,770,000)

Filming Dates: June 2-10; September 7, 1983

"Surfing, sun, girls in bikinis."

-K.I.T.T.

Crew: Robert Foster (Executive Producer), Joel Rogosin (Supervising Producer), Robert W. Gilmer (Co-Producer), Stephen Downing (Co-Producer), Gian R. Grimaldi (Coordinating Producer), Bernadette Joyce (Associate Producer), Robert Ewing (Associate Producer), William Schmidt (Story Editor), Don Peake (Music), H. John Penner (Director of Photography), Russell Smith (Art Director), Stanley Wohlberg (Film Editor), Ron Martinez (Unit Production Manager), Robert Villar (1st Assistant Director), Bruce Humphrey (2nd Assistant Director), R. Lynn Smartt (Set Decorator), Stan Gordon (Sound), April Webster (Casting), John Shouse (Sound Effects Editor), Richard Lapham (Music Editor), Barry Downing (Costume Supervisor), Judie Champion (Costume Supervisor), Robert Bralver (Stunt Coordinator), Jack Gill (Co-Stunt Coordinator), Jeremy Swan (Make-up), Allen Payne (Hairstylist)

Guest Cast: Dana Elcar (Edward Strock), Joe LaDue (Jack Kragen), Deborah Allison (Camela/Amelia Clermont), Linden Chiles (Albert Ebersol), Kurt Smildsin (Sam Richards), John Wesley (U.S. Marshal)

Michael teams up with Camela Clarmont to investigate her mother's mysterious disappearance in Arizona.

Knight Knotes:

- Alan Myerson on filming the semi set on Stage 1: "I remember it as being hot and tedious work. The long narrow set (which didn't have wild walls as I recall) made it really laborious to shoot the scene, which was primarily an expository scene, which meant that most of the staging of the actors was somewhat arbitrary to get a little movement into what was essentially a very static scene."
- April supplies K.I.T.T. with Ultra Magnesium Charges and managers to increase the strength of the Micro Jam.

Script to Screen:

- The SX-411 is described in the script as "awesome, a full-blown attack helicopter, the K.I.T.T., as it were, of helicopters."
- The script notes that Camela's name is "pronounced Pamela with a 'C'."
- When K.I.T.T. first introduces himself to Camela, he speaks in French and then she replies. K.I.T.T. is actually asking, "Am I correct in assuming you speak French?" and Camela replies, "Yes. Actually, I think of English as my second language."

Déjà Vu:

- Joe LaDue returns in "Knightlines".

Featured Songs:

"California Girls" by The Beach Boys

"Breakdown" by Tom Petty and The Heartbreakers

K.I.T.T.'s Capabilities:

- Audio Playback, Auto Cruise, Auto Phone, Auto-Roof Right, Map Search, Micro Jam, Picture Sharpen, Point-of-Impact Analysis, Pursuit, Radar, Rocket Fire, Ski Mode, Smoke Release, Surveillance Mode, Telephone Trace, Turbo Boost, Ultra Magnesium Charges, Voice Analyzer, X-Ray

PROD. #57809

{ EPISODE
25 }

Script History:

August 27, 1983 (F.R.)

BLIND SPOT

Working Title: "Insights"

Written By: Jackson Gillis

Directed By: Bernard L. Kowalski

Original Airdate: October 23, 1983 (Sunday, 8:00 PM) (22.2%; 18,600,000)

NBC Rerun #1: January 1, 1984 (Sunday, 8:00 PM) (20.3%; 17,010,000)

Filming Dates: August 26 – September 7, 1983

"My tweeters are sealed."

-K.I.T.T.

Crew: Robert Foster (Executive Producer), Joel Rogosin (Supervising Producer), Robert W. Gilmer (Co-Producer), Gian R. Grimaldi (Co-Producer), Bernadette Joyce (Associate Producer), Robert Ewing (Associate Producer), Janis Hendler (Executive Script Consultant), Don Peake (Music), H. John Penner (Director of Photography), Russell Smith (Art Director), Beryl Gelfond (Film Editor), Ron Martinez (Unit Production Manager), Robert Villar (1st Assistant Director), Bruce Humphrey (2nd Assistant Director), R. Lynn Smartt (Set Decorator), Pat Somerset (Sound), April Webster (Casting), John Shouse (Sound Effects Editor), Richard Lapham (Music Editor), Barry Downing (Costume Supervisor), Judie Champion (Costume Supervisor), Jack Gill (Stunt Coordinator), Jeremy Swan (Make-up), Allen Payne (Hairstylist)

Guest Cast: Elyssa Davalos (Julie Robinson), Sam Vlahos (Alfredo Diaz), John Milford (Louis R. Gastner), Michael J. London (David Dudley), Arthur Taxier (Mel), Christopher Coffey (John Murray), Javier Grajeda (Ramon), David J. Partington (Officer Peter Gray), Akosua Busia (Nurse)

Michael must protect a young blind woman who accidentally stumbles into an evidence drop gone wrong.

A Look Back:

Viewers of this episode may notice that Hasselhoff was in K.I.T.T. while the car was in the crusher. The production team had to take some extra steps to ensure that he wouldn't be injured during this dangerous scene. Jack Gill recalls, "The only thing I remember about K.I.T.T. in the crusher is that I, as stunt coordinator, was very worried about stopping the crusher once it started moving with David inside the car. We wanted to see just how far we could go with David in the car and all it would take is one small malfunction and how do you really get him out of there? You couldn't put a failsafe on it because any type of steel rod that we put in there to try and stop it was just going to get crushed as well. We had to disconnect a bunch of hydraulic lines so it didn't have the kind of pressure that it would normally have. This meant that if it did go haywire it would just bend a little bit and not crush."

Knight Knotes:

- Michael utilizes the Trajectory Guide to escape the car compactor. This feature is introduced in the season finale "Big Iron", which was actually one of the first episodes produced for the season.

Script to Screen:

- After K.I.T.T. comments about how it's a crime to leave cars in a parking lot on a hot day, he then adds, "I happen to be a car, and crimes against cars bother me."

Featured Songs:

"Oye Como Va" by Santana

"Maniac" by Michael Sambiello

K.I.T.T.'s Capabilities:

- Audio/Video Record, Auto Cruise, Pursuit, Radar, Trajectory Guide, Turbo Boost

PROD. #57801

[EPISODE
26]

Script History:

May 2, 1983 (F.R.)

May 5, 1983 (F.R.)

May 6, 1983 (F.R.)

RETURN TO CADIZ

Working Title: "To Forgive, Devine"

Written By: Larry Forrester

Directed By: Alan Myerson

Original Airdate: October 30, 1983 (Sunday, 8:00 PM) (23.4%; 19,610,000)

NBC Rerun #1: March 11, 1984 (Sunday, 8:00 PM) (21.4%; 17,930,000)

Filming Dates: May 10-19, 1983

"You didn't sink buddy! You didn't sink!"

-Michael

Crew: Robert Foster (Executive Producer), Joel Rogosin (Supervising Producer), Robert W. Gilmer (Co-Producer), Stephen Downing (Co-Producer), Gian R. Grimaldi (Coordinating Producer), Bernadette Joyce (Associate Producer), Robert Ewing (Associate Producer), William Schmidt (Story Editor), Don Peake (Music), H. John Penner (Director of Photography), Russell Smith (Art Director), Lawrence J. Gleason (Film Editor), Ron Martinez (Unit Production Manager), Robert Villar (1st Assistant Director), Bruce Humphrey (2nd Assistant Director), R. Lynn Smartt (Set Decorator), Stan Gordon (Sound), April Webster (Casting), Sam Gemette (Sound Effects Editor), Richard Lapham (Music Editor), Barry Downing (Costume Supervisor), Judie Champion (Costume Supervisor), Robert Bralver (Stunt Coordinator), Jack Gill (Co-Stunt Coordinator), Jeremy Swan (Make-up), Allen Payne (Hairstylist)

Guest Cast: Anne Lockhart (Jennifer Shell), Guy Stockwell (Zachary Sloate), Nicolas Coster (Paul Manley), Michael Bowen (Bobby Shell), Marion Yue (Nurse Tracy), Ken Scott (Karl Roessler), Jack Gill (Jack)

When a young scuba diver is nearly killed diving an old shipwreck, Michael investigates and realizes that his accident was no accident at all.

A Look Back:

English born actor Nicolas Coster landed the role of bad guy Ross Manley in this episode, the first produced for the season. "I decided to act when I was in high school. I was a bit of a naughty boy and my mother and I mutually decided I should return to England and live with my father. I attended RADA and the rest... should have been history."

Coster admits that he may have his scuba diving skills to thank for getting him the role on the show. "I became an instructor in 1974 and went on to form the modern scuba diving program at Columbia University, The

West Side YMCA and Pan Aqua Divers in New York. I believe I got the role in 'Return to Cadiz' because I was a scuba instructor at that time."

Alan Myserson directed the episode, a man who Coster knew very well. "Alan was a personal friend of mine. We had worked on an improvisational and fun pilot show about guys living in a junk yard. It didn't sell but it was way ahead of its time. Alan was a good director and a nice guy."

There is one infamous scene in "Return to Cadiz" where K.I.T.T. is seemingly driving on water. "I vaguely remember we shot a trailer in the water of sorts. Thereafter it was 'the magic of movies', wherein they create whole objects and backgrounds (miniatures) and all sorts of illusions to make us believe."

Coster says he remembers David Hasselhoff as someone who oozed confidence on the set. "David had achieved a level of TV stardom by then which he handled very well. He was unapologetic about his quick rise and seemed to handle it as though he belonged up there. His longevity has proved that. He is clever at handling a career, much better than some of us," jokes Coster.

Coster once used his scuba diving skills to teach one very famous person. "I taught John F Kennedy Jr. who, until his tragic death, remained a friend. He was a magnificent young man. His family was delightful to me and came to see all my shows in New York thereafter."

At the time of filming "Return to Cadiz", Coster was an actor in demand - he had worked on *Hardcastle and McCormick* and *TJ Hooker* before appearing in *Knight Rider*. "At that time, I was working constantly. I remember having to use my professional water skills at the beginning of the episode. In those situations, there is little fooling around. There is too much risk to body and mind (your own and others) and too much chance of things going awry and that's when liability is involved. We do our job, and in the process try to have a jolly good time and a few beers afterward."

Despite this episode airing fifth in *Knight Rider's* second season, it was actually the first to be filmed, and as such, the first episode for series regular Rebecca Holden. "The first day on ANY new job can be nerve-wracking, regardless of whether the job is a television series or not," says Holden. "So, of course, I was nervous getting out of my trailer to walk to the set at the beach to shoot our very first scene. (Plus of course, in that first scene, I was wearing shorts and a little midriff shirt!) But everyone was so welcoming and made me feel so at ease. I think from the very first moment, there was such chemistry, and I knew right away that we were all going to be a great team." April also got to leave the F.L.A.G. semi and go undercover as a nurse. "It was so gratifying to play a nurse, because both my mother and sister are register nurses. Nursing is such a noble career choice. They possess such kindness and compassion, so in playing her I just wanted to honor the profession," says Holden.

"Return to Cadiz" featured K.I.T.T. riding on the ocean surface with the help of his newly installed Third Stage Aquatic Synthesizer. The majority of these scenes were shot using miniatures, however the close ups of Hasselhoff in the car required some Hollywood magic. Stunt coordinator Jack Gill recalls, "The only thing I remember doing with David to do with water was on a sound stage with the car in a tank. We sprayed lots of water on the windshield and side windows for his coverage. The miniatures looked so bad that nobody really liked them, but the producers were committed to the miniatures for a while. We would protest as much as we could about it. They finally went the other way by the time we got to our last year. The miniatures on the water looked pretty bad." Alan Myerson, adds, "I believe the water illusion was accomplished by several gimmicks: having K.I.T.T. actually drive a short distance on a platform submerged under the water for wider shots and some rear projection for the closer work inside the cabin of the car."

Knight Knotes:

- Director Alan Myerson on the casting of Rebecca Holden: "Another beautiful woman -- but this one does bring back some recollection. As I recall, she was very excited to be part of a now-successful series and anxious to do her job well."
- Myerson on K.I.T.T. driving on the beach: "The car didn't run well on the loose sand and often got stuck. It was decided not to try to run the car on the wet but harder and more manageable sand so as not to leave tracks in the sand for subsequent takes."
- The Chemical Analyzer debuts in this episode.

Script to Screen:

- A second diver named Axel Wicks helps Roessler attack Bobby Shell at the start of the episode. Roessler's hand is tattooed with a skull and crossbones.
- The script states that K.I.T.T. cleans the gold coin in his Chemical Analyzer. In the episode, K.I.T.T. merely tells Michael that he can examine the object in a more presentable state.

Déjà Vu:

- Ken Scott returns in "Knight in Disgrace".

Featured Songs:

"Every Breath You Take" by The Police

K.I.T.T.'s Capabilities:

- Auto Cruise, Auto-Roof Left, Chemical Analyzer, Eject Left, Electronic Pilot Override, Linguistic Analyzer, Map Search, Medical Scan, Printer, Pursuit, Radar, Surveillance Mode, Third Stage Aquatic Synthesizer, Trunk Lid, Turbo Boost

PROD. #57824

```
[ EPISODE ]
[   27    ]
```

Script History:

August 29, 1983 (F.R.)

August 31, 1983 (F.R.)

September 7, 1983 (F.R.)

K.I.T.T. THE CAT

Working Title: "An Attractive Nuisance"

Written By: Janis Hendler

Directed By: Jeffrey Hayden

Original Airdate: November 6, 1983 (Sunday, 8:00 PM) (22.0%; 18,440,000)

NBC Rerun #1: April 29, 1984 (Sunday, 8:00 PM) (16.8%; 14,080,000)

Filming Dates: September 13-21, 1983

"Valet parking? Caterers? Orchestra? Do we really need an orchestra?"

-Devon

Crew: Robert Foster (Executive Producer), Joel Rogosin (Supervising Producer), Robert W. Gilmer (Co-Producer), Gian R. Grimaldi (Co-Producer), Bernadette Joyce (Associate Producer), Robert Ewing (Associate Producer), Janis Hendler (Executive Script Consultant), Don Peake (Music), H. John Penner (Director of Photography), Russell Smith (Art Director), Howard B. Anderson (Film Editor), Ron Martinez (Unit Production Manager), Charles Watson Sanford, Jr. (1st Assistant Director), Bruce Humphrey (2nd Assistant Director), R. Lynn Smartt (Set Decorator), Pat Somerset (Sound), April Webster (Casting), John Shouse (Sound Effects Editor), Richard Lapham (Music Editor), Barry Downing (Costume Supervisor), Judie Champion (Costume Supervisor), Jack Gill (Stunt Coordinator), Jeremy Swan (Make-up), Allen Payne (Hairstylist)

Guest Cast: Geena Davis (Grace Fallan), Keene Curtis (Griffin), Jack Starrett (Lieutenant George Barth), Bill Wiley (Maxwell Elliot), Terry Moore (Molly Friedrich), Paul Pepper (Ricky), Kopi Sotiropulos (Kopi the Gardener), Wally Taylor (Security Guard)

Michael tries to weed out a cat burglar who has been stealing valuable jewelry from the wealthy and using the M.O. of a deceased criminal.

A Look Back:

April Curtis once again leaves the confines of the Foundation and goes undercover during a dinner party. Rebecca Holden recalls, "Pretending to be Devon's fiancée was hilarious--we had such a ball with it! (And of course that episode was exciting for another reason as well--April got to dress up! She was known for her mechanic's jumpsuits, so it was terrific to get to put my hair up and wear a sparkly dress!) The humor and teasing was one of the things that made the show special. Beyond all the action and the technical gadgets, the show was really about the camaraderie, the humor, and the friendships. We were united in spirit; we were dedicated professionals on a mission for good, but along the way, we certainly had a whole lot of fun."

Knight Knotes:

- Rebecca Holden on Geena Davis: "Geena Davis was terrific--so nice and very professional and it was easy to see that she would go on to have a great career."

Script to Screen:

- The name of the stolen necklace is spelled "Sangre de Coeur".
- Maxwell Elliot was originally named James Elliot.

Featured Songs:

"Telephone (Long Distance Love Affair)" by Sheena Easton

K.I.T.T.'s Capabilities:

- Auto Cruise, Chemical Detectors, Heat Sensors, Medical Scan, Pursuit, Radar, Turbo Boost

PROD. #57821

{ EPISODE
28 }

Script History:

September 16, 1983 (Spec. Run)

September 19, 1983 (F.R.)

CUSTOM K.I.T.T.

Teleplay By: William Schmidt

Story By: William Schmidt and Robert Specht

Directed By: Georg Fenady

Original Airdate: November 13, 1983 (Sunday, 8:00 PM) (22.5%; 18,860,000)

NBC Rerun #1: April 1, 1984 (Sunday, 8:00 PM) (19.9%; 16,680,000)

Filming Dates: September 27 – October 5, 1983

"You wanted to steal a car, and now you've stolen the ride of your lives!"

-K.I.T.T.

Crew: Robert Foster (Executive Producer), Joel Rogosin (Supervising Producer), Robert W. Gilmer (Co-Producer), Gian R. Grimaldi (Co-Producer), Tom Greene (Co-Producer), Bernadette Joyce (Associate Producer), Robert Ewing (Associate Producer), Janis Hendler (Executive Script Consultant), Don Peake (Music), H. John Penner (Director of Photography), Russell Smith (Art Director), Lawrence J. Vallario (Film Editor), Ron Martinez (Unit Production Manager), Robert Villar (1st Assistant Director), Bruce Humphrey (2nd Assistant Director), R. Lynn Smartt (Set Decorator), Pat Somerset (Sound), April Webster (Casting), John Shouse (Sound Effects Editor), Richard Lapham (Music Editor), Barry Downing (Costume Supervisor), Judie Champion (Costume Supervisor), Jack Gill (Stunt Coordinator), Jeremy Swan (Make-up), Allen Payne (Hairstylist)

Guest Cast: Denise Miller (Carrie Haver), Melinda O. Fee (Suzanne Westen), Angel Tompkins (Nora Rayburn), Bernard Fox (Commander Henry Ashburton Smythe), Michael Huddleston (Hector), Albert Salmi (Buck Rayburn), Brian Cutler (Dobie), Robert Pastorelli (Leroy)

When a car loaned to Devon is stolen, K.I.T.T. goes undercover as a custom hot rod to find the ones responsible.

A Look Back:

Brian Cutler returned to *Knight Rider* in season two's "Custom K.I.T.T." He played the role of bad guy Dobie, where Cutler was given much more screen time and a meatier role than in the Pilot. "Fortunately for me, I had been on the show before which gave me a better shot for the role. I remember the crew was great when I got the job. They all remembered me and suggested I get a silk *Knight Rider* jacket because of my second appearance. I did order one."

Cutler enjoyed himself in the role of Dobie. "Absolutely, bad guys are always more fun. It took me a long time to get to the point where some casting people didn't just think of me as another 'pretty face'. Bad guys always have more depth and character development".

"Custom K.I.T.T." was directed by Georg Fenady, a man who Cutler fondly remembers. "Georg and I go way back. He was one of the regular directors of the hit series *Emergency!* I was lucky enough to be a recurring regular on *Emergency!* for 3 years and always loved working with Georg. So, to get to work with him again was a pleasure".

Cutler's boss in "Custom K.I.T.T." was played by the late Albert Salmi, and Cutler only has the highest regard and fondest memories of Salmi. "Throughout your career in this crazy business, there are always people you admire and hope to work with some day. Albert was one of those people for me. We hit it off immediately and became dear friends. I was very sad when he passed. Working with Albert was everything I hoped and thought it would be. The only acting coach I have ever studied with was Charles E. Conrad and he taught us to work, moment-by-moment and impulse-by-impulse, without a preconceived idea or predetermined outcome. That is the way Albert worked and we had a ball".

Cutler has many fond memories of "Custom K.I.T.T.", including one scene where he is driving a deluxe limousine. "In LA, there are several custom car companies that supply studios with all types of vehicles. I don't know which one supplied the limo but it was fun to drive, especially with the hot tub...what a ride!" And for Cutler, the fun did not stop there. "I got to beat David (Hasselhoff) up, fire a .45 at K.I.T.T. and work with a director who I had always enjoyed working with. The best part of all though was to work with Albert Salmi. As an actor in LA, your next job is as good as your most recent credit. Of course, guest starring on one of the hottest shows at the time helped my career immeasurably".

Photo courtesy of Rebecca Holden

Knight Knotes:

- The aftermarket rims seen on K.I.T.T. in this episode are Borlem 7JJ 15x7 rims.
- The custom car show seen here was actually filmed in a parking lot at Universal Studios. This parking lot is reused again as Circus Major in season three's "Circus Knights".

- Guest star Angel Tompkins ran against William Daniels for Screen Actors Guild president in 1999. Daniels won.

Script to Screen:
- Devon believes that the woman who hit him was intoxicated.
- April investigates the car left behind by Nora Rayburn after she steals the Pennington and discovers a strand of fake blonde hair.
- K.I.T.T. expresses more of his distaste of car customizing after initially leaving the semi. "Do you have any idea what is done to these cars? They're painted, cut, molded, covered with decals and chrome."
- Two blonde surfers named Jan and Dean pull up in a customized van and hit on Carrie.
- A guard named Don Jensen watches over the cars at night, but is sleeping when Carrie's car is stolen.
- A hobo witnesses Michael and K.I.T.T.'s turbo boost over the train. Cutting it close, K.I.T.T. warns Michael, "If we fail to reach the necessary height for clearance we'll end up customized by a freight train."
- As K.I.T.T. is chasing the motorcycle rider, a milk truck heading towards him forces a ski mode.
- Carrie is falsely arrested for Grand Theft Auto when the police find a suitcase of blonde wigs in her room.
- Commander Smythe is described as "a cross between John Houseman, Winston Churchill and an English Bulldog."
- K.I.T.T.'s new appearance is described as follows: "For a moment we can't believe our eyes. The car drawing all the attention is K.I.T.T. -- recognizable but distinctively customized, bright red and yellow flames, altered air scoops, chrome extension pipes, etc. The smoked

windows glide down, revealing Carrie behind the wheel, waving to the impressed crowd."

Featured Songs:

"One Thing Leads to Another" by The Fixx

"Promises, Promises" by Naked Eyes

K.I.T.T.'s Capabilities:

- Auto Cruise, Chemical Analyzer, Pursuit, Radar, Turbo Boost, Voice Projection

PROD. #57829

> EPISODE
> 29

Script History:

September 28, 1983 (F.R.)

September 29, 1983 (F.R.)

October 5, 1983 (F.R.)

October 5, 1983 (2nd rev.)

October 6, 1983 (F.R.)

SOUL SURVIVOR

Written By: Robert Foster and Robert W. Gilmer

Directed By: Harvey Laidman

Original Airdate: November 27, 1983 (Sunday, 8:00 PM) (24.4%; 20,450,000)

NBC Rerun #1: March 25, 1984 (Sunday, 8:00 PM) (19.3%; 16,170,000)

NBC Rerun #2: August 12, 1984 (Sunday, 8:00 PM) (12.5%; 10,480,000)

Filming Dates: October 6-14, 1983

"I am the Knight Industries Two Thousand. My serial number is Alpha Delta 227529. I am unauthorized to allow access to my Central Processing Unit."

-K.I.T.T.

Crew: Robert Foster (Executive Producer), Joel Rogosin (Supervising Producer), Robert W. Gilmer (Co-Producer), Gian R. Grimaldi (Co-Producer), Tom Greene (Co-Producer), Bernadette Joyce (Associate Producer), Robert Ewing (Associate Producer), Janis Hendler (Executive Script Consultant), Don Peake (Music), H. John Penner (Director of Photography), Russell Smith (Art Director), Stanley Wohlberg (Film Editor), Ron Martinez (Unit Production Manager), Charles Watson Sanford, Jr. (1st Assistant Director), Bruce Humphrey (2nd Assistant Director), R. Lynn Smartt (Set Decorator), Pat Somerset (Sound), April Webster (Casting), John Shouse (Sound Effects Editor), Richard Lapham (Music Editor), Barry Downing (Costume Supervisor), Judie Champion (Costume Supervisor), Jack Gill (Stunt Coordinator), Jeremy Swan (Make-up), Allen Payne (Hairstylist)

Guest Cast: Ann Turkel (Adrianne Margeaux), Brian Robbins (Randy Merritt), Jon Cypher (George Atherton), Janet Carroll (Denise Merritt), Carl Strano (Fredericks), Frank Birney (Assistant Manager), Jim Nabors (Elmer)

Michael is lured to an attractive woman's house, where he is drugged and K.I.T.T. is stolen.

A Look Back:

Actress and model Ann Turkel made her first of three appearances on *Knight Rider* in "Soul Survivor", where she played the evil Adrianne Margeaux. In front of the camera, Turkel was best known for her role in the John Frankenheimer movie *99 and 44/100% Dead*, where she starred alongside her soon to be husband Richard Harris. "I always loved to act," says Turkel. "I started dancing when I was 5 years old and by the time I was eleven I was taking acting lessons. I never once thought whilst studying in the theatre that I would be in films and TV shows."

Before Turkel ventured into television and film, she was one of the most glamorous and most famous models in the world. "I had a wonderful life. I was discovered by the editor of *Vogue* magazine and before I knew it I was flying all around the world and being paid to do so. I worked in Tahiti, Japan, France and England to name a few. I was photographed by Helmut Newton and David Bailey shot his first Vogue cover with me."

A chance conversation with an agent would change Turkel's life once more. "At this time, I was living and working in London. I was dating David Niven's brother and David's friend, who was an agent, talked to me and suggested that I move to Los Angeles and get into television and movies."

Turkel's career took off and in 1983 she was approached to star in one of the hottest shows on prime time television. "To be honest with you, I didn't have to audition for *Knight Rider*," confirms Turkel. "I think that was due to the fact that I was a known name before *Knight Rider*. The process was that my agent would give me the script and then I would read it and thereafter it was my decision if I would take the job. I read my part as Adrianne Margeaux and loved it, so I accepted."

Before starring in *Knight Rider,* Turkel already had connections with the show as one of her best friends was and still is Glen Larson. "Glen is just wonderful. I'm good friends with him and I have known him for a long time. Back in the 80's, my brother, my boyfriend (at the time) and I would go over to Glen's place sometimes three or four times a week and hang out and watch movies. We used to watch a lot of films together. They were great times."

We are first introduced to *Knight Rider's* leading female villain when she sabotages her own car so it won't start in order to lure Michael Knight back to her house and use K.I.T.T. for her own purposes. "It's funny, because starting from this period of my career, I was always being hired to play the evil character," notes Turkel. "Adrianne was very centrally evil as oppose to being nasty and bad. I was really happy to be working on the show. From the first scene, David and I got on so well. I remember that scene vividly because Adrianne's car was a classic Rolls Royce and I actually don't like them. My ex-husband, Richard Harris, was given a Rolls Royce as part of a deal for a film that he did but I never liked them. I always assumed that they were driven by old people."

Turkel's sidekick was a computer whiz kid named Randy Merritt, played by a young Brian Robbins. "Brian was excellent and really accomplished. I never felt that I had to give him pointers or encouragement. But that was also back in the 80's. Perhaps if it were now and I was acting alongside someone like Brian, maybe I would act more as a guardian and give out some advice."

Turkel also confirms that a long standing rumor that Robbins took K.I.T.T. for a joyride between takes is just that. "No, I don't believe that story was true. I never heard of that. I guess it would have been funny though if it had happened."

Adrianne and Randy spend a few scenes in the "Rodents Raiders" van where they attempt to control K.I.T.T., and although many set ups like this were usually studio based, this scene appears to have been on location. "When we did 'Soul Survivor' and indeed on all my time shooting *Knight Rider,* I don't ever recall shooting in a studio. We always seemed to be on location," says Turkel.

One of Adrianne's most memorable lines in "Soul Survivor" comes when she is trying to convince Randy to stick with her plans. "'Your genius is your power, never forget that!' You know, we had a great script and I think we all did our part and acted it out very well. I put a lot of feeling into Adrianne's character and I was able to give her an evil streak," says Turkel. She was also fond of the episode's director. "Harvey was great to work with, he had a way of keeping the story flowing. Of course he was very professional and kind. I watched 'Soul Survivor' when it first aired and I have to say that I was very satisfied with how it turned out and I liked my performance. Adrianne was quite an evil character. It was a great episode to be involved in and to watch."

"This is my favorite episode," says director Harvey Laidman. "The plot is clever and the humor is fresh." Indeed, "Soul Survivor" is remembered fondly by fans of the show, almost thirty years after it aired.

Ann Turkel guest starred as Adrianne Margeaux, a ruthless villain intent on acquiring K.I.T.T. for her own purposes. She would become one of *Knight Rider's* most popular guest stars, re-appearing later in the season in "Goliath Returns" and in the following season in "Knight in Retreat". Laidman has nothing but fond memories of working with her. "Ann Turkel was fantastic. She was friendly, professional and amusing. I remember at the time of filming, she was manufacturing a line of bathing suits that passed sunlight through for tanning. The suits were very attractive. I worked with Ann many times."

Laidman remembers the magnificent house that posed for Turkel's residence. "I remember that house well. It was in Trancas, just a little north of Malibu. I believe at that time, the house was vacant and for sale. The Universal location department found it and I approved it. We shot inside and out for one full day."

When Adrianne invites Michael into her house, she uses a trance-like music piece that puts Michael to sleep in order to steal K.I.T.T. "The music was recorded specifically for the show. A certain number of shows were actually scored by an orchestra."

Brian Robbins, who played the character of Randy Merritt, was Turkel's sidekick and was the brains behind K.I.T.T.'s theft. "I worked with Brian several times. He is a very talented guy. His father was an actor and was his guardian during the filming of the episode." There has been a long standing rumor amongst the *Knight Rider* fan community that Robbins had taken K.I.T.T. for a joyride between takes. To that rumor, Laidman remarked, "No, not at all."

If the studio had its way, Robbins' character would have been controlling K.I.T.T. in a different way. "I remember having an argument with the producers. They wanted Brian to use a mouse to remotely control K.I.T.T. They had never even heard of a joystick!"

In the episode, Adrianne and Randy disguised their mobile headquarters as an exterminator's truck. Laidman confesses, "The 'Rodent Raiders' on the van was just a joke. In those days, there was no product placement. It was considered 'payola'. The van belonged to the Universal transportation department."

"Soul Survivor" is unique in that Michael's quest to find and capture the bad guys is largely done without K.I.T.T.'s direct help, as his CPU had been separated from the car. "To be honest, there was nothing really special about the boom box", says Laidman. "Everything was done in post-production."

The episode featured a number of turbo boosts, a stunt in which Laidman recalls were very hard on the cars. "Universal had purchased a trainload of Trans Ams from the manufacturer that were damaged and not saleable. If you look closely at those turbo boost jumps, which were done off a ramp with a 'kicker', you can see just how hard it was on the frame."

Filming for this episode was as regular as ever. "All of the one hour episodes of *Knight Rider* were photographed in seven days - an assortment of 11, 12 and 14 hour days. Woe to the director who went over seven days. I don't think anyone ever did," says Laidman.

Despite being nemesis' on screen, Rebecca Holden thinks nothing but the best of guest star Ann Turkel. "I had worked with Ann once before on an episode of *Mike Hammer* and we had really enjoyed working together," recalls Holden. "But all of us, the 'Ladies of *Knight Rider*', have actually come to know each other much better in the years since the show. I think at the time when you are in production, especially on a dramatic episodic series which requires such long hours, you are so focused on the work and concentrating on your scene, that there is really very little time for socializing. Ann is a precious person and Catherine (Hickland) is so fun-loving and a joy to be around. We have gotten to be good friends. I admire and respect them both, and I always look forward to the *Knight Rider* festivals and conventions when we can catch up and have some 'girl talk'. I love spending time with them. And of course, let's not forget the glamorous and elegant Barbara Rush, who played Garthe's mother. I had always thought she was such a beautiful actress in the old movies. By the way, I saw her not too long ago--- and she is still as beautiful as ever!"

Knight Knotes:

- The vehicle that Adrienne and Randy occupy throughout the episode is disguised as an exterminator's van sporting the fake company name of Rodent Raiders. They even went so far as to apply slogans to the side of the van: "If it crawls, it falls" and "If it flies, it dies."

- The armored truck seen in this episode sports a license plate number of CA 5Z39398. This plate is seen again on the circus van in "Silent Knight", the caterer's chase car in "A Knight in Shining Armor" and Simpson's truck in "Burial Ground".

- The episode begins with Michael playing "Pac-Man" on K.I.T.T.'s dash, a fact which he remembers in *Knight Rider 2000*.

- The turbo boost seen in the final seconds of this episode is actually the same one used when K.I.T.T. jumps over the Mercedes earlier in the episode.

- K.I.T.T.'s portable television set seen in this episode would be back in "Junk Yard Dog" and "Knight of the Juggernaut". The set was built from a JVC CX-710 portable television.
- Jim Nabors, most remembered for his roles on *The Andy Griffith Show* and *Gomer Pyle, U.S.M.C.,* has a small role here as the man who trades his Studebaker for Michael's Mercedes.

Script to Screen:

- The episode originally starts with Randy feverishly working in his computer lab as Adrianne walks in. He doubts his programming skills, but the scene ends with 3 black monitors lighting up with pictures of K.I.T.T. The scene then transitions to Michael playing Pac-Man.
- The synthesized music that hypnotizes Michael was intended to sound similar to Vangelis or Tangerine Dream.
- In addition to Randy opening K.I.T.T.'s door and hood, he also activates the windshield wipers and horn.
- As soon as K.I.T.T. denies access to his CPU, and Adrianne says that they don't need the CPU because he controls the car, Randy remarks, "But, Adrianne, you told me the Knight Industries Two Thousand is one of the most fantastic computers in the world. I've gotta get inside, get to know it...." Adrianne's tone changes and she tells Randy to destroy it.
- Devon informs Michael that George Atherton has been on the Foundation's Board of Directors for fifteen years and he was Wilton Knight's good friend.

Déjà Vu:

- Ann Turkel returns in "Goliath Returns" and "Knight in Retreat".

K.I.T.T.'s Capabilities:

- Auto Cruise, Auto-Roof Right, Composite Identification, Eject Right, Laser, Map Search, Pursuit, Telephone Trace, Turbo Boost

PROD. #57810

{ EPISODE
30 }

Script History:

May 18, 1983 (F.R.)

RING OF FIRE

Written By: Janis Hendler

Directed By: Winrich Kolbe

Original Airdate: December 4, 1983 (Sunday, 8:00 PM) (19.1%; 16,010,000)

NBC Rerun #1: July 8, 1984 (Sunday, 8:00 PM) (12.7%; 10,640,000)

Filming Dates: May 20-31, 1983

"I'm in no mood to be pushed past my boiling point!"

-Michael

Crew: Robert Foster (Executive Producer), Joel Rogosin (Supervising Producer), Robert W. Gilmer (Co-Producer), Stephen Downing (Co-Producer), Gian R. Grimaldi (Coordinating Producer), Bernadette Joyce (Associate Producer), Robert Ewing (Associate Producer), William Schmidt (Story Editor), Don Peake (Music), H. John Penner (Director of Photography), Russell Smith (Art Director), Lawrence J. Vallario (Film Editor), Ron Martinez (Unit Production Manager), Charles Watson Sanford, Jr. (1st Assistant Director), Bruce Humphrey (2nd Assistant Director), R. Lynn Smartt (Set Decorator), Stan Gordon (Sound), April Webster (Casting), Sam Gemette (Sound Effects Editor), Richard Lapham (Music Editor), Barry Downing (Costume Supervisor), Judie Champion (Costume Supervisor), Robert Bralver (Stunt Coordinator), Jack Gill (Co-Stunt Coordinator), Jeremy Swan (Make-up), Allen Payne (Hairstylist)

Guest Cast: Leslie Wing (Layla Charon Callan), Robert Reynolds (Christopher "Cray" Callan), George Murdock (Judge Oliver Callan), Joseph Hindy (Reverend Tom Baylor), Beau Starr (Jacques Charon), Will MacMillan (Sheriff Casey), Larry Moss (Henri Lecroix), Dick Durock (Officer Brown), Jack Gill (Paul Lecroix), Harold "Hal" Frizzell (Poacher), Dick Durock (Brown), Larry Turk (Cajun Man)

Michael and K.I.T.T. are stranded in the Louisiana bayou after a chase involving an escaped murderer lands them in a swamp.

A Look Back:

The last scene in this episode features Rebecca Holden's character, April, scolding Michael for the damage he inflicted upon K.I.T.T. Holden remarks, "I think April really thought of K.I.T.T. as 'her baby', which triggered all my maternal and protective instincts. April even scolded Michael when he was too mischievous or adventurous or did things that she thought were too risky or dangerous for them. I think she genuinely loved both Michael and K.I.T.T., and I think it would have devastated her if one of her inventions for them ended up getting one or both of them hurt in any way. In another episode ["Return to Cadiz"], K.I.T.T. calls April 'motherly', and I think she WAS when it came to protecting those she cared about. Again, beyond the action, jumps and high speed chases, the show was really about the RELATIONSHIPS."

Knight Knotes:

- April installs a pyroclastic lamination that protects his occupants for temperatures up to 600 degrees.
- As Michael is entering Fleur de Lac, a Datsun sporting the license plate of CA 286 995 can be seen. Only a few minutes earlier, that same plate is seen on the prison truck with the chain gang.
- The bayou festival where Layla was kidnapped was filmed at a barn on the Universal Studios' backlot.

Script to Screen:

- K.I.T.T. interfaces with a computer called Omni-comp to obtain information on Christopher Callan.
- Judge Callan is described as dressing in "Colonel Sanders white".
- K.I.T.T. jumps over a fallen tree while in pursuit of Callan before landing in the swamp.
- Michael and Layla stop at the poacher's shack and eat some peaches. Michael asks about the dynamite and when Layla tells him that everyone knows about the shack, they leave.
- A description of Michael and K.I.T.T. pulling up to the Cajun settlement: "As the Trans Am pulls into the center of the settlement,

we hear that the car's engine is missing badly. Finally, the car dies, and the hum of its engine is replaced by strange Cajun music wafting out of a nearby barn. Michael and Layla climb out and Michael crosses to open the Trans Am's hood, tinker with the complicated engine."

Déjà Vu:

- George Murdock returns in "Mouth of the Snake" and *Team Knight Rider's* "The A List"; Dick Durock is back in the finale "Voo Doo Knight".

Featured Songs:

"Mr. Radio" by Trisha Yearwood

"Personally" by Karla Bonoff

"I'm So Lonesome" by Willie Nelson

K.I.T.T.'s Capabilities:

- Audio Playback, Auto Cruise, Auto-Roof Left, Energy System Override, Grappling Hook, Integrated Micronetic Navigational Circuit, Printer, Pursuit, Pyroclastic Lamination, Self-Diagnostic Analyzer, Surveillance Mode, Turbo Boost, Voice Analyzer

PROD. #57830

{ EPISODE 31 }

Script History:

October 10, 1983 (F.R.)

October 12, 1983 (F.R.)

October 14, 1983 (F.R.)

October 17, 1983 (F.R.)

October 17, 1983 (2nd Rev.)

October 19, 1983 (F.R.)

October 21, 1983 (Shooting)

KNIGHTMARES

Written By: Tom Greene and Janis Hendler

Directed By: Sidney Hayers

Original Airdate: December 11, 1983 (Sunday, 8:00 PM) (22.5%; 18,860,000)

NBC Rerun #1: April 13, 1984 (Friday, 8:00 PM) (13.2%; 11,060,000)

NBC Rerun #2: July 29, 1984 (Sunday, 8:00 PM) (15.1%; 12,650,000)

Filming Dates: October 17-25, 1983

"My whole world is turned upside down, and now I am talking to a car."

-Michael

Crew: Robert Foster (Executive Producer), Joel Rogosin (Supervising Producer), Robert W. Gilmer (Co-Producer), Gian R. Grimaldi (Co-Producer), Tom Greene (Co-Producer), Bernadette Joyce (Associate Producer), Robert Ewing (Associate Producer), Janis Hendler (Executive Script Consultant), Don Peake (Music), H. John Penner (Director of Photography), Russell Smith (Art Director), Lawrence J. Gleason (Film Editor), Ron Martinez (Unit Production Manager), Robert Villar (1st Assistant Director), Bruce Humphrey (2nd Assistant Director), R. Lynn Smartt (Set Decorator), Pat Somerset (Sound), April Webster (Casting), John Shouse (Sound Effects Editor), Richard Lapham (Music Editor), Barry Downing (Costume Supervisor), Judie Champion (Costume Supervisor), Jack Gill (Stunt Coordinator), Jeremy Swan (Make-up), Allen Payne (Hairstylist)

Guest Cast: Laura Bruneau (Cara Caulfield), Mike Genovese (Frank Poole), Susan Kellermann (Nurse Langly), Nick Dimitri (Duke), J. Jay Saunders (Officer Bowman), William Boyett (Desk Sergeant), Marty Schiff (Taxi Driver), Bruce Paul Barbour (Police Officer)

After nearly being killed in an explosion, Michael reverts back to his former identity as Michael Long.

A Look Back:

Rebecca Holden had the distinct honor of driving K.I.T.T. briefly in this episode. While it may seem that driving a car would be an easy task, the entire process was a bit more difficult since it had to be captured on screen. "Driving a car in a scene is more complex than one might think," admits Holden. "The actor must follow the director's instructions--driving the right speed, staying in the camera angle, hitting the mark, etc. What I was required to do was relatively simple, comparatively speaking, and I am incredibly awed by the guys who drove K.I.T.T. in the action scenes--all the chases and jumps. The stunt drivers like Jack Gill are breathtaking to watch and their feats are simply amazing! So just driving down the street, as I did, was elementary, of course, but I was concentrating so hard to do just as I was told. (Can you even imagine if April had wrecked K.I.T.T.?! Ha!) I always liked to get things right on the first take as well, so I really wanted to do it right the first time and was focusing especially hard. So I think it wasn't until the director yelled, 'Cut!' and I was headed off the set, that it really sunk in...'Hey I actually drove K.I.T.T.! History making!'"

Marty Schiff starred as the taxi driver who drops Michael Knight off at his 'home', and then lets him off his taxi fare when Michael, suffering from amnesia, realizes that he has no money. "If the fare was worth the effort and depending on the day, I would probably go after a person who skipped on it," jokes Schiff.

Schiff's acting career began in the late 1970's with a few roles in horror movies, namely *Dawn of the Dead* and *Creepshow*. "I am a horror fan and growing up in Pittsburgh, you must do at least one zombie movie if you want to be taken seriously. I have the zombie triple crown - I've been a zombie, I've killed a zombie and I have been killed by a zombie."

Schiff believes a mixture of moving to Hollywood at a young age and possessing an 8mm camera threw him into the world of acting. "I knew by the age of ten that I was moving to Hollywood and that I wanted to act. I watched a lot of TV and would go to the movies at least once a week. When I was 12, my father gave me an 8mm Kodak camera. I was hooked."

Apart from working on the CBS show *The Book of Lists* (which was hosted by Bill Bixby), *Knight Rider* was one of Schiff's first TV roles. "The audition was straightforward. I showed up, did a few lines and went home and waited for the phone to ring. I didn't have to do a call back and I got the role on the first audition."

Schiff only shares his scene with David Hasselhoff, which meant that he did not get to meet the rest of the cast but he did get a quick glimpse of K.I.T.T. "David was great to work with," confirms Schiff. "Even though it's a short scene, we actually spent most of the day riding around in the cab. David was very friendly and, unlike many stars, a genuinely nice guy. I'm glad he has had a successful career. He deserves it. I did not meet the other cast, but I did get an education that day learning that there was more than just one K.I.T.T. There were various sections of the car to make shooting easier. They had them all on a flatbed truck."

"Knightmares" was directed by Sidney Hayers and Schiff still remembers how he received motivation from the Scotsman. "At that time, I was still very 'green' and had come from a heavy stage background, so even if you had one line, you labored over it. So, I was working on my character relationship and objective. I walked up to Sidney and asked him, 'What is my motivation in the scene?'. Sidney, who had been in the business forever and was a seasoned pro, looked at me and with his thick UK accent said, 'Motivation? You're a cab driver. You drive the bloody cab!'".

Though Schiff's scene is just over a minute long, he confirms just how long that minute means in work time. "We were on the road for most of the morning and just beyond lunch. I remember we did many takes from many different angles." Schiff drives for the fictional cab company Tower Taxi's. "I'm sure there was lots of research done to be sure there wasn't an actual Tower Taxi anywhere that could sue them." Albeit a small role, Schiff is thankful for his time on *Knight Rider*. "For me, it was my job. It was what I did. Every role is a victory. There are actors that audition for decades that do not get a role on a TV series. I was very lucky to have a 1:10 ratio, meaning that I usually got a job every ten auditions."

Schiff has had a career spanning over thirty years, but there are two significant TV roles that stick out for him. "I liked playing Hern Burford in

Nickelodeon's *Out of Control*. It was fun to be at the beginning of something that you knew would be really big," confesses Schiff. "The other role that I liked was playing Mr. Del Grecco in *Dallas*. I was in several episodes and ended up playing JR's roommate in a mental institution. I worked with Larry Hagman all week for each episode. He's a lot of fun and has a great sense of humor. I ran into him a few years ago at a film convention in New Jersey, and out of a crowd of thousands he picked me out and introduced me to his wife. I loved every role I have done," concludes Schiff.

Knight Knotes:

- The hospital where Michael is treated is named the Hoff Medical Center.
- This episode features scenes from "Brother's Keeper".
- The dam featured here, Sepulveda Dam in Los Angeles, reappears in "Redemption of a Champion".

Script to Screen:

- A description of how Michael finds the secret door at the dam: "He climbs to the bottom and walks against the wall of the mound, seeking an entry into the dam. He runs his hand across a row of bolts jutting out in a straight line the length of the wall. Long rust stains flow down from the bolts like red tears. Eyeing the bolts, Michael stops. We see what he's spotted -- a group of bolts exactly like the others, except that these do not have the rust stains under them. Beneath them, he discovers a space in the wall, like the crack of a door. Michael pries the crack with his fingers, finds a hidden release; applies pressure, and with a click, the concrete door comes ajar. He swings it open and carefully walks into the dam."

- As the taxi cab pulls away, Michael has a flashback of K.I.T.T. pulling away as well.

- While en route to the police station with April and Devon, K.I.T.T. comments, "The thought of Michael forgetting everything is quite distressing. If I were to experience total file loss, I would simply switch an auxiliary data bank." Devon replies, "In a manner of speaking, that's just what Michael did. Only in his case, his auxiliary data bank is missing two years."

K.I.T.T.'s Capabilities:

- Auto Cruise, Auto-Roof Left, Chemical Analyzer, Comprehensive Configuration Analysis, Computer Graphics, Hydraulic Seat, Infrared, Micro Jam, Police/Radio Frequency, Pursuit, Radar, Tinted Windows, Turbo Boost

PROD. #57817

Script History:

October 12, 1983 (F.R.)

October 20, 1983 (F.R.)

October 21, 1983 (F.R.)

{ EPISODE
32 }

SILENT KNIGHT

Working Title #1: "The Fiddler"

Working Title #2: "Fiddler's Dream"

Working Title #3: "Knight and the Gypsy"

Teleplay By: Robert W. Gilmer and Janis Hendler

Story By: Stephen B. Katz

Directed By: Bruce Kessler

Original Airdate: December 18, 1983 (Sunday, 8:00 PM) (22.6%; 18,940,000)

Filming Dates: October 26 – November 4, 1983

"That is a phone and I am not a booth."

-K.I.T.T.

Crew: Robert Foster (Executive Producer), Joel Rogosin (Supervising Producer), Robert W. Gilmer (Co-Producer), Gian R. Grimaldi (Co-Producer), Tom Greene (Co-Producer), Bernadette Joyce (Associate Producer), Robert Ewing (Associate Producer), Janis Hendler (Executive Script Consultant), Don Peake (Music), H. John Penner (Director of Photography), Russell Smith (Art Director), Beryl Gelfond (Film Editor), Ron Martinez (Unit Production Manager), Charles Watson Sanford, Jr. (1st Assistant Director), Bruce Humphrey (2nd Assistant Director), R. Lynn Smartt (Set Decorator), Pat Somerset (Sound), April Webster (Casting), John Shouse (Sound Effects Editor), Richard Lapham (Music Editor), Barry Downing (Costume Supervisor), Judie Champion (Costume Supervisor), Jack Gill (Stunt Coordinator), Jeremy Swan (Make-up), Allen Payne (Hairstylist)

Guest Cast: Paul LaGreca (Tino Petro), Janet DeMay (Marta Petro), Stephen Liska (Casey), Giorgio Tozzi (Stephano Petro), Robert Miranda (Paolo), Lloyd Alan (Nick), David Proval (Skip)

Michael and K.I.T.T. take a break from their Christmas shopping to help a young gypsy boy being targeted by a trio of bank robbers.

A Look Back:

Stephen Liska had starred in many television shows of the 1980's, including *Street Hawk* and *The A-Team,* as well as such Hollywood blockbusters as *Beverly Hills Cop 2* and *Lethal Weapon 4*. His acting career began with a move to Los Angeles. "I was new to the process of auditions in Hollywood," says Liska. "I had just moved to LA in 1980 after a decade in New York City doing stage work. I believe the casting director at *Knight Rider* was Joe Reich. They were all very helpful to me in our early meetings."

Liska played a crook named Casey in "Silent Knight". Along with his partners in crime, Paolo and Skip, the trio robs a bank during the Christmas season. "We all meshed well," remembers Liska. "Our 3 antagonists had three different approaches to our roles that stressed different colors. There was Robert Miranda, who played Paolo. I had worked with him a number of other times. He took the serious 'muscle' approach. David Proval (who was not credited in the episode) was an actor I looked up to. He was outstanding in Martin Scorsese's *Mean Streets*. He was the quiet, menacing thug. Then there was me, Casey. I tried to be the manic driving force of the trio. Casey was a bit of a James Wood type."

"Silent Knight" was directed by Bruce Kessler, a man whom Liska has good memories working with. "Bruce Kessler was fun to work with," recalls Liska. "I believe at the time of shooting that someone mentioned that he had a background in racing cars, and I think you can see that in the K.I.T.T. action sequences."

As for K.I.T.T., Liska was perplexed at how the car drove without a driver and he was determined to get to the bottom of the mystery while filming his episode. "I was fascinated with K.I.T.T. I couldn't figure out how they controlled the car without a driver. You could have knocked me over with a feather after I found out. They removed the driver's seat and replaced it with an identical one, only it was larger and hollowed out. The stunt driver would just slide into the seat from the back. In reality, K.I.T.T. always had a driver in the seat, it's just that most of the time, he couldn't be seen. Fun, eh?"

Liska and his gang of thugs spend nearly the entire episode chasing Tino (played by Paul LaGreca), a young gypsy boy who has himself stolen a gold watch from them. Since the watch links the gang to the crime, it becomes a priority for them to retrieve it back. "Paul La Greca was very much like his character - animated, full of energy, friendly and ready to try anything during our chase sequences. I remember that we were pressed for time shooting the episode. I think we had 7-8 days to wrap it up. It was a tight schedule and the stunt car scenes involving K.I.T.T. took a long time to set up. It was very hot in the San Fernando Valley and time is of importance when shooting an episodic for TV."

Saving Tino from the robbers was, of course, K.I.T.T. and Michael. "I must say that David Hasselhoff was just great, a real pro. So easy to work with and he knew his stuff from A-Z. Every day on the set, he was at his peak in every scene. The best I can say about David was that he really knew how to handle the daily grind of TV work and make it look real and easy. Quite a talent. Lastly, after a long day in the heat and rolling around in fight sequences, David could be found at the end of the day taking time to talk and sign autographs to the kids visiting the set. There were always children visiting the set the week I worked."

The chase for Tino comes to a head in a corn field, when Casey and his gang track down the youngster and aim to end the chase there and then. "I remember having to drive that corn thrasher for the final sequence. My stunt driver did most of the driving, but I had a ball doing the startup and stopping sequence. Acting in an action sequence was a new experience for me since I came from the stage, and I found it both fun and stressful at first."

Liska has a lot of respect for the stunt people on *Knight Rider.* "There was real technique to the fight sequences and the fight coordinator on *Knight Rider* really knew his stuff and took the time to show me the best ways of taking a fall and/or throwing a punch." Liska watched the episode when it aired a week before Christmas in 1983. "I did watch the airing of the show and I don't normally do that. Normally, I have it taped and then look at it months later. This time, I wanted to see it as soon as possible. I attempted, in my characterization, to make more use of my body, arms, hands, etc. in order to convey a slight manic sensibility, so I wanted to see if that approach worked.

(Photo courtesy of Stephen Liska)

Unfortunately, I wasn't happy with the results. I felt my movements were a bit large and strained. I would have preferred a more subtle movement, but I don't think it hurt the main concept and it did teach me a valuable lesson for my future work in television. Less can be better."

Jack Gill recalls the turbo boost into a corn field, seen near the end of this episode. "We had a shot of Pat Romano doubling the little kid in the corn field and I put a flag up behind him so I could see him. I jumped the car into the corn field and I couldn't see anything because the corn was 8 feet tall. So, I'm just looking for the flag and I said to Pat, 'You be to the right of the flag'. Well, he was turned around and he thought that the right was over there. All I see is the corn go down and I hit him. He goes up over the top of the car and lands behind it. The car was so low that it didn't really do anything to him. He got up, ran around the car, jumped in and I went, 'I just hit you!' He didn't have a scratch on him, just bruised up a little bit. I said, 'What happened to being on the right?' He said, 'I was on the right!' I said, 'No, my right!'"

Knight Knotes:

- When Michael confronts Stephano about selling Tino out to the bank robbers, viewers can spot the staircase leading to the Bates House from *Psycho,* as this scene was shot on Universal Studios' back lot.
- Stephen Liska starred in 1993's *Street Knight* alongside fellow *Knight Rider* alums Grainger Hines ("No Big Thing"/"Knight Racer") and Sal Landi ("White-Line Warriors").

Script to Screen:

- The side of the robber's van says "The Amazing Banducci Brothers -- World's Smallest Circus".
- The gold watch was originally intended to be a wrist watch, not a pocket watch.

- The viewer is first introduced to Tino when he attends his father's viewing at the funeral parlor. He puts a religious medal in his father's hand and promises to take care of Marta and become a real gypsy.

- Instead of Tino stealing the gold watch from the robbers, he finds it on the ground once they leave.

- Tino tries to convince Michael that the robbers are a gang called The Bombers and they are after him.

- The police officer that Michael talks to at the station is named Lt. Weber.

- The character of Nick was originally named David.

- April's speech to Michael about the importance of the Foundation Ball comes from Devon instead.

- The script says that during one of the driving scenes, "Frosty the Snowman" or "Jingle Bells" should be playing on the radio. K.I.T.T. asks if it's hard to get in the Christmas spirit when it's 70 degrees out, but Michael says it's worth living in that part of the country because he can surf all year long.

Featured Songs:

"Owner of a Lonely Heart" by Yes

"Gypsy" by Fleetwood Mac

"Eye of the Tiger" by Survivor

K.I.T.T.'s Capabilities:

- Auto Cruise, Auto-Roof Left, Auto-Roof Right, Chemical Analyzer, Map Search, Medical Scan, Police/Radio Frequency, Pursuit, Smoke Release, Turbo Boost

PROD. #57832

| | EPISODE 33 | |

Script History:

October 31, 1983 (F.R.)

A KNIGHT IN SHINING ARMOR

Written By: Janis Hendler and Tom Greene

Directed By: Bernard McEveety

Original Airdate: January 8, 1984 (Sunday, 8:00 PM) (21.4%; 17,930,000)

NBC Rerun #1: June 3, 1984 (Sunday, 8:00 PM) (13.1%; 10,980,000)

Filming Dates: November 8-16, 1983

"So is my motor oil, but he didn't leave anything to me."

-K.I.T.T.

Crew: Robert Foster (Executive Producer), Joel Rogosin (Supervising Producer), Robert W. Gilmer (Co-Producer), Gian R. Grimaldi (Co-Producer), Tom Greene (Co-Producer), Bernadette Joyce (Associate Producer), Robert Ewing (Associate Producer), Janis Hendler (Executive Script Consultant), Don Peake (Music), H. John Penner (Director of Photography), Russell Smith (Art Director), Lawrence J. Vallario (Film Editor), Ron Martinez (Unit Production Manager), Robert Villar (1st Assistant Director), Bruce Humphrey (2nd Assistant Director), R. Lynn Smartt (Set Decorator), Pat Somerset (Sound), April Webster (Casting), John Shouse (Sound Effects Editor), Richard Lapham (Music Editor), Barry Downing (Costume Supervisor), Judie Champion (Costume Supervisor), Jack Gill (Stunt Coordinator), Jeremy Swan (Make-up), Allen Payne (Hairstylist)

Guest Cast: Daphne Lee Ashbrook (Katherine Granger), Art Lund (Charlie Granger), Lance LeGault (Christopher Stone), David Cowgill (Scott), Thomas F. Wilson (Chip), Julie Ronnie (Stacey)

Michael helps a young co-ed unlock the secret behind a mysterious treasure left to her by her late father.

A Look Back:

The star of this episode was a young actress named Daphne Ashbrook, who played the strong willed Katherine Granger. As it turned out, Ashbrook came very close to missing out on one of her first television roles. "My agent sent me out and I auditioned for *Knight Rider*," remembers Ashbrook. "April Webster cast me and I had to audition many times for the role. I thought that it went very well but, during the meeting, I learned that April was concerned about how young and inexperienced I was as an actress. It was clear from the acting part of the audition that I could play the part, but it was obvious to everyone that I was very young." Indeed, Ashbrook was just 20 years old when she came up for the audition process. "April took a chance on me and *Knight Rider* became my first 'guest starring' role. When I got the call that I had the part, I was thrilled. I'm sure that I screamed or something similar. I called my dad to tell him the good news," remembers Ashbrook.

Ashbrook's first scene in "A Knight in Shining Armor" is on horseback being rescued by Michael Knight and K.I.T.T. after an attempted assassination. The would-be assassin was named Christopher Stone, played by TV veteran Lance LeGault. "I believe that we shot that first scene in Griffith Park," recalls Ashbrook. "Lance LeGault was a very professional actor. We worked together again on *The A-Team*".

Part of Ashbrook's role required her to ride a horse, which was not foreign to her. "I started western style riding when I was a young kid," says Ashbrook. "My dad had gotten me horseback riding lessons and I just loved it. When I got the part they told me that I'd have to ride English style, so they had to give me just a couple of pointers for the scene."

Knight Rider veteran Bernard McEveety directed the episode and Ashbrook remembers him fondly. "I loved Bernie. His brother Vince directed as well and I believe I also worked with him later on in my career. Bernie was like a father figure to me on the set. He was just great." When asked about her time working with David Hasselhoff, Ashbrook commented, "I really liked working with David. He was so relaxed on set. I remember how he would crack jokes in between takes. It really set the tone for the set. He was very laid back and so tall."

One of Ashbrook's co-stars was the now comedian Thomas F. Wilson, and it was not until recently that Ashbrook was able to recall how she knew him. "Tom was very funny even back then," recalls Ashbrook. "I did recognize him from the *Back to the Future* movies but I could never put my finger on where I had actually worked with him. It wasn't until I recently viewed this episode that I said, 'Now that's where we worked together!'"

David Cowgill and Thomas F. Wilson standing next to their dressing rooms on the set of "A Knight in Shining Armor" (Photo courtesy of David Cowgill)

For much of the episode, Ashbrook's character resents her father for abandoning her, even though he had just passed away. In a scene towards the end of the episode, Michael finally convinces her that her father did indeed love her. It is here where we see Katherine Granger finally mourn for her father's passing. Ashbrook explains her technique in bringing those emotions to the screen. "In those days, I used a technique called 'transference', where I would use personal experience with my own father to drum up emotion. However, I quit using that technique shortly after we filmed the episode because I found transference to be unreliable. It would short change my imagination which, in turn, I found to be a more reliable and impactful technique."

Though Ashbrook would be one of the lucky few to be a passenger in K.I.T.T., she never got to drive the most sophisticated car on television. "K.I.T.T. was a Trans Am and that meant that the bucket seats were low, so it was not easy to drive K.I.T.T. I remember that during filming, there was a lot of 'acting' because the special effects and William Daniels' voice would be put in afterwards. But K.I.T.T. and I got along just fine," jokes Ashbrook.

In the episode's climax, Michael and K.I.T.T., with Katherine's help, finally locate her father's hidden treasure. "The exterior shots of the cave were filmed in Bronson Canyon in the Hollywood Hills. The interior with the treasure was filmed at the Universal lot," confirms Ashbrook. "That cave has been used many times on different TV shows. Again, the special effects required were added in later, so I learned to react to something that wasn't really there. That became a staple for me later on in my career with roles in *Star Trek: Deep Space Nine* and *Doctor Who*.

David Cowgill's career had only just begun when he landed the small role of Scott on *Knight Rider*. "I don't remember much about the audition, apart from the casting director, April Webster. To this day, she is one of the nicest casting people I have ever come across." Despite winning a role on one of the hottest shows on television, Cowgill did have some mixed emotions. "I wasn't as nervous as I was excited," he recalls. "Working on 'A Knight in Shining Armor' was one of my first jobs and it was such a thrill just to be working in Hollywood."

Cowgill's scenes are brief, but he did share screen time with a then unknown actor named Thomas F. Wilson, who would go on to play Biff in the hugely popular *Back To The Future* trilogy. "I do remember Tom, he was a nice guy. His success came rather quickly and I was very happy for him." Of course, Cowgill also remembers working with David Hasselhoff. "I distinctly remember him being very friendly and welcoming. Always ready to chat and he didn't act like a star. I really appreciated the hard work he did on that show and yet had time to chat and be friendly to 'the new kid'."

David Cowgill and Thomas F. Wilson prepare for filming (Photo courtesy of David Cowgill)

In the final scene of the episode, Cowgill asks Michael Knight for a race and is dumbfounded when K.I.T.T. blasts ahead of him. "It was one of my great regrets in life, that *I* didn't get to drive K.I.T.T. In an unrelated story, I did an episode of *Viper* in the late 90's and because of my regrets of never having driven K.I.T.T., I made sure I got to drive the Dodge Viper."

Cowgill enjoyed his time on the original show and would be asked to come back into the *Knight Rider* universe years later. "It was a thrill for me to work on the show. It was a huge show at the time and I was honored to be even a small part of it. I guest starred some 13 years later on *Team Knight*

Rider as detective Kovacs, I believe. *Knight Rider* is the gift that keeps on giving!"

A scene near the end of this episode has K.I.T.T. performing a *reverse turbo boost* to escape from a collapsed cave. This is the one and only time that a reverse car jump was performed on the series ("Goliath Returns" also featured a reverse turbo boost, but the production utilized a miniature car as opposed to the real thing). Stunt coordinator Jack Gill was the man behind the wheel for this feat. "The reverse turbo boost was an interesting feat for me only because I was trying to figure out what parts of my head were going to rattle the hardest when I was in the blind driver's seat. The hardest thing was trying to get a small helmet inside the blind driver's seat because inside that thing was only steel and some tiny pieces of rubber that I put my head around. There wasn't a whole lot of room to get a helmet in there, so what I did was I got a tiny bicycle helmet and wore that. Just imagine that you are looking in the mirrors and lining up the ramp. I was probably doing 40-45 when I hit the mini ramps. It's a whole other ball game trying to line up ramps going backwards. But it all came out great and the car landed good and I didn't get hurt. I guess that's all that really matters."

Knight Knotes:

- This episode features the TV debut of Thomas F. Wilson, who was only a year away from rising to fame playing Biff in *Back to the Future*.
- Stacey makes a reference to 1939's *Gone with the Wind* when she says that Michael "carried Katie out like Scarlett O-Hara".
- Michael refers to the 1966 movie *A Man for All Seasons* in his confrontation with Christopher Stone at his house.
- Christopher Stone's Cadillac has the license plate number of CA 1W15153 – the same plate as Lauren's Mazda in "Diamonds Aren't a

Girl's Best Friend", the commando's van in "Goliath Returns" and Raleigh's truck in "Knight Strike".

Script to Screen:

- The episode begins with Charlie's room, the camera panning over old newspaper articles of Charlie with former world leaders. The scene then cuts to a man in a Jaguar XJS pulling into the Foundation grounds, at which point the scenes actually shown in the episode begin.

- Charlie leaves a letter addressed to Devon in the desk before he is killed. The letter reads, "I bequeath you the greatest treasure I ever encountered, on that day twenty-one years ago when you were born. You're now old enough to value it. The key to the treasure is in the locket you've worn since birth. Katherine, you were always the treasure in my eyes. Please forgive me. Charles Granger."

- After Michael's long assignment, April asks K.I.T.T. if he needs any adjustments. K.I.T.T. replies that his RTA is on scope, but that his ultraphonic gear could use some tweaking. Michael looks at the notes that April is taking, and notices that she's not doing a circuit check, but a road test. Michael complains that he just got back and isn't ready to go out again.

- Charlie Granger was the Foundation's groundskeeper and lived in the groundskeeper's cabin behind F.L.A.G.

- Christopher Stone hires a man named Micky to start digging for the treasure.

- Michael still chases Katherine and stops her horse, but originally, there wasn't anyone shooting at her.

- The sniper shows up at Katherine's dorm and is about to fire when K.I.T.T. senses the man. Michael puts K.I.T.T. in reverse a heads to the dorm. When a golf cart stops in his path, K.I.T.T. performs a reverse turbo boost over the cart to block the shooter.

- When Michael and Katherine arrived at the Foundation, she gets out, looks up at the house and says, "It's just like I pictured it. When I used to meet girls in school, I'd describe the house my father lived in. I always described it exactly like this house."

- Katherine and Michael form more of a romantic bond than what is seen in the episode.

- Michael figures out that the secret to the treasure lies in the eyes of the photograph in the locket, because of how Charlie mentioned in his letter that Katherine was "always the treasure in my eyes." Instead of a code hidden in the eyes, it's simply a reflection of the map in Charlie's eyes.

- The treasure is not located in the side of a mountain, but rather underneath the ground. K.I.T.T. spins his wheels while remaining stationary in order to "sink" into the ground to the treasure room. Once in the room, Stone comes to and dynamites the hole, leaving Michael, K.I.T.T. and Katherine trapped. K.I.T.T. comments that a reverse turbo boost isn't powerful enough for them to escape and there's no room to turn around. Michael tries doing a 180 as he turbo boosts in order to escape.

Déjà Vu:

- David Cowgill returns in *Team Knight Rider's* "Choctaw L-9"; Julie Ronnie is back in "The Wrong Crowd".

K.I.T.T.'s Capabilities:

- Audio Record, Auto Cruise, Auto-Roof Left, Chemical Analyzer, Eject Left, Map Search, Micro Jam, Pursuit, Reverse Turbo Boost, Speed Reading Program, Surveillance Mode, Telephone Call-Intercept, Tinted Windows, Trunk Lid, Turbo Boost

PROD. #57833

[EPISODE
34]

Script History:

November 11, 1983 (F.R.)

November 16, 1983 (F.R.)

DIAMONDS AREN'T A GIRL'S BEST FRIEND

Written By: Robert Foster and Robert Gilmer

Directed By: Jeffrey Hayden

Original Airdate: January 15, 1984 (Sunday, 8:00 PM) (20.1%; 16,840,000)

NBC Rerun #1: April 22, 1984 (Sunday, 8:00 PM) (14.3%; 11,980,000)

Filming Dates: November 17-28, 1983

"That young man was talking to his car, Maurice. Can you imagine? Talking to
something that can't talk back?"

-Mable

Crew: Robert Foster (Executive Producer), Joel Rogosin (Supervising Producer), Robert W. Gilmer (Co-Producer), Gian R. Grimaldi (Co-Producer), Tom Greene (Co-Producer), Bernadette Joyce (Associate Producer), Robert Ewing (Associate Producer), Janis Hendler (Executive Script Consultant), Don Peake (Music), H. John Penner (Director of Photography), Russell Smith (Art Director), Stanley Wohlberg (Film Editor), Ron Martinez (Unit Production Manager), Charles Watson Sanford, Jr. (1st Assistant Director), Bruce Humphrey (2nd Assistant Director), R. Lynn Smartt (Set Decorator), Pat Somerset (Sound), April Webster (Casting), John Shouse (Sound Effects Editor), Richard Lapham (Music Editor), Barry Downing (Costume Supervisor), Judie Champion (Costume Supervisor), Jack Gill (Stunt Coordinator), Jeremy Swan (Make-up), Allen Payne (Hairstylist)

Guest Cast: Cameron Mitchell (Bernie Mitchell), Jo Ann Pflug (Nina Jurgenson), Wendy Kilbourne (Lauren Janes), Elizabeth Lindsey (Rachel Robinson), Rene Assa (Miller), Nicholas Guest (Chris Carlsen), Nancy Ellison (Photographer), Lu Leonard (Mable), Deborah Ludwig Davis (Singer), Quinn O'Hara (Mary Potter), Patricia Ayame Thomson (Model)

After a young model is found dead in her apartment, Michael turns his suspicions toward the head of a modeling agency.

A Look Back:

K.I.T.T. crosses into Mexico, but has trouble returning. A properly placed phone call from Devon is needed as he is looked over with a fine tooth comb before the car is allowed to pass by the Mexican authorities at the border. This is the first episode in which we learn that K.I.T.T. is afraid of flying (a character trait we later learn was programmed by Bonnie).

Knight Knotes:

- Rachel's apartment complex is actually the Universal Park and Terrace Complex on Bluffside Drive, across the street from the north gate of Universal Studios, Hollywood. This location is used again as Karen Forester's apartment building in "K.I.T.T.nap".

- Miller's car wears a license plate number of CA 1WWY819. This plate is seen again on the 4x4 that Mace is handcuffed to in "White-Line Warriors", Sonny Martin's van in "Dead of Knight" and Nick O'Brien's delivery van in "Knight of the Rising Sun".

- Bernie's Lincoln sports a license plate number of CA 9Y58311. This plate is seen again on the Michael's Jeep in "Lost Knight".

Script to Screen:

- Bernie's last name was original Michels. It was changed to Mitchell in the episode, however a computer graphic seen near the end of the episode still lists Michels.

- Rachel Robinson's last name is originally Robbins.

- K.I.T.T. doesn't understand the need for humans to constantly change their fashion sense and that they should be content with what they have. Michael comments that if Detroit had been content, then he would still be a Model T.

Déjà Vu:

- Rene Assa is back in "Knight By a Nose".

Featured Songs:

"Ain't Nobody" by Chaka Khan and Rufus

"Human Touch" by Rick Springfield

K.I.T.T.'s Capabilities:

- Audio Record, Auto Cruise, Infrared, Map Search, Micro Jam, Oil, Pursuit, Radar, Telephone Call-Intercept, Telephone Trace, Turbo Boost

PROD. #57828

{ EPISODE 35 }

Script History:

November 25, 1983 (F.R.)

November 28, 1983 (F.R.)

WHITE-LINE WARRIORS

Working Title #1: "Mister Alarm"

Working Title #2: "Weekend Warriors"

Written By: Richard C. Okie

Directed By: Robert E.L. Bralver

Original Airdate: January 8, 1984 (Sunday, 8:00 PM) (21.8%; 18,270,000)

NBC Rerun #1: September 23, 1984 (Sunday, 8:00 PM) (18.4%; 15,620,000)

Filming Dates: November 29 – December 7, 1983

"You know, K.I.T.T., sometimes I think I've got the best job in the whole world.

A lot of men would die for duty like this."

-Michael

Crew: Robert Foster (Executive Producer), Joel Rogosin (Supervising Producer), Robert W. Gilmer (Co-Producer), Gian R. Grimaldi (Co-Producer), Tom Greene (Co-Producer), Bernadette Joyce (Associate Producer), Robert Ewing (Associate Producer), Janis Hendler (Executive Script Consultant), Don Peake (Music), H. John Penner (Director of Photography), Russell Smith (Art Director), Howard B. Anderson (Film Editor), Ron Martinez (Unit Production Manager), Robert Villar (1st Assistant Director), Bruce Humphrey (2nd Assistant Director), R. Lynn Smartt (Set Decorator), Pat Somerset (Sound), April Webster (Casting), John Shouse (Sound Effects Editor), Richard Lapham (Music Editor), Barry Downing (Costume Supervisor), Judie Champion (Costume Supervisor), Jack Gill (Stunt Coordinator), Jeremy Swan (Make-up), Allen Payne (Hairstylist)

Guest Cast: Mary Beth Evans (Cindy Mattheson), Woody Brown (Ron Prescott), Hugh Gillin (Chief Rupert Craig), Allyn Ann McLerie (Marietta Mattheson), Sammy Jackson (Handsome Anson James), Sal Landi (Ty), Tim Gillin (Officer Apted), Milt Oberman (Manny Carmichael), Frank Garret (Mace Beaudry)

Michael investigates a string of burglaries in Vista Beach after the main suspect claims to be a scapegoat.

A Look Back:

"White-Line Warriors" is a great episode that deals with a group of racers who are using the competitions as a cover for a string of burglaries. The radio station makes K.I.T.T. an offer to become their permanent news person after broadcasting Chief Craig's confession. Michael is constantly bothered by Manny Carmichael, a car alarm salesman who won't take no for an answer. Michael tries to convince him that he already has the best alarm system, but Manny keeps trying to break in to K.I.T.T. and almost manages to get arrested!

Knight Knotes:

- K.I.T.T. gets his Silent Mode in this episode.
- The license plate seen here on the Sheriff's car – CA 104007 – appears again in both "Race for Life" and "K.I.T.T. vs. K.A.R.R."
- A scene cut from this episode, with Devon remarking that, "Michael may not always take the conventional approach" has surfaced on a blooper reel.

Script to Screen:

- The description of the first time we meet Ron and Mace: "In one car -- with a "REBELS" plate on the corner of windshield is Ron Prescott, early twenties, good looking in a James Dean vulnerable kind of way. In the other car is Mace Beaudry, local boy, a little younger, intense."
- The Sunspot Club was originally named the Hurricane Club.
- The trigger song to commit the robberies was supposed to be Michael Sembello's "Maniac".

Déjà Vu:

- Mary Beth Evans guest stars in "Deadly Knightshade".

Featured Songs:

"Maniac" by Flashdance

"Breakdown" by Tom Petty

"Little Red Corvette" by Prince

"Crumblin' Down" by John Cougar Mellencamp

"Rhiannon" by Fleetwood Mac

"Love Is A Battlefield" by Pat Benetar

"I've Got It" by Andrae Crouch and The Disciples

K.I.T.T.'s Capabilities:

- Audio Record, Auto Cruise, Auto-Roof Left, Grappling Hook, Infrared, Micro Jam, Radar, Silent Mode, Trunk Lid, Turbo Boost

PROD. #57826

{ EPISODE 36 }

Script History:

December 2, 1983 (F.R.)

December 5, 1983 (F.R.)

December 7, 1983 (F.R.)

December 8, 1983 (F.R.)

RACE FOR LIFE

Working Title: "Short Notice"

Written By: Bruce Belland and Roy M. Rogosin

Directed By: Georg Fenady

Original Airdate: February 5, 1984 (Sunday, 8:00 PM) (24.9%; 20,870,000)

NBC Rerun #1: June 17, 1984 (Sunday, 8:00 PM) (15.0%; 12,570,000)

Filming Dates: December 8-16, 1983

"Your lesson in checkers paid off. Devon never knew what hit him."

-Becky Phillips

Crew: Robert Foster (Executive Producer), Joel Rogosin (Supervising Producer), Robert W. Gilmer (Co-Producer), Gian R. Grimaldi (Co-Producer), Tom Greene (Co-Producer), George Crosby (Associate Producer), Robert Ewing (Associate Producer), Janis Hendler (Executive Script Consultant), Don Peake (Music), H. John Penner (Director of Photography), Russell Smith (Art Director), Beryl Gelfond (Film Editor), Ron Martinez (Unit Production Manager), Charles Watson Sanford, Jr. (1st Assistant Director), Bruce Humphrey (2nd Assistant Director), R. Lynn Smartt (Set Decorator), Pat Somerset (Sound), April Webster (Casting), John Shouse (Sound Effects Editor), Richard Lapham (Music Editor), Barry Downing (Costume Supervisor), Judie Champion (Costume Supervisor), Jack Gill (Stunt Coordinator), Jeremy Swan (Make-up), Allen Payne (Hairstylist)

Guest Cast: Lynne Marta (Laura Phillips), Scott Getlin (Rick), James Arone (Tony), Hank Brandt (Dr. Carney), Robyn Lively (Becky Phillips), Mario Marcelino (Julio Rodriguez), Jesse Aragon (Santos Rodriguez), Toni Nero (Terri), Vincent Barbour (Conqueror), Frank Lugo (Shopkeeper), William Harlow (Trooper)

It's a race against time as Michael and K.I.T.T. must search Los Angeles for a suitable donor match for April's ailing niece.

A Look Back:

Mario Marcelino played Julio Rodriguez in "Race for Life", a role that he will never forget. "Once again, I was stereotyped as a gang member who is not really a lost soul or someone who has really gone bad. My first professional job was guest starring on *CHiPS*, where I played an 18 year old gang member who was trying to go the straight and narrow rather than continue my involvement with gangs."

Marcelino believes that he succeeded in his audition because of the focus he put into it. "I auditioned for Georg Fenady, the director. He liked that I never lost my focus during my audition reading. Something that I recommend to all students of acting is to stay in character until you hear cut."

Veteran director Georg Fenady liked Marcelino so much that he asked him back to work on another show. "George was one of the first television directors that I had great respect for," says Marcelino. "He dealt with actors as if we were doing a film. He gave us motivation and encouraged us to take chances. He didn't just tell us to go to a mark and say our lines, as if we were on a conveyor belt. Back in those days, series' episodes were wrapped in one week, so time was of the essence. Georg liked my work so much that a year later he called me out for *Airwolf*. He chose me without going to callbacks because of his working experience with me on *Knight Rider*. I must say that that was the only time in my career that has ever happened. We got along great."

Marcelino's first scene was in the red brick church where he is hiding from the rival gang. It was here that he also meets Michael Knight for the first time. "I think the church was somewhere in East L.A.," says Marcelino. "As for David Hasselhoff, I had worked with him years before on *The Young and the Restless*. I was the show's production supervisor at the time. The first morning when we shot "Race for Life", I wasn't sure that David would recognize me. Immediately, he came over and said, 'Mario, so are you on the production team over here now?' and I said, 'No I'm your guest star'. We had a wonderful reunion and he was absolutely great to work with. He was patient, attentive and very respectful of his co-stars - many stars aren't you know. I remember laughing a lot when the cameras were not rolling, especially as my character was very serious."

(Photo courtesy of Mario Marcelino)

Aside from costarring with David Hasselhoff, Marcelino shared scenes with actress Toni Nero, who played his girlfriend Terri, and actor Jesse Aragon, who played his best friend Santos. "I never saw Toni after we filmed the episode. She was very sweet and pretty as you can see. I got to know

Jesse Aragon fairly well over the years. We were always on the same auditions. However, his story is a tragedy. He was killed some years later on his motorcycle, I believe by a truck driver. So unfortunate as he was a very good actor and a nice guy. I liked him very much."

Marcelino is a passenger in K.I.T.T. in quite a few scenes as Michael Knight does his best to get Julio to the hospital to save April's niece, Becky, who needs a bone marrow transplant. Marcelino was also involved in a few stunts, such as the scene where K.I.T.T. drives on a train track. "I remember that very well. Some of that scene was actually shot on a real track. We had so much fun – it was such an adventure. For the stunt scenes, they would never allow us to do that. I was glad as I didn't want to get hurt. It meant that the stunt guys got to have a job as well - spread it all around so to speak."

Eventually, Michael saves the day and succeeds in getting Julio to the hospital for the bone marrow transplant that Becky, played by Robyn Lively, needs. The scene played out is arguably one of the most emotional in any *Knight Rider* episode, and as Marcelino explains, it was closer to home than any of his co-stars would realize. "Nobody on the set knew that at the time that my two and a half year old son was very sick with hydrocephalous and seizures. He had been through two shunting operations. So, in my scenes with Robyn, I am imagining my son at her age and what he might say to me if I was the only one who could help him. It was a sort of a catharsis for me. At one point in the scene, I think I was supposed to say something in response to her question about me being scared and nothing came out. I think that was the perfect choice because there was nothing I could say that would be appropriate at the time. It was an emotional scene for me, and of all my scenes, this is the one that I am the most proud of. Robyn Lively was a wonderful actress and I loved doing this scene with her."

The Vengadores (Photos courtesy of Mario Marcelino)

At the end of the episode, we tragically learn that Marcelino's son passed away during filming. The episode was dedicated to his memory. "Everyone in the cast and crew were so thoughtful to me. They, along with David Hasselhoff, made donations. I asked for donations to go to a children's hospital that cares for sick children. People sometimes think negatively of the cast and crew of TV shows in Hollywood, but I found them to be very generous, kind, compassionate and understanding. Their dedication to my son will remain as one of the wonderful gestures toward me in my career. I will always give thanks to David and Georg for their kindness."

Marcelino's career has been a roller coaster ride, working alongside the likes of Tom Cruise and Leonard Nimoy. "I starred in *Star Trek 3* after *Knight Rider* and I told Leonard Nimoy in my callback audition that I'd do the job for free, because it meant so much to me to work on a project that I had loved since I was a kid. He laughed and said I was perfect and said I would get paid anyway. It was an incredible experience."

The experiences don't end there for Marcelino, though. "I came to Hollywood to be a songwriter and someone suggested I try acting. I'm glad I did. I first worked at CBS as a production supervisor, but I would see all the actors having so much fun and making so much money that I was ready to go on the other side of the camera. I also liked to write poetry and read novels. In 1987, after receiving my MA in English, I got it into my head that I could get a PhD. My friends said no way, but I proved them wrong. By 1991 I was a regular on *Hunter* as Sgt. Jimmy Rivera, but the show was canceled the following year. The same week, I had won a Fulbright award for my dissertation on the poetry of Jorge Luis Borges. I went to Madrid and whilst studying I got a role on *Zorro*. Between 1993 and 2000, I did not act." Since 2000, Marcelino rebooted his career to star in some of the most watched TV series of the last decade. "I've done great roles on *Dexter*, *The Shield*, *Dragnet* and *ER*."

Knight Knotes:

- Rebecca Holden on this episode: "Robyn was a lovely girl, a wonderful actress and she did an admirable job in a very heartwarming episode, which, yes, was more serious in tone and had a tender storyline. It also showed an even more sensitive side of Michael."
- Robyn Lively was nominated for a 1985 Young Artist Award (Best Young Actress - Guest in a Television Series) for her role in this episode.
- This episode's working title was "Short Notice". It was no doubt changed when the producers realized that there was already a season one episode with this title.

Script to Screen:

- Dr. Carney's name is originally Dr. Kiley.
- When K.I.T.T. is blocked in by the Conqueror's vans outside of the church, instead of pushing one of them out of the way, Michael recommends a double turbo boost. His exact quote from the script: "Kitt, what about a double turbo? One to pop the angle, and the other to clear the vans?" K.I.T.T. says that he's never tried it before. Michael presses the Turbo Boost button once and K.I.T.T. arches back on his rear wheels. He presses it again and K.I.T.T. flies over the other van to freedom.

Déjà Vu:

- William Harlow returns in "The Nineteenth Hole".

L to R: Jesse Aragon, David Hasselhoff, Mario Marcelino (Photo courtesy of
Mario Marcelino)

K.I.T.T.'s Capabilities:

- Auto Cruise, Auto Phone, Auto-Roof Right, Map Search, Polyphonic Synthesizer, Printer, Pursuit, Radar, Turbo Boost

PROD. #57837

{ EPISODE
37 }

Script History:

December 15, 1983 (F.R.)

December 16, 1983 (F.R.)

SPEED DEMONS

Working Title: "The Speed Demons"

Written By: Tom Greene and Janis Hendler

Story By: Stephen B. Katz

Directed By: Bruce Seth Green

Original Airdate: February 12, 1984 (Sunday, 8:00 PM) (26.2%; 21,960,000)

NBC Rerun #1: June 10, 1984 (Sunday, 8:00 PM) (16.7%; 13,990,000)

Filming Dates: December 21-30, 1983

"The fact that Devon would choose that two wheeled can opener over the comfort of an automobile is completely mystifying."

-K.I.T.T.

Crew: Robert Foster (Executive Producer), Joel Rogosin (Supervising Producer), Robert W. Gilmer (Co-Producer), Gian R. Grimaldi (Co-Producer), Tom Greene (Co-Producer), George Crosby (Associate Producer), Robert Ewing (Associate Producer), Janis Hendler (Executive Script Consultant), Don Peake (Music), H. John Penner (Director of Photography), Russell Smith (Art Director), Lawrence J. Vallario (Film Editor), Ron Martinez (Unit Production Manager), Gary Grillo (1st Assistant Director), Bruce Humphrey (2nd Assistant Director), R. Lynn Smartt (Set Decorator), Pat Somerset (Sound), April Webster (Casting), John Shouse (Sound Effects Editor), Richard Lapham (Music Editor), Barry Downing (Costume Supervisor), Judie Champion (Costume Supervisor), Jack Gill (Stunt Coordinator), Jeremy Swan (Make-up), Allen Payne (Hairstylist)

Guest Cast: John Macchia (Kelly Travis), Lydia Cornell (Sabrina Travis), Bruce Bauer (Lee Carstairs), Madison Mason (Roger Floyd), Christine DeLisle (Darlena Webster), Michael Champion (Wade Fontaine), Ethan Wayne (Danny Duvall), Kurt Fuller (Cameraman), Larry Huffman (Race Announcer)

On the one year anniversary of a motocross rider's suspicious death, Michael and K.I.T.T. join the race to uncover the killer.

Knight Knotes:

- Rebecca Holden on this episode: "The turbo boost was always a blast, wasn't it? Devon was such a dignified and proper English gentleman, so it was such a riot to see him go crazy on a motorcycle. Loved that scene."
- The turbo boost over the lake is a scene reused from "Good Day at White Rock". Coincidentally, Michael Champion, who played Wade Fontaine, also guest starred in that same episode as a biker.

- The helmet Devon wears at the end of the episode is the same one worn by Michael in "Slammin' Sammy's Stunt Show Spectacular".

- When Michael is getting out of K.I.T.T. to go into the warehouse, a close eye can spot a hand reach out from the back seat and pull the door shut!

- K.I.T.T. gets a boost with the installation of April's High Traction Drop Downs.

- Ethan Wayne, who played Danny Duvall in the opening of the episode, is the real-life son of John Wayne.

Script to Screen:

- Wade Fontaine's last name is originally Fortuno. There's also a female European racer named Gene Tourvald. She spars with Fontaine instead of Lee Carstairs.

- A description of the first time we meet the news anchors: "They're Roger Floyd and Darlena Webster, and look like they've just escaped from the top of a wedding cake. Roger is midthirties, too many teeth, styled hair and tanned to a crisp. The only thing natural about the well-built Darlena is her tongue, which she can't control. She wears a bright red tailored jumpsuit and a five-hour hairdo."

- Michael tells Carstairs that he had a poster of him in his garage over a work bench when he was growing up.

- An elimination round before the real race results in Tourvald being seriously injured when someone mysteriously tampers with her bike.

- Devon was known as "Dusty Miles" during his motocross days, which he revealed was in 1939.

- The script calls the overhead console that descends from the semi's roof as the "circuit analyzer" and the tall computers in the back of the semi as "the computer module area".

- Instead of calling it "Ski Mode", the script simply says that, "Michael flips the left side booster switch."

- Instead of Michael pushing Carstairs into the water, he instead opens the sunroof and pulls him into the car. He then has K.I.T.T. close the sunroof, which hits Carstairs on the head and he passes out!

- The High Traction Drop Downs are originally called "Drop-Down High Traction Wheels". The script describes how they work: "Angle on K.I.T.T. as large, high-traction wheels drop down, covering the standard wheels which then retract up into K.I.T.T.'s shell. As Michael accelerates, we see them spin for a beat, then catch the dirt, push the Trans Am up the mountain with surging power."

K.I.T.T.'s Capabilities:

- High Traction Drop Downs, Pursuit, Radar, Ski Mode, Sonar, Turbo Boost, Video Playback

PROD. #57839

EPISODE 38	

Script History:

December 28, 1983 (F.R.)

GOLIATH RETURNS (TWO HOURS)

Working Title #1: "Deja Vu All Over Again"

Working Title #2: "Deja Vu"

Working Title #3: "Return of Goliath"

Written By: Robert Foster, Robert W. Gilmer, Tom Greene, and Janis Hendler

Directed By: Winrich Kolbe

Original Airdate: February 19, 1984 (Sunday, 8:00 PM) (26.9%; 22,540,000)

NBC Rerun #1: May 4, 1984 (Friday, 8:00 PM) (Rating Unavailable)

Filming Dates: January 4-20, 1984

"I don't escape, Adrianne. I attack."

-Garthe Knight

Crew: Robert Foster (Executive Producer), Don Peake (Music), Russell Smith (Art Director), Robert W. Gilmer (Co-Producer), Gian R. Grimaldi (Co-Producer), Tom Greene (Co-Producer), Lawrence J. Gleason (Film Editor), Stanley Wohlberg (Film Editor), H. John Penner (Director of Photography), Joel Rogosin (Supervising Producer), George Crosby (Associate Producer), Robert Ewing (Associate Producer), Bernadette Joyce (Associate Producer), Janis Hendler (Executive Script Consultant), Ron Martinez (Unit Production Manager), Robert Villar (1st Assistant Director), Bruce Humphrey (2nd Assistant Director), R. Lynn Smartt (Set Decorator), Pat Somerset (Sound), April Webster (Casting), John Shouse (Sound Effects Editor), Richard Lapham (Music Editor), Barry Downing (Costume Supervisor), Judie Champion (Costume Supervisor), Jack Gill (Stunt Coordinator), Jeremy Swan (Make-up), Allen Payne (Hairstylist)

Guest Cast: Peter Mark Richman (Dr. Klaus Bergstrom), Suzanne Barnes (Christina Bergstrom), Ann Turkel (Adrianne Margeaux), Cyndi James-Reese (Kathy Cunningham), John M. Banach (Technician #1), Cris Capen (Technician #2), Henry G. Sanders (Hotel Security Guard), Vicki McCarty (Hotel Clerk)

Garthe Knight escapes from prison with the help of Adrianne Margeaux and his indestructible rig, Goliath.

A Look Back:

"Goliath Returns" marked the return of Ann Turkel, who reprised her role as Adrianne Margeaux from "Soul Survivor". Turkel recalls, "'Goliath Returns' was amazing to shoot," says Turkel. "It was a special double episode and ran as long as a movie." Fans were certainly excited to find out that along with a second helping of Michael Knight's evil brother, Garthe, they would also be treated to the return of Adrianne. "It was cool to have that continuation with the same character," remarks Turkel. "It meant that everyone knew me and I could just step right back into that role again."

Adrianne certainly doesn't mess around in her return by first using Goliath to free Garthe from prison and then delivering Garthe to her high-tech hidden retreat. "In my first scene in the hot tub, I was quite nervous," confirms Turkel. "I don't like men with facial hair and I blame that fact on this scene where I kiss Garthe who has a full beard. I didn't even like it later in the episode when Garthe just had a moustache. The men in my life need to be clean shaven."

Normally, all actors and actresses that starred in the series were dressed with costumes from the Universal Studios wardrobe department, but in the hot tub scene, Turkel was wearing her own clothing. "I'm wearing the N suit which I made. It was the only time in all of my episodes that I wore my own clothing. It became a huge brand and featured on the front page of the Wall Street Journal. You can guarantee that when I promote something, it will be huge. For the rest of the scenes where Adrianne changes frequently, I would go to wardrobe and carefully pick out what I thought a woman like Adrianne would wear. I would try different clothes out and make sure it looked right because I am 6 foot tall so not everything would be suitable. Also, I always did my hair myself. I wouldn't let anyone else touch it. In fact, the only time there was an exception is when I shot an episode of *Highlander* where we were whisked back in time and then I needed a professional to style my hair so it reflected the period we were filming in."

"Goliath Returns" features a few violent moments, including Garthe confronting April in the cell and his fight with Adrianne. "He was really holding Rebecca aggressively but that was what was called for and it made the whole scene in the cell more intense. For our fight, before we shot the scene, I called David over and I said to him, 'Let's not pretend here. Let's do it for real or it's going to look phoney.' No one wanted that and David agreed.

So, I slapped him for real and he slapped me back and I just went flying. If you watch that scene again you can see I go flying right out of the camera frame. It was a very intense scene. I didn't think the slap would be that hard. I can tell you it hurt. After we did that scene, David rushed over to me and asked if I was alright. We were able to laugh and joke about it afterwards. I'm proud of that scene though because we were both evil characters and it brought a reality to the episode. It was a lot of fun and a very unique experience having two David's – one evil, one good. David did a terrific job in making Garthe so evil. I would say that David really upped his game on this episode, as oppose to the normal, sweet and caring David as Michael."

Turkel also had the opportunity to work alongside Edward Mulhare and Rebecca Holden in the cell scene. "Edward! What a phenomenal star. He was from a different school of acting and he had such a wonderful voice. I wished that I had had more scenes with him. It was great to work with Rebecca. We met on the show and got along very well. It wasn't until a few years ago in Las Vegas at the *Knight Rider Festival* that we met up again and became really close friends. It was at that very same festival that I became friends with Catherine Hickland also."

"Goliath Returns" was directed by Winrich Kolbe, who ended his *Knight Rider* career with 11 directorial episodes to his name. "Working with Winrich was great. He was very technical and professional. He made a 90 minute episode flow really well." The episode also starred TV veteran Peter Mark Richman, who still acts today. "Peter was just amazing. He played, of course, the character that we would clone. He was such a good actor and you could see how well he was playing two different characters. Peter was very professional and so easy to work with."

With Adrianne effectively cloning Dr. Klaus Bergstrom, Turkel comments, "I'd like to think that years from now, that there would be another Ann Turkel around. I'd like the idea. It's possible to clone dogs now but they say that the dog only has a short life span."

Though one of Adrianne's "weapons" in the episode is Goliath, given a choice between that and K.I.T.T., the decision is simple. "I think I would have to go for K.I.T.T., and in the present day, I love the two-seater Audi R8. That would be my dream car."

Adrianne is finally killed alongside Garthe Knight when Goliath careens off a cliff. Turkel would have preferred that her character was not killed off. "I told them, 'Don't kill Adrianne off'. But, I guess after going over a cliff in Goliath, that it's hard to come back from that. Having said that, I'm sure there could have been a way to bring her back."

For "Goliath Returns", almost every scene was filmed on location, something guest star Peter Mark Richman was happy to do. "Location work is no different than studio work. Personally, I feel freer when I am not at a studio shooting". Richman is all too aware the trials of location work, especially when that work involves stunts. "As an actor, you have to be aware of the elements of location work. The director can wish for a particular shot that may be dangerous, so you have to be selective in what you will do without a stunt double. In the past, I have put my life in jeopardy, but as I got older, I said 'no more'. Horses, cars, helicopters - that's what they pay stunt doubles for!"

The role of Richman's character, Klaus Bergstrom, required that he speak in a Swedish accent. "I am a dialectician. Accents have fascinated me since working on radio as a youngster. Sometimes I would play three voices in one show. I am not sure how successful I was with the Swedish dialect".

In the episode, Klaus Bergstrom is kidnapped and replaced with a doppelganger, also played by Richman. He recalls, "Bad guys are more interesting to do and are generally meatier roles, especially in TV. I remember the scene when I played two roles. I opened the door and there was the other guy staring me in the face. I got a kick out of that!"

Even though this episode was a two-hour feature, it was shot very quickly. "I believe it was filmed in ten days, possibly two weeks. I saw "Goliath Returns" when it aired. It was not the most meaningful show I've ever done".

Richman worked with all of the regular cast members and remembers them fondly. "Edward Mulhare was a nice guy, very warm and friendly, and David Hasselhoff was a charming fellow. We worked well together and we had a lot of laughs. His career was just beginning".

A scene in this episode shows Garthe really being rough with April during her plea to let Devon go from Garthe and Adrianne's prison. Rebecca Holden recalls, "Since I adored David and he is such a sweetheart, I had to really concentrate to suspend reality and imagine him as the evil twin, since he played the dual role. I think Michael cared about April deeply, so it was probably equally difficult for David to play Garthe and shove me against the wall and throw me around. So I encouraged him before the scene to not hold back and get as rough as necessary to make the scene real."

In a dramatic scene towards the episode's conclusion, Michael Knight rescues Klaus Bergstrom from Goliath's trailer while traveling down the road at highway speeds. Jack Gill recalls, "The guy that was doubling Michael Knight was Tim Gilbert and I was blind driving the car. We drove to the back of the truck for the transfer and it was critical that we got it right. Al Jones was driving the truck and I'm in the blind drive car, so he sets the speed I do all the rest and put Tim Gilbert there so he can do the transfer to the truck and it worked really well."

Knight Knotes:

- Adrianne tells Garthe that her only interest in Michael Knight is in re-acquiring K.I.T.T. for herself. Her plan is to combine K.I.T.T.'s CPU with Goliath's body for unlimited power.

- Garthe's limo wears a license plate number of CA 1XWY815. This plate is seen again on one of the caterer's cars in "A Knight in Shining Armor".

- This episode marks the first and only time that two villains from two prior episodes team up in an attempt to take down Michael and K.I.T.T.

Script to Screen:

- Adrianne's last name is spelled Margot, not Margeaux, in some instances.

- An earlier script reveals the name for April's parachute device - the Emergency Parachute Deployment (EPD).

- The man who drives Goliath into the prison wall in order to allow Garthe to escape is named Halverson.

- The scene where April fixes K.I.T.T.'s parachute in the semi was originally envisioned to be in the Foundation's lab. The script notes, "If possible, the same location used as the 'heat room' in 'Ring of Fire'."

- The script's description of the first time we see Adrianne again: "A woman, her back to camera, is luxuriating in the spa part of the pool. She turns as Garthe walks out of the house toward her, moving across the lawn like a conquering soldier taking possession of his spoils. He walks toward the pool and, without hesitating a moment, steps into the spa, takes the woman in his arms and kisses her. She is Adrianne Margeaux (from 'Soul Survivor' fame.) She kisses back for a moment, then breaks the embrace."

- A doctor named Adrian Moritz explains the facial reconstruction surgery to Garthe, not Adrianne. In the episode, Moritz does not have a speaking role and is mentioned briefly by Adrianne.

- Michael is questioned by a Lt. Chatsworth at the Foundation before leaving in K.I.T.T. to track the coolant drops.

- Michael gets out to investigate the mannequins dressed as Devon and April, at which time K.I.T.T. begins to sink. K.I.T.T. shoots out his grappling hook and it lands in some brush, so once Michael makes it to harder ground, he attaches the grappling hook to a tree and K.I.T.T. backs himself out.

- In the original script, the SUV sinks into the bog as a commando watches Michael and K.I.T.T. escape from the mountain. Remnants of these original scenes still remain in the episode – the SUV just barely starts to sink before the scene is cut and a commando pops up in the far distant background on top of the mountain as Michael and K.I.T.T. leave.

- Adrianne comments to Garthe that her only interest in Michael is to re-acquire the Knight Industries Two Thousand.

- Goliath manages to hit the rear end of K.I.T.T., which forces him to lose control and careen off the cliff. Once they land and Michael is captured, he looks down at K.I.T.T.'s dash where he sees "the malfunction light blinking, the buzzer going -- then all lights on the dash blow out."

- In the dungeon, Adrianne talks more about her offer to Michael to join forces: "If we were to work together there is no end to the power we would have. Add to that the mind of K.I.T.T. transplanted into the body of Goliath, and you and I will have the world at our fingertips."

Déjà Vu:

- Peter Mark Richman returns in "Many Happy Returns".

Featured Songs:

"Heart and Soul" by Huey Lewis and the News (1983)

"Gimme Shelter" by The Rolling Stones (1969)

K.I.T.T.'s Capabilities:

- Audio Editing Mode, Audio Playback, Audio Record, Auto Cruise, Auto Phone, Auto-Roof Left, Auto-Roof Right, Chemical Detectors, Comprehensive Configuration Analysis, Emergency Parachute Deployment, Grappling Hook, Magnetic Analyzer, Medical Scan, Micro Jam, Pursuit, Radar, Sonar, Surveillance Mode, Telephone Tap, Telephone Trace, Turbo Boost

PROD. #57840

EPISODE
39

Script History:

January 13, 1984 (F.R.)

January 18, 1984 (F.R.)

January 20, 1984 (F.R.)

A GOOD KNIGHT'S WORK

Working Title: "Sneak Attack"

Written By: Richard Okie

Directed By: Sidney Hayers

Original Airdate: March 4, 1984 (Sunday, 8:00 PM) (20.5%; 17,180,000)

NBC Rerun #1: September 16, 1984 (Sunday, 8:00 PM) (10.8%; 9,170,000)

Filming Dates: January 23-31, 1984

"How am I going to get down from here?"

-K.I.T.T.

Crew: Robert Foster (Executive Producer), Joel Rogosin (Supervising Producer), Robert W. Gilmer (Co-Producer), Gian R. Grimaldi (Co-Producer), Tom Greene (Co-Producer), Bernadette Joyce (Associate Producer), George Crosby (Associate Producer), Robert Ewing (Associate Producer), Janis Hendler (Executive Script Consultant), Don Peake (Music), H. John Penner (Director of Photography), Russell Smith (Art Director), Howard B. Anderson (Film Editor), Ron Martinez (Unit Production Manager), Robert Villar (1st Assistant Director), Bruce Humphrey (2nd Assistant Director), R. Lynn Smartt (Set Decorator), Pat Somerset (Sound), April Webster (Casting), John Shouse (Sound Effects Editor), Richard Lapham (Music Editor), Barry Downing (Costume Supervisor), Judie Champion (Costume Supervisor), Jack Gill (Stunt Coordinator), Jeremy Swan (Make-up), Allen Payne (Hairstylist)

Guest Cast: John Vernon (Cameron Zachary), Alexa Hamilton (Gina Adams), Robert O'Reilly (Jake Simpson), Dana Gladstone (Dave Collins), Rosalind Ingledew (Car Buyer)

Michael is targeted for death by the bitter ex-lover of the woman who shot Michael two years prior.

Knight Knotes:

- Michael Long was born on January 9, 1949 and "died" on August 8, 1982.
- Michael's middle name, Arthur, is mentioned only in this episode and in the Pilot.

Script to Screen:

- Michael originally hides in K.I.T.T. to catch the man at the beginning of the episode, as opposed to leaning against a pillar. He chases the man in K.I.T.T. and leaps out the sunroof to tackle him.
- Mighty Mouth was originally called Talking Teddy.
- Gina's Carrot Top doll grossed eighteen million dollars.
- When Devon tells April that Michael Long's grave was robbed, April replies that she didn't realize there was a grave to rob. Devon responds that they planted a body to protect Michael's identity.
- Brummel's first name is Bob.
- Cameron Zachary was Tanya Walker's boss, not just her lover.
- Michael talking about Wilton: "I only knew Wilton Knight for a few days, but that old man taught me a hell of a lot about fighting. About using your fear and anger to spur you on instead of being crippled by them."
- Zachary confronts Michael with details of his old life in order to obtain K.I.T.T. His uncle lived at 410 Chesapeake Road, while his niece attended the Burnley school; his old police sergeant was named Charlie Hart.

Déjà Vu:

- John Vernon returns in "Voo Doo Knight"; Robert O'Reilly is back in "KITTnap"; and Rosalind Ingledew guest stars in "Knight Behind Bars".

K.I.T.T.'s Capabilities:

- Auto Cruise, Auto-Roof Left, Auto-Roof Right, Chemical Analyzer, Computer Tap, Eject Left, Eject Right, Hydraulic Seat, Micro Jam, Printer, Pursuit, Surveillance Mode, Turbo Boost

PROD. #57831

⌠ EPISODE ⌡
⌠ 40 ⌡

Script History:

December 13, 1983 (F.R.)

January 19, 1984 (F.R.)

February 4, 1984 (F.R.)

February 13, 1984 (F.R.)

MOUTH OF THE SNAKE (TWO HOURS)

Working Title: "All That Glitters"

Written By: Robert Foster and Robert W. Gilmer
Directed By: Winrich Kolbe

Original Airdate: April 8, 1984 (Sunday, 8:00 PM) (Rating Unavailable)

Rerun: September 2, 1984 (Sunday, 8:00 PM) (9.6%; 8,040,000)

Filming Dates: February 16 – March 8, 1984

"I guess my sense of humor needs a tune-up."

-Michael

Crew: Robert Foster (Executive Producer), Don Peake (Music), Lawrence J. Gleason (Film Editor), Lawrence J. Vallario (Film Editor), Russell Smith (Art Director), Robert W. Gilmer (Co-Producer), Gian R. Grimaldi (Co-Producer), Tom Greene (Co-Producer), H. John Penner (Director of Photography), Joel Rogosin (Supervising Producer), George Crosby (Associate Producer), Robert Ewing (Associate Producer), Bernadette Joyce (Associate Producer), Janis Hendler (Executive Script Consultant), Ron Martinez (Unit Production Manager), Charles Watson Sanford, Jr. (1st Assistant Director), Bruce Humphrey (2nd Assistant Director), R. Lynn Smartt (Set Decorator), Pat Somerset (Sound), April Webster (Casting), John Shouse (Sound Effects Editor), Richard Lapham (Music Editor), Barry Downing (Costume Supervisor), Judie Champion (Costume Supervisor), Jack Gill (Stunt Coordinator), Jeremy Swan (Make-up), Allen Payne (Hairstylist), Jean-Pierre Dorleac (Costume Designer)

Guest Cast: Joanna Pettet (Joanna St. John), L. Charles Taylor (David Dalton), George Murdock (Archibald Hendley), Robert Colbert (Elton Matthews), Patty Kotero (Tiara D'Arcy), Pedro Armendariz (Eduardo O'Brian), Emily Banks (Priscella Ragsdale), Robert Clarke (John Ragsdale), Chuck Lindsly (Steward), Luis Contreras (Coyote), Arell Blanton (Frank), Tom Gilleran (Arthur Abrahms), Todd Martin (Elmo Elliott), Alan Graff (Highway Patrolman), Vance David (Security Man), Rick Holly (Pilot), Joel Kramer (Commando #1), Spike Silver (Commando #2), Mario Roberts (Commando #3), Rick Avery (Commando #4), John Sherrod (Truck Driver #1), Jeff Jensen (Truck Driver #2), Kenny Rossall (Van Driver #1)

Michael teams up with a mysterious drifter to find out what happened to a federal agent who disappeared near the Mexico border.

A Look Back:

There were five novels released throughout the course of the series, each one based on an episode. The book <u>All That Glitters</u> is essentially a novelization of this episode. In each of the books, many details are added to help flesh out the characters, such as April being related to Devon. Rebecca Holden believes that having her character as Devon's daughter wouldn't have been a bad idea for on screen. "I think the revelation that April is Devon's daughter is very plausible. She was so devoted to him, to the Foundation and to their work...and she had such a profound respect and admiration for him personally. Edward, of course, was British, and I am of English and Irish descent, so casting-wise, we certainly could have been related as father/daughter. It would please me a great deal to think we were. I would be quite honored to consider him not only mentor and friend, but father as well."

Knight Knotes:

- L. Charles Taylor reprised his role as David Dalton in *Knight Rider's* first spin-off, *Code of Vengeance*.
- Carl Ciarfalio won the award for "Best Fight Sequence (Television) at the 1985 Stuntman Awards for his work on this episode.

Script to Screen:

- In early versions of the script, David Dalton's last name was Brighton.

Déjà Vu:

- Chuck Lindsly guest stars in "Voo Doo Knight"; Luis Contreras is back in "Knight of the Juggernaut".

Featured Songs:

"Stay With Me Tonight" by Jeffrey Osborne

K.I.T.T.'s Capabilities:

- Auto Cruise, Auto Phone, Auto-Roof Right, Chemical Analyzer, Micro Jam, Pursuit, Radar, Turbo Boost, X-Ray

PROD. #57834

EPISODE
41

Script History:

January 28, 1984 (F.R.)

January 31, 1984 (F.R.)

February 1, 1984 (F.R.)

February 6, 1984 (F.R.)

LET IT BE ME

Working Title #1: "Dream Life"

Working Title #2: "It's Only Rock and Roll"

Teleplay By: Robert Foster and Robert W. Gilmer

Story By: William Elliott

Directed By: Bernard McEveety

Original Airdate: May 13, 1984 (Sunday, 8:00 PM) (18.8%; 15,750,000)

NBC Rerun #1: August 26, 1984 (Sunday, 8:00 PM) (11.0%; 9,220,000)

Filming Dates: February 1-9, 1984

"I'll see you in the supermarket."

-Stevie Mason

Crew: Robert Foster (Executive Producer), Joel Rogosin (Supervising Producer), Robert W. Gilmer (Co-Producer), Gian R. Grimaldi (Co-Producer), Tom Greene (Co-Producer), Bernadette Joyce (Associate Producer), George E. Crosby (Associate Producer), Robert Ewing (Associate Producer), Janis Hendler (Executive Script Consultant), Don Peake (Music), H. John Penner (Director of Photography), Russell Smith (Art Director), Stanley Wohlberg (Film Editor), Grant Hoag (Film Editor), Ron Martinez (Unit Production Manager), Robert Villar (1st Assistant Director), Bruce Humphrey (2nd Assistant Director), R. Lynn Smartt (Set Decorator), Pat Somerset (Sound), April Webster (Casting), John Shouse (Sound Effects Editor), Richard Lapham (Music Editor), Barry Downing (Costume Supervisor), Judie Champion (Costume Supervisor), Jack Gill (Stunt Coordinator), Jeremy Swan (Make-up), Allen Payne (Hairstylist)

Guest Cast: Catherine Hickland (Stevie March/Mason), Michael C. Gwynne (Paul Block), Shanna Reed (Barbara Bellingham), John Patrick Reger (Greg Noble), Joseph Burke (Band Member), Randy Polk (Jimmy), Steven Ameche (Steve), Alana Crow (Concert Woman)

Michael's former fiancée, Stevie Mason, returns and needs Michael's help after her boyfriend is found dead in his dressing room.

A Look Back:

Throughout the run of the series, many expository scenes took place on Stage 1 at Universal Studios, home to the sets for Devon's office and the interior of the F.L.A.G. mobile command center. Rebecca Holden recalls, "The semi set is probably where April spent the majority of her time---working on K.I.T.T. So stepping onto this particular set each week felt like her home. It was fun reading each script and anticipating what technology would be awaiting my character for each episode. I would look forward to seeing what the guys would come up with in the way of physical gadgetry to fit the script. There were also always a lot of made up technological words to go along with the gadgets, too...so it was always fun!"

Knight Knotes:

- Rebecca Holden on the gadgets: "Loved all the gadgets! The writers were so imaginative in inventing new devices and contraptions for April to use with K.I.T.T., and the prop guys were simply ingenious in creating the fulfillment of the writers' imaginations!"
- The end credits list a special note for the concert hall filming location seen in this episode: "Location Site Furnished By Universal Amphitheatre".
- The songs heard in this episode from the "Night Rocker" album include "Our First Night Together", "No Way to Be In Love", and "Let It Be Me".
- Although there is still one more episode left in the second season, this is the last time that Rebecca Holden would be seen as computer whiz April Curtis.

Script to Screen:

- The script notes the first time we see Michael in this episode: "Michael's behind the wheel. He's wearing his baseball hat (Dodgers, of course)." There's a dialog where Michael tries to convince K.I.T.T. that baseball is a great sport. K.I.T.T. asks, "Grown men in funny costumes swinging sticks of wood at pieces of horse-hide is American?". Michael replies, "You're weird. Are you sure you weren't assembled overseas somewhere?"

- Stevie fills Michael in on what happened with the criminals seen in "White Bird": "When they'd arrested and convicted everyone I'd testified against, it was safe for me to 'resurface' again. I kept my new name and just sort of slipped back into life."
- The first song that Michael and Stevie sing on stage is called "Stay the Night".
- Instead of Michael stopping to save the girl from her burning car, Michael is originally stopped by an old lady pulling out in front of him in a van. Michael wants to jump over the van, but K.I.T.T. says they can't due to the overhead electrical wires.
- Greg Noble's first name was originally Tommy.

Featured Songs:

"No Way to Be In Love" by David Hasselhoff and Catherine Hickland

"Our First Night Together" by David Hasselhoff and Catherine Hickland

"White Bird" by It's a Beautiful Day

"Runaway" by Del Shannon

"Let It Be Me" by David Hasselhoff and Catherine Hickland

K.I.T.T.'s Capabilities:

- Audio/Video Playback, Audio/Video Record, Auto Cruise, Auto Phone, Comprehensive Configuration Analysis, Micro Jam, Pursuit, Radar, Turbo Boost

PROD. #57804

EPISODE 42

Script History:

June 6, 1983 (F.R.)

BIG IRON

Working Title: "Amber Waves"

Written By: Julie Friedsen

Directed By: Bernard L. Kowalski

Original Airdate: May 27, 1984 (Sunday, 8:00 PM) (16.6%; 13,910,000)

NBC Rerun #1: August 5, 1984 (Sunday, 8:00 PM) (11.8%; 9,890,000)

Filming Dates: June 13-21, 1983

"To put it in your terms, Michael, I'm trashed."

-K.I.T.T.

Crew: Robert Foster (Executive Producer), Joel Rogosin (Supervising Producer), Robert W. Gilmer (Co-Producer), Gian R. Grimaldi (Co-Producer), Bernadette Joyce (Associate Producer), Robert Ewing (Associate Producer), Janis Hendler (Executive Script Consultant), William Schmidt (Story Editor), Don Peake (Music), H. John Penner (Director of Photography), Russell Smith (Art Director), Beryl Gelfond (Film Editor), Ron Martinez (Unit Production Manager), Charles Watson Sanford, Jr. (1st Assistant Director), Bruce Humphrey (2nd Assistant Director), R. Lynn Smartt (Set Decorator), Stan Gordon (Sound), April Webster (Casting), John Shouse (Sound Effects Editor), Richard Lapham (Music Editor), Barry Downing (Costume Supervisor), Judie Champion (Costume Supervisor), Robert Bralver (Stunt Coordinator), Jack Gill (Co-Stunt Coordinator), Jeremy Swan (Make-up), Allen Payne (Hairstylist)

Guest Cast: Stuart Whitman (Frank Sanderson), Patch MacKenzie (Lucy Sanderson), Myron Healey (Lloyd Newald), Alex Kubik (Sam), Michael Rider (Vance Burke), Kaaren Lee (Mary Beth Graves), Gene LeBell (Junior)

Michael helps out a construction company owner when his equipment is stolen.

A Look Back:

Julie Friedgen penned what would ultimately become *Knight* Rider's second season finale, "Big Iron". This episode was one of the first to be filmed for the season, but was held back for unknown reasons. Friedgen was a secretary when she thought about writing scripts for television. "I was a secretary on *The Streets of San Francisco* and my job was to retype scripts for the producers. I would think to myself, 'I could do this', but since I didn't have a college education I was intimidated to try."

Though Friedgen had a stable job within the industry, she never gave up her dreams of writing television shows. "A few years later, I worked myself up to Junior Executive in prime time programming at NBC, but I still wanted to go to college. I applied to Occidental College and was accepted. At the end of my college years, I wrote a few spec comedy scripts and contacted agencies but I didn't get any replies. Then Kismet! The editor of a local newspaper for whom I had done a few restaurant reviews invited me to a party. I sat next to a woman who would end up being my agent. She told me to send my specs. My first writing specs were for half hour comedy shows, but that market was getting too expensive to produce. So, I was advised to start writing for one hour specs. I wrote a *Magnum P.I.* spec and against all advice sent it to the show. Writers are always told never to send a spec to shows because the producers can write their own show better than anyone else."

Nevertheless, Friedgen's initiative paid off and she met Joel Rogosin. "Joel was the producer of *Magnum* at the time. He called me and the first thing he said was, 'Did you write this by yourself?' He liked it and said it sounds like a man wrote it and that I had nailed *Magnum's* psyche and voice as well as the other characters. I didn't know whether to be offended or pleased. After Joel told me that if I could write like this, he would keep me busy, he brought me in to pitch and before I could say anything he said they had an idea and if I could make it work I had an assignment. He told me that he had a meeting down the hall and that he would be back in 15 minutes. I thought he meant that I could go home and work on it. When he returned, I had figured out how to make the idea work. He loved it and ran it past Don Bellasario who also loved it and that's how I started writing one hour shows."

Friedgen reveals that Rogosin had big ideas for "Big Iron". She recalls, "Joel had an idea that he wanted to do. He had read an article about how heavy construction equipment was being stolen from job sites. He loved the idea of K.I.T.T. going up against an earth mover. So, I took Joel's idea and had fun with it. Working with Joel was easy because he insisted that the outlines be very well developed, so by the time I got to the first draft we knew where we were going. The episode reflected the script absolutely," says Friedgen. She greatly enjoyed working for Rogosin and even made a few sacrifices along the way to help him. "I loved working with Joel so much that I even gave up a trip to Brazil to do this episode."

"Big Iron" is notable in that it is the only episode of *Knight Rider* where Michael Knight does not wear his black leather jacket. "That was unrelated, I don't remember that being in the script," confirms Friedgen.

This episode featured K.I.T.T. being pushed over a cliff by a bulldozer and subsequently buried. Jack Gill comments, "My recollection of this was that it was done by miniatures. A miniature car and miniature bulldozer as I recall. I could be wrong because we did have many cars that were no use to us anymore, and there wouldn't have been anyone in it. They may have used the manual transmission car. We blew the transmission out of that thing and it never really worked right after that. It was a jump car."

Knight Knotes:

- April makes no appearance in this episode but is mentioned. The only other second season episode where she is not present is "Mouth of the Snake".
- This is the only episode in the series' entire run where Michael's leather jacket is not seen.

Script to Screen:

- Joe Gluber's last name is originally Graves and Frank Sanderson's last name is Gunderson.

- Michael complains to April about K.I.T.T.'s new Ultraphonic Chemical Analyzer when K.I.T.T. object's to Michael eating a doughnut. April says they will test it for a month to get the bugs out, and Michael comments that he will starve to death. K.I.T.T. later uses his analyzer to detract Michael from swimming in the motel's pool, as it "contains more bacteria than a petri dish."

- A scene in the semi has April explaining K.I.T.T.'s new Trajectory Guide system. "I've also adapted a trajectory guide to Kitt's turbo boost system. By adjusting the angle here you should be able to launch him at any angle within a ninety degree arc. This is a prototype, designed for normal application only. So, don't get any ideas...."

- K.I.T.T. originally has enough air for 1 hour plus 4 hours of reserve, instead of the 5 minutes seen on screen.

-

Featured Songs:

"Mammas Don't Let Your Babies Grow Up To Be Cowboys" by Willie Nelson and Waylon Jennings

K.I.T.T.'s Capabilities:

- Auto Cruise, Chemical Detectors, Energy System Override, Oil, Pursuit, Self Diagnostic Analyzer, Sonar, Telephone Trace, Trajectory Guide, Turbo Boost, Ultraphonic Analyzer

Behind the KNIGHT: Klaus and the Clone

Actor Peter Mark Richman made two appearances on *Knight Rider*, the first of which was as Dr. Klaus Bergstrom in season two's "Goliath Returns". In this episode, Richman had to play both a Swedish scientist and an evil clone of the scientist. The original script that he used for memorizing his lines provides a great insight into how he was able to pull off playing both characters. The following pages show some examples.

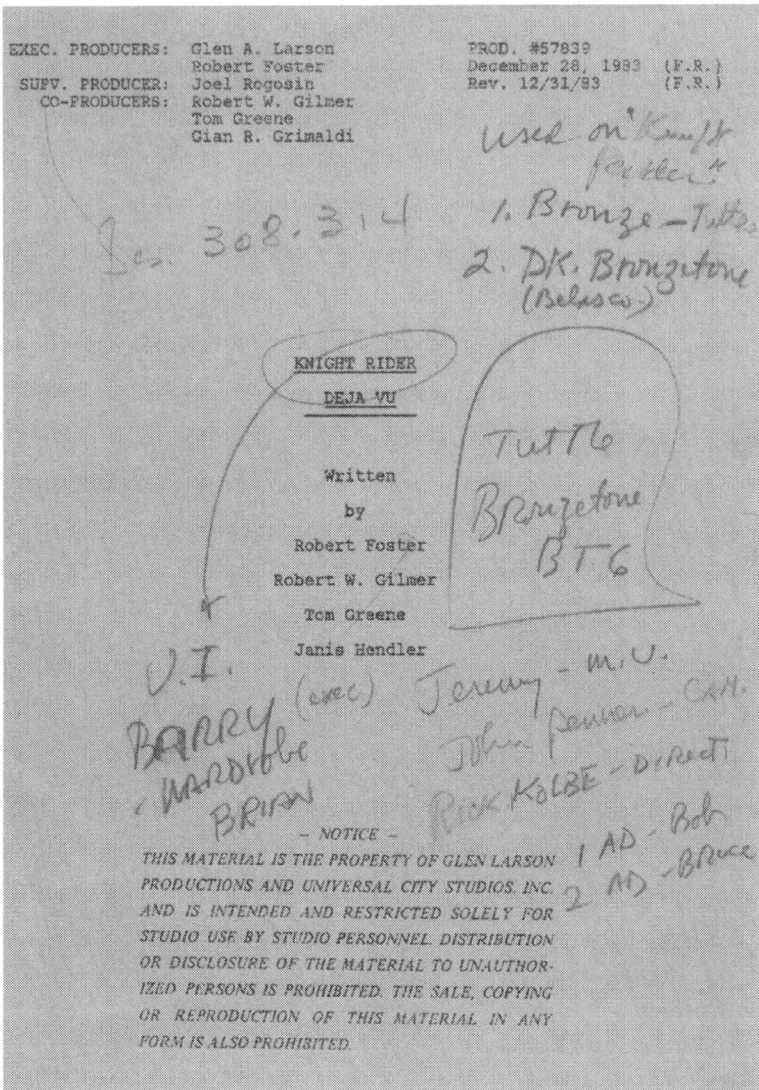

```
EXEC. PRODUCERS:   Glen A. Larson          PROD. #57839
                   Robert Foster           December 28, 1983   (F.R.)
SUPV. PRODUCER:    Joel Rogosin            Rev. 12/31/83       (F.R.)
   CO-PRODUCERS:   Robert W. Gilmer
                   Tom Greene
                   Gian R. Grimaldi



                        KNIGHT RIDER

                         DEJA VU



                         Written

                           by

                      Robert Foster

                      Robert W. Gilmer

                        Tom Greene

                        Janis Hendler




                       - NOTICE -
         THIS MATERIAL IS THE PROPERTY OF GLEN LARSON
         PRODUCTIONS AND UNIVERSAL CITY STUDIOS, INC.
         AND IS INTENDED AND RESTRICTED SOLELY FOR
         STUDIO USE BY STUDIO PERSONNEL. DISTRIBUTION
         OR DISCLOSURE OF THE MATERIAL TO UNAUTHOR-
         IZED PERSONS IS PROHIBITED. THE SALE, COPYING
         OR REPRODUCTION OF THIS MATERIAL IN ANY
         FORM IS ALSO PROHIBITED.
```

Above: The cover page of Peter Mark Richman's personal script for "Goliath Returns". On the right side, he lists a bronze toner by the William Tuttle corporation, used to make his skin darker. Richman also makes note of some of the crew members: Barry [Downing] for wardrobe, Jeremy [Swan] for make-up, John Penner for camera, Rick Kolbe as director, Bob [Villar] as 1st assistant director and Bruce [Humphrey] as 2nd assistant

#57829

HAPPY → HAH PEH
BAD → BEHt
THIRST → TURST
WORD → VURT
BIRD → BURT
FRIEND → FRANT
GET → GAT

NO DIALOGUE CHANGES ARE TO BE MADE
WITHOUT THE EXPRESS APPROVAL OF THE
EXECUTIVE PRODUCER OR SUPERVISING
PRODUCER. IN THE EVENT THAT NEITHER
IS AVAILABLE ANOTHER MEMBER OF THE
PRODUCING STAFF SHOULD BE CONTACTED.
IF NO CONSULTATION IS POSSIBLE, DUE
TO THE LOCATION OF THE COMPANY, ETC.,
ANY CHANGES SHOULD BE IN ADDITION TO
THE ORIGINAL, RATHER THAN INSTEAD OF.
IN OTHER WORDS, "SHOOT IT BOTH WAYS."

is said
W = V

SAD is SEH.t
Doctor → DAWKTUHR

Z is S
Has. HEHs (sibilant s)
R. is rolled slightly
S- more sharp and sibilant
+H → D

Richman also made notes in his script to help him with Klaus Bergstrom's Swedish accent. Above: Richman's notes on some common words, such as "Doctor" being pronounced "Dawktuhr" and to make sure that his "R's" are rolled slightly and his "W's" sound like "V's".

EXT. HOTEL - NIGHT

as Michael gets out, opens the door and helps Christina
out. Klaus climbs out, leans back into the car.

                    KLAUS
          Good night, Kitt. Perhaps a fast   *FEST*
          game of chess before I leave.

INT. HOTEL ROOM - NIGHT   *No dialect?*

Christina is carefully going through Klaus #2's coat pocket
which is draped over the living room easy chair. Just as
she is about to lift the wallet from the breast pocket, he
appears from his bedroom in a robe.

*Top: Richman made a note to ensure that he pronounces "fast" as "fest".
Above: When the Klaus clone first shows up, Richman makes a note to
confirm that Klaus #2 does not have a dialect in this scene.*

```
#57839                      32

CONTINUED                                                84
                    CHRISTINA
               (to Klaus)
          That's strange.

No response.

                    CHRISTINA
          He said he'd call. Where do you
          suppose he could be?

Still no response. She crosses.

ANGLE FROM LIVING ROOM                                   85

as she enters. Klaus hasn't moved.

                    CHRISTINA
          Uncle Klaus?

He grunts absently, absorbed. She shakes her head, smiles;
crosses to turn down the TV.

                    CHRISTINA
          Look at you. A man of your intelli-    (X)
          gence, your vision -- you come to
          America to enlighten the world on
          laser technology and before I know it
          you're like every other American
          male...glued to a TV set watching
          football.
```
Ankle sprain (X)

*Above: Richman makes a note to remember that Klaus now has an ankle
sprain. He also notes that the real Klaus enjoys football.*

KLAUS #2
Michael?

She shakes her head, disappointed.

CHRISTINA
(into phone)
I'll tell him. Thank you.

She hangs up.

CHRISTINA
That was Mr. Andrews. He wanted you
to know the press conference has been
finalized.

KLAUS #2
I hate press conferences.

He puts his notes down, rises, stretches.

KLAUS #2
The thing I'm going to miss the most
when I get back to Sweden is football
...especially the beer commercials.
I don't know which is more violent,
the games or the commercials.

CONTINUED

How does he know Klaus #1 liked football? Did He.

INT. SUITE - DAY

The door opens and Christina hurries in.

CHRISTINA
Uncle Klaus...!

Klaus #2 is seated in front of the TV. He looks up at her
absently, smiles.

KLAUS #2
What is it, Christina?

1st scene as K-2 91

Top, Richman makes a note: "How does he know Klaus #1 liked football? Did he?" Above: Richman marks the first scene as "K-2", the evil Klaus clone.

KNIGHT RIDER

SEASON THREE (1984-1985)

Starring:

David Hasselhoff as Michael Knight

Edward Mulhare as Devon Miles

Patricia McPherson as Bonnie Barstow

William Daniels as the voice of K.I.T.T.

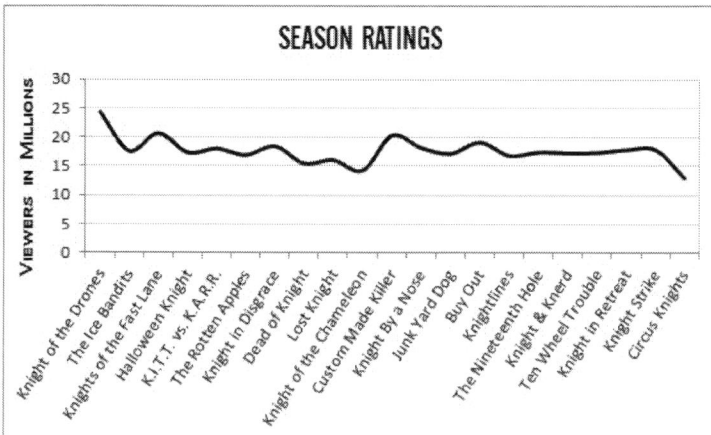

SEASON RATINGS

PROD. #58621

EPISODE
43

Script History:

July 16, 1984 (F.R.)

July 19, 1984 (F.R.)

EN July 24, 1984 (F.R.)

July 25, 1984 (F.R.)

July 27, 1984 (F.R.)

July 29, 1984 (F.R.)

July 30, 1984 (F.R.)

July 30, 1984 (2nd rev.)

July 31, 1984 (F.R.)

August 7, 1984 (F.R.)

KNIGHT OF THE DRONES (TWO HOURS)

Written By: Robert Foster and Gerald Sanford

Directed By: Sidney Hayers

Original Airdate: September 30, 1984 (Sunday, 8:00 PM) (28.6%; 24,280,000)

NBC Rerun #1: April 21, 1985 (Sunday, 8:00 PM) (24.8%; 21,060,000)

"Michael, a car doesn't drive by itself."

-K.I.T.T.

Crew: Robert Foster (Executive Producer), Gerald Sanford (Producer), Gino Grimaldi (Producer), Ron Martinez (Associate Producer), Robert Ewing (Associate Producer), Richard Okie (Story Editor), Don Peake (Music), H. John Penner (Director of Photography), Frank Grieco, Jr. (Art Director), R. Lynn Smartt (Set Decoration), Joe Reich (Casting), Lawrence J. Gleason (Film Editor), Lawrence J. Vallario (Film Editor), Pat Somerset (Sound), Ron Martinez (Unit Production Manager), Zane Radney (Unit Production Manager), Robert Villar (1st Assistant Director), Bruce Humphrey (2nd Assistant Director), John Shouse (Sound Editor), Richard Lapham (Music Editor), Barry Downing (Costume Supervisor), Karen Braverman (Costume Supervisor), Jack Gill (2nd Unit Director-Stunt Coordinator), Jeremy Swan (Make-Up), Allen Payne (Hairstylist)

Guest Cast: Jared Martin (Dr. David Halston), Jim Brown (C.J. Jackson), Evan Kim (Peter Wong), Barbara Stock (Margo Sheridan), The Barbarian Brothers (Clifton and Turk), Joseph Ruskin (Bubba), Arnie Moore (Prison Guard Jim Carter), Wood Moy (Fong), Harry D.K. Wong (Ho Chin), Chuck Dorsett (Arthur), Grace Bauer (Henrietta), Joan Chen (Su-Lin), Al Leong (Karate Twin #1), Harold "Hal" Frizzell (Cab Driver)

K.I.T.T. is destroyed while on a mission to San Francisco to investigate Bonnie's mentor.

A Look Back:

In the Summer of 1984, *Knight Rider* was gearing up for its third season and, similar to other season premieres, they took Michael and K.I.T.T. out of Los Angeles. For this season's premiere, "Knight of the Drones", the production moved to San Francisco. Among the many locations that needed to be found was Margo Sheridan's mountain retreat. As luck would have it, the crew chose a house whose occupants included an eight year old boy who was about to have his childhood hero in his living room. That boy was named Tyler Ham. So how did this all happen? Though he was young, Ham has vivid memories of this highlight from his childhood.

Tyler Ham sitting in the Hero K.I.T.T. car (#1177) on the set of "Knight of the Drones" (Photo courtesy of Tyler Ham)

"I believe the story was that when they went to film this episode, there was a strike in L.A. by one of the unions that made filming impossible," recalls Ham. "So, they decided to film this episode in the bay area. At the time, our house had been used for a few commercials, so it was a 'known' location, but my parents never actively pursued it. Every once in a while, they would let a small crew use it because my mom and dad always thought it was fun watching the productions happen. Generally, those were just one-day shoots. So, when the strike happened, I guess they needed a nice, large house that was semi-secluded. Our house was big and at the end of a cul-desac with few neighbors, so it was an easy location to set up and block off. My dad originally was going to turn their offer down, but he knew I was a huge fan of the show and so he agreed to let them film." It also turns out that Margo Sheridan and the Ham family had a lot of the same tastes. "The set decorators didn't really change the house for filming. A few personal effects were moved but all the furniture, paintings, etc. that you see were ours and they were always right where you saw them on the show."

And so, this eight year old boy had the likes of David Hasselhoff, Jim Brown, The Barbarian Brothers and more in his living room. "It was a really fun cast," says Ham. "Jim Brown was there as a 'Special Guest' and he was very, very friendly. The body building twins, 'The Barbarian Brothers', were also guest stars, and again they could not have been nicer. My dad really enjoyed talking with them. As for the actress who played Margo, I don't remember as much but me being just 7 or 8, and her being SUPER pretty, I'm sure I just shied away from her. I have a photo of me giving her a kiss on the cheek and I remember it took ALL of my bravery inside to do that." Regarding David Hasselhoff, Ham says that he couldn't have been nicer. "Finally, the Hoff was SO nice. I'm sure I drove him nuts being a star struck kid, but he did all sorts of stuff with me, took pictures with me, and was just a generally really friendly happy guy. It was sad to see him go through all those problems as I got older, having such fond memories of him. I get people asking me (after they find out about it) if he was a jerk or drunk on set. I always tell them that I never ever got even the slightest inkling of him being anything less than a really cool guy who was just enjoying his job and life. Not that I know him at all - mind you, I just spent 3 days with him as an 8 year old - but to this day, I defend him whenever anyone says anything bad about him. He left an impression for sure."

How cool it must have been to have Michael Knight literally in your back yard?

(Photo courtesy of Tyler Ham)

Along with having Michael Knight at his house, Ham was also lucky enough to have a certain four wheeled sidekick there as well. However, as he was about to find out, the magic of Hollywood that made K.I.T.T. the way he was on-screen didn't completely translate to real life. "I LOVED the show before it filmed at my house. As I said, me being a fan was the only reason my dad agreed to it. I had *Knight Rider* lunchboxes, toys, etc. As you can probably guess, most of my presents that year were *Knight Rider* themed. Funny enough, having K.I.T.T. in the driveway was both cool, and in a way disappointing. When it is in front of you, it LOOKS like K.I.T.T., but I got inside and the buttons didn't do anything and he didn't talk. I saw the hollow seat the stunt driver sat in to make K.I.T.T. look like he was driving himself. It was a conflict for sure, even at a young age. I remember a scene where K.I.T.T. ejects something for Michael and it comes out from under the car. I always thought it was a secret door or something in the bumper, but it was just a skinny guy under the car literally handing out the item to Hasselhoff. Illusion shattered!"

Ham was around for the filming of all of the scenes at his house, and accidentally ruined one scene by accident. "Our house was big and a few rooms had multiple entrances. While they were shooting in what was our dining room, I opened a door on the other end of the room. Like any kid, I got super scared and hid behind the curtains. Well, the scene was long and went on and on - It felt like forever to me and I kept thinking how much longer this scene felt than any of the other ones. Looking back, I'm sure I was hiding for multiple takes - I didn't know. I felt like I was back there forever when I suddenly hear the director ask, 'Is there a kid behind the curtain?' I got caught red handed. I remember thinking that everyone was going to be SO MAD at me, but they all laughed about it. Truth be told, it may have just been rehearsals but I was so little and scared that I didn't know. I just remember that no one cared in the end and I didn't get banned from the set or anything!"

Another amusing story comes from the scene where Michael Knight escapes from the house by jumping over the pool patio ledge. Ham recalls, "They shot the down angle with a low MM lens so it looked like a really far drop, but in reality it was really not that far, probably only 8 feet or so. Well, I guess David was not a fan of heights, so they had to build up mattresses, boxes, ANYTHING to make it as small of a jump as possible. Being afraid of heights myself, I totally get it. But as a kid, it was a trip to see Michael Knight afraid of something. I remember him laughing about it."

(Photo courtesy of Tyler Ham)

Being so young, Ham has snippets of other memories from their 3 days of filming at the house. "There are a lot of great memories that are just bits and pieces. Coincidentally, my grandparents lived right down the street from us, and the crew set up their craft services there. They would come out at lunch time and the crew had them (and us) sit and eat with all of them. It was a neat experience getting to have my whole family eat lunch with Michael Knight! The whole crew was very good to us. I also remember that David would actually drive himself to set dressed in his Knight outfit, and driving a hero K.I.T.T. car. He would drive really slow and kids were running with him and following like he was the pied piper. Tiburon is a small town and when a BIG show came, everyone knew. David would get out, talk to the kids and sign autographs. Again, I can't say enough of how nice of a man he was. When the kids found out it was MY house, that also earned me a lot of 'playground cred' at school. Even all these years later when I mention it to people I work with, everyone gets all 'retro' and asks me everything about it. It is really a wonderful childhood memory."

Knight Knotes:

- This episode is one of only a handful that was filmed outside of the Los Angeles area. Here, it was San Francisco; in "Goliath", the crew went to Las Vegas and in "Knight of the Juggernaut" they visited Chicago.
- A San Francisco police car bearing the license plate CA 507297 is seen in this episode. That plate appears again as Jim Courtney's cruiser in "Knights of the Fast Lane" and on a cruiser in "K.I.T.T. vs. K.A.R.R."
- Bonnie drives K.I.T.T. for the first and only time in the series.

(Photo courtesy of Tyler Ham)

- The producers attempted to make it appear that Clifton and Turk were smoking during their electrocution scene by running hidden tubing underneath their clothes, but they were unable to get the desired effect and cut it.

- The fake gun that Michael uses to threaten Clifton and Turk is a Speeder Bike Gun toy from *Star Wars: Return of the Jedi*.

- Watch Patricia McPherson's reaction when David Hasselhoff tosses her the drone car's CPU – McPherson's hands were tender as she was practicing for her part in NBC's *Circus of the Stars #9*.

- One of the drone cars, same license plate and all, reappears as Alana's car in season four's "Knight Racer".

- The helicopter seen in the climax of this episode is a 1972 Bell 206B Jet Ranger III, registration number N2917W, serial number 806. It was damaged beyond repair in an accident in San Francisco on August 13, 1990. No fatalities were reported.

Script to Screen:

- The prison guard's name is Jim Carter.
- The transforming radio walks across the guard desk.
- Halston originally created three drone cars, not two.
- A police cruiser intercepts Jackson as he escapes from prison, but the drone car accelerates and forces the cruiser into a fire hydrant.
- It's not Babette that picks C.J. up in the Silver Phantom, but Margo herself.
- The script specifically references the movie *Bullitt* in regards to the chase through San Francisco.
- Margo has blonde hair, not brown.
- Former F.L.A.G. agent Ken Franklyn was tailing Jackson because of a major diamond robbery the night he was killed.
- A reunion scene between Bonnie and K.I.T.T. was written. K.I.T.T. tells Bonnie that it wasn't the same without her around. He opens the door and she gets in. Bonnie comments, "I see April kept you in top shape" and K.I.T.T. replies, "Yes, but now she's accepted an offer with a French firm. It's hard to find good help these days."
- Bonnie examines the drone car that Michael stopped and pulls out a small semiconductor unit.
- The drone car's CPU smokes in K.I.T.T.'s backseat instead of the lab. K.I.T.T. forces Michael and Bonnie to get out. As soon as they do, the CPU explodes with so much force that it lifts K.I.T.T. off the ground.
- The maps of the Chinese tunnels originally belonged to Peter Wong's great-grandfather, Lee Ho Wong. Peter now owns them and that's why Halston and Sheridan pulled him into the scheme.

- Peter's girlfriend is named Fu Sing Wu, not Sue Lin.
- Peter tells a skeptical Halston that he saw K.I.T.T. driving by himself and speaking Chinese to Fong's bodyguards. Halston is intrigued and said that he wants to see the car.
- The main space in the semi is referred to as the "working area", while the room towards the front of the trailer is known as the "rest area".
- K.I.T.T. has a new feature called "Vertical Dynamics" which lifts K.I.T.T.'s front two wheels off the ground at a 45 degree angle.
- Some of K.I.T.T.'s new features include a Directional Audibilizer and an Ultrasonic Destabilizer.
- Halston seduces a young co-ed named Kelly Wilson in order to get her father's plans for a security system that guards the bank that they are trying to rob. The vault holds $100 million dollars. It is this, not the Tri-S Satellite, that Halston is after.
- Clifton and Turk do not appear in early drafts of the script.
- Halston and company escape on a barge from Sheridan Enterprises with the money, but K.I.T.T. turbo boosts on to the barge to stop them.

Featured Songs:

"Torture" by The Jacksons

"Jump (For My Love)" by The Pointer Sisters

"Little Red Corvette" by Prince

K.I.T.T.'s Capabilities:

- ATX Surveillance Equipment, Auto Cruise, Auto Phone, Auto-Roof Left, Eject Left, Electrical Generating Mode, Grappling Hook, Image, Infrared Tracking Scope, Interactive Graphics Plotter, Linear

Predictive Graphics Routine, Passive Laser Restraint System, Police/Radio Frequency, Polyphonic Synthesizer, Pursuit, Radar, Self-Analyzing Probe, Self-Diagnostic Routine, Ski Mode, Surveillance Mode, Thermo Dynamic System, Traffic Control System, Turbo Boost, Voice Projection, Voltage Induction Coil, Winch

PROD. #58603

Script History:

June 28, 1984 (F.R.)

July 5, 1984 (F.R.)

July 7, 1984 (F.R.)

{ EPISODE
44 }

THE ICE BANDITS

Working Title: "Knight of a Thousand Diamonds"

Written By: Gerald Sanford

Directed By: Georg Fenady

Original Airdate: October 7, 1984 (Sunday, 8:00 PM) (20.7%; 17,570,000)

NBC Rerun #1: April 12, 1985 (Friday, 8:00 PM)

"Pursuit Mode? Turbo Boost? Eject button? Truly the design of a

supreme being!"

-Brother Francis

Crew: Robert Foster (Executive Producer), Gerald Sanford (Producer), Gino Grimaldi (Producer), Ron Martinez (Associate Producer), Robert Ewing (Associate Producer), Richard Okie (Story Editor), Don Peake (Music), H. John Penner (Director of Photography), Frank Grieco, Jr. (Art Director), R. Lynn Smartt (Set Decoration), Joe Reich (Casting), Domenic G. DiMascio (Film Editor), Pat Somerset (Sound), Ron Martinez (Unit Production Manager), Zane Radney (Unit Production Manager), Louis Race (1st Assistant Director), Bruce Humphrey (2nd Assistant Director), John Shouse (Sound Editor), Richard Lapham (Music Editor), Barry Downing (Costume Supervisor), Karen Braverman (Costume Supervisor), Jack Gill (2nd Unit Director-Stunt Coordinator), Jeremy Swan (Make-up), Allen Payne (Hairstylist)

Guest Cast: Bruce Fairbairn (Charley Winters), Bruce M. Fischer (Eric Sanders), Alex Henteloff (Brother Francis), Paul Koslo (Lyle Austin), Janet Julian (Jody Tompkins), Tom Reese (Brother Carey), Al Checco (Brother Juliano), Julian Barnes (Dr. Fellows), Tip Kelley (Brother Tyrone), Mindi Miller (Nurse Jones), John H. Evans (Charley Winters #2)

Michael and K.I.T.T. go deep into the heart of wine country when a pair of robbers steal some diamonds earmarked for a Foundation auction.

A Look Back:

Janet Lansbury appeared in this installment as Jody Tompkins, a young artist who is dating a wanted diamond thief. At the time of filming, Lansbury wasn't married yet and went by the last name of Julian. "I ended up marrying the nephew of one of the original producers of the show, Bruce Lansbury," confirms the former actress.

Knight Rider was a stepping stone in Lansbury's career, a career that seen her star in over 25 productions over a twenty two year career. "In all honesty, I was ill suited for the entertainment business," confesses Lansbury. "I don't remember much about my experience on *Knight Rider*. It was never my dream to be an actress."

Lansbury would go on to be a regular cast member in both *Falcon Crest* and *Swamp Thing*, but a career in Hollywood was never her desired dream. "That whole acting career was rather torturous for me."

Knight Knotes:

- The turbo boost over some stalled cars is reused footage from last season's "Diamonds Aren't a Girl's Best Friend".
- The car carrier that K.I.T.T. lands on near the middle of the episode is the same carrier that the production staff used to haul the numerous K.I.T.T. cars to the shooting locations.

Script to Screen:

- After Michael catches Lyle Austin, he interrogates him, hoping that Austin will reveal the name of his accomplice. He doesn't.
- K.I.T.T. speaks a line of French during the drive to Napa. Translated, he says, "The wine is the elixir of love."

Featured Songs:

"The Politics of Dancing" by Reflex

K.I.T.T.'s Capabilities:

- Auto Cruise, Auto-Roof Left, Auto-Roof Right, Grappling Hook, Hemometer (Heat Sensors), Interactive Graphics Plotter, Linear Predictive Graphics Routine, Medical Scan, Pursuit, Turbo Boost

PROD. #58601

{ EPISODE
45 }

Script History:

August 8, 1984 (F.R.)

KNIGHTS OF THE FAST LANE

Written By: Richard Okie

Directed By: Winrich Kolbe

Original Airdate: October 14, 1984 (Sunday, 8:00 PM) (24.3%; 20,630,000)

NBC Rerun #1: June 23, 1985 (Sunday, 8:00 PM) (14.0%; 11,890,000)

"I've got a little present for you. It used to belong to a partner of mine. You remind me of him a lot. Michael Long. A special guy, by any standard."

-Jim Courtney

Crew: Robert Foster (Executive Producer), Gino Grimaldi (Producer), Gerald Sanford (Producer), Larry Mollin (Executive Story Consultant), Ron Martinez (Associate Producer), Robert Ewing (Associate Producer), Richard Okie (Story Editor), Don Peake (Music), H. John Penner (Director of Photography), Frank Grieco, Jr. (Art Director), R. Lynn Smartt (Set Decoration), Joe Reich (Casting), Howard B. Anderson (Film Editor), Pat Somerset (Sound), Ron Martinez (Unit Production Manager), Louis Race (1st Assistant Director), Bruce Humphrey (2nd Assistant Director), John Shouse (Sound Editor), Richard Lapham (Music Editor), Barry Downing (Costume Supervisor), Karen Braverman (Costume Supervisor), Jack Gill (2nd Unit Director-Stunt Coordinator), Jeremy Swan (Make-up), Allen Payne (Hairstylist)

Guest Cast: Alan Feinstein (Mark Taylor), Lory Walsh (Diane Landreaux), Cliff Osmond (Jim Courtney), Allen Williams (Jack Lehigh), Tim Rossovich (Tom Bloodworth), Elaine Welton Hill (Nikki La Donna), Dani Douthette (Stacy Courtney), Julie Gray (Kitten #1)

Michael receives a blast from the past when he meets up with his old police partner while investigating a hit and run.

A Look Back:

Alan Feinstein had been acting since the sixties, and had starred in television shows such as *Kojak* and *The Streets of San Francisco* before getting the part of bad guy Mark Taylor in "Knights of the Fast Lane". "I remember in those days a casting director could offer a role directly to an actor without any auditioning, and that is what happened in my case with *Knight Rider*," recalls Feinstein.

Feinstein is very convincing as the evil Taylor. "Playing the bad guy is usually much more interesting as my inspirations when I was growing up were Marlon Brando and Burt Lancaster."

Feinstein's greatest memory of "Knights of the Fast Lane" is the episode's climax. Michael Knight and his old police partner, Jim Courtney (played by Cliff Osmond), team up to bring Mark Taylor to justice. "I remember the fight scene at the end of the episode - it took some time with retakes."

He has been in show business for almost 50 years, but has one stand out moment from his years in acting. "My favorite show was a 2 hour drama I did called *Fans of the Kosko Show*," reveals Feinstein.

Writer Richard Okie comments on the inspiration for this episode by saying, "That episode was actually ripped right out of the headlines. It came out of a Los Angeles article. At that time, people were taking their cars out at three o'clock in the morning and drag racing them on the streets. Robert Foster gave me the idea for it and I started researching. Casting the other cars was fun. People came by with their cars and in the end we had our choice of about eight of them. Where else would someone be willing to rent out their $200,000 sports car?"

Knight Knotes:

- Mark Taylor's complex is actually the College of the Canyons in Valencia, CA. This location has been used in numerous other episodes, including "Deadly Maneuvers", "Junkyard Dog", "Knight of the Chameleon", "Knight Strike" and "The Wrong Crowd".
- The Dagger DX is actually a gold Ferrari owned at the time by George Barris.

Script to Screen:

- In an earlier draft of the script, Mark Taylor was initially named Mark Tanner and Michael was attacked by two Dobermans while investigating "The Racer's Edge" (Originally called "Beyond the Limit").

- Mark Taylor's Dagger DX was originally envisioned as a 600HP green sports car with gullwing doors known as the Vector Twin Turbo W-2.

- Instead of Lehigh being killed in a car explosion, he is instead run over by Bloodworth behind La Donna's building. Michael chases Bloodworth, turbo boosting through a water bottling truck, but loses him shortly after.

- During the argument between Bonnie and Michael after K.I.T.T. is lost in the race, Michael comments, "Bonnie, I love having you back. You're great at your job. But every minute we argue is a minute we don't find Kitt."

- Michael stops Taylor's car from going off the cliff by turbo boosting in front of him and then slowing him down with his brakes.

Featured Songs:

"Talking in Your Sleep" by The Romantics

"Ghostbusters" by Ray Parker, Jr.

K.I.T.T.'s Capabilities:

- Auto Cruise, Auto-Roof Right, Chemical Analyzer, Chemical Detectors, Eject Right, Homing Device, Load Jettison, Map Readout, Micro Jam, Power, Pursuit, Signal, Turbo Boost

PROD. #58624

$$\left[\begin{array}{c} \text{EPISODE} \\ 46 \end{array} \right]$$

Script History:

August 23, 1984 (F.R.)

August 25, 1984 (F.R.)

August 29, 1984 (F.R.)

HALLOWEEN KNIGHT

Written By: Bill Nuss

Directed By: Winrich Kolbe

Original Airdate: October 28, 1984 (Sunday, 8:00 PM) (20.4%; 17,320,000)

NBC Rerun #1: July 14, 1985 (Sunday, 8:00 PM) (16.1%; 13,670,000)

"If you ask me, she has newts in her belfry."

-K.I.T.T.

Crew: Robert Foster (Executive Producer), Gino Grimaldi (Producer), Gerald Sanford (Producer), Larry Mollin (Executive Story Consultant), Ron Martinez (Associate Producer), Bruce Golin (Associate Producer), Robert Ewing (Coordinating Producer), Richard Okie (Story Editor), Don Peake (Music), H. John Penner (Director of Photography), Frank Grieco, Jr. (Art Director), R. Lynn Smartt (Set Decoration), Joe Reich (Casting), Grant Hoag (Film Editor), Pat Somerset (Sound), Ron Martinez (Unit Production Manager), Louis Race (1st Assistant Director), Bruce Humphrey (2nd Assistant Director), John Shouse (Sound Editor), Richard Lapham (Music Editor), Barry Downing (Costume Supervisor), Karen Braverman (Costume Supervisor), Jack Gill (2nd Unit Director-Stunt Coordinator), Jeremy Swan (Make-up), Allen Payne (Hairstylist)

Guest Cast: Jason Evers (Edward Joseph Grant), John Calvin (Simon Grant), Kurt Paul (Norman Baines), Dallas Cole (Esmerelda/Jean), Linda Alberici (Linda Ramsden), Jim Gatherum (Barry), Gillian Grant (Teenage Girl), Taaffe O'Connell (Denise Reynolds), William Winckler (Trick-or-Treater)

On Halloween, Bonnie is targeted when she witnesses a murder in her apartment building.

A Look Back:

Taafe O'Connell was unforgettable as the wise cracking party host Denise Reynolds. O'Connell recalls how she got the role. "My agent, Ernest Dade, literally would haunt the offices of the casting directors making sure that his clients got a shot at the great roles. This was back in the days when agents were still allowed to visit the casting directors, look at the scripts and pitch their clients. Joe Reich was the casting director and he thought of me as an actress who was great at playing the 'wise cracking bombshell with an edge'. He personally called me for the role, but there was a bit of a delay because the producers wanted to cast actors that looked like they were related. Luckily, I looked like John Calvin's sister! They also needed tall people to play against David Hasselhoff. Luckily, being 5'9' really helped!"

O'Connell was known as a "Scream Queen" in the 1980's after starring in *New Year's Evil* and *Galaxy of Terror*, so she was accustomed to starring in a Halloween themed *Knight Rider* episode. "I love horror and Sci-fi. It's like big kids playing. Growing up, I watched *The Twilight Zone* and *The Outer Limits*. The cast and crew on *Knight Rider* were amazing. I was totally energized because there was such electricity on the set."

Working on the show could sometimes mean long shoots as O'Connell recalls. "One night, we worked until 2am when we were shooting the apartment scene with me and David. What I loved about David was that he was a physically gorgeous man, so they used what was called glamour lighting. So, even at two in the morning when in person I might have looked a little bedraggled, I was in heaven. When I saw the final footage, it was pure glamour and beauty." This scene was memorable for another reason as well. "I remember that I really had to use the bathroom during a break in the scene. David had briefly gone to his dressing room and time was tight. I didn't have enough time to go back to my dressing room, so I ran down the stairs and quickly relieved myself in the grass. At least I thought it was the grass. It turned out to be a concrete walkway. It was dark so no one had noticed. But when David came back in for the next take, he shook the bottom of his shoe and asked if it had been raining outside!"

O'Connell remembers the cast and crew well. "Winrich Kolbe (the episode's director) was amazing. He knew how to work with and motivate actors. He also knew when to just let the actor 'run with it'. His sense of setting up the mystery was incredible and he was so very kind. He gave me plenty of close-ups. David Hasselhoff was the consummate professional. At that time, he was a big singing sensation in Europe, so he was going back and forth, which meant that we didn't have time for second and third takes. We usually got what Winrich wanted in the first take. Kurt Paul was perfectly cast as the spoof of Norman Bates. He was sensitive and introverted and you never quite knew what he was thinking," jokes O'Connell.

David Hasselhoff cooling off on set (Photo courtesy of Tyler Ham)

Then there was the character of Esmerelda, played by Dallas Cole, who O'Connell had previously known. "It was great and a little eerie to reconnect with Dallas. Years earlier, I had been to her home. She had a wonderful Italian husband named Geno. I had visited her with my boyfriend at the time, who was Geno's cousin. When asked of his profession, he had told me that he was a 'business man'. Later, we lost touch and I should have suspected something when he gave me a phone number to see if I had been 'tapped'! He later called me from prison when one of my shows aired to tell me that 'dead people' had been found in his pool in Las Vegas and he was doing hard time. I decided not to ask Dallas how he was when we met back up on the set."

There was one scene towards the end of "Halloween Knight" that was delayed because of a zooming van and O'Connell's then boyfriend. "I remember when we shot at Denise's father's house. A scene had been set up where David had to cross the street to get to the front door. Suddenly a big customized van came zipping through the shot and was honking. It was none other than the plastic surgeon that I had been dating at the time. He hadn't understood that he was supposed to have stopped! When he got on the set, it was like old home week, because he had done the face of Jason Evers (Denise's father)."

Even though O'Connell did not get to drive K.I.T.T., she did get a pleasant surprise. "No I didn't get to drive K.I.T.T., but once when I walked past him, he whistled and commented on my legs. I was in love."

Knight Knotes:

- The F.L.A.G. ballroom set is also used as the setting for the jewelry store in "The Ice Bandits", LaSalle's computer lab in "Knight in Disgrace, Armand's basement in "Knight of the Chameleon", The room in the Foundation where Devon calls Michael in "Junk Yard Dog"; Dutton's home in "Out of the Woods", Peralta's capital building in "Knight Flight to Freedom", F.L.A.G.'s computer lab in

"Hills of Fire" and as Harana's party in "Voo Doo Knight". A quick eye can also spot the set in the background of the studio in "Fright Knight".

- A Camaro parked at the drive-in sports a license plate of CA UHH 563. This same plate appears on a different Camaro later this season in "The Nineteenth Hole".

Script to Screen:

- A few cut scenes have Michael discussing with K.I.T.T. possible Halloween costumes for F.L.A.G.'s party. Among the suggestions are Long John Silver and St. Francis Assisi. Michael threatens that if he goes as Assisi, K.I.T.T. will be going as the witch mobile.
- Michael and Bonnie originally fall through a trap door on the porch of the Fairview house where they find Linda's body. The episode has them finding her in the shed.
- Devon calls Michael to inform him of the murder that Bonnie witnessed. Devon tells him that he called Bonnie's doctor and the doctor told Devon that the medication could have caused a hallucination.
- Michael is nearly caught by a guard at Central Costume, but has K.I.T.T. animate a suit of armor to distract the guard so he can escape.
- Esmerelda puts a curse on K.I.T.T. after he asks her to remove her cat. K.I.T.T. replies that it's making him "sick to my transmission". She continues with her chant, "Prince of Darkness, Angel of the Bottomless Pit, Devil, Satan, let's all welcome K.I.T.T.!"
- The description of Grant's mother's house, in reality, the *Psycho* house: "A dilapidated house on the hill. Boy, this place looks familiar."

- The movie on the drive-in screen was supposed to depict a nurse getting into a black Camaro. She then starts driving towards the audience, and which time K.I.T.T. turbo boosts through the screen.

Featured Songs:

"Self Control" by Laura Branigan

K.I.T.T.'s Capabilities:

- Audio Playback, Auto Cruise, Chemical Analyzer, Grappling Hook, Infrared Tracking Scope, Medical Scan, Pursuit, Surveillance Mode, Turbo Boost

PROD. #58617

$$\left[\begin{array}{c} \text{EPISODE} \\ 47 \end{array} \right]$$

Script History:

May 21, 1984 (F.R.)

May 24, 1984 (F.R.)

May 26, 1984 (F.R.)

May 29, 1984 (F.R.)

May 31, 1984 (F.R.)

June 1, 1984 (F.R.)

June 5, 1984 (F.R.)

K.I.T.T. VS. K.A.R.R.

Written By: Richard Okie

Directed By: Winrich Kolbe

Original Airdate: November 4, 1984 (Sunday, 8:00 PM) (21.2%; 18,000,000)

NBC Rerun #1: January 20, 1985 (Sunday, 8:00 PM) (17.3%; 14,690,000)

Filming Dates: May 31- June 11, 1984

"Get in. Let me show you what I can really do."

-K.A.R.R.

Crew: Robert Foster (Executive Producer), Gino Grimaldi (Producer), James M. Miller (Producer), Gerald Sanford (Executive Story Consultant), Ron Martinez (Associate Producer), Robert Ewing (Associate Producer), Richard Okie (Story Editor), Tom Lazurus (Story Editor), Don Peake (Music), H. John Penner (Director of Photography), Frank Grieco, Jr. (Art Director), R. Lynn Smartt (Set Decoration), Joe Reich (Casting), Lawrence J. Gleason (Film Editor), Pat Somerset (Sound), Ron Martinez (Unit Production Manager), Robert Villar (1st Assistant Director), Bruce Humphrey (2nd Assistant Director), John Shouse (Sound Editor), Richard Lapham (Music Editor), Barry Downing (Costume Supervisor), Karen Braverman (Costume Supervisor), Jack Gill (2nd Unit Director-Stunt Coordinator), Jeremy Swan (Make-up), Allen Payne (Hairstylist)

Guest Cast: Jeffrey Osterhage (John Stanton), Jennifer Holmes (Mandy Moran), Ed Crick (Eddie Dexter), Georgia Schmidt (Little Old Lady), Vincent Howard (CHP Officer), Laura Kamins (Female Rollerskater), Paul Frees (Voice of K.A.R.R.)

A young couple accidentally re-activate the Knight Automated Roving Robot (K.A.R.R.) while relaxing on a beach.

A Look Back:

Before endearing himself to *Knight Rider* fans as John Stanton in "K.I.T.T. vs. K.A.R.R.", Detroit native Jeff Osterhage already had some impressive film credits to his name, such as 1978's *True Grit* and the 1979 mini-series *The Sacketts*, the latter of which is considered to be one of the best Westerns of the 1970's. While fans of *Knight Rider* know him best as the man who resurrects K.A.R.R. from the beach, he was very close to landing an even bigger role in the series. "I auditioned for the role of Michael Knight in the Pilot," says Osterhage. "I remember thinking that it was very heavy in terms of the drama and just a damn good script. I had studied Stanislavski and had done Shakespeare and was proud to be known as a dramatic actor, so I felt that the original, heavier script of *Knight Rider* was the perfect fit for me."

Osterhage was one of the final four actors up for the role. His competition included Don Johnson and, of course, David Hasselhoff. "We were being called in, one at a time, for our screen tests," recalls Osterhage. "Don Johnson went first. We performed three scenes at our screen test, to include a scene where Michael hears the car talking for the first time and a scene with Michael speaking to Devon. I remember that Hasselhoff was so nervous and was pacing back and forth. I went in to my screen test and Don Johnson was just finishing up. I did my screen test and really thought that I nailed it. A few weeks went by and I hadn't heard anything so I called my agent and was informed that the network turned all four of us down!" Weeks later, Osterhage learned that they re-considered and offered the part to Hasselhoff.

Fast forward two years, and Osterhage gets a call from his agent saying that they were looking for someone to play the role of John Stanton in "K.I.T.T. vs. K.A.R.R." Osterhage recalls, "I got to skip the preliminary auditions and went straight to the screen test. I had to perform the scene on Malibu Road where I was talking to K.A.R.R. and I remember being sick with the flu. I was so sick, in fact, that I forgot my lines. I finally had to tell the producers and director that I was so sick and I apologized. Apparently, they didn't care as I got the part anyways!"

With Osterhage over his illness, filming was sent to commence on Thursday, May 31, 1984. However, once they arrived on set, they weren't sure that filming would occur at all. "My first scene was with Mandy on the beach with the metal detector. We were setting up and hadn't started filming yet. The producer came over and said that they weren't sure if we would be filming today as Hasselhoff was 'sick'. In reality, Hasselhoff was in contract negotiations so the entire schedule was up in the air. Finally, Hasselhoff showed up and they announced that they could begin filming."

Photo courtesy of Jeff Osterhage

Osterhage spent the rest of the week filming around the Malibu area with a hot Trans Am and a bevy of beautiful women. "The day we shot the scene where a girl on roller skates comes up to me and says something like, 'Hot car' was a good day. There were lots of beautiful women on set that day," jokes Osterhage. "If you watch the scene, you can see that I am laughing a bit, even though that wasn't in the script. And, of course, Jennifer Holmes was one of those beautiful women, and she was wonderful to work with as well." Holmes played John's girlfriend, Mandy Moran.

While not in front of the camera, Osterhage did hang around the set to witness some of the incredible stunts that men like Jack Gill were able to pull off. "Jack Gill was amazing. I learned so much from watching him. It was so interesting to see how he made the car appear to drive by itself, that he was actually tucked inside the seat behind the wheel. I also remember the scene where K.A.R.R. was supposed to crash into a bridge post. We got to the set and the posts were there, but there was no bridge! I asked the crew what the posts were for and they replied that it's for the bridge. Another lesson in special effects technology!"

Following *Knight Rider*, Osterhage guest starred in a number of other hit television shows such as *Murder, She Wrote* and *Moonlighting* before landing a starring role as Vic Daniels in the 1989 remake of *Dragnet*, which lasted two years. These days, Osterhage is still acting and recently finished work on the crime thriller *Taken By Force*.

Ed Crick had a decade of acting in such series as *The Rockford Files*, *Simon & Simon* and *The A-Team* under his belt before appearing in "K.I.T.T. vs. K.A.R.R." as Eddie Dexter, owner of Mr. D's Marine. Crick recalls, "It was a terrific experience. David Hasselhoff and Jeff Osterhage were great. I had done other shows such as *Airwolf*, but *Knight Rider* was by far the biggest sci-fi show at the time." Despite the fact that Crick's episode aired fifth in the season, it was actually the first one shot. As such, an ongoing contract negotiation from the summer hiatus spilled into the new filming season. "I do recall that there was a stand-off with Hasselhoff's agents to try and secure him some more money. This was a very common occurrence when you are a few years into a hit show. So, this may have delayed the shooting somewhat." Indeed, "K.I.T.T. vs. K.A.R.R." took eight days to film, when most one hour installments usually took five.

The first scene that Crick shot for the episode was his scene in the hospital bed. "Rick Kolbe wanted to reshoot that scene and make my performance better. I had the first day jitters and wanted to have another crack at it. On the last day of filming, there was no time to return to the set on stage at Universal so we left the scene as is. That's showbiz!"

In Crick's final scene in the episode, his character is shoved against a wall by Michael Knight and forced to reveal his armored truck heist plans. Crick recalls that the scene was more realistic than many would believe. "In that scene, I am pushed against a rusty door by Hasselhoff. You'll notice that when I turn around, I have blood on my cheek. That was real. I cut my cheek on the rusty door and had to get a tetanus shot at the Universal Studios infirmary after filming that scene was complete. A small piece of that door lodged in my face and I think it's still there to this day."

In 2000, Crick turned 55 and received an early pension from the Screen Actors Guild. He moved his family back to his hometown of Huntsville, Alabama. He is currently the spokesperson for a local credit union and teaches acting classes to aspiring young students. Crick also works for a local food bank in the Huntsville area.

K.A.R.R. is reintroduced to viewers when he is found buried in the sand on the beach. Bringing this scene to life had some challenges of its own, as Jack Gill recalls. "The scene with K.A.R.R. buried in sand was done a few times. I couldn't get enough traction so we ended up digging a huge pit, then laid down some plywood and put sand over the plywood. Then I backed the car into the spot and then they gingerly laid sand all over the top with some false pockets, so I didn't have a whole lot of sand on top of me. I was then going to drive out, but the first time I drove the car, it just spun and it couldn't push all that sand out of the way. So we had to put a cable on the front of the car with me driving so we could get the car out without any issues. One of the times we attempted it we were down at Paradise Cove in Malibu by the ocean. You can still see the spot if you go there and go to the restaurant and sit out there looking out to the ocean. Off to the right is where we buried it."

Knight Knotes:

- John makes a reference to the 1953 TV series *Candid Camera*, thinking that K.A.R.R. speaking to him is a prank.

- Richard Okie on bringing K.A.R.R. back: "We were trying to think of some interesting premises for episodes, and I mentioned the return of K.A.R.R. Everyone said, 'Of course!' I was the first to pitch the idea so I was assigned the project. Paul Frees did the voice, which was a great honor. Since William Daniels' voice was very 'proper', we had to go with a very gutsy voice for the other car. It was Robert Foster's idea to leave the blinking light at the end to signify that K.A.R.R. was still alive. The producers never capitalized on it once I left the series, though."

Script to Screen:

- Though not mentioned in the episode, Eddie's last name is revealed in the script as Dexter. Earlier drafts listed it as Dayton.

- The description of the first time the viewers are reintroduced to K.A.R.R.: "Protruding from the sand at the waterline are the roof and window posts of a very familiar black Trans Am. Even three-quarters buried, its sleek lines are recognizable and despite its position, it is free of rust and corrosion. It glistens in the morning light as a froth of foam splashes around it."

- K.A.R.R.'s scanner doesn't initially pulsate after John and Mandy find him, but rather, an ominous yellow light appears from a slit in the window.

- As John looks for a place to attach the tow truck's chain, he brushes away the sand on the license plate to reveal the letters "KARR".

- The description of K.A.R.R. roaring to life and driving out of the sand pit: "Suddenly the scanner flashes on and a throaty turbine roars. John jumps back in amazement as K.A.R.R. starts to shake, digs in, and rises slowly from its sandy grave like a dark Phoenix. It glides up onto the flat beach and its engine lowers to a throbbing idle."

- The store that Mandy works at, called Endless Summer in the episode, is named Bikinimania here.

- Instead of Devon re-briefing Michael on K.A.R.R., viewers are treated to a flashback via K.I.T.T.'s monitor, using scenes from "Trust Doesn't Rust".

- The description of the scene after K.A.R.R. tears into the back of the semi: "K.I.T.T. is parked nearby, red scanner flashing a warning to the night. Beware. We've been hurt. Proceed at your own risk."

- In the script, Michael is guilt-ridden after K.A.R.R.'s attack on the semi and apologizes to Devon. He states, "Now KARR's got a modified laser and we've got a banged-up mobile unit we can't even get a picture out of."

- A comment that Michael makes alludes to the fact that the Alpha Circuit is what allows K.A.R.R. to make other repairs on his own: "KARR's probably having his Alpha circuits repaired right now. Once that's done he can make the rest of his repairs himself. He'll be at full strength and more dangerous than ever."

- John was arrested in 1978 for grand theft auto and he served 6 months in prison.

- Instead of K.A.R.R. trying to run down Michael at Mr. D's Marine, in the script, K.A.R.R. is gone but Michael finds a corroded Alpha circuit on the ground.

- During the climax, Michael opens the t-top and stands up to address K.A.R.R. In the episode, Michael makes his speech over K.I.T.T.'s speaker.
- Description of the final scene: "Residue of the confrontation, quiet and peaceful now, just the whistle of the wind. Then a faint noise, a weak electronic pulse, and camera finds a twisted black box about the size of a pack of cigarettes lying in the rocks, wires sheared off and tangled. It can't still be functioning, but it continues to emit a pulse and a faint red light. It is K.A.R.R.'s CPU, his Central Processing Unit, and incredibly it's still alive."

Featured Songs:

"Jump (For My Love)" by The Pointer Sisters

"Self Control" by Laura Branigan

"Cruel Summer" by Bananarama

K.I.T.T.'s Capabilities:

- **By K.I.T.T.:** Audio/Video Record, Auto Cruise, Chemical Detectors, Chemical Scan, High-Tensile Reflectors, Pursuit, Remote Monitors, Self-Analyzing Probe, Signal, Surveillance Mode, Turbo Boost, Voice Projection
- **By K.A.R.R.:** Anharmonic Synthesizer, Audio Playback, Auto Cruise, Interior Temperature Control, Laser, Manual Override, Medical Scan, Micro Jam, Power, Sonar, Surveillance Mode, Turbo Boost, Tinted Windows, Voice Projection

PROD. #58611

$$\left[\begin{array}{c} \text{EPISODE} \\ 48 \end{array}\right]$$

Script History:

August 17, 1984 (F.R.)

THE ROTTEN APPLES

Working Title #1: "The Wild Bunch"

Working Title #2: "The Bad Apples"

Teleplay By: Gerald Sanford

Story By: Peter L. Dixon

Directed By: Robert E.L. Bralver

Original Airdate: November 11, 1984 (Sunday, 8:00 PM) (19.2%; 16,900,000)

NBC Rerun #1: April 28, 1985 (Sunday, 8:00 PM) (12.8%; 10,870,000)

"My name is Marilyn, like in Monroe."

-Marilyn

Crew: Robert Foster (Executive Producer), Gino Grimaldi (Producer), Gerald Sanford (Producer), Larry Mollin (Executive Story Consultant), Ron Martinez (Associate Producer), Bruce Golin (Associate Producer), Robert Ewing (Coordinating Producer), Richard Okie (Story Editor), Don Peake (Music), H. John Penner (Director of Photography), Frank Grieco, Jr. (Art Director), R. Lynn Smartt (Set Decoration), Joe Reich (Casting), Domenic G. DiMascio (Film Editor), Pat Somerset (Sound), Ron Martinez (Unit Production Manager), Robert Villar (1st Assistant Director), Bruce Humphrey (2nd Assistant Director), John Shouse (Sound Editor), Richard Lapham (Music Editor), Barry Downing (Costume Supervisor), Karen Braverman (Costume Supervisor), Jack Gill (2nd Unit Director-Stunt Coordinator), Jeremy Swan (Make-up), Allen Payne (Hairstylist)

Guest Cast: Terri Treas (Rebecca Hammond), Denny Miller ("Big" Ed Barton), Robert Symonds (Cat Holliday), Richard Lineback (Sheriff Lance Barton), Russ McCubbin (Alfred Barton), Lana Clarkson (Marilyn), Tobie Norton (Blue), Reginald T. Dorsey (Magic Fingers), Mimi Kinkade (Star), James LeGros (Thrasher), Michelle Newkirk (Joanna), Richard Coca (Diablo)

Michael and K.I.T.T come to the rescue of Rebecca Hammond, a young rancher whose cattle are being stolen by a crooked sheriff and his gang.

Knight Knotes:

- This episode features two Bigfoot-style monster trucks brought in from Illinois.
- Gerald Sanford wrote the words to the song, "If You Leave Me Tonight, I'll Cry", sung by Marilyn in this episode.
- Michael references *The Lone Ranger* as he is escaping from Big Ed's office ("Hi Ho, K.I.T.T., Away!")

David Hasselhoff joking in between takes (Photo courtesy of Tyler Ham)

Featured Songs:

"C.C. Waterback" by Merle Haggard and George Jones

"No Words For Love" by David Hasselhoff

"If You Leave Me Tonight, I'll Cry" by Jerry Wallace

"I'm So Excited" by The Pointer Sisters

"The Heart of Rock and Roll" by Huey Lewis and the News

K.I.T.T.'s Capabilities:

- Aim Laser, Auto Cruise, Auto-Roof Left, Brite, Chemical Analyzer, Eject Left, Electrical Generating Mode, Geological Analyzer, Grappling Hook, Homing Signal, Image, Map Search, Micro Jam, Microlock, Printer, Pursuit, Radar, Range, Ski Mode

PROD. #58622

$$\left[\begin{array}{c} \text{EPISODE} \\ 49 \end{array}\right]$$

Script History:

June 15, 1984 (F.R.)

June 20, 1984 (F.R.)

June 20, 1984 (2nd rev.)

June 21, 1984 (F.R.)

June 21, 1984 (2nd rev.)

June 21, 1984 (3rd rev.)

June 22, 1984 (F.R.)

June 25, 1984 (F.R.)

June 25, 1984 (2nd rev.)

June 28, 1984 (F.R.)

KNIGHT IN DISGRACE

Written By: Simon Muntner

Directed By: Harvey Laidman

Original Airdate: November 18, 1984 (Sunday, 8:00 PM) (21.7%; 18,420,000)

NBC Rerun #1: May 12, 1985 (Sunday, 8:00 PM) (14.7%; 12,480,000)

"Given a choice, I prefer alligators."

-K.I.T.T.

Crew: Robert Foster (Executive Producer), Gino Grimaldi (Producer), Gerald Sanford (Producer), Ron Martinez (Associate Producer), Robert Ewing (Associate Producer), Richard Okie (Story Editor), Tom Lazurus (Story Editor), Don Peake (Music), H. John Penner (Director of Photography), Frank Grieco, Jr. (Art Director), R. Lynn Smartt (Set Decoration), Joe Reich (Casting), Howard B. Anderson (Film Editor), Pat Somerset (Sound), Ron Martinez (Unit Production Manager), Robert Villar (1st Assistant Director), Bruce Humphrey (2nd Assistant Director), John Shouse (Sound Editor), Richard Lapham (Music Editor), Barry Downing (Costume Supervisor), Karen Braverman (Costume Supervisor), Jack Gill (2nd Unit Director-Stunt Coordinator), Jeremy Swan (Make-up), Allen Payne (Hairstylist)

Guest Cast: John Considine (Boyd Lasalle), Kitty Moffat (Linda), Ken Foree (Danton), Lee Ryan (Charles Wallyburton), Casey Sander (Sergeant), Ken Scott (Gino the Bartender), Jean Lubin (Carmen), Elizabeth Frazier (Mary Beth), Richard Camphuis (Mansion Guard), Michael Horsley (Guard), Charles Picerni (Willis)

Michael is suspended from the Foundation after a crook plants some evidence on him during a drug bust.

A Look Back:

The beginning of "Knight in Disgrace" featured a scene that was used only once in the entire show's history. Michael Knight is sitting in K.I.T.T. and we see the image of Devon Miles on the monitor in the car speaking to him. Director Harvey Laidman explains, "In those days, we only did it two ways - a 'burn-in' where the monitor picture is composited in post-production or by photographing the monitor with a camera. The camera would have a modified shutter that converted 30 frames (NTSC) to 24 frames. Every monitor shot on *Knight Rider* was a burn in. I also remember that this scene was unusual for the show, but within the conventions established for other shows. That scene was the writer/producer's idea."

The episode was based in New Orleans, but not filmed there. *"Knight Rider* never went to New Orleans. Parts of Pasadena look like New Orleans so we shot there. We even had New Orleans police cars but they were straight out of the Universal transportation department."

It could be argued that "Knight in Disgrace", with its scenes of drugs, deception and alcohol, is one of the more mature episodes in the show's history. "Testing the censor has always been a sport in television," says Laidman. "Compared to what was developing in U.S. television, this was fairly mild. I don't think the producers considered *Knight Rider* a children's show. All television is truly on the level of the prepubescent teenage boy - a stage that a vast majority of men never outgrow. As for drugs - they were always plot devices in prime time melodramas anyway. The plot result was that Michael was undercover - I am sure that the audience probably understood this from the outset."

Boyd LaSalle's beautiful mansion was featured heavily here and acquiring the mansion for filming was not difficult. "People love to rent to the movies. They get a tax break and get a pot of money. The house was in Pasadena near downtown. Every house there is very elaborate. I cannot count how many times I have shot there. If I am being honest, those houses are so elaborate that I would never consider living in such opulence. I believe the owners were having some financial trouble at the time."

K.I.T.T. on set (Photo courtesy of Tyler Ham)

During a scene on the grounds of the estate, there was a scene in which K.I.T.T. turbo boosted over a hedge. This scene was a bit difficult for Laidman. "For the turbo boost, the car we used was essentially a 'dune buggy' with the Trans Am skin. That baby could really jump. There was stock footage, as I recall, and the rest was stunt driving with the camera over cranked for slow motion or under cranked to speed it up. That turbo boost attracted the Pasadena police. They came and made us cut the stunt down. It was supposed to be more elaborate - like the house."

As a director, Laidman worked closely with stunt man Jack Gill, although Laidman thought that Gill's talents could be put to use in front of the camera as well. "I used to kid with Jack, but it's true - he was so good looking that he should have quit the stunt business to become an actor. However, Jack was aware of his acting abilities! In my mind, a stuntman should look like Corey Loftin – big, angular, hatchet-faced and gruff. Jack really was the complete opposite. He is married to the incredibly beautiful Morgan Brittany."

Laidman was content on shooting scenes on location, although as with everything, there were pros and cons. "Location shooting, if well planned and weather and ambient noise is mild, is great. Overcast skies mean easy lighting and the look is fresh. Also, everyone doesn't suddenly split for the local restaurants for lunch. Everyone's there and according to the budget, you get two extra hours. Normally, studio days are 10-12 hours and location days are 12-14. Of course, you have to be aware of losing light. Then, you can shoot a bit of night exterior shots. It certainly takes careful scheduling. Because of union rules, night exteriors were usually scheduled for Friday nights."

Between shots, the actors took time out to marvel at the location of the house. "I remember John Considine and David standing on the patio of the mansion, just looking out at the mini Versailles. It was a nice place to shoot and John was great."

Knight Knotes:

- The ski mode seen during Chuck Wallyburton's test drive of K.I.T.T. is reused footage from "Chariot of Gold".

Script to Screen:

- K.I.T.T.'s final line ("Given a choice, I prefer alligators") was added late in production. The script originally ended with Chuck's line ("Hey little buddy, look who's here").
- As Michael leaves the Foundation after being told of his suspension, Devon makes a comment that they will both be laughing about it in a week. This line would have provided a hint to the viewer that the suspension was all an act.

- The technician who brings LaSalle his spy briefcase at the mansion is named Poole. He is described as "a twenty-three-year old computer expert, thin, long hair and John Lennon glasses".

- During Devon and Bonnie's conversation about Michael's suspension, Devon goes on to say, "Bonnie, I'm going to miss him, too...but the integrity of the Foundation is more important that any one man -- including Michael Knight."

- After LaSalle agrees to pay Michael $50,000 to steal K.I.T.T., LaSalle continues by saying, "The Knight Industry Two Thousand. Or as you so fondly call it...K.I.T.T."

- A special note accompanies a description of the scene where Michael arrives at the F.L.A.G. garage in a limo. "Note: This limo should not have Louisiana plates."

Déjà Vu:

- John Considine returns in "Knight of the Juggernaut"; Ken Foree returns in "Redemption of a Champion".

Featured Songs:

"Owner of a Lonely Heart" by Yes

"Won't You Please Come Home" by Bill Bailey

K.I.T.T.'s Capabilities:

- Anharmonic Synthesizer, Auto Cruise, Auto Phone, Auto-Roof Left, Eject Left, Homing Signal, Manual Override, Micro Jam, Pursuit, Ski Mode, Turbo Boost, X-Ray

PROD. #58607

[EPISODE
50]

Script History:

September 10, 1984 (F.R.)

September 11, 1984 (F.R.)

DEAD OF KNIGHT

Teleplay By: Peter Baloff and David W. Wollert

Story By: Janis Hendler and Tom Greene

Directed By: Bernard L. Kowalski

Original Airdate: December 2, 1984 (Sunday, 8:00 PM) (18.2%; 15,450,000)

NBC Rerun #1: June 9, 1985 (Sunday, 8:00 PM) (15.6%; 13,240,000)

"Why are you talking to your arm?"

-Rosemary

Crew: Robert Foster (Executive Producer), Gino Grimaldi (Producer), Gerald Sanford (Producer), Larry Molin (Executive Story Consultant), Ron Martinez (Associate Producer), Bruce Golin (Associate Producer), Robert Ewing (Coordinating Producer), Richard Okie (Story Editor), Don Peake (Music), H. John Penner (Director of Photography), Frank Grieco, Jr. (Art Director), R. Lynn Smartt (Set Decoration), Joe Reich (Casting), Dayle Mustain (Film Editor), Pat Somerset (Sound), Ron Martinez (Unit Production Manager), Robert Villar (1st Assistant Director), Bruce Humphrey (2nd Assistant Director), John Shouse (Sound Editor), Richard Lapham (Music Editor), Barry Downing (Costume Supervisor), Karen Braverman (Costume Supervisor), Jack Gill (2nd Unit Director-Stunt Coordinator), Jeremy Swan (Make-up), Allen Payne (Hairstylist)

Guest Cast: Tony Young (Paul Renard), Karen Kopins (Cindy Morgan), Aarika Wells (Ava Bennett), Stanley Kamel (Sonney Martin), Victor Campos (Colonel Faisur), Jean Hasselhoff (Rosemary), Bob Larkin (Colonel Jennings), Richard Peabody (Security Guard), Guylaine Sanford (Michele), Joanie Allen (Lori Meadows), Richard Brose (Arnold), Ed McCready (Tourista), Clay Lacy (Pilot)

After a dancer is killed by an exotic poison, Michael's investigation leads him to a botanist – and the deadly serum.

Knight Knotes:
- K.I.T.T. states that he has 1000 Mega Bits of memory, and a 1 nano-second access time.
- Rosemary the receptionist is actually Jean Hasselhoff, David's sister.
- Guylaine Sanford, who played Michele, is producer Gerald Sanford's wife.
- A keen eye can spot a *He-Man and the Masters of the Universe* piñata hanging from the ceiling of the Mexican cantina.

Script to Screen:

- The description of the first appearance of Sonny Martin: "He's a cross between Troy Donahue and Charles Manson. An earring in one ear, a lot of keys on his belt, and a silver mesh glove on his right hand. Why? We'll find out later."

- A scene with Sonny and Rosemary where Sonny practices throwing his razor blade Frisbee was originally included after Lori is killed.

- The scene with Sonny's runaway van was originally envisioned as the following: Sonny leads Michael to a sparsely populated area. Sonny crests a hill, gets out and lets the van drift down the hill. Michael throws it in reverse as the van comes barreling towards him and veers out of the way. The van hits an embankment and stops.

- The body builder asks K.I.T.T. how much he weighs. K.I.T.T. responds, 3200 pounds.

- Michael ingests the poison in the orange juice, as well as Cindy. K.I.T.T. notices an imbalance in his metabolism eventually realizes what happened.

- The description of K.I.T.T.'s drive to Mexico: "The black Trans Am twists through the Sequaro desert on an asphalt ribbon much smaller and lonelier than the previous highway. We know we're south of the border from the scenery and the music: maybe the Grateful Dead's "Mexicali Blues" or J.J. Cale's "Bringin' It Back From Mexico". As the sound alike fades..."

- K.I.T.T. tells a few additional jokes: "Speaking of Vegas, you know the only way to make any money there? When you walk off the plane, walk into the propeller!" The other is: "And how 'bout those show girls in Vegas....I saw one with beautiful blonde hair all down her back. None on her head, all down her back." Also, Arnold reappears at the end of the episode as K.I.T.T. tells this joke: "Did you hear the one about the weight lifter who tried to press his own weight, but burned himself with the iron?"

- K.I.T.T. turbo boosts through the wing of the plane instead of crashing head on into it.

Featured Songs:

"Rebel Yell" by Billy Idol

"Torture" by The Jacksons

"When Doves Cry" by Prince

K.I.T.T.'s Capabilities:

- Anharmonic Synthesizer, Auto Cruise, Auto Phone, Chemical Scan, Infrared Tracking Scope, Medical Scan, Microlock, Printer, Pursuit, Tinted Windows, X-Ray

PROD. #58619

{ EPISODE
51 }

Script History:

May 30, 1984 (F.R.)

EN June 6, 1984 (F.R.)

June 8, 1984 (F.R.)

June 11, 1984 (F.R.)

LOST KNIGHT

Working Title: "K.I.T.T. Phone Home"

Written By: Robert Foster and James M. Miller

Directed By: Sidney Hayers

Original Airdate: December 9, 1984 (Sunday, 8:00 PM) (18.9%; 16,050,000)

NBC Rerun #1: June 30, 1985 (Sunday, 8:00 PM) (10.1%; 8,570,000)

Filming Dates: June 12-21, 1984

"A talking car...if that's not a mind blower."

-Doug Wainwright

Crew: Robert Foster (Executive Producer), Gino Grimaldi (Producer), James M. Miller (Producer), Gerald Sanford (Executive Story Consultant), Ron Martinez (Associate Producer), Robert Ewing (Associate Producer), Richard Okie (Story Editor), Tom Lazurus (Story Editor), Don Peake (Music), H. John Penner (Director of Photography), Frank Grieco, Jr. (Art Director), R. Lynn Smartt (Set Decoration), Joe Reich (Casting), Grant Hoag (Film Editor), Lawrence J. Vallario (Film Editor), Pat Somerset (Sound), Ron Martinez (Unit Production Manager), Louis Race (1st Assistant Director), Bruce A. Humphrey (2nd Assistant Director), John Shouse (Sound Editor), Richard Lapham (Music Editor), Barry Downing (Costume Supervisor), Karen Braverman (Costume Supervisor), Jack Gill (2nd Unit Director-Stunt Coordinator), Jeremy Swan (Make-up), Allen Payne (Hairstylist)

Guest Cast: Jason Bateman (Doug Wainwright), Lenore Kasdorf (Lori Wainwright), Anthony James (Bobby Pell), Karl Johnson (Julius Korso), Duncan Gamble (Jim Turner), Bill Cross (Conrad Marrs), Anne Wyndham (Ms. Jordon), Pamela Bowman (Angel), Alice Nunn (Nurse)

Michael is devastated when an accident short circuits K.I.T.T.'s memory, leaving the supercar in the hands of a young teenager.

A Look Back:

Lenore Kasdorf was already an established and well respected performer before making her first appearance on *Knight Rider,* having been seen on other Universal shows such as *Magnum, P.I., The A-Team* and *Airwolf.* "In those days, I worked a lot at Universal," recalls Kasdorf. "I then went to New York for five years. When I returned to California, I auditioned for 'Lost Knight' and got the part."

(Photo courtesy of Lenore Kasdorf)

In the episode, Kasdorf played Lori Wainwright, the owner of a nursery and mother to Doug Wainwright, played by a young Jason Bateman. "You know, it's funny. I don't know that I had ever seen this episode until recently. I knew Jason played my son in something, but I thought it had been in an episode of a show called *FBI* with Efrom Zimbalist, Jr. way back in 1974. I recall being amazed at how polished and good he was for such a young actor. I felt the same way years later when I worked with Anne Hathaway and

Hillary Swank. Now, they are all big stars! Perhaps I had something to do with that," jokes Kasdorf.

Besides running a nursery and dealing with a teenage son, Lori Wainwright must also contend with her boyfriend, Jim, an overly protective man who is suspicious of Michael's intentions with the Wainwright family. "Boy, my boyfriend on the show was absolutely miserable!" laughs Kasdorf. "From the first time we saw him at the nursery, he was not nice! I don't know why on earth she was with him?"

Knight Knotes:

- NBC promoted this episode as follows: "An accident destroys K.I.T.T.'s memory. Can guest star Jason Bateman help Michael save him?"
- The license plate on Peli and Korso's Chevy 4x4 changes from 1JKN550 to 1JKN551 throughout the episode.
- Here, we see K.I.T.T.'s "Evade" button for the first (and only) time.

Script to Screen:

- The scene with Ms. Jordan demonstrating the nitro-plastique was drawn out a bit further originally. Devon explains that F.L.A.G. is involved to ensure the substance is used for non-military use only. Two observers named Mr. Iamoto and Mr. Schmitt ask about the stability of the substance – Ms. Jordan throws it on the ground to prove it's safe.
- Bob's Plumbing Supply was changed from Kellog's Plumbing Supply on the side of Korso's Bronco (a Jeep in the episode). Their vehicle was outfitted with a supercharger instead of nitrous oxide.
- When K.I.T.T. is electrocuted, his dash sparks and smokes.

- Once Pell and Korso return from the heist, they peel a white skin from the top of their Bronco, making the SUV all red, and remove the plumbing logo from the door.

- Bonnie brings Michael's Jeep to the hospital. When he asks her how far K.I.T.T. could go, Bonnie responds, "His turbine has nothing to do with his memory banks, Michael. As long as it's working, he can go as far as he wants."

- Devon warns Michael that if he can't find K.I.T.T., he must follow Wilton Knight's orders so that K.I.T.T. does not end up in the wrong hands. As such, they created a "Terminate and Destroy" button at the Foundation. Bonnie contacts every computer supply outlet in the area and tells Michael and Devon that if someone tries to repair him, they would know about it. Devon responds, "Kitt could be transferred out-of-state and repaired. He could be repaired from existing CPU components. I have no choice. If Kitt can't be recovered by 9:00 AM tomorrow, I'll be forced to activate his self-destruct mode."

- When Michael describes K.I.T.T. to Doug, he says, "It wouldn't have been too hard to spot. Might even've had a flashing red light in its grill."

- A description of when Doug presses the Pursuit button: "A dazzling display of K.I.T.T.'s capabilities intercut with Doug at the wheel, expression changing from fear to exhilaration to absolute wonder. This is an experience beyond his wildest dreams."

- Michael pleads with Doug to tell him where K.I.T.T. is: "Doug, listen to me. If you were, you'll know what I'm talking about...Kitt's my friend. My best friend. He's been hurt and he needs help. He's saved my life more times than I can count and now I've got to save his."

Déjà Vu:

- Lenore Kasdorf returns in "Fright Knight".

Featured Songs:

"Caribbean Queen (No More Love on the Run)" by Billy Ocean

K.I.T.T.'s Capabilities:

- Audio Playback, Auto Cruise, Auto-Roof Right, Chemical Detectors, Eject Right, Energy System Override, Evade, Map Search, Micro Jam, Police/Radio Frequency, Pursuit, Radar, Surveillance Mode, Turbo Boost

PROD. #58631

$$\left[\begin{array}{c} \text{EPISODE} \\ 52 \end{array} \right]$$

Script History:

October 10, 1984 (F.R.)

KNIGHT OF THE CHAMELEON

Working Title: "The Chameleon"

Written By: Robert Sherman

Directed By: Winrich Kolbe

Original Airdate: December 30, 1984 (Sunday, 8:00 PM) (16.8%; 14,260,000)

NBC Rerun #1: June 2, 1985 (Sunday, 8:00 PM) (13.9%; 11,800,000)

Filming Dates: October 24- November 2, 1984

"Oh Michael, where did I go wrong?"

-K.I.T.T.

Crew: Robert Foster (Executive Producer), Gino Grimaldi (Producer), Gerald Sanford (Producer), Richard Okie (Executive Story Consultant), Robert Sherman (Executive Story Consultant), David Bennett Carren (Story Editor), Ron Martinez (Associate Producer), Bruce Golin (Associate Producer), Robert Ewing (Coordinating Producer), Don Peake (Music), H. John Penner (Director of Photography), Frank Grieco, Jr. (Art Director), R. Lynn Smartt (Set Decoration), Joe Reich (Casting), Lawrence J. Gleason (Film Editor), Pat Somerset (Sound), Ron Martinez (Unit Production Manager), Robert Villar (1st Assistant Director), Bruce A. Humphrey (2nd Assistant Director), John Shouse (Sound Editor), Richard Lapham (Music Editor), Barry Downing (Costume Supervisor), Karen Braverman (Costume Supervisor), Jack Gill (2nd Unit Director-Stunt Coordinator), Jeremy Swan (Make-up), Allen Payne (Hairstylist)

Guest Cast: Dick Gautier (J. Gordon Baxter/Chameleon), Kimberly Foster (Tonie Baxter), Byron Webster (Armand Pressler), Nicholas Worth (Ryals), Don Gibb (Gibbs), Shari Shattuck (Ingrid), Dominick Brascia (Harry), Alice Backes (Judge Edith Webster), Alan Jordon (Major William Anderson), Raymond Lynch (Bryson), James Williams (John Maxwell), Gustaf Unger (Gustaf), Bertil Unger (Bertil), Eric Lawrence (M.P. Guard)

Michael and K.I.T.T. face a former enemy nicknamed "The Chameleon", who can disguise himself as anyone or anything.

A Look Back:

The episode's main foe was played by Dick Gautier, a veteran character actor well-known at the time for playing Hymie the Robot in the 1960's *Get Smart* television program. Here, he played a master of disguise known as the Chameleon. "I liked playing the Chameleon", says Gautier. "[There were] lots of disguises. The makeup was on occasion tiring but Ken

Diaz (the makeup artist) was a good guy and made the time go faster. It really was a pleasant experience being on set".

One of Gautier's fondest *Knight Rider* memories took place when he was filming a scene with his on-screen daughter, played by Kimberley Foster. "I had a speech that went something like, 'Honey, I have to go to the high desert and I'll see you when I get back and we will have dinner, OK?'. Well, I totally messed up the lines, and at one point, I added the following to save myself from the cast and crew: 'And honey, while I'm gone, get a dictionary and look up the word incest'. I exited to waves of laughter from the cast and crew".

Between takes, Gautier was introduced to David Hasselhoff's new invention. "David was charming and especially nice to the kids who came around on location. He had invented a product called a 'rag ball'. It was a ball that felt like a hardball but was soft and couldn't do any damage in a game of catch. He gave them out to all the kids".

As for Gautier's on-screen daughter, he recalls, "The pretty blonde girl that played my daughter was the center of attention. She looked nothing like me. I was her evil - or at least criminal – father. It was an enjoyable shoot".

The climax of "Knight of the Chameleon" featured the Chameleon attempting an escape using a military jet pack. Michael Knight ejected out of K.I.T.T. and forced the Chameleon to land in a lake, a scene in which Gautier wasn't too comfortable with. "The lake was up in Valencia near Magic Mountain. I'm a rotten swimmer and have always been, so they had to double me. I simply waded out of the lake and onto dry land. Before I went into the water, the set doctor took me aside and guided me into a makeshift tent. They proceeded to give me several injections in my arm. I asked what the shots were for and the doctor explained that the lake was stagnant and polluted".

Finally, when asked about using the jet pack, Gautier revealed that the "Master of Disguise" was, in fact, somebody completely different. "The owner, who was also the inventor, was on set and he doubled me. That was a real jet pack, but it wasn't me. No one was allowed to use it but one guy. It was quite dangerous. You're aloft for something like nine seconds tops and then you plummet like a rock. He's the guy who did the spectacular entrance into the L.A. Coliseum for the Olympics. I had it on though and it was very heavy and unwieldy. And you thought making TV shows was easy!"

Knight Knotes:

- Armand's Cafe is an homage to the classic movie *Casablanca*; actor Byron Webster was cast because of his likeness to actor Sidney Greenstreet. Michael meets a young lady there named Ingrid (as in Ingrid Bergman).

Script to Screen:

- Michael is on a date with a girl named Julie at a golf range. She is bored but has the hots for Michael, but Michael insists on her getting out once in a while. Michael goes to hit the ball, but K.I.T.T. rings in saying he forgot the tee.
- Bonnie asks Devon that if he could disguise himself as anyone, who would it be? She suggests Laurence Olivier and Winston Churchill. Michael suggests Boy George. Bonnie says that she would like to become Madam Curie or poet Elizabeth Barrett Browning. Michael then says he would like to be Count Dracula and asks Bonnie if he may kiss her on the neck!
- Bonnie reminds Michael that the first time the Chameleon was loose, he tried to steal K.I.T.T.'s master control.

- Michael is locked in a generator room with 3 million volts of electricity and K.I.T.T. activates the MEC (Magnetic Energy Concentrator), an unseen function that forced the 3 million volts directly into K.I.T.T.
- During Michael's final chase of Baxter, he originally turbo boosts through an ice truck filled with seafood.

Déjà Vu:

- Nicholas Worth guest stars in "Knight of the Juggernaut", and Dominick Brascia is in "Knight Behind Bars".

Featured Songs:

"The Lucky One" by Laura Branigan

K.I.T.T.'s Capabilities:

- Air Vac, Anharmonic Synthesizer, Auto Cruise, Auto Phone, Auto-Roof Left, Eject Left, Infrared, Interactive Graphics Plotter, Linear Predictive Graphics Routine, Map Search, Medical Scan, Pursuit, Radar, Surveillance Mode, Telephone Monitor, Telephone Trace, Trunk Lid, Turbo Boost

PROD. #58640

$$\left[\begin{array}{c} \text{EPISODE} \\ 53 \end{array} \right]$$

CUSTOM MADE KILLER

Written By: Burton Armus

Directed By: Harvey Laidman

Original Airdate: January 6, 1985 (Sunday, 8:00 PM) (23.9%; 20,290,000)

NBC Rerun #1: September 13, 1985 (Friday, 8:00 PM) (17.2%; 14,770,000)

"Dancers pirouette on their toes to the strains of violins and flutes. They do not gesticulate wildly to the throbbing beat of bongo drums and saxophones."

-Devon

Crew: Robert Foster (Executive Producer), Gino Grimaldi (Producer), Burton Armus (Producer), Gerald Sanford (Producer), Richard Okie (Executive Story Consultant), Gregory S. Dinallo (Executive Story Consultant), Ron Martinez (Associate Producer), Bruce Golin (Associate Producer), Robert Ewing (Coordinating Producer), Don Peake (Music), H. John Penner (Director of Photography), Frank Grieco, Jr. (Art Director), R. Lynn Smartt (Set Decoration), Joe Reich (Casting), Domenic G. DiMascio (Film Editor), Grant Hoag (Film Editor), Pat Somerset (Sound), Ron Martinez (Unit Production Manager), Robert Villar (1st Assistant Director), Bruce Humphrey (2nd Assistant Director), John Shouse (Sound Editor), Richard Lapham (Music Editor), Barry Downing (Costume Supervisor), Karen Braverman (Costume Supervisor), Charles Picerni, Sr. (2nd Unit Director-Stunt Coordinator), Jeremy Swan (Make-up), Allen Payne (Hairstylist)

Guest Cast: James Luisi (D.G. Grebbs), Elaine Giftos (Debra Sands), Alan Oppenheimer (Joe Lewis), Kai Wulff (Flood), Viveca Parker (Joan Keahey), Phil Rubenstein (Joe), Michael Fox (Phil), Guerin Barry (Photographer), Jimmy Murphy (Tom O'Malley), Maria Lauren (Model), Ron Lunceford (Attendant)

Michael and K.I.T.T. are asked to investigate the death of a fashion designer after the burnt out shell of his car is found at the bottom of a cliff.

A Look Back:

Harvey Laidman had the pleasure of directing three veteran television actors in this episode. "James Luisi (D.G Grebbs) was bright, fun and easy to work with. I was very pleased that we were able to cast him. I remember trying to get Kai Wulff (Flood) for another show and could not. I actually think that Kai was under contract to Universal at the time. I worked with Alan Oppenheimer (Joe) many times. He was quiet and funny and was a regular on a show I did called *Eischied*. There are many times when you work on a tight schedule like this and you suffer with a difficult cast. This was never the case with *Knight Rider*. I can't remember a single instance when there were difficulties with the cast. I think this goes back to the producers who allow competent actors to be hired and don't 'stunt cast'."

"Custom Made Killer" opens with a car chase in which Flood is driving the custom car and ends up pushing another car off a cliff. Laidman explains the difficulties of this shoot, especially since it was shot at night. "It's very difficult to shoot at night and back in those days, film and lenses required much more light. It took a long time to light each shot. We were limited to the amount of shots we could accomplish. I believe this scene was filmed on the Universal back lot."

The majority of the episode was shot on location at a shopping mall. "We shot at the famous fashion mart in downtown Los Angeles. It's in the area where all the 1940's film noir pictures were made - the Bradbury Building. It was fun being in that venue and they were so used to the filming that they completely ignored us! The mart is a great place to visit in LA."

One striking scene involving the character of Flood occurred when he pushed Tom O'Malley and his car into the path of a moving train. "This was a street crossing in Burbank, not too far from the studio. I shot all the pieces up to the crash. The crash was miniature footage as it was very hard to get cooperation from the railroads."

Laidman directed six episodes of *Knight Rider*, with many of those shoots taking place in the Foundation semi. "When K.I.T.T. was inside, there was hardly enough room to open the doors. We shot one angle then removed a wall and then shot another. Of course, the set was raised above the stage floor so that K.I.T.T. could ramp up into it. The interior was just a set and any wall could be removed for filming. K.I.T.T. was driven into it on a soundstage with a translucent backing behind."

As Laidman explains, the residents of Burbank were treated to quite a show on their streets during most shoots. "All of the driving shots were achieved by having K.I.T.T. being towed by a camera car with two cameras on the back facing K.I.T.T. We were quite a parade coming down Burbank Boulevard - two motorcycle cops, a van full of hair, makeup and wardrobe personnel, and the infernal contraption of a camera car! Crew would be hanging on for dear life towing K.I.T.T., followed by zigzagging extras creating traffic from behind. Most of the time, there were two huge arc lights on top of the camera car - a bit like Mickey Mouse's ears."

As was often the case in *Knight Rider,* while Michael left K.I.T.T. unattended, his trusty Trans Am would encounter every walk of life from animals to car thieves. In "Custom Made Killer", K.I.T.T. was used as a prop for a model's photo shoot. The woman was portrayed by real life model Maria Lauren and the photographer was played by Guerin Barry. "I remember the shoot fairly well, but oddly enough, I don't remember the model at all," confesses Barry.

Barry has been acting for over 30 years and even as a child knew deep down what he wanted to do as a career when he grew up. "I suppose I was attracted to performing as a young boy. I loved Ernie Kovacs, Jackie Gleeson and Sid Caesar on TV. I didn't have any athletic ability, so I had to do something. As an adult, I was working in New York at an advertising agency. I conducted casting sessions for commercials that were so serious and tense, it occurred to me that the actors were having lots more fun than I was. That is when I finally decided I wanted to be an actor and I moved to Los Angeles."

Though Barry is known as a photographer whose antics annoy K.I.T.T., Barry confesses that the voice belonging to K.I.T.T. may have come from himself. "I was the voice of the Alex 7000 computer for *The Bionic Woman.* One day, Universal's casting director, Marc Malis, asked me if I would read the K.I.T.T. part for him. At that time, there was no talk of anyone else for the part, so I left thinking that I had gotten the job. How sad I was to learn that William Daniels, who was already working on *St. Elsewhere,* got it." Barry, who went on to star in such shows as Glen Larson's *The Fall Guy*, *Matlock* and *Columbo,* was later pleased with how Daniels gave K.I.T.T. an identity. "I think Bill did a wonderful job with K.I.T.T. I have met him at SAG meetings but we've never spoken about it."

(Photo courtesy of Guerin Barry)

Barry knew Glen Larson fairly well. "Glen produced quite a few shows that I worked on. One was a short lived show called *Fitz and Bones* that was set in San Francisco and starred the Smothers Brothers. Glen was also a singer with the group *The Four Preps* and they had a big hit with the song ' 26 Miles Across the Sea'."

Oddly enough, Barry played a photographer three times in three different shows. Including *Knight Rider*, Barry played the same role in *Quincy* and *Simon and Simon*. "I had lived with a fashion model in New York and we often socialized with her friends who included fashion photographers, stylists and make-up men. I portrayed fashion photographers, modeling instructors, florists and many of those roles were described as 'colorful', 'flamboyant', 'artistic' or 'sensitive'." Barry believes there was a certain campiness to his role. "In Hollywood at that time, many gay actors were not interested in playing gay roles for fear they would 'out' themselves and not be able to get other work. Most straight actors were incapable of playing gay roles. I, it seemed, knew the secret. I believed all one had to do was to play the human being, not the stereotype. Later, the gay community became more comfortable in society and I was relegated to roles which I call 'people you just want to slap'." In real life, Barry does indeed enjoy photography.

So, what did Barry think of the car? "I don't believe that all the cars were working. I never saw the car move. I did think that it was snappy looking, but at the time I think I was driving a Honda Civic."

Because Barry spent just one day on the episode, he had little interaction with director Harvey Laidman. "Very often, a director will watch a rehearsal and make adjustments with the actors when necessary. I don't remember Mr. Laidman making any suggestions. My scene was not time consuming and was done over one day. So, I would not have been with Mr. Laidman very long."

Barry did not have a scene with David Hasselhoff, but he did leave the set with his shirt. "In the episode, I am wearing a striped shirt that was bought for David. It had his name in it. I got to take it home after the shoot. As a young actor getting to take home a piece of wardrobe was very important and very memorable," says Barry.

Barry is very snap happy in "Custom Made Killer" but he has something to confess. "The camera was empty. No film was harmed in the making of this TV show," jokes Barry.

Along with being an actor, Barry has also been a member of *Sha Na Na,* a retro 1950's rock group. Barry is also a professional whistler, working for composers of TV and film music.

Knight Knotes:

- The Killer car sports the license plate CA 1ALE458. The car that attacks Michael at the drive-in in "Sky Knight" wears the same plate.

- When K.I.T.T. runs a search on fashion companies in the L.A. area, the monitor displays the following: MCA International, run by Lew Wasserman (the real head of the company in 1985); Blowhard, Inc., run by a G. Larson; Inserts Unlimited; Titles and Opticals; Retardo Graphics; Borg Janitorial; Whamtronix, Inc. and Digital Gorilla.

Script to Screen:

- The ramming plate on the killer car is described in the script as "a hi-tech cowcatcher".

- The interior of the killer car is described as "stripped to a shell...A heavily padded roll bar, netting brackets the driver's seat, which is the semi-reclined bucket seat, shoulder and lap straps with heavy double buckles, and next to the driver is a booster fuel tank containing ether (or whatever fuel would boost an engine's speed) which the driver is now turning down..."

- Flood's car originally turns beige in the car wash, not green.

Featured Songs:

"What's Love Got to Do With It" by Tina Turner

K.I.T.T.'s Capabilities:

- Anharmonic Synthesizer, Auto Cruise, Chemical Detectors, Map Search, Medical Scan, Police/Radio Frequency, Priority Override, Pursuit, Record, Telephone Tap, Tinted Windows

PROD. #58604

{ EPISODE
54 }

Script History:

October 1, 1984 (F.R.)

KNIGHT BY A NOSE

Written By: William Elliott

Directed By: Bernard McEveety

Original Airdate: January 13, 1985 (Sunday, 8:00 PM) (21.4%; 18,170,000)

NBC Rerun #1: July 7, 1985 (Sunday, 8:00 PM) (12.7%; 10,780,000)

"Let's just say that I have a hot system."

-K.I.T.T.

Crew: Robert Foster (Executive Producer), Gino Grimaldi (Producer), Gerald Sanford (Producer), Richard Okie (Executive Story Consultant), Robert Sherman (Executive Story Consultant), Larry Mollin (Executive Story Consultant), Ron Martinez (Associate Producer), Bruce Golin (Associate Producer), Robert Ewing (Coordinating Producer), Don Peake (Music), H. John Penner (Director of Photography), Frank Grieco, Jr. (Art Director), R. Lynn Smartt (Set Decoration), Joe Reich (Casting), Domenic G. DiMascio (Film Editor), Pat Somerset (Sound), Ron Martinez (Unit Production Manager), Robert Villar (1st Assistant Director), Bruce A. Humphrey (2nd Assistant Director), John Shouse (Sound Editor), Richard Lapham (Music Editor), Barry Downing (Costume Supervisor), Karen Braverman (Costume Supervisor), Jack Gill (2nd Unit Director-Stunt Coordinator), Jeremy Swan (Make-up), Allen Payne (Hairstylist)

Guest Cast: Patrick St. Esprit (Tommy Lee Burgess), Toni Hudson (Maxine Flemming), F. William Parker (Dr. Harley Thorpe), Don Gordon (Randy Cavanaugh), Dave Cass (Louis), Rene Assa (Rashid), John Allen (Gino), Floyd Levine (Oscar), Leigh Lombardi (Croupier), Roger Rose (Valet)

When Maxine Flemming's horse, King Jack, takes a fall during a routine run, Michael volunteers to help her find the real reason behind the accident.

A Look Back:

Dave Cass returned to *Knight Rider* two years later to play hard man Louis. Cass had some memorable scenes including hitting actor Patrick St. Espirit and knocking out Michael Knight at the illegal gambling house. "We did those scenes more than once, using different angles etc. No one was hurt. I used to get those parts because of my stunt background."

Bernie McEveety directed "Knight By a Nose". "I remember Bernard McEveety well. I did a lot of parts for Bernie and his brother Vince. They both directed a hell of a lot of television including *Gunsmoke* and *Disney MOWS*."

Cass' boss was played by the TV veteran Don Gordon, another returning *Knight Rider* guest star. "I did not know Don very well on a personal basis, but we did work together previously in *Starsky and Hutch*. On set, he was very nice and very professional."

In one scene where Michael and K.I.T.T. are chasing Cass, K.I.T.T. turbo boosts over Cass' car. "I was not there during the filming of that scene. I believe they did that on a 2nd unit."

Cass has fond memories of working in Hollywood at that time. "Those were wonderful years for television in Hollywood. Each network had two or three drama/action shows on each night and movies of the week. This supplied work for hundreds of people. Not just actors and stuntmen, but crew folks, drivers, grips, electricians...I could go on and on. It was a great learning ground for those like myself. We learned things to put into our 'bag of tricks' that are still used today. Directors had their favorite supporting players and used them from show to show and producers would do the same. It was a tighter knit community back then."

When Michael and K.I.T.T. find the illegal gambling house being run by Randy Cavanaugh, he decides to partake in a few spins of the roulette wheel and uses K.I.T.T.'s technology to pick out the winning numbers in order to get Cavanaugh's attention. The croupier was played by Leigh Lombardi. "I don't remember having any training (for the wheel), and I think it was a real one," confirms Lombardi.

Lombardi had previously starred in *Blue Thunder* and *Falcon Crest* before landing a role in *Knight Rider*. "The head of casting at Universal liked me and recommended me to the casting director. I remember wearing really high heels. I was trying to look tall like David Hasselhoff. In order to get a job with David, you had to be at least 5'7", since he is over 6 feet."

Lombardi only stars in a few minutes of the episode, but as she explains, shooting took longer than one would initially think. "Although my part ended up being brief, I actually worked for 2-3 days and that one scene is what they ended up editing it down to." Lombardi ended up sharing all of her on screen time with Hasselhoff. "He was a nice person on set and off," confirms Lombardi. "I was in a restaurant in New York City called Michael's a couple of years ago and he was there. I said 'hello' and reminded him that we had worked together. He was very cordial and he nicely played like he remembered me."

Lombardi remembers one line that gave everyone a laugh. "I had a line that read, 'Close only counts in horse shoes and hand grenades, handsome'. However, on my first take, I said, 'Close only counts in horse grenades and hand shoes, handsome.' It was one of my first jobs and I got tongue tied. Everyone laughed, but I still felt like an idiot. It was one of the most embarrassing moments in my career."

Lombardi remembers her former roles and directors fondly. "My favorite experience was shooting an episode of *T.J. Hooker* on location at Saddle Rock. It is an amazing place with lots of unique animals and antique carriages." Coincidentally, Saddle Rock appeared in *Knight Rider* as Adrianne Margeaux's mansion in "Goliath Returns" and as "The Retreat" in "Knight in Retreat". Lombardi continues, "My favorite TV role was playing Anne Devon in 2002's *Ocean Ave*. It was shot in and around Miami Beach. My favorite movie role was *The Radicals*. It was a period piece and I played the role of Margaretha Sattler. It was based on a true story about Michael and Margaretha Sattler. We filmed in France, Switzerland and Germany in the winter and I almost froze to death! I have worked with so many great directors throughout my career - Mel Brooks, Henry Winkler, Michael

Tuchner, J. Lee Thompson, Art Linson and Peter Douglas. It was a wonderful career."

Knight Knotes:

- Tommy Lee's horse trailer wears a license plate number of CA 3Y83955. This plate is seen again on a van at the start of "Dead of Knight".

- Michael says that he met Maxine while on the "Grimaldi Case", a reference to Gino Grimaldi, show's producer.

- Toni Hudson, who played Maxine, was married to *The A-Team's* Dirk Benedict from 1986 until 1995.

Script to Screen:

- Maxine's horse is a three year old colt named Knightrider. Early on in the script, Michael makes the comment to K.I.T.T., "How can I horse named Knightrider lose?"

- K.I.T.T. distracts Doc Thorpe while Michael investigates his shotgun by calling his office and pretending to be a female checking on her cow. When Doc Thorpe asks what is wrong with the cow, K.I.T.T. responds, "All she does is mooo all day long. Mooo, mooo."

Featured Songs:

"Still the Same" by Bob Seger

K.I.T.T.'s Capabilities:

- Auto Cruise, Auto Currency Dispenser, Auto-Roof Left, Chemical Analyzer, CO2, Infrared, Micro Jam, Oil Slick, Pursuit, Silent Mode, Tinted Windows, Turbo Boost

PROD. #58641

$$\left\{ \begin{array}{c} \text{EPISODE} \\ 55 \end{array} \right\}$$

Script History:

December 4, 1984 (F.R.)

EN December 10, 1984 (F.R.)

December 11, 1984 (F.R.)

December 12, 1984 (F.R.)

December 13, 1984 (F.R.)

December 13, 1984 (2nd rev.)

December 14, 1984 (F.R.)

JUNK YARD DOG

Working Title: "Junkyard Dog"

Written By: Calvin Clements, Jr.

Directed By: Georg Fenady

Original Airdate: February 3, 1985 (Sunday, 8:00 PM) (20.2%; 17,150,000)

NBC Rerun #1: August 9, 1985 (Friday, 8:00 PM)

"You know, Bonnie, it's funny. Sometimes it takes something like this to make you realize how much you take people for granted. I'd forgotten how good you really are."

-Michael

Crew: Robert Foster (Executive Producer), Gino Grimaldi (Producer), Calvin Clements, Jr. (Producer), Gerald Sanford (Producer), Burton Armus (Producer), Richard Okie (Executive Story Consultant), Gregory S. Dinallo (Executive Script Consultant), Ron Martinez (Associate Producer), Bruce Golin (Associate Producer), Robert Ewing (Coordinating Producer), Don Peake (Music), H. John Penner (Director of Photography), Frank Grieco, Jr. (Art Director), R. Lynn Smartt (Set Decoration), Joe Reich (Casting), Lawrence J. Gleason (Film Editor), Domenic G. DiMascio (Film Editor), Pat Somerset (Sound), Ron Martinez (Unit Production Manager), Louis Race (1st Assistant Director), Bruce A. Humphrey (2nd Assistant Director), John Shouse (Sound Editor), Richard Lapham (Music Editor), Barry Downing (Costume Supervisor), Karen Braverman (Costume Supervisor), Jack Gill (2nd Unit Director-Stunt Coordinator), Jeremy Swan (Make-up), Allen Payne (Hairstylist)

Guest Cast: Ramon Bieri ("Acid" John Birock), Heather McNair (Fran), Curt Lowens (Dr. Von Voorman), Alex Kubik (Mike "The Torch" Zoormagian), Jim B. Raymond (Arthur Stiles), Kathy Shower (Tori), Louis Elias (Chuck)

K.I.T.T. is eaten alive in an acid pit when Michael investigates a businessman suspected of dumping illegal chemicals into the ground.

A Look Back:

In this installment, viewers are exposed to K.I.T.T. being dumped into a corrosive acid pit and nearly destroyed. Later on, he's seen in a primer undercoat. Stunt coordinator Jack Gill remembers having these uniquely dressed cars on set. "The *Knight Rider* car that was dropped into corrosive acid was the art director's work. He had just seamed the car to make it look like it was being rotted from the inside. That car was still very useable. You could clean that car up and bring it back to pristine condition fairly easily. So it was just made to look like it was all coming apart. As far as the primered car, that was actually just painted that color. I had a few of them there and I just kind of played in the parking lot and then built some obstacles and drove around them. It wasn't a thin skin - that was the actual paint that was on the car."

David Hasselhoff prepares for filming. (Photo courtesy of Tyler Ham)

Knight Knotes:

- Gerald Sanford on this episode: "They kept changing the show, trying to find a way to build an audience. They had a terrific new script by Calvin Clements called 'Junk Yard Dog'. It was darker and more aimed at the things Foster and I were trying to do. However, they just did it that one show and then went right back to the safe, *Knight Rider* premise."

- A quick eye can spot a set of keys in the ignition of K.I.T.T.'s gutted interior when Michael examines the damage. The keys sport a

Universal Studios tag. Also of note – the car used to simulate K.I.T.T.'s shell was a manual transmission, as evidenced by the larger driveshaft tunnel cut-out.

Script to Screen:

- After K.I.T.T.'s shell was pulled from the acid pit, Michael originally reaches for the remains of his voice box only to have it crumble at his touch.

- At the start of the episode, Michael tries to convince K.I.T.T. to allow him to airbrush a surfing scene on his door with the words "K.I.T.T. – the love machine" on the side. When K.I.T.T. says that the conversation is straining his audio sensors, Michael agrees to stick with basic black.

- During the scene in the semi where Bonnie shows Michael a tape of Birock, the script says that Bonnie should either have "a video disc (or VCR cassette)" to put in the machine.

- The description of the tractor used to lift K.I.T.T. into the acid pit: "It's (literally) a custom tractor truck, (figuratively) the meanest 'junk yard dog' to K.I.T.T.'s 'pedigree.'"

- The description of K.I.T.T. going under in the acid pit: "The last of him sinks into the bubbling smoking mess...and, finally, his red scanner grows pale, then stops as he disappears from sight."

- The description of the first time we see K.I.T.T. after being dumped into the acid pit: "K.I.T.T. has only (steel belt) shreds of an interior left. Shreds of other 'stuff' (trim, wiring) hang festooned from the car. There are only splotches of paint. There is no upholstery. The car might well have been burned to its metal skeleton, which, in fact, is pretty much what happened."

- Bonnie sits at a computer console, trying to access K.I.T.T.'s memory. She types, "YOU ARE THE KNIGHT INDUSTRIES TWO-THOUSAND. WHO ARE YOU?" into the computer, but gets no response.

Déjà Vu:

- Kathy Shower is back in "Knight of a Thousand Devils".

K.I.T.T.'s Capabilities:

- Audio/Video Record, Auto Cruise, Micro Jam, Silent Mode, Ski Mode, Turbo Boost

PROD. #58643

$$\left[\begin{array}{c} \text{EPISODE} \\ 56 \end{array} \right]$$

Script History:

January 7, 1985 (F.R.)

BUY OUT

Working Title: "Buyout"

Written By: Gregory S. Dinallo

Directed By: Jeffrey Hayden

Original Airdate: February 10, 1985 (Sunday, 8:00 PM) (22.5%; 19,100,000)

NBC Rerun #1: August 23, 1985 (Friday, 8:00 PM) (13.2%; 11,210,000)

"Melanie. The heat chamber. Open that door. Not now. Open that door, then

you have my permission to faint."

-K.I.T.T.

Crew: Robert Foster (Executive Producer), Burton Armus (Producer), Gino Grimaldi (Producer), Gerald Sanford (Producer), Richard Okie (Executive Story Consultant), Gregory S. Dinallo (Executive Script Consultant), Ron Martinez (Associate Producer), Bruce Golin (Associate Producer), Robert Ewing (Coordinating Producer), Don Peake (Music), H. John Penner (Director of Photography), Frank Grieco, Jr. (Art Director), R. Lynn Smartt (Set Decoration), Joe Reich (Casting), Lawrence J. Vallario (Film Editor), Pat Somerset (Sound), Ron Martinez (Unit Production Manager), Louis Race (1st Assistant Director), Bruce A. Humphrey (2nd Assistant Director), John Shouse (Sound Editor), Richard Lapham (Music Editor), Barry Downing (Costume Supervisor), Karen Braverman (Costume Supervisor), Jack Gill (2nd Unit Director-Stunt Coordinator), Jeremy Swan (Make-up), Allen Payne (Hairstylist)

Guest Cast: Clu Gulager (Eugene Hanson), Jesse Vint (Hank Kagan), Susanne Reed (Lilah Graham), John vanDreelen (Hans Kleiser), Robin Dearden (Melanie Mitchell), Than Wyenn (Theo Corelli), Bernie White (Eddie Deskey), Jack Gill (Ray Jordan, Limo Driver)

Michael and K.I.T.T. investigate the explosion of a supposedly indestructible armored limousine.

A Look Back:

A quick eye can spot stunt coordinator Jack Gill behind the wheel of the doomed limo at the episode's introduction. Gill appeared in numerous other bit parts throughout the course of the series and explains why he took on the additional work. "What really happened is that I needed a stunt driver to play this part. David Hasselhoff said, 'Why don't you do it and you can get your face on camera at the same time and have a little fun?'. That was the only reason I really did it. I still needed a stunt guy to play it, so I just went ahead and jumped into the clothes and did it myself. It wasn't out of convenience, just that Hasselhoff said to do it. In the past, I had driven limousines and different vehicles on the show. It was about having fun on the show, and the scene was fun for me and David."

Knight Knotes:

- The limo that takes the potential buyers to the airport sports the license plate CA 095XID – which happens to be the same plate that is on Soltis' limo in "Knightlines".
- The name of Clu Gulager's character, Gene Hanson, is the same as an uncredited writer of the previous episode "Junk Yard Dog".

Script to Screen:

- The name of the driver in the doomed limo at the start of the episode is revealed to be Ray Jordan.
- Armborbuilt was originally named Armorclad.
- It is revealed that Michael and K.I.T.T. were returning from a successful mission in Washington, D.C. when this episode starts.
- Michael and K.I.T.T.'s "audition" for Armorbuilt originally included a turbo boosts and both left and right profile ski modes (as they are called in the script) before performing the continuous 360's as seen in the episode. They also catch the attention of Lonnie Londell, an automobile circus performer who is driving by the test track at that particular time. It is Lonnie, not Eddie Deskey, who persistently tries to buy K.I.T.T.

K.I.T.T.'s Capabilities:

- Audio Playback, Auto Cruise, Chemical Scan, Map Search, Micro Jam, Pursuit, Radar, Turbo Boost

PROD. #58644

$$\left[\begin{array}{c} \text{EPISODE} \\ 57 \end{array}\right]$$

Script History:

January 17, 1985 (F.R.)

January 21, 1985 (F.R.)

KNIGHTLINES

Written By: Richard Okie

Directed By: Charles Watson Sanford

Original Airdate: March 3, 1985 (Sunday, 8:00 PM) (19.8%; 16,810,000)

NBC Rerun #1: July 28, 1985 (Sunday, 8:00 PM) (14.8%; 12,570,000)

"Are you expecting something to fall on your head?"

-K.I.T.T.

Crew: Robert Foster (Executive Producer), Gino Grimaldi (Producer), Burton Armus (Producer), Gerald Sanford (Producer), Richard Okie (Executive Story Consultant), Gregory S. Dinallo (Executive Script Consultant), Ron Martinez (Associate Producer), Bruce Golin (Associate Producer), Robert Ewing (Coordinating Producer), Don Peake (Music), H. John Penner (Director of Photography), Frank Grieco, Jr. (Art Director), R. Lynn Smartt (Set Decoration), Joe Reich (Casting), Domenic G. DiMascio (Film Editor), Pat Somerset (Sound), Ron Martinez (Unit Production Manager), Robert Villar (1st Assistant Director), Bruce A. Humphrey (2nd Assistant Director), John Shouse (Sound Editor), Richard Lapham (Music Editor), Barry Downing (Costume Supervisor), Karen Braverman (Costume Supervisor), Jack Gill (2nd Unit Director-Stunt Coordinator), Jeremy Swan (Make-up), Allen Payne (Hairstylist)

Guest Cast: Taylor Miller (Janet Morgan), Joe LaDue (Dan Hannegan), Hank Garrett (Stephen Barnes), Frank Annese (Soltis), Andre Gower (Billy), Bob Delegall (Lieutenant Rayford), Sally Hampton (Seline), Roy David (Jack the Cop)

Michael investigates a young widow's claim that her husband's supposed accidental death at a construction site was in actuality a murder.

A Look Back:

Near the episode's conclusion, K.I.T.T. is seen turbo boosting through a pile of concrete blocks. Jack Gill explains how this scene was set up. "This effect was a jump into concrete blocks. It was supposed to be concrete blocks, but what we created was a material called pyrocel and it's a really lightweight, air raided kind of Plaster of Paris material that looks very similar to concrete. When it comes apart, it looks exactly like concrete and makes powder but it's not as damaging as concrete. It's very lightweight and brittle.

Pyrocel is what the effects guys made all those props out of and this scene is essentially just a mini ramp jump into concrete blocks."

Knight Knotes:

- Andre Gower played a character named Billy only five months earlier in *The A-Team* episode "Timber!".

Script to Screen:

- Megafax Industries was originally called Megatron, assumingly changed due to the name being the same as a character on *Transformers,* which had premiered a year prior. When Devon tells Michael about the company, he says that it sounds like a *Masters of the Universe* toy.
- The giant crane that hits K.I.T.T. is known as the Mega-4.

K.I.T.T.'s Capabilities:

- Air Vac, Audio/Video Record, Auto-Roof Left, Micro Jam, Printer, Trunk Lid, Turbo Boost, Ultrasonic Frequency, Zoom-In

PROD. #58627

{ EPISODE
58 }

Script History:

October 12, 1984 (F.R.)

THE NINETEENTH HOLE

Written By: Gerald Sanford and Robert Foster

Directed By: Georg Fenady

Original Airdate: March 10, 1985 (Sunday, 8:00 PM) (20.5%; 17,400,000)

"Michael, I've heard of automatic drive before, but this is ridiculous!"

-Jamie Downs

Crew: Robert Foster (Executive Producer), Gino Grimaldi (Producer), Gerald Sanford (Producer), Richard Okie (Executive Story Consultant), Robert Sherman (Executive Story Consultant), Ron Martinez (Associate Producer), Bruce Golin (Associate Producer), Robert Ewing (Coordinating Producer), Don Peake (Music), H. John Penner (Director of Photography), Frank Grieco, Jr. (Art Director), R. Lynn Smartt (Set Decoration), Joe Reich (Casting), Grant Hoag (Film Editor), Pat Somerset (Sound), Ron Martinez (Unit Production Manager), Louis Race (1st Assistant Director), Bruce A. Humphrey (2nd Assistant Director), John Shouse (Sound Editor), Richard Lapham (Music Editor), Barry Downing (Costume Supervisor), Karen Braverman (Costume Supervisor), Jack Gill (2nd Unit Director-Stunt Coordinator), Jeremy Swan (Make-up), Allen Payne (Hairstylist)

Guest Cast: Wendy Schaal (Jamie Downs), Michael McManus (Danny "Rooster" Roskovich), Cliff Carnell (Joey Rome), Albert Paulsen (Mr. Caesar), Brendon Boone (Motel Clerk), Rebecca Perle (Daisy Doolittle), John La Motta (Benji Bomper), Borah Silver (Nick), Bill Harlow (Man)

After receiving threatening letters ordering her to cancel a car race, Jamie Downs calls the Foundation to help her find the ones who wrote the letter and ensure that the race is a success.

David Hasselhoff receives a last minute touch-up before filming (Photo
courtesy of Tyler Ham)

A Look Back:

"The Nineteenth Hole" featured guest star Wendy Schaal, who had appeared in numerous television productions (including Glen Larson's short lived series *Cover Up*) before landing the role in *Knight Rider*. "My agent submitted me for the role. I remember that David Hasselhoff was very tall and they needed girls over 5'7", so I did fib about my height by a couple of inches. Thank heavens they didn't have a measuring tape at the casting session!"

Schaal's character, Jamie Downs, is a no fear newspaper reporter who seemingly stops at nothing to get her story, a determination that Schaal shares with the character. "Once I go into something, you're not going to tell me to stop," confirms Schaal. But that's where Schaal and Jamie Downs go their separate ways. "As far as taking risks? I'm a mamby pamby wuss, unlike Jamie."

Schaal remembers director Georg Fenady well. "I remember Georg as easy going and very pleasant. We had lots of physical work to do and it was a large cast. That can make some directors pretty fussy, but not Georg."

"The Nineteenth Hole" is entirely shot on location, something Schaal prefers. "I always liked working on location. They feel like a paid camping trip. I think the motel we filmed in was real. We just changed the sign at the front. I also must have blocked out the sign wearing my hair like that - shocking!" jokes Schaal.

Most of Schaal's on screen time is with Michael Knight. "David was enthusiastic about everything. He approached ideas and his other projects (singing at the time) like it was something else 'neat' to do. It was like he never saw a barrier to doing anything - almost childlike. He made working on the show fun."

Schaal's character has an eventful time in the episode to include her almost being blown up, getting kidnapped, organizing a road race and taking on gangsters. "I remember having a stunt double for the more dangerous moves, so I don't remember having to worry about getting hurt due to the explosions and the mafia threats." As for the gangsters themselves? "We all worked on a quilt together under a tree," jokes Schaal. "I remember between takes they would tell me that if I didn't make my stitches smaller, they were going to pop me one!"

Schaal was a passenger in K.I.T.T., but did she get the opportunity to drive the car? "No way," says Schaal. "The production company wasn't stupid!"

Schaal remembers Patricia McPherson and Edward Mulhare fondly. "Unfortunately, we only had that one scene together, but it was such an easy one that I remember it being very relaxed and friendly. And remember, we got French fries! How bad could it have been?"

Jack Gill directed the big scene where K.I.T.T. jumps over Rooster's car and into an electric fence. Gill recalls the challenges of this scene. "This was a jump that my brother Andy did. He was jumping over Mike Tillman, who is not with us anymore. Mike was in the red car with the big blower on it. This jump had to be timed precisely because the car had to land directly in front of the electric wire that was strung across the road so we had to time it so Andy was jumping over Mike Tillman. I was directing 2nd unit at the time, so we did some practice runs with Andy driving past the ramp and not hitting the ramp. Then, we tried to figure out where he would actually land. He can't land on the wires - he had to land in front of them and Andy can't land on Mike Tillman, so this was a tough shot. But it came out perfectly and the timing was perfect. Andy landed in front of the wires, tripped them, and K.I.T.T. took the brunt of the electricity and not the red car, which is what we wanted."

Andy Gill, who was helming K.I.T.T. during this stunt, recalls working through the logistics of the stunt to ensure it went off without a hitch. "I jumped K.I.T.T. over the Camaro and landed in front of the sparking wires. We did the jump out on a dirt road that is now Avenida De Los Arbolus and the surrounding housing community. It was just a ranch with nothing but one paved road when we filmed there in the 80's. The jump was one of my favorites. Jack was directing 2nd unit and we were running out of time. He asked me if I could jump over the Camaro, land and go through the wires that FX would rig to spark in one shot. We had planned on filming the jump over the Camaro stunt and then, in a separate shot, film a mini ramp landing and then going through the sparks. I said I could do it and he told me to tell FX where to place the wires. A good friend and one of the finest stuntmen I ever met was driving the Camaro under me. His name was Mike Tillman. Mike and I discussed how to make this shot work. We set the aluminum split ramps that we always used for the take-off. It was going to be one of the longer type jumps we normally performed so we set the ramps accordingly. The aluminum ramps were 14' long and 32" high in the standard positions. This was good for 60-80' long jumps about 6-8' high in the air. We needed more so we put our 2' ramp extension on the front of the ramp making it 16' long. We raised the height of the ramp to 36" as well. This configuration would normally get the car to travel 80-110' (the faster you went, the further you would travel) and about 10-14' high. I wanted to jump the car and land between the 90' to 110' marks so I told the FX crew where I thought I would land and then gave myself a few more car lengths to get the car controlled and then picked the spot to place the wires. Jack didn't want the wires too far from the landing so he asked me to place them as close as I could without jumping over them. I picked the spot, Jack placed his cameras accordingly and then Mike Tillman and I began discussing how we were going to get K.I.T.T. to jump over the top of the Camaro (not beside it), land in front of it and then go through the wires. The problem was the Camaro wasn't going to hit the jump ramps so he would have to drive beside the ramp and then dive in underneath K.I.T.T. , then slow down so the flying K.I.T.T. has time to pass over the top and land in front. We discussed speeds and we decided on coming in at the ramp at 50mph. The best way to do the jump would be for Mike to drive to the right side of the ramps about one car length ahead of me. This way, when I was hitting the ramp and gassing it on the ramp, Mike would already be clear of the ramp so he could slide under me and let off the gas. We had a mark at 60' and 80' for Mike. If he didn't see me enter his windshield view at the 60' mark he would slow. If he didn't see me when he was approaching the 80' mark he was to dive to the right and stop. The reason we picked these marks was I know I was going to make the 90' landing mark. If he didn't see me then he would probably be too far in front of me so he would be driving and entering my landing zone. This was our out if things didn't time out correctly. We performed the stunt and it went perfectly! Mike was dead on with his timing and I was dead on with the jump distance. Because of the time crunch, this is one of the shots in the *Knight Rider* series where you see K.I.T.T. take on damage when it lands but in the next shot K.I.T.T. is perfect again."

Knight Knotes:

- Watch the chase between Rooster and Michael –Michael's clothes change from a green and white jacket to his black leather jacket!

Script to Screen:

- The restaurant where the car owners are parked is known as Manny's Drive-In.

Déjà Vu:

- Cliff Carnel returns in "Knight Racer".

Featured Songs:

"Shout at the Devil" by Motley Crue

K.I.T.T.'s Capabilities:

- Anharmonic Synthesizer, Auto Cruise, Chemical Analyzer, Geological Analyzer, Image Enhancement Software Program, Laser Modulator, Map Search, Medical Scan, Micro Jam, Passive Laser Restraint System, Pursuit, Silent Mode, Suspension Synchronizer, System – Protect, Telephone Trace, Turbo Boost, Voice Projection, XK100 Thermal Printer

PROD. #58630

$$\left[\ \begin{array}{c} \text{EPISODE} \\ 59 \end{array}\ \right]$$

Script History:

September 24, 1984

KNIGHT & KNERD

Working Title: "Knight And Knerd"

Written By: Larry Mollin

Directed By: Georg Fenady

Original Airdate: March 17, 1985 (Sunday, 8:00 PM) (20.3%; 17,230,000)

"If you've got it, flaunt it."

-Elliott Sykes

Crew: Robert Foster (Executive Producer), Gino Grimaldi (Producer), Gerald Sanford (Producer), Larry Mollin (Executive Story Consultant), Richard Okie (Story Editor), Ron Martinez (Associate Producer), Bruce Golin (Associate Producer), Robert Ewing (Coordinating Producer), Don Peake (Music), H. John Penner (Director of Photography), Frank Grieco, Jr. (Art Director), R. Lynn Smartt (Set Decoration), Joe Reich (Casting), Edward Nassour (Film Editor), Pat Somerset (Sound), Ron Martinez (Unit Production Manager), Louis Race (1st Assistant Director), Bruce A. Humphrey (2nd Assistant Director), John Shouse (Sound Editor), Richard Lapham (Music Editor), Barry Downing (Costume Supervisor), Karen Braverman (Costume Supervisor), Jack Gill (2nd Unit Director-Stunt Coordinator), Jeremy Swan (Make-up), Allen Payne (Hairstylist)

Guest Cast: Arye Gross (Elliott Sykes), Steve Sandor (Mac Gifford), Tawny Moyer (Ali Raymond), Victoria Bass (Vanessa Mary Sutton), Lou Felder (Thomas Raymond), Cheryl M. Lynn (Jeanie)

Michael must protect a woman after a group of ninjas kill her father in search of a rare crystal.

A Look Back:

Starting at the beginning of season three, the *Knight Rider* crew began using a new Trans Am for interior driving shots. This car was a stock black and gold Trans Am on the outside, with a dash shell and overhead console inside. This is also the car that featured Pontiac's split rear seat, a 1983 and up feature. Jack Gill explains why they didn't bother converting the exterior. "We did this because, back then, we had to pump so much light into the inside of the hero car so that you could see the actors. But, it melted the paint on the outside of the car and you couldn't really use that as an extra because the paint would bubble up. You don't have to use those kind of lights anymore because the camera and film are so much better, but back then, we had 8 lights mounted to the car. They would generate intense heat, especially in the summer. I can remember sitting in the car and watching the paint bubble up and melt the rubber molding around the windshield, so it was pretty hot."

Knight Knotes:

- Knerd was created from a 1983 50cc Derbi Variant moped.
- The green 4x4 used at the end of this episode sports a license plate of CA 819 TJD. This same plate is used as the front plate on Bianca's red 4x4 in "Knight in Retreat".

Script to Screen:

- In early scripts, a special refracting windshield was developed to protect K.I.T.T. from the thermal laser instead of the chemical insulating formula seen in the episode.
- Another cut scene has K.I.T.T. asking permission from Michael to eject him out if the laser is going to hit K.I.T.T.'s body. Michael denies his request, telling him to not be so negative.
- K.I.T.T. asks Michael if there's anyone that he's ever admired for a well-rounded accomplishment to which Michael responds, "Belinda." K.I.T.T. dryly responds, "Yes... very accomplished" and Michael finishes with, "Not to mention well-rounded."
- The description of the first time we see Elliott Sykes: "Elliott is dressed like your quintessential nerd: white shirt with top button buttoned. Pocket filled with pens. Calculator on his belt and glasses which are currently steamed over in the smoky room."
- Elliott's laugh is described as "nervous" and "asthmatic".

- When Gifford's men kidnap Ali and Elliott runs out after her, Michael and K.I.T.T. originally don't stop to talk with Elliott, but rather speed by, and, according to the script, "splash a puddle of water onto his new Knight Rider shirt."

- The insulating solution that Bonnie and Elliott create was originally a polarized refracting windshield that they install on K.I.T.T.

- Michael, fearing for K.I.T.T.'s safety, originally shuts him down when they arrive in Mars Canyon. Later, K.I.T.T. asks Michael for permission to eject him out if he believes that Michael will die when they confront Gifford and Sutton at the diamond exchange.

Déjà Vu:
- Victoria Bass returns in "Knight Behind Bars".

Featured Songs:
"Run To You" by Bryan Adams

K.I.T.T.'s Capabilities:
- Anharmonic Synthesizer, Auto Cruise, Medical Scan, Signal, Silent Mode, Turbo Boost, X-Ray Mode

PROD. #58645

$$\left[\begin{array}{c} \text{EPISODE} \\ 60 \end{array} \right]$$

Script History:

January 28, 1985 (F.R.)

TEN WHEEL TROUBLE

Written By: Burton Armus

Directed By: Robert Bralver

Original Airdate: March 24, 1985 (Sunday, 8:00 PM) (20.4%; 17,320,000)

NBC Rerun #1: September 6, 1985 (Friday, 8:00 PM) (15.0%; 12,890,000)

"K.I.T.T. is his. I just put him back together again."

-Bonnie

Crew: Robert Foster (Executive Producer), Gino Grimaldi (Producer), Burton Armus (Producer), Richard Okie (Executive Story Consultant), Gregory S. Dinallo (Executive Script Consultant), Ron Martinez (Associate Producer), Bruce Golin (Associate Producer), Robert Ewing (Coordinating Producer), Don Peake (Music), H. John Penner (Director of Photography), Frank Grieco, Jr. (Art Director), R. Lynn Smartt (Set Decoration), Joe Reich (Casting), Lawrence J. Gleason (Film Editor), Pat Somerset (Sound), Ron Martinez (Unit Production Manager), Louis Race (1st Assistant Director), Bruce A. Humphrey (2nd Assistant Director), John Shouse (Sound Editor), Richard Lapham (Music Editor), Barry Downing (Costume Supervisor), Karen Braverman (Costume Supervisor), Jack Gill (2nd Unit Director-Stunt Coordinator), Jeremy Swan (Make-up), Allen Payne (Hairstylist)

Guest Cast: Robert Hogan (Shatner), Babette Props (Sally Flynn), Jamie Cromwell (Mike Curtis), Ji-Tu Cumbuka (Trucker), Christopher McDonald (Joe Flynn), Cliff Emmich (My. Lyndon), Diane McBain (Mama Flynn), Darwin Joston (Burgers), Bruce Neckels (Phil Janetti)

Michael must clear a trucker accused of cutting the brake lines on a truck and killing the man inside.

A Look Back:

When Babette Props won the role of Sally Flynn in "Ten Wheel Trouble", she was over the moon. "I grew up watching *Knight Rider,* so I was so excited to be in the show and work with K.I.T.T. I kept thinking, 'Oh yeah, it is going to be like the Batmobile! Welcome to Hollywood, kid!'".

As Flynn, Props played a hopeful and feisty 15 year old who taps into F.L.A.G.'s computers to ask for help. In real life, Props had just turned 23. "I didn't land my first adult role until I was 26 years old," confirms Props.

"Nobody would hire me for roles over the age of sixteen. I remember that I auditioned for *Knight Rider* coming off a picture with John Hughes [*Weird Science*] and another film with Laurent Hutton, where I played a 15 year old."

Props shared most of her screen time with David Hasselhoff and recalls one scene in particular where she really let him have it. "David was great and very funny. We had one scene where I had to hit him in the face and I really let him have it. He was shook up a bit but he rolled with it." Her character's scene in the semi also meant working with Edward Mulhare, Patricia McPherson and, of course, K.I.T.T. "Patricia and Ed were great to work with - very giving actors. K.I.T.T. was a shell of a car and the script supervisor sat on the sidelines on an apple box and fed me the lines!"

Props recalls the final scene of the episode where she had to kiss David Hasselhoff. "David was a tall guy. I had to stand on top of three apple boxes for the end scene where my character says goodbye. I think I still have the head shot David gave me of himself signed, 'To Props - the best kisser'."

When the episode first aired in March of 1985, Props was watching with her own family. "I remember watching it with my three year old daughter, Charlee. Now she has a daughter about the same age."

Props was already establishing her resume with impressive TV and movie appearances before *Knight Rider* and she would go on to star in such diverse fare as *Santa Barbara* and *Seinfeld*. She also starred alongside an all-star cast in 1995's *Get Shorty*. "I enjoyed playing the role of Nikki with John Travolta, Danny DeVito and Renee Russo. We laughed so much and I also remember having lunch with Gene Hackman. He was so down to Earth and ate with the crew and was sexy in person." Theater remains Props' first love. "The role of Erica in *Bogosians Suburbia* at the Lincoln Center was amazing. Theater is my first and true love."

Knight Knotes:

- K.I.T.T.'s impact with the two sedans near the end of the episode is reused from "A Plush Ride".

- Sally mentions to Michael that his next stop is at Armorbuilt – a reference to the company featured only a few episodes earlier in "Buy Out". In another odd coincidence, the radio broadcaster at the start of the episode is named Eugene Hanson – the same name as the antagonist in "Buy Out".

- Joe Flynn is seen throughout the episode wearing a yellow hat with the Leute Corporation insignia. Erik Whitby can be seen wearing this same hat in the next season episode "Out of the Woods".

Script to Screen:

- Curtis' first name is revealed to be Mike, while the African American trucker is named Frank Dial.

- Shatner is originally given the name of Edmund Jordon.

- During the scene where Michael stops Joe Flynn on the road, K.I.T.T. was originally to use his turbo boosters for speed to pass the truck. This variation of the turbo boost hasn't been used since the first season.

- During the final convoy scene where the F.L.A.G. semi is being used, Michael calls Devon from K.I.T.T. Devon responds, "Michael, if you're talking to me on the monitor, who's driving my F.L.A.G. vehicle?" Devon becomes nervous when Michael tells her that Mama Flynn is driving.

K.I.T.T.'s Capabilities:

- Anharmonic Synthesizer, Audio/Video Playback, Audio/Video Record, Auto Cruise, Auto-Roof Left, Homing Device, Infrared, Map Search, Micro Jam, Pursuit, Radar, Record, Signal, Ski Mode, Telephone Monitor, Telephone Tap, Telephone Trace, Turbo Boost

PROD. #58642

Script History:

December 26, 1984 (F.R.)

December 30, 1984 (F.R.)

KNIGHT IN RETREAT

Working Title: "Weekend Dreams"

Written By: Gerald Sanford

Directed By: Roy Campanella Jr.

Original Airdate: March 29, 1985 (Friday, 8:00 PM) (21.0%; 17,830,000)

NBC Rerun #1: August 4, 1985 (Sunday, 8:00 PM) (14.4%; 12,230,000)

"Michael, whatever happened to the good old days when we simply turbo boosted over fences and crashed through walls?"

-K.I.T.T.

Crew: Robert Foster (Executive Producer), Gino Grimaldi (Producer), Burton Armus (Producer), Gerald Sanford (Producer), Richard Okie (Executive Story Consultant), Gregory S. Dinallo (Executive Script Consultant), Ron Martinez (Associate Producer), Bruce Golin (Associate Producer), Robert Ewing (Coordinating Producer), Don Peake (Music), H. John Penner (Director of Photography), Frank Grieco, Jr. (Art Director), R. Lynn Smartt (Set Decoration), Joe Reich (Casting), Grant Hoag (Film Editor), Pat Somerset (Sound), Ron Martinez (Unit Production Manager), Robert Villar (1st Assistant Director), Bruce A. Humphrey (2nd Assistant Director), John Shouse (Sound Editor), Richard Lapham (Music Editor), Barry Downing (Costume Supervisor), Karen Braverman (Costume Supervisor), Jack Gill (2nd Unit Director-Stunt Coordinator), Jeremy Swan (Make-up), Allen Payne (Hairstylist)

Guest Cast: Ann Turkel (Bianca Morgan), Don Galloway (Harley Freeman), Randi Brooks (Tanya), Sandra Kronemeyer (Monica Brown), Dani Minnick (Veronica), David Hedison (Ted Cooper)

Michael infiltrates a retreat run by three beautiful women who are working to acquire parts to form a dangerous missile.

A Look Back:

After starring as Adrianne Margeaux in two separate episodes in season 2, Ann Turkel returned for a third and final time in season three's "Knight in Retreat". But, with Adrianne killed off at the end of "Goliath Returns", Turkel would play a completely different character named Bianca Morgan. She still, however, reprised the role of the villain. "Thinking back, that may have confused some fans with the fact that the same person was playing a different character. I think all they had to do was a quick flashback to the cliff and have Adrianne running from the scene. I think that could have worked and would have been easy. It sure would have been a great way to have the character return for a third time."

Though Turkel was becoming a somewhat regular face on the show, she confirms that she did not have much of a chance to improvise. "That never really happened. David and I would simply rehearse our lines together and we would take it from there, ready for the next scene."

"Knight in Retreat" was directed by Roy Campnella Jr. "Roy was a very good director. He knew what had to be done and did a great job. I remember that I worked alongside his father, who was a very famous baseball player." The episode also meant that Turkel would be required to work alongside animals. "I love animals," says Turkel. "I love dogs and wild animals. I'm not a huge fan of cats, yet I love wild cats. I remember once doing an advert with a lion. And when I looked over at the lion, I became frightened as he did not look as docile and tame as I was led to believe."

Turkel has had quite a distinguished career as a model and actress, working in television and film for over 40 years, and she has wonderful memories of her time as perhaps the greatest *Knight Rider* villain ever. "It was very interesting watching the episodes again. It's the first time in nearly 30 years that I viewed them. I got very engrossed in watching them and I am proud and happy that I starred in *Knight Rider*."

Sandra Kronemeyer played Monica Brown in this episode and has fond memories of her time on set. "I was first shown to the casting director and then I got a call back from the producers," says Kronemeyer. "The audition process was exciting and scary at the same time, but everyone was very kind."

Kronemeyer had already starred in Glen Larson's *The Fall Guy* and had also appeared in such popular TV shows as *T.J. Hooker* and *Hart to Hart* before landing a job on *Knight Rider*. "Before acting, I had been an International Flight Attendant and a successful model and commercial actress in San Francisco." It was here where Kronemeyer's career would change forever. "ABC was doing a nationwide talent search in San Francisco and they told me that I should move to Los Angeles and find an agent. Before I was able to move to L.A., I was cast in a small part in the movie *The Right Stuff*. I tried out to play Sally Rand, a blonde fan dancer. Mind you, I was not a dancer, nor was I blonde. I am 5' 11" and a redhead so after the audition, I stuck my head in the room and asked if there was anything else that I might be right for and he let me go for another part and that's how it all started."

Kronemeyer starred opposite Ann Turkel, who was appearing in her third and final *Knight Rider* episode. "Ann was very approachable and very business-like. All of us girls got along very well." Kronemeyer also has kind words for David Hasselhoff and director Roy Campanella. "David was such a kick! He worked very hard and played hard. He was funny and kind as well. Roy was a terrific director. Very easy to work with and I had the opportunity to do so more than once. Things on set always moved along well and he always got the right take."

While "Knight in Retreat" appears to have been shot on a typically sunny California day, Kronemeyer explains that conditions were far from perfect. "I remember the shoot being very cold outside and the water was cold in the hot tub scene." The episode is also unique as the episode's "bad guys" were actually "bad women". Kronemeyer reflects, "Why shouldn't women be the bad girls? We can be just as devious as the men. My nature is good and kind so it is less of a challenge."

(Photo courtesy of Sandra Kronemeyer)

After *Knight Rider*, Kronemeyer went on to co-star in a host of other prime time shows, but it is perhaps her recurring role in *Airwolf* where she is best remembered by her fans. "I played Lydia in a recurring role in *Airwolf*. I flew in helicopters and drove limousines. What a ball!"

Stunt coordinator Jack Gill drove K.I.T.T. during the big parachute scene and recalls some of the challenges associated with it. "The scene with K.I.T.T. pulling Michael Knight up on a parachute was done on Cayman Dune Road right by Calamino's Ranch where they did a lot of filming. The scene was actually shot on Mulholland Highway – it's an offshoot of Cayman Dune Road. We shot this on a two lane road."

One of the things that was touchy during the shoot was that it was pretty windy that day. "We had already done the scene of the parachutist jumping out of the helicopter and parachute in as if he is going over the fence to the inside of the compound. But we still needed to do the blind drive of Michael Knight being pulled up by K.I.T.T. to start this thing. I had David run behind the car with the parachute and I'm blind driving the car. I said to him that the parachute wouldn't really pick him up in the air and even if it did, I would be looking in my mirrors and trying to slow down. I didn't want David to be 10-15 feet high in the air and then the parachute stalls on him. So we were very careful about that, but David did have to run pretty fast behind me to get some air in the parachute."

When they were ready to shoot the scene, the production got a real parachutist in and Gill ended up dragging him up in the air. "The minute he disconnected from the cable," recalls Gill, "I got above the mountain range. On the right hand side of K.I.T.T. was a high mountain range and there was a lot of wind blowing over the top of that range. So, as soon as he got enough altitude to hit that wind, it pitched him sideways and he swayed right and left really bad and came in for a really hard landing. Luckily he wasn't hurt, but it scared all of us because he flopped pretty hard with the wind. It's a good thing that I didn't let David go up because it probably would have killed him. But we had a skilled parachutist - he had a hard time with it, but luckily everything was ok."

"Knight in Retreat" is also one of the few episodes to feature animals in some of its scenes. In this episode, it was a tiger cub that gets caught inside K.I.T.T. "Every kind of animal we had on the show was a little different because they like to chew on things," recalls Gill. "They would chew on the seats inside the cars and the apparatus. It was always good to see animals because it was fun to see how K.I.T.T. would deal with them. Once, we had a panther on the show ["Deadly Knightshade"] and it was kind of a handful because he was a little feisty with people. Other than that, we didn't have any problems with them trying to get away, only that they loved to chew on things."

Knight Knotes:

- When Michael shows Bonnie the photograph of Bianca near the beginning of the episode, her face is looking up. A few minutes later, Michael shows her the same photo and Bianca's face is looking down!

- When K.I.T.T. uses his Sub-Zero feature, all the windows ice up except the rear hatch.

- TV Guide described this episode as follows: "Michael poses as a space-weapon scientist to gain access to a club operated by a woman dealing in blackmail and top secret weapon systems".

- The retreat used here by Bianca can also be seen as Adrianne and Garthe's mansion in "Goliath Returns".

- Megafax Industries is also mentioned in "Knight of the Drones".

Script to Screen:

- As Michael is describing parasailing to K.I.T.T., he accuses K.I.T.T. of not having an imagination. K.I.T.T. replies, "If turning yourself into a human kite is imagination, Michael, then the lack of one is surely the least of my problems."

- In terms of looks and physicality, the script ranks the ladies at the retreat, from least to greatest: Monica, Veronica, Tanya and Bianca.

- A note accompanies the script during the scene where Tanya attacks the courier: "Note: During the action that follows, Tanya will never get a good look at Michael's features, and he will not see her behind the windshield."

- K.I.T.T. apologizes for not getting a photo of the driver who attacked the courier and states that "there just wasn't time for me to make use of my Thermal One Hundred Hard Copier."

- Bianca pulls up a computer file on Michael's cover that reads: "Doctor Michael Knightwood: PhD in Physics from the Washington University of Technology. Most recent publication: The Journal of Military Science. Subject matter: Space Weaponry. Star Wars."

- In the scene where Ted Cooper and Bianca are embracing in the hot tub, a note accompanies the script: "Note: This will, of course, be done tastefully."

Featured Songs:

"Careless Whisper" by Wham!

"Strut" by Sheena Easton

K.I.T.T.'s Capabilities:

- Audio/Video Record, Auto Cruise, Auto-Roof Left, Homing Signal, Map Search, Medical Scan, Micro Jam, Pursuit, Sub Zero, Surveillance Mode, Turbo Boost

PROD. #58647

$$\left[\begin{array}{c} \text{EPISODE} \\ 62 \end{array} \right]$$

Script History:

February 7, 1985 (F.R.)

KNIGHT STRIKE

Written By: Gregory S. Dinallo

Directed By: Georg Fenady

Original Airdate: April 5, 1985 (Friday, 8:00 PM) (21.0%; 17,830,000)

NBC Rerun #1: August 16, 1985 (Friday, 8:00 PM) (12.6%; 10,700,000)

"I did not strike that man's car."

-K.I.T.T.

Crew: Robert Foster (Executive Producer), Gino Grimaldi (Producer), Burton Armus (Producer), Richard Okie (Executive Story Consultant), Gregory S. Dinallo (Executive Script Consultant), Ron Martinez (Associate Producer), Bruce Golin (Associate Producer), Robert Ewing (Coordinating Producer), Don Peake (Music), H. John Penner (Director of Photography), Frank Grieco, Jr. (Art Director), R. Lynn Smartt (Set Decoration), Joe Reich (Casting), Grant Hoag (Film Editor), Pat Somerset (Sound), Ron Martinez (Unit Production Manager), Robert Villar (1st Assistant Director), Bruce A. Humphrey (2nd Assistant Director), John Shouse (Sound Editor), Richard Lapham (Music Editor), Barry Downing (Costume Supervisor), Karen Braverman (Costume Supervisor), Jack Gill (2nd Unit Director-Stunt Coordinator), Jeremy Swan (Make-up), Allen Payne (Hairstylist)

Guest Cast: Judy Landers (Sheila Gutherie), Jack O'Halloran (Rawleigh), Logan Ramsey (Edgar), Katherine Baumann (Tyler Jastrow), Richard Herd (Lyle Jastrow), Paul Tuerpe (Fletcher), Biff Yeager (Tom O'Mally), Mark Giardino (Sergeant Gottlieb), Wendy Oates (Clerk), Michael Masters (Tuxedo), Virginia Peters (Martha), Harold "Hal" Frizzell (Man Waiting for Elevator), Jack Gill (Camo Pedestrian)

When a shipment of high powered weapons is stolen from a military depot, Michael is assigned to investigate the theft.

A Look Back:

"Knight Strike" is notable for a guest appearance by veteran TV actor Richard Herd, who played the character of Lyle Jastrow. Herd had just finished shooting the science fiction movie *Trancers*, as well as starring in the ongoing TV series *TJ Hooker,* when he got the role. "We had a fine production coordinator on *TJ Hooker* who was able to rearrange my shooting days so I could do *Knight Rider*", recalls Herd.

The episode was directed by Georg Fenady, and Herd has nothing but good memories from his time on the set. "I liked playing the part of the bad guy. George was a no nonsense guy who knew his job. I enjoyed working with him".

The episode would see Herd pilot everything from jeeps to helicopters. Herd remembers the climax well. "We had a mock up helicopter on location that was moved about to suggest motion. The rope was looped to my landing gear to make my escape impossible".

Veteran TV actress Judy Landers makes a return appearance in this episode, having previously filled the role of Micki Bradburn in season one's "Forget Me Not". "It was easier to land this role because I had proven myself previously with the producers," remembers Landers. "There were only about four other girls auditioning for that role."

At the beginning of "Knight Strike", Landers is seen parading guns at the fair in the hotel - something that she felt uncomfortable with. "I believe we shot that scene at the Hyatt in Westlake Village. I remember feeling scared and uncomfortable about the guns. David reassured me that although the guns were real, they were non-functioning with the exception of a few of them that only the very qualified stuntmen were using."

Landers was happy to play the role of Sheila. "I loved playing Sheila because the character had many dimensions. There was more than one side to her personality, which is always more fun and challenging for an actress. I really loved that my character was able to surprise everyone by getting the bad guys and saving the day!" One of the bad guys was actor Richard Herd. "I was very excited to work with Richard Herd. He is such a respected actor and it was an honor to work with him."

Whenever possible, Landers wanted to go over scenes multiple times in order to make sure it was done correctly. "The writers and producers always preferred for us to stick with the lines in the script. But after they got a take done and they were happy with it, I would always ask if I could do a take with my own improvisations and line changes."

Landers was a passenger in K.I.T.T. in both of the episodes that she starred in, so it only felt right that she would get the opportunity to go behind the wheel. "Yes, I remember driving the car. The cast and crew were on a lunch break and a stunt supervisor let me drive K.I.T.T. It was so much fun!"

Though Judy Landers would go on to star in many more television shows after *Knight Rider,* she made a decision to change the course of her career. "After about 10 years of being in the limelight, my focus changed and being an actress was not my top priority anymore. I wanted to be a wife and mother. I got married to Major League Baseball player Tom Niedenfuer (a World Series champion with the Los Angeles Dodgers in 1981) and have two wonderful daughters, Lindsey and Kristy Landers-Niedenfuer."

Seasoned actor Jack O'Halloran starred as bad guy Rawleigh in "Knight Strike". "I didn't have to take an audition for the role," confirms O'Halloran, who is perhaps best known as the mute Non from the first two *Superman* movies. At that, O' Halloran was not interested in acting for television. "To be honest with you, I was getting a lot of calls about being in this and that, everything really. But I had absolutely no interest in acting in television. I had starred in many films and I didn't see the point. You know when you are lucky enough to work alongside such actors as Robert Mitchum and Marlon Brando then television just seemed a step down. The reason I took the job for *Knight Rider* was because of the fantastic crew that was involved in the show. I knew some of them and I did like *Knight Rider.* I would catch some episodes when I could. Other than that, working on TV compared to film was like 'wham bam, thank you ma'am', because the filming was all done in one week."

Before acting, O'Halloran was a famous heavyweight boxer, facing legends like George Foreman. "It was funny because when I was through with boxing, talent agents came to me. They would offer me roles for certain parts and I would always turn them down. I met Steve McQueen and together with Robert Mitchum they were the guys that made it a reality and gave me the belief that I could carve out a career in acting," says O'Halloran.

Not only would O'Halloran work alongside David Hasselhoff, but 'Knight Strike' also had an interesting pairing that included Richard Herd and Judy Landers. "Richard is a wonderful person. He was very busy back at that time and very versatile. He is a genuinely good guy. Judy was hilarious on set and I remember that she was such a sweetheart. David, well, you know, it was his show. He would look in the mirror a lot. He worked hard and knew what he wanted."

After *Knight Rider*, O'Halloran went on to make more prime time television appearances, but it is his early film career that makes him proud. "I loved doing the *Superman* films. It was my idea to have Non not speak so he would appear more childlike. After all, the movies were for children. You couldn't just have plain evil everywhere. My favorite role though was working with Mitchum on the movie *Farewell, My Lovely*. I don't have a priority on different roles. Because of that, I haven't been typecast. I can happily play the bad guy and then play the good guy or the mute guy," jokes O'Halloran.

Knight Knotes:

- The climax of this episode takes place at the Anderson Precious Metals Depository. In reality, it's the campus of the College of Canyons in Valencia, CA. This location was one of the most frequented by the *Knight Rider* crew, and can be seen in "Deadly

Maneuvers", "Knights of the Fast Lane", "Knight of the Chameleon", "Junkyard Dog" and "The Wrong Crowd".

Script to Screen:

- Sheila's last name is revealed to be Gutherie.

- Michael tells Edgar that the Foundation has an entire department that deals in fraudulent accident claims. Edgar then backs off his accusations of injury.

- The scene where Fletcher fires the laser at K.I.T.T.'s scanner is described as "shattering the crystal". K.I.T.T. also mentions that his gyro circuits are down. The following scene in the semi states that, "Bonnie slides a new scanner unit into position".

- Another scene with Edgar and Martha has Michael offering $200 for the damage, which K.I.T.T. states is $100 over blue book value. Edgar tries to show them how solid the car is my hitting its hood, at which time the bumper falls off.

- The entire ending scene was not written during the release of the first draft; instead, a paragraph describing how the scene should play out is included.

Déjà Vu:

- Paul Tuerpe returns in "Knight of the Rising Sun".

Featured Songs:

"Neutron Dance" by The Pointer Sisters

K.I.T.T.'s Capabilities:

- Audio Playback, Audio/Video Record, Auto Cruise, Auto-Roof Left, Laser System Override, Map Search, Micro Jam, Pursuit, Radar, Surveillance Mode, Tinted Windows, Turbo Boost, Winch

PROD. #58633

{ EPISODE
63 }

Script History:

October 28, 1984 (F.R.)

CIRCUS KNIGHTS

Written By: David R. Toddman

Directed By: Harvey Laidman

Original Airdate: May 5, 1985 (Sunday, 8:00 PM) (15.3%; 12,990,000)

NBC Rerun #1: July 21, 1985 (Sunday, 8:00 PM) (15.2%; 12,900,000)

Filming Dates: November 5-13, 1984

"Bang? An orangutan named Bang?"

-K.I.T.T.

Crew: Robert Foster (Executive Producer), Gino Grimaldi (Producer), Gerald Sanford (Producer), Richard Okie (Executive Story Consultant), Robert Sherman (Executive Story Consultant), David Bennett Carren (Story Editor), Ron Martinez (Associate Producer), Bruce Golin (Associate Producer), Robert Ewing (Coordinating Producer), Don Peake (Music), H. John Penner (Director of Photography), Frank Grieco, Jr. (Art Director), R. Lynn Smartt (Set Decoration), Joe Reich (Casting), Lawrence J. Vallario (Film Editor), Pat Somerset (Sound), Ron Martinez (Unit Production Manager), Louis Race (1st Assistant Director), Bruce A. Humphrey (2nd Assistant Director), John Shouse (Sound Editor), Richard Lapham (Music Editor), Barry Downing (Costume Supervisor), Karen Braverman (Costume Supervisor), Jack Gill (2nd Unit Director-Stunt Coordinator), Jeremy Swan (Make-up), Allen Payne (Hairstylist)

Guest Cast: Michelle NiCastro (Terry Major), James Callahan (Jeff Barnes), Chuck McCann (Bombo), Sharon Hughes (Tiger), Tom Williams (Ringmaster)

Michael goes undercover as "Turbo Man" at a circus when the main attraction is mysteriously killed.

A Look Back:

Harvey Laidman was behind the camera for this episode and recalls the challenges in creating a circus in downtown Los Angeles. "The circus was set up in the rear Universal studio parking lot. All the tents, midway, seating and trapeze were all rentals. The incredible Bob Yerkes was a circus performer and teacher as well as stuntman. He provided all the trapeze equipment and talent. Bob has a house in the north west corner of Los Angeles where he teaches and trains circus performers. He's an amazing guy who handles stress extremely well. We also had Buzz Bundy, who specialized in balancing cars on two wheels. He would drive up a ramp to tip the car to one side and then balance it that way by shifting his body weight."

The actual circus performance was filmed at night, both to add a sense of dazzle to the episode and for financial reasons, as well. "The studio did not want to pay for all the extras required to fill the tent and seeing the empty seats was a problem," says Laidman. "We changed the performances to night for that reason, but we still saw lots of empty seats."

In order to make the circus believable, the production team knew that they would need to bring some animals in. But there was a certain orangutan that Laidman would rather forget. "I love working with animals, but there was a problem. An orangutan developed a big crush on me, and whenever he saw me, he wanted to give me a big hug and kiss. I'm not kidding! I had to hide when I was directing scenes with him, otherwise he would run to me and give me a big, wet kiss!"

The bad guy in the episode is played by the late great veteran television actor James Callahan, whose previous roles had included everything from *The Twilight Zone* to *Charles in Charge*. "I worked with Jimmy many times. A great professional and lots of fun on the set," recalls Laidman. Michelle NiCastro also appeared as Terri Major, Michael's love interest and part of the circus team. "I cast her in the show", recalls Laidman. "I also worked with her on *Airwolf*. Tragically, she died in 2010. She was only 50. She was a fantastic singer and very sweet. I adored her."

One scene in "Circus Knights" involves Michael facing off with the Tiger Lady, an encounter that left him a little hot under the collar. "One of the producers was searching for a menacing moment to put David in peril and decided to create the deadly flaming twirling baton attack. I had a hard time with that one - how to make it believable, how to shoot it from obscure angles. It is what it is. David was very well coordinated, but there was an entire stunt crew and a double (Joel Kramer) who looked just like him. He let them do their jobs - which they did very well."

Knight Knotes:

- TV Guide described this episode as follows: "Michael and K.I.T.T. join a circus as a daredevil act to find out who's trying to force it into bankruptcy".

Script to Screen:

- Michael is very reluctant to go to the circus, citing many other things he'd rather be doing, to include: skiing, sailing, snorkeling, hang-gliding, horseback riding or "anything else in the whole wide world".
- K.I.T.T. originally meets Bang the orangutan at the dress rehearsal where Peter Major is killed. To ward him off, K.I.T.T. opens and closes his hood and makes jungle noises.
- Bombo the Clown is named Blippo.
- The scene with Devon watching the footage of Peter's fall plays out differently – originally, Devon is up late into the night examining the footage while Bonnie brews him some tea.
- Michael volunteers to look into Peter's death, even though Devon tells Michael that he hasn't had a day off in over a month and he doesn't have to work this case.
- Michael originally wanted to go undercover as a human cannonball and K.I.T.T. would catch him.
- Michael turbo boosts into the circus instead of using ski mode. That's why he decides on the name "Turbo Man".
- A twenty-five year old rock music lover named Chuck Foley is the one who sets the fire in the costume tent, not Tiger.

- Bang attacks K.I.T.T. with a can of white spray paint, but he escapes unscathed.\
- When Michael captures Foley, he locks him in K.I.T.T. When he refuses to talk, K.I.T.T. activates his climate control and takes the temperature below freezing until he cracks.

Déjà Vu:

- Tom Williams returns in "Knight Racer".

K.I.T.T.'s Capabilities:

- Anharmonic Synthesizer, Audio/Video Record, Auto Cruise, CO_2, Medical Scan, Pursuit, Pyroclastic Lamination, Self Diagnostic Analyzer, Ski Mode, Surveillance Mode, Turbo Boost, Voice Projection

Behind the KNIGHT: Jack Gill and the Blind Drive Cars

The blind-drive seat was probably the most innovative idea that we came up with. Up until *Knight Rider*, everyone was trying to drive with video cameras or cutting a portion of the grill away and laying down to drive. I had a car for blind-driving from the driver's side and blind-driving from the passenger's side. My role was to tell them where to put the steering columns, how far back they had to be and where the pedals had to be. The special effects department actually constructed them for me, but we had a bit of R and D on it too.

One thing we had to figure out was if the viewers could actually see me. We put a blind driver seat on the right side because obviously they are not interchangeable. I had to get up inside of one of them, so you didn't want to see the right or the left of it. We had three or four blind driver seats because it just took way too long to try and pull a blind driver's seat out and stick it on the other side. The cars were all ready and set up to go and each one had a specific role. The driver's side blind drive car had the telescoping steering column. There was a lever that I could drop down right to my lap so you couldn't actually see the wheel.

You may have heard the story of me passing out in the blind driver's seat one summer. They had already called "action" and I took off and it was 110-115 degrees in the car. I passed out and luckily the car just went into a ditch and stopped, but it could get quite hot in there on occasion.

The cars did have an emergency break lever, although I never used it. I always used the line lock device. There were some stunt guys when I directed that liked to use that thing but the problem we had was that the minute they went over to reach for the emergency break lever you could see their hands moving inside the car. If I had my brother, Andy, or somebody else, I would try and get them used to using the line lock.

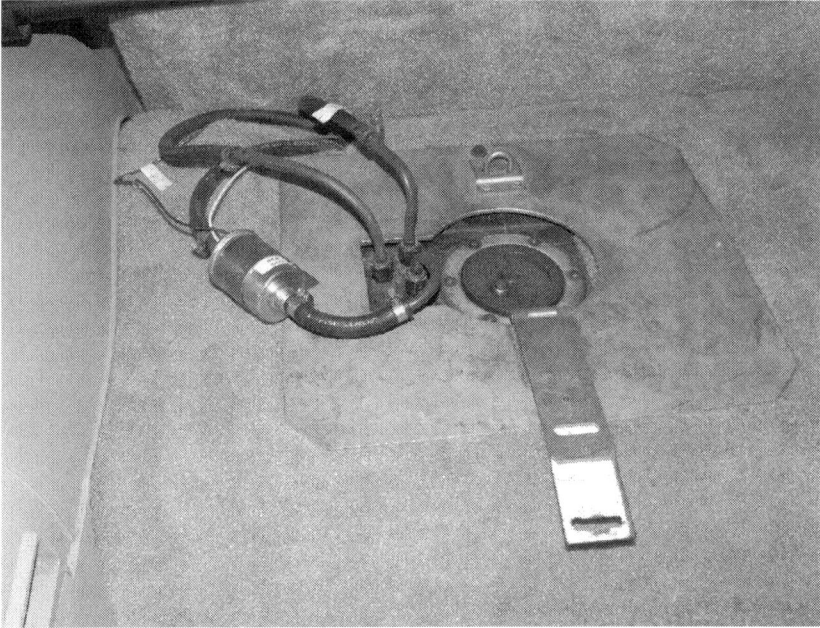

Close up shot of the fuel cell in an original stunt K.I.T.T.

On the right hand blind drive car, there was a toggle switch that was on the blue box to the left of the wheel, which was the scanner control box. But what that also served a purpose for was that it gave me control of the actual brakes, because in the driver's seat on the left hand side I had all the controls over there. Once you're in the right hand seat driving, you can't really get to the line lock or any of the other controls, so we put a whole set of controls on that box so that I didn't have to reach across the console and figure out all the buttons that were there. So the toggle switch actually armed the line lock device and then that button was a buzzer. When I pushed it, it gave out a loud buzzer noise, knowing that I only had rear brakes. A lot of the time the car is screaming, going down rough terrain and I can't really look for a light, or sometimes there would be too much bright sun in the car. So we went to a buzzer and the toggle switch. All it did was arm it so I knew to switch from the left side to the right side. Anytime David Hasselhoff would say, "K.I.T.T., come get me", I would come up in the right side blind-drive car. He'd jump in and have a steering wheel on his side. The minute he jumped in, we were fighting for the wheel, trying to get out of the shot!

Jack Gill

June 28, 2011

Close up shot of the line lock activator from an original stunt K.I.T.T.

Behind the KNIGHT: Blind Driving with Andy Gill

Over the years, I doubled many different characters and had the extreme pleasure of driving K.I.T.T. when K.I.T.T. was supposed to be driving himself. We called this "Blind Driving" and I took the job over when Jack became too busy directing or coordinating. I would sit INSIDE the driver's seat and look out of the headrest to drive. Jack had a seat made that the driver actually sat inside. The front covering of the seat would flip up and I would slide in under the leather and work my head up into a custom made headrest. The headrest was built wide to put my head in it and the front of the headrest had mesh on it so I could see through it. Once I was in the seat with my head in the headrest, I would reach up and drop the front leather covering down to cover my upper body completely. I even had armrests that slipped onto my arms and we had a very small round steering wheel that sat just over the top my legs. I would drive with my elbows tucked into my sides and hold the bottom of the small steering wheel. I learned to shuffle turn the wheel when sliding around corners in order to keep your hands hidden below the dash.

We started with a left side blind drive car but we eventually ended up with a left side blind drive car and a right side blind drive car. This came about because at first we would blind drive K.I.T.T. whenever K.I.T.T. would drive without anyone inside. This was usually when Michael called K.I.T.T. to come to his aid. We would blind drive K.I.T.T. and slide up to Michael. As we stopped, we would sling the door open and Michael would start to jump in. That would be a cut because Michael would be sitting on top of the blind driver and couldn't really fit in the car. So we made a right side blind drive car to fix the problem. That opened up a whole new level of shots that we could do. Now, Michael could jump in and drive away! We also learned Michael could transfer into a moving blind driven K.I.T.T.! Over the years, I drove

K.I.T.T. from both the right and left side blind drive seats for many transfers, slides, mini jumps, and runbys. The blind drive seat was an amazing idea that worked so well that it changed the course of the action sequences. The writers started coming up with more and more uses for the blind drive seats. I still use the same setup in cars today when I set up blind drive cars.

Photo sequence above courtesy of Andy Gill

David Hasselhoff was a big supporter of the Make a Wish Foundation. Make a Wish Foundation reached out and tried to give terminally ill cancer patients a last wish. One of his contributions to Make a Wish was to invite a young person to the set that wished to see K.I.T.T. and Michael Knight. David would hang out with the kids and Jack would drive up in the left side blind drive car. The kid would get in the passenger side and Jack would slide around the parking lot or set and give the kids a thrill. I don't think any of them ever realized that Jack was really driving K.I.T.T. from the blind driver seat. They were too excited about being in K.I.T.T.!!! and having K.I.T.T. slide them around!!!. It was great seeing their faces when they stepped out of the car. I remember David telling everyone on the set one day that a little girl that came out with Make a Wish had passed away. She had asked to be buried in her *Knight Rider* jacket that David gave her. Somehow, *Knight Rider* touched everyone's lives in one way or another.

Andy Gill

October 7, 2011

KNIGHT RIDER

SEASON FOUR (1985-1986)

Starring:

David Hasselhoff as Michael Knight

Edward Mulhare as Devon Miles

Patricia McPherson as Bonnie Barstow

Peter Parros as Reginald Cornelius III (RC3)

William Daniels as the voice of K.I.T.T.

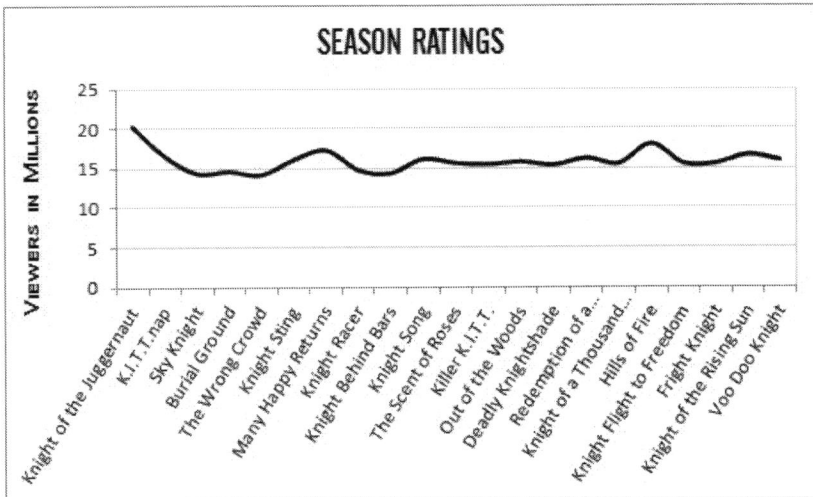

SEASON RATINGS

PROD. #60214

$$\left[\begin{array}{c} \text{EPISODE} \\ 64 \end{array} \right]$$

Script History:

June 7, 1985 (F.R.)

June 12, 1985 (F.R.)

June 18, 1985 (F.R.)

June 21, 1985 (F.R.)

June 25, 1985 (F.R.)

June 26, 1985 (F.R.)

July 5, 1985 (F.R.)

July 11, 1985 (F.R.)

KNIGHT OF THE JUGGERNAUT (TWO HOURS)

Working Title: "The Juggernaut"

Written By: Robert Foster and Burton Armus

Directed By: Georg Fenady

Original Airdate: September 20, 1985 (Friday, 8:00 PM) (23.6%; 20,270,000)

Rerun: February 28, 1986 (Friday, 8:00 PM) (21.3%; 18,300,000)

Filming Dates: June 24 - July 16, 1985

"I'm the Knight Industries Two Thousand, sure enough. Ready to ramble,

ready to roll, ready to strut my stuff!"

-K.I.T.T.

Crew: Don Peake (Music), Lawrence J. Vallario (Editor), Lawrence J. Gleason (Editor), Lou Montejano (Art Director), H. John Penner (Director of Photography), Robert Foster (Executive Producer), Burton Armus (Supervising Producer), Bruce Lansbury (Supervising Producer), Gino Grimaldi (Producer), Glen A. Larson (Creator), Gregory S. Dinallo (Co-Producer), Mark Jones (Co-Producer), Robert Ewing (Coordinating Producer), Michael Eric Stein (Story Editor), Ron Martinez (Associate Producer/Unit Production Manager), Bruce Golin (Associate Producer), Stu Phillips (Theme), Louis Race (First Assistant Director), Bruce A. Humphrey (Second Assistant Director), Donna Dockstader (Casting), R. Lynn Smartt (Set Decorator), John Shouse (Sound Editor), Richard Lapham (Music Editor), Barry Downing (Costume Supervisor), Karen J. Braverman (Costume Supervisor), Jack Gill (2nd Unit Director/Stunt Coordinator), Pat Somerset (Sound), Jeremy Swan (Make-up), Allen Payne (Hairstylist)

Guest Cast: John Considine (Philip Nordstrom), Nicholas Worth (Jim Hower), Pamela Susan Shoop (Marta Simmons), Mary Kate McGeehan (Jennifer Knight), Richard Fullerton (Frank), Blair Underwood (Potts), Joe Shea (Cabbie), Michael Dickson (Ardell), Robert Kim (Technician), Tom Noga (Messenger), Sandy Maschmeyer (Receptionist), R. Chandler Garrison (Head Butler), Luis Contreras (Voice #2), RCB (Voice #1), V.C. Dupree (Gang Member), Wren Brown (Gang Member), Marco Hernandez (Gang Member), Rick Plastina (Guard), Mary Woronov (Dr. Von Furst), Laurence Haddon (John Lloyd), Angelo De Meo (Thug)

Devon is kidnapped and replaced with a clone while Michael is in Chicago safeguarding a rare isotope.

A Look Back:

Of all the new additions included in the final season of *Knight Rider,* the most significant was the addition of a new regular cast member who would be employed as part of the F.L.A.G. team. Peter Parros, who played RC3, was 24 at the time of his audition. He had briefly appeared in such television shows as *The Facts of Life,* but a leading role on *Knight Rider* would make Parros a household name. "I was thrilled to get the job," says Parros. "*Knight Rider* was my big break and being cast as RC3 allowed me to be a full time professional actor because at that time I was working as an office clerk at a law firm."

Parros competed with a then unknown actor named Blair Underwood for the chance to act alongside David Hasselhoff and the team. The audition went down to the wire until Parros impressed the network with a cheeky but inspiring poem. "The audition process was very exciting for me. I always wanted to play an action hero, and that's how I saw RC3. This was a role I really wanted and felt I was perfect for. I had read for Donna Dockstader, the casting director, a couple of times before, and she liked my work. As I recall, I had four auditions and at my final audition, it was down to me and Blair Underwood. The network and the producers were all there. It was a morning audition and we were told that whoever got the part would be leaving for Chicago that afternoon. So, I did my scenes and just before I walked out of the room, I turned back and announced, 'I'm badder than Mr. T. and prettier than Ali, so hire me for RC3'. I was young and crazy but my corny poem worked! I won the role for RC3 and that afternoon I was on a plane to Chicago." Though Underwood had lost the audition, he did retain a small part in the season opener. "The next morning, I was on set shooting my first TV series. Blair Underwood was also cast in 'Knight of the Juggernaut' as one of the car thieves."

David Hasselhoff on the set of "Knight of the Juggernaut" (Photo courtesy of Christopher Orlando)

Parros was overwhelmed and thrilled on his first day of shooting *Knight Rider* on the streets of Chicago. "It was like a dream. *Knight Rider* was a hit show and wherever we were shooting, crowds of people lined the streets, hoping to meet David Hasselhoff and get a peek at K.I.T.T." Though RC3 was supposed to be a Chicago native and would go on throughout season 4 wearing Chicago related clothing, Parros has something to confess. "I'd actually never been to Chicago. I had no connection with the city before the show. Within hours of being cast, I was flown there by first class and then I went to wardrobe to be fitted for my 'Street Avenger' costume."

Before shooting started, Parros was introduced to his new co-stars. "I was excited to meet everyone. David Hasselhoff is a great person and was tons of fun from day one. He's got a smile that really made me feel welcome and we grew to be personal friends. I was in awe of Edward Mulhare because I grew up watching his TV show *The Ghost and Mrs Muir* where he played the captain. He was a classy professional and everything I had hoped he would be. He helped me a lot. Patricia McPherson was cool and caring, though I didn't work with her as much." And then there was the little matter of meeting K.I.T.T. "My initial impression of K.I.T.T. was the surprise that there were so many K.I.T.T. cars," says Parros. "I didn't realize that there were different cars for different purposes. There were jump cars, tinted window cars, blind drive cars, cars to be destroyed, a special skin for bullet hits and a computer car. Plus, the new versions added for this season, so I think there were more than 20 cars in all." One of those new versions was of course the Super Pursuit Mode. "The Super Pursuit Mode car was kept under wraps," confirms Parros. "They didn't want the secret out about changes to K.I.T.T. I thought it was cool."

Parros was surprised by the Chicago weather when shooting did take place. "Early the next morning, I arrived on set. My first day of shooting would be on the streets of Chicago. I expected it to be cold and windy, but it was sunny and hot," confirms Parros. As RC3, Parros makes a dramatic entrance in his first episode but, as he explains, not everything went to plan. "The fighting in the alley was the very first scene that I shot. We actually shot the sequence out of order. It was my first screen fight, and we rehearsed it at half speed several times. When it came time for the actual shoot at full speed, our timing and positioning got a bit off and after I tackled the bad guy, I actually punched him in the mouth and split his lip! I was horrified. The stunt man was bleeding and the crew thought it was funny. That stunt guy was a pro because he finished the scene then they took him off to hospital to get stitches. I'm sure he got a bonus for his injury, but that was definitely not the way to start the day. In fact, I thought I was going to get fired." Parros did not get his marching orders but did earn a nickname. "After that incident, Burton Armus jokingly started calling me 'Peter one-punch', a nick name that stuck through the rest of the season," recalls Parros. Though cast members hardly ever did their own stunts, Parros was an exception. "I've always been athletic and grew up working out. I loved the physicality of RC3 and wanted to do as many of the stunts as they would let me do. One of these was the truck leap jump while chasing the bad guys into the alley."

Georg Fenady returned behind the lens to direct Parros' debut episode and the new kid on the block was very impressed with the veteran director. "Georg was an unforgettable character. As a kid, I was a fan of Spider-Man comics. Fenady immediately reminded me of J. Jonah Jameson, Peter Parker's editor at the Daily Bugle. Both sported military style crew cuts and smoked a cigar. At first, Fenady came off as gruff, but maybe that was me projecting Jameson onto him. He was really a nice guy and a terrific director. As far as directors go, I would say Georg and Chuck Bail were my favorites on the show."

At the episode's climax, Devon officially gives RC3 the job to join the F.L.A.G. team back in Los Angeles. It is here where RC3 and Bonnie reveal to Michael what the 'C' button is for. "I loved it that RC3 had that secret addition on K.I.T.T. that he could go convertible, because at the time I owned a 1963 Ford Falcon convertible," jokes Parros.

Parros was thrilled to watch the show when it first premiered. "I watched my first episode with a bunch of friends. I loved the way RC3 came off, but at the same time the most exciting part for me was seeing myself on the opening credits!"

While the addition of a new cast member and new tricks for K.I.T.T. would have been enough, the producers also decided to expand upon the *Knight Rider* universe by introducing us to Jennifer Knight, Wilton Knight's daughter and the person in control at F.L.A.G. headquarters. The role of Jennifer Knight went to Mary Kate McGeehan. "I remember feeling really connected to the role of Jennifer Knight," says McGeehan, who was surrounded by acting at an early age. "My mom and dad were both in radio, so while I was growing up, acting was always part of our family. I knew somehow that I would be an actress since I was a little girl. We had an actual stage in our home basement that we called 'The Cadillac Theatre'. I have fantastic memories of it as it was a great, creative space with curtains and everything - a real little theatre. My mom would write plays and my dad would direct and we would perform for the neighborhood."

As Jennifer Knight, McGeehan recalls noting the importance of her role in the *Knight Rider* universe. "I was excited at the auditions, especially as it was for the daughter of the man who invented K.I.T.T. I felt as if I owned who she was and, in the audition, I could actually feel that the producers felt the same way, so that was a great moment for me. I knew that Jennifer's father had passed away and now she was left in control of F.L.A.G., but her lack of experience and naivety led her to trusting those around her, who of course would turn out to be evil. When I got the role, I knew we would be doing a special double episode and that we would travel to Chicago to film, so it was very exciting."

McGeehan's first scene in "Knight of the Juggernaut" takes place in the board room, where she tells Michael Knight that the Knight Foundation will freeze funds for F.L.A.G. and that he will be suspended. The scene went well, but, unbeknownst by viewers, McGeehan had only just learned her lines. "I had memorized the scene, which was an important one as it was the true introduction to Jennifer. Before we shot the scene, I was running over my lines when I noticed that the lines I had were not the lines we were just about to shoot. I'm not sure exactly what happened or why, but somewhere along the line, someone forgot to give me the rewrite. So, it was sheer panic time as I quickly had to learn an entire new scene, including that long monologue speech. Also, I needed to do it in record time as the entire cast and crew waited and time is money. I dug deep and managed to pull it off and, in watching it, I don't think anyone could ever tell that I had just learned it. I was proud of myself for getting it together and for making it work."

McGeehan was impressed with her costar David Hasselhoff and enjoyed working with him, but "Knight of the Juggernaut" was not the first time that the two of them had worked together. "We had worked together years before on *The Young and the Restless*. David was so accommodating, open, friendly and funny. He was the same sweet guy on *Knight Rider*. Actually, he was genuinely excited and proud that I was doing *Knight Rider* because when I'd worked on *The Young and the Restless'*, I was an 'under-five' nurse, which meant saying 5 words or less. As an actress, I had graduated to bigger roles and he couldn't be happier or more supportive of me. It was a great time. He was more confident on *Knight Rider*, but he wasn't cocky or full of himself, just truly happy to be working and to be on his own hit show. He was also a very generous and supportive actor, too, David was the same confident, happy guy I'd always known him to be. I had a fantastic time."

Whilst McGeehan and David Hasselhoff had a clearly friendly relationship off screen, it was another story on screen as their characters would disagree with the proposed future of F.L.A.G. Though McGeehan's character would change her mind later in the episode, McGeehan prefers playing the ruthless role. "I must admit that it is always more fun to play the tough, don't mess with me bitch role, which I was definitely like at the beginning of the episode." McGeehan also shared screen time with Edward Mulhare. "I feel very lucky to have had the opportunity to work with Edward Mulhare. What a truly wonderful, gifted and elegant actor. He was an absolute joy to work with, very giving and supportive and always with a twinkle in his eye. I think he had a fantastic time in "Knight of the Juggernaut" playing the two Devon's."

(Photo courtesy of Mary Kate McGeehan)

Even though Chicago is widely known as "the windy city", McGeehan remembers the weather during shooting as incredibly hot. "We shot a lot of scenes in LA at Universal and then we traveled to Chicago. It was in the summer and it was very hot and humid. I had never really experienced humidity like that before and wow, was it intense. But what a great city! I loved being there - it was a terrific experience."

In the final scene of the episode, Jennifer Knight is a passenger in the newly refurbished K.I.T.T. convertible. "I was very lucky, it was so much fun to have been able to do that," recalls McGeehan. She will always have fond memories of being such an important character on the series. "I can honestly say working on this show as Jennifer Knight was one of the most wonderful experiences in my career, and I am very grateful to the powers that be who cast me."

Stunt coordinator Jack Gill and his brother, Andy, were the ones piloting the Juggernaut and K.I.T.T. during the scene where K.I.T.T. was destroyed. Gill recalls, "The Juggernaut was one of the most lethal weapons we ever used on *Knight Rider*, only because it went very, very fast and was indestructible. The battering ram at the front is what was so dangerous because it liked to punch through parts of the vehicle. If it had a bigger surface, it probably would only push the car around. But it was a tiny piece of metal and it would try and punch through the doors, so we had to put roll bars inside the doors to protect the driver. I drove the Juggernaut and my brother Andy drove K.I.T.T. We set up a bunch of shots where I would just beat the car to death and do as much damage as I could without actually hurting the driver."

Richard Fullerton starred as bad guy Frank in this episode, a man who is punished by Phillip Nordstrom for failing a mission. "As far as I recall, I went through the standard interview process for the role. My agent submitted me, then I was called in to the audition and subsequently received notice that I had been cast." Fullerton was unaware that the show would be a double episode, "I had no idea that there was anything special about the episode. In fact, I do not believe that I had seen *Knight Rider* previously," admits Fullerton.

Fullerton's character Frank appears in one scene near the beginning of the episode where we are introduced to Philip Nordstrom, played by John

Considine. "It was another day at the office for me. I do not have any distasteful memories of working alongside John. I do not remember him to be particularly warm or a chatty sort of guy either."

Fullerton's scene is brief but also shows the viewer first "hand", if you will, just how powerful his boss, Nordstrom, is. After Nordstrom is dissatisfied with Frank's work, he uses his bionic hand to crush Frank's hand and throws him across the room. "I remember that the close-up of his bionic hand squeezing my poor fist took a few takes to get right. The director, Georg Fenady, was particular about the exact positioning and lighting for that shot. John's hand was just make up applied over it but if you look closely some of it is peeling away. We finished the dialogue in roughly three takes."

Fullerton did not use any regular *Knight Rider* stunt men for his character's fall into the barrels after being struck by Nordstrom. "I have played a lot of 'heavies' in my career, and in those days, I often described my roles as first heavy or second heavy to the left," jokes Fullerton. "It was my habit to do a lot of my own fights and falls just to ease the boredom of watching someone else pretend to be me. I would always make certain there was a double on the set and pulling a salary, and then I would make my final decision as to whether or not I would take it myself based upon how much peril and skill seemed to be involved in the scene. I remember telling the guy that the barrels were all his. I let my stunt man, Pat McGroaty, take that punch. I'm not easy to double, what with my very curly hair and small nose. Pat possessed both and was well respected in the Hollywood stunt community." Fullerton adds, "It's much easier to remember personal pain instead of the double variety."

Much to McGroaty's chagrin, the fall into the barrels took several attempts to get it right. "It took poor Pat more takes than usual to go flying through the barrels in just the right way. They always seem to resent it if a stunt man can't get it done in one take every time. Pat was embarrassed that they had to set up the barrels several times."

The other thug in the scene and showing pity to Fullerton's character was the late Nicholas Worth. "I remember him more on the lines of 'ah, I've seen this guy around a lot'," remembers Fullerton, "but it wasn't like we had many discussions. He was certainly a distinctive character type. That whole scene was shot in LA."

Producer Burton Armus co-wrote the script with Executive Producer Robert Foster. Armus recalls, "We worked hand in hand. For example, I would write act 1 and he would write act 2 and so on. That is how it worked for that episode and then we would pitch more ideas to each other. We had Georg Fenady directing 'Juggernaut' so we were in good hands. Because it was the first episode of the season, we flew out on location to Chicago. We had a Chicago based crew who were excellent and very professional. There were no problems on set or the location. It went very smoothly because we had a great set of people around us. The shoot did not take too long because most of the interiors were shot before in LA. But we did use real buildings in Chicago also."

Knight Knotes:
- NBC's comments on the script: "Location dailies made good use of Chicago but some re-shooting may be required in the opening sequence on the lot. The disappointing juggernaut has been redesigned. The production team is still learning how to use the 'super pursuit mode' effectively."
- Producer Burton Armus on the SPM car: "We had 12 K.I.T.T.'s and they all did different things. For Season 4, we introduced the Super Pursuit Mode. I drove one of them and let's just say that I didn't handle it very well."

- A September 20, 1985 press release for this episode read, "Michael Knight (David Hasselhoff) & Marta (Susan Marie Shoop) deal with Third World Terrorists in a two-hour season premiere of *Knight Rider*." Note the misspelling of Pamela Susan Shoop's name.
- TV Guide described this episode as follows: "In the fourth-season opener, Michael hopes a street gang can rebuild K.I.T.T. in time to prevent a criminal mastermind from stealing a radioactive isotope. Peter Parros joins the cast in a recurring role as RC3".
- Jennifer Knight's board meeting videotape combines scenes from several episodes, including "Knightmares", "A Good Knight's Work", "Lost Knight", and unused footage of K.I.T.T.'s jump through a train from "A Knight In Shining Armor".
- Peter Parros was chosen for the role of RC3 sometime between June 21 and July 31, 1985.
- The Juggernaut was previously used in the 1983 movie, *Spacehunter: Adventures in the Forbidden Zone*.
- Patricia McPherson: "I got to ride a mounted officer's horse while we were shooting in Chicago. I asked and he allowed me. It was quite an experience."

Script to Screen:

- K.I.T.T. describes himself to the car thieves as "the most advanced automobile known to mankind. I have capabilities beyond your wildest dreams."
- The process of K.I.T.T.'s changeover as described in the script: "An Air Dam slides down on K.I.T.T.'s front end. The rear fin converts to a new aerodynamic shape as the rear end lifts up to expose two jet exhausts...Side vents slide outward. An air intake vent pops up from the hood. The Super Pursuit Mode transformation complete, we see

a whole new K.I.T.T. - sleeker, meaner, a car out of the future dropped into today."

- Hower initially tries to bribe the guard at the beginning of the episode before using the Juggernaut to kill him.

- The description of the first time we see The Juggernaut: "Half-tank, half-armored vehicle, it's an awesome sight, a sixteen-foot battering ram protruding from its turret. The driver, Hower, faces a control panel that rivals K.I.T.T.'s."

- When K.I.T.T. informs Michael that he picked up a bank robbery where the suspects were being chased by a man in a strange costume, Michael asks if he looks like a bat.

- When Michael meets up with Devon at the vault, Michael wants answers as to why Jennifer Knight wants to close down the Foundation. Michael comments, "Devon, you tell me to come to Chicago ASAP, Jennifer Knight's taking an active role in the Foundation and number one on her agenda -- I quote 'number one' -- is to phase out the Foundation for Law and Government. That's us -- you, me, Bonnie and Kitt." Devon replies, "We deserve to exist -- how could anyone, particularly anyone named Knight, decide differently?"

- When Jennifer first meets Michael, she vocalizes her displeasure in sharing the same last name: "Please be seated, Michael. I hope you don't mind my calling you Michael, I have difficulty attaching the family name to you." Michael responds, "Since your father saw fit to give it to me, and since he had it long before you -- I think we should both respect his wishes." Jennifer then says, "My father, as you well know is dead. I'm not. I carry the name now -- and I refuse to have it attached to violence and a vigilante state of mind."

- Michael talks more about Wilton's dream than what makes it into the final script: "He chose to save the basis of charity and caring - the law. Without it there's nothing. No 'cusps' or 'quantum leaps'. With it, there's a chance. That's all we want - to guarantee that chance. If it takes going through a wall, we go through a wall. Walls can be fixed."

- The real name of the man who takes Devon's place is Jonathan Elliott.

- An additional scene shows Devon's palm prints being copied and Elliott listening to recordings of Devon's voice.

- A scene was written where Dr. Von Furst produces the neutralizer for K.I.T.T.'s molecular bonded shell: "A destabilizing agent that will make Michael Knight's super car exceedingly mortal on contact."

- The description of K.I.T.T.'s destruction: "The battering ram punches into the defenseless K.I.T.T. time and again, rending huge holes in a ruthless, brutalizing attack. The rear wheels try to dig in...K.I.T.T. swings in a weak half circle, not enough to elude the full force of the Juggernaut; it blasts into what little is left of K.I.T.T., flipping him over and over. K.I.T.T. comes to a stop on his roof, one wheel spinning slowly. A series of shots graphically detailing the carnage: K.I.T.T., once so invulnerable, now lies at a grotesque angle, pierced and punctured at will, as if torn apart by a savage beast."

- RC3 tells his workers, "Now remember, if Michael or Bonnie notices the 'C' button, play dumb -- which from my own personal experience I know you're good at. I want it to be a surprise."

- In the scene where Bonnie is inside K.I.T.T. asking what the 'C' button is for, she is re-installing K.I.T.T.'s CPU.

- K.I.T.T. originally doesn't fire up when he's rebuilt. Bonnie makes an adjustment under the hood and then he starts.

Featured Songs:

"We Don't Need Another Hero" by Tina Turner

K.I.T.T.'s Capabilities:

- Auto Cruise, Comprehensive Configuration Analyzer, Convertible Mode, Emergency Braking System, Heat Sensors, Infrared, Micro Jam, Oil Slick, Passive Laser Restraint System, Police/Radio Frequency, Protect, Pursuit, Radar, Self-Analyzing Probe, Super Pursuit Mode, Turbo Boost

PROD. #60216

$$\Big[\begin{array}{c} \text{EPISODE} \\ 65 \end{array}\Big]$$

Script History:

July 26, 1985 (F.R.)

July 30, 1985 (F.R.)

July 31, 1985 (F.R.)

August 2, 1985 (F.R.)

August 5, 1985 (F.R.)

August 6, 1985 (F.R.)

KITTNAP

Written By: Skip Webster

Directed By: Bernard McEveety

Original Airdate: September 27, 1985 (Friday, 8:00 PM) (19.3%; 16,580,000)

NBC Rerun #1: March 21, 1986 (Friday, 8:00 PM) (17.1%; 14,690,000)

Filming Dates: August 6-14, 1985

"No wonder I've been feeling itchy lately."

-Michael

Crew: Robert Foster (Executive Producer), Burton Armus (Supervising Producer), Bruce Lansbury (Supervising Producer), Gino Grimaldi (Producer), Glen A. Larson (Creator), Gregory S. Dinallo (Co-Producer), Robert Ewing (Coordinating Producer), Michael Eric Stein (Story Editor), Ron Martinez (Associate Producer/Unit Production Manager), Bruce Golin (Associate Producer), Stu Phillips (Theme), Don Peake (Music), H. John Penner (Director of Photography), Lou Montejano (Art Director), Edward Nassour (Editor), Roberto Villar (First Assistant Director), Bruce A. Humphrey (Second Assistant Director), Donna Dockstader (Casting), R. Lynn Smartt (Set Decorator), John Shouse (Sound Editor), Richard Lapham (Music Editor), Barry Downing (Costume Supervisor), Karen J. Braverman (Costume Supervisor), Jack Gill (2nd Unit Director/Stunt Coordinator), Pat Somerset (Sound), Jeremy Swan (Make-up), Allen Payne (Hairstylist)

Guest Cast: Daniel Faraldo (Julian Martin), Janine Turner (Karen Forester), Robert O'Reilly (Snyder), Denise Galik (Jodi Hopkins), Robert F. Lyons (Jeffery Cavanaugh), Nick Angotti (Councilman), Nick Savage (Lukas Hall), Jim Bullock (Dog Catcher)

Michael's relaxing afternoon is interrupted when a former foe escapes from prison.

A Look Back:

Robert F. Lyons played bad guy Jeffrey Cavanaugh in this installment, a man who breaks out of prison with the help of Julian Martin. "I don't mind being the bad or good guy, any role and the bigger the challenge, the better." Lyons had been acting for almost thirty years when he got the role, starring in everything from *The Monkees* TV series to acting alongside Charles Bronson in both *Death Wish 2* and *Ten to Midnight*.

"As a teenager in Albany, New York, all I wanted to do was become an actor", recalls Lyons. "In 1965, I went to Hollywood and started in television right away. I had a very strong drive to do it and love it." One of Lyons' first roles was in the TV classic *I Dream of Jeannie.*

Lyons partner in crime was Julian Martin, played by actor Daniel Faraldo. "I remember Daniel well. We were different actors and had different training," says Lyons.

Faraldo ends up turning on his old friend when he shoots him dead towards the end of the episode. Lyons says that his character's demise is something very familiar to him. "I have to laugh at this. My dear mother watched me get 'killed' in so many different films and TV shows, that her first question to me was always, 'Honey, do you die in this one?'. I can recall a time I was visiting home and a show was to air one of the nights I was there and she told a person, 'You have to watch this one. He doesn't die in it'."

Lyons says that he got along very well with David Hasselhoff. "I did meet him and he was a wonderful person, very cordial and very grateful that I was doing his show. He knew how to treat his guest stars well. I like the guy a lot."

Still acting, Lyons also teaches the art and has recently gone into the world of children's publishing with his first book, Polar Dog.

In "KITTnap", viewers got the chance to see RC3 behind the wheel of the F.L.A.G. semi. "The studio actually sent me to truck driving school and I earned a real license to drive a semi," says Peter Parros. "The hardest part of driving it was backing up, which I never did on camera. It was fun to drive it, but my license has since expired. At the truck driving school, they told me, 'If you ever want to get into truck driving, you'd do really well'."

Knight Knotes:

- The helicopter used to pick up Cavanaugh at the beginning of the episode is a Bell 206B Jet Ranger III, registration number N230CA, serial number 2779. This same helicopter can also be seen in *Blue Thunder*, *Commando*, *Lethal Weapon*, *Darkman* and the first episode of *MacGyver*. This helicopter was damaged beyond repair in September 2005 when it crashed while documenting the damage that Hurricane Katrina caused in New Orleans.
- Cavanaugh's getaway car seen at the start of the episode wears three different license plates during the chase: 1MCU745, 1MCU770 and 1MCU767.
- RC3 mentions to Michael that he misses the Street Avenger action - a reference to "Knight of the Juggernaut".

Script to Screen:

- The dog that hides in K.I.T.T. is named Scruffy.
- When K.I.T.T. asks Michael is he should microlock Cavanuagh's brakes, Michael replies, "No, he might crash into those tanks." However, if you watch his lips, he's actually saying, "No, we don't know what's in those tanks", which is what is written in the script.

K.I.T.T.'s Capabilities:

- Anharmonic Synthesizer, Auto Cruise, Auto Phone, Auto-Roof Left, Auto Vac. System, Convertible Mode, Emergency Braking System, Homing Signal, Passive Laser Restraint System, Police/Radio Frequency, Super Pursuit Mode, Tinted Windows, Turbo Boost

PROD. #60219

⎧ EPISODE ⎫
⎩ 66 ⎭

Script History:

August 6, 1985 (F.R.)

August 8, 1985 (F.R.)

August 12, 1985 (F.R.)

August 13, 1985 (F.R.)

August 14, 1985 (F.R.)

August 15, 1985 (F.R.)

August 15, 1985 (2nd rev.)

August 16, 1985 (F.R.)

SKY KNIGHT

Working Title: "Doomsday"

Written By: Carlton Hollander and Dennis Rodriguez

Directed By: Jeffrey Hayden

Original Airdate: October 18, 1985 (Friday, 8:00 PM) (16.7%; 14,350,000)

NBC Rerun #1: June 6, 1986 (Friday, 8:00 PM) (14.4%; 12,370,000)

Filming Dates: August 15-22, 1985

"I'm the only sworn officer in these here parts to ticket a talkin' car??? It just don't get any better'n that."

-Sheriff Amos

Crew: Robert Foster (Executive Producer), Burton Armus (Supervising Producer), Bruce Lansbury (Supervising Producer), Gino Grimaldi (Producer), Glen A. Larson (Creator), Gregory S. Dinallo (Co-Producer), Robert Ewing (Coordinating Producer), Michael Eric Stein (Story Editor), Ron Martinez (Associate Producer/Unit Production Manager), Bruce Golin (Associate Producer), Stu Phillips (Theme), Don Peake (Music), H. John Penner (Director of Photography), Lou Montejano (Art Director), Lawrence J. Gleason (Editor), Louis Race (First Assistant Director), Bruce A. Humphrey (Second Assistant Director), Donna Dockstader (Casting), R. Lynn Smartt (Set Decorator), John Shouse (Sound Editor), Richard Lapham (Music Editor), Barry Downing (Costume Supervisor), Karen J. Braverman (Costume Supervisor), Jack Gill (2nd Unit Director/Stunt Coordinator), Pat Somerset (Sound), Jeremy Swan (Make-up), Allen Payne (Hairstylist)

Guest Cast: Ron O'Neal (Charles Zurich), Robbie Rist (Nick), Dennis Pratt (Steven), Macon McCalman (Calvin Holmes), Barbara Townsend (Mrs. Swanson), Jeffrey Alan Chandler (Lloyd Swanson), Susan Blu (Mary), Will Gill Jr. (Security Officer), Brian Thompson (Kurt), Bob Coker (Ticket Agent), Pope Freeman (Captain Bill Rogers), Jack Starrett (Sheriff Amos)

Michael and Devon begin a frantic search for a hijacked plane containing many passengers – including Bonnie.

A Look Back:

Series co-star Peter Parros recalls working with Supervising Producer Burton Armus. "Burt's a tough guy. He was a New York homicide cop who worked his way from technical advisor, to writer, to show runner. He really knows how to write a story and has very strong patriotic ideals. I think that is reflected in his writing. I owe my being cast as RC3 on *Knight Rider* to Burt.

After *Knight Rider*, Burt hired me to work for him on the syndicated series *Adam-12* the 90's, which was also shot at Universal. Over the years, Burt has been a very good friend."

The right hand blind drive car (Photo courtesy of Christopher Orlando)

Knight Knotes:

- The scenes where Michael is avoiding the missiles just prior to entering the compound is reused footage from "Deadly Maneuvers" and "Knight Strike".

- From an October 1, 1985 NBC memo: "First draft filled with action but lacked logic in spots. Re-write improved although production costs have necessitated several changes. This episode will require a great deal of post-production (and miniature) work. This episode is slow to start but ends fairly well. Notes given to strengthen the opening with some pick-ups being considered."

- Listen to the announcements in the airport terminal at the beginning of the episode - one of the names mentioned is Robert Ewing, the fourth season producer. He's also paged in the hotel lobby in the earlier episode "Knight Strike".

- The police report on the airport bombers can only be seen briefly on the semi's computer screen, but this is what it said:

CRIME REPORT

SUITCASE BOMB

ATTEMPTED HIJACKING

SUSPECTS VEHICLE: LATE MODEL TAN VAN

SUSPECTS: DAN SACKHEIN & BRICE RUSSELL

LOCATION: LAX

DATE/TIME: 9/23/85 11:00 A.M.

SUSPECTS BELONGINGS: (2) 45 CALIBER AUTOMATIC WEAPONS

NO IDENTIFICATION

(6) PACKS OF CIGARETTES

DRIVE IN MOVIE STUBS FOR SAME MOVIE (6) DAYS IN A ROW

NO OTHER POSSESSIONS

SUSPECTS ATTEMPTED TO BRING SUITCASE BOMB ON BOARD AIRCRAFT

WERE APPREHENDED JUST OUTSIDE AIRPORT TERMINAL AFTER SHORT

CHASE.

VAN WAS STOPPED BY BLACK T-TOP BELONGING TO F.L.A.G.

Script to Screen:

- The plane disappears from the radar after Zurich uses some sophisticated equipment in his attaché case.

- The name of the two men who are caught at the airport after trying to run a fake bomb through security are named Larry and Eddie.

- Devon asks RC3 if he should be behind the wheel of the semi, but he comments that the semi is on auto pilot, just as he does in "Burial Ground".

- Zurich lands the plane at an abandoned military compound called Harris Field.

- The description of K.I.T.T. switching to Super Pursuit Mode: "An air dam slides down on K.I.T.T.'s front end. The rear fin converts to a new aerodynamic shape as the rear end lifts up to expose two jet exhausts. Side vents slide outward. An air intake vent pops up from the hood. The Super Pursuit Mode transformation complete, K.I.T.T. explodes."

- K.I.T.T. originally turbo boosts into the Doomsday room to stop the device from exploding, instead of Michael taking the elevator.

- After Sheriff Amos tells K.I.T.T. that he's the only officer around to give a ticket to a talking car, K.I.T.T. moans and drives away by himself. In the episode, the scene cuts before K.I.T.T. drives away. However, a sharp eye can spot that they used the blind drive K.I.T.T. in that scene anyways.

K.I.T.T.'s Capabilities:

- Auto Cruise, Electrical Generation Mode, Electronic Pilot Override, Microlock, Micropulse, Passive Laser Restraint System, Super Pursuit Mode, Surveillance Mode, Protect, Tinted Windows, Voice Analyzer

PROD. #60204

{ EPISODE
67 }

Script History:

June 25, 1985 (F.R.)

July 10, 1985 (F.R.)

July 16, 1985 (F.R.)

July 18, 1985 (F.R.)

July 24, 1985 (F.R.)

July 25, 1985 (F.R.)

July 26, 1985 (F.R.)

BURIAL GROUND

Written By: Michael Eric Stein

Directed By: Chuck Bail

Original Airdate: October 25, 1985 (Friday, 8:00 PM) (17.0%; 14,600,000)

NBC Rerun #1: June 13, 1986 (Friday, 8:00 PM) (10.0%; 9,360,000)

Filming Dates: July 25-August 5, 1985

"Throwing me out could prove hazardous to your health."

-Michael

Crew: Robert Foster (Executive Producer), Burton Armus (Supervising Producer), Bruce Lansbury (Supervising Producer), Gino Grimaldi (Producer), Glen A. Larson (Creator), Gregory S. Dinallo (Co-Producer), Mark Jones (Co-Producer), Robert Ewing (Coordinating Producer), Michael Eric Stein (Story Editor), Ron Martinez (Associate Producer/Unit Production Manager), Bruce Golin (Associate Producer), Stu Phillips (Theme), Don Peake (Music), H. John Penner (Director of Photography), Lou Montejano (Art Director), Domenic G. DiMascio (Editor), Louis Race (First Assistant Director), Bruce A. Humphrey (Second Assistant Director), Donna Dockstader (Casting), Rochelle Moser (Set Decorator), John Shouse (Sound Editor), Richard Lapham (Music Editor), Barry Downing (Costume Supervisor), Karen J. Braverman (Costume Supervisor), Jack Gill (2nd Unit Director/Stunt Coordinator), Pat Somerset (Sound), Jeremy Swan (Make-up), Allen Payne (Hairstylist)

Guest Cast: Robert Pine (Cyrus Oakes), Gina Gallego (Susan Christopher), Ron Soble (Dr. Thorne), George O. Petrie (Dr. Quentin Tanner), Michael Horse (Jonathan Eagle), Ivan Naranjo (Simpson), Ron Joseph (Thomas), Greg Finley (Chauffeur/Henchman), Signy Coleman (Barbara Ralston), Joshua Gallegos (Lucas), Frank Roach (Jim), Jerado Decordovier (Blue Feather), Lesa Weis (Lisa)

Michael's vacation is once again interrupted when a young woman needs the Foundation's help in order to stop a greedy businessman from gaining control of sacred Indian territory.

A Look Back:

Peter Parros' only scenes in this episode were inside the semi. But he confirms that shooting in the semi was not as small and awkward as it looked on screen. "Shooting the semi shots was pretty easy. It does look tight but there were only three walls and several wall sections were movable. The funny thing is we have a conversation about the semi rolling down the highway driverless, but the shot of the semi rolling down the highway shows a driver!"

Producer Bruce Golin, onboard since season three's "Halloween Knight", also worked to make sure that the close up shots that involved the studio dash and other props worked perfectly. "Having the responsibility for filming everything on the 'camera-ready' dashboard from the turbo boost button to K.I.T.T.'s voice box and all of K.I.T.T.'s various added features was so much fun. When K.I.T.T. sprouted wings after being re-built, I had the camera-ready K.I.T.T. from George Barris on the back lot at Universal filming as many of the functions that could be captured in close up. We shot hundreds of inserts during the course of the television season which had to do with either K.I.T.T. or some story point."

Knight Knotes:

- NBC's comments on the initial script: "First draft was adequate with sufficient action and jeopardy. Notes given to make some of the specific beats more creative and to tighten the story structure."
- Peter Parros on Associate Producer Bruce Golin: "I remember Bruce was just getting started. He was a fun producer and one of the younger guys on the production side."

Script to Screen:

- The Indian who thinks that K.I.T.T. is the "God of the Wind" is named Blue Feather.

Featured Songs:

"Country Road" by James Taylor

K.I.T.T.'s Capabilities:

- Auto Cruise, Comprehensive Configuration Analyzer, Convertible Mode, Electrical Generation Mode, Emergency Braking System, Hydraulic Lift, Infrared, Micro Jam, Passive Laser Restraint System, Smoke Release, Super Pursuit Mode, Surveillance Mode, Turbo Boost, Zoom In

PROD. #60221

{ EPISODE
68 }

Script History:

August 19, 1985 (F.R.)

August 23, 1985 (F.R.)

August 27, 1985 (F.R.)

THE WRONG CROWD

Written By: Gregory S. Dinallo

Directed By: Chuck Bail

Original Airdate: November 1, 1985 (Friday, 8:00 PM) (16.5%; 14,170,000)

NBC Rerun #1: May 9, 1986 (Friday, 8:00 PM) (17.0%; 14,600,000)

Filming Dates: September 9-17, 1985

"Now I know how Michael felt when K.I.T.T. was destroyed. It's like part of me

is missing."

-Bonnie

Crew: Robert Foster (Executive Producer), Burton Armus (Supervising Producer), Bruce Lansbury (Supervising Producer), Gino Grimaldi (Producer), Glen A. Larson (Creator), Gregory S. Dinallo (Co-Producer), Robert Ewing (Coordinating Producer), Michael Eric Stein (Story Editor), Ron Martinez (Associate Producer/Unit Production Manager), Bruce Golin (Associate Producer), Stu Phillips (Theme), Don Peake (Music), H. John Penner (Director of Photography), Lou Montejano (Art Director), Grant Hoag (Editor), Louis Race (First Assistant Director), Bruce A. Humphrey (Second Assistant Director), Donna Dockstader (Casting), R. Lynn Smartt (Set Decorator), John Shouse (Sound Editor), Richard Lapham (Music Editor), Barry Downing (Costume Supervisor), Karen J. Braverman (Costume Supervisor), Jack Gill (2nd Unit Director/Stunt Coordinator), Pat Somerset (Sound), Jeremy Swan (Make-up), Allen Payne (Hairstylist)

Guest Cast: Mark Schneider (Scott Hollander), Gary Hershberger (Nicholas Arkett), Scott Valentine (Colton), Charles Fleischer (Hitchhiker), Julie Ronnie (Erika), William Joyce (Glen Arkett), Suzanne Rogers (Lydia Arkett), Kandace Kuehl (Ann Galloway), Ted Petersen (Pop Galloway), Nancy Omi (Ferret Technician)

While searching the road for a shipment of vodka, Scott Hollander and his cohorts unknowingly hijack the Foundation semi.

A Look Back:

In "The Wrong Crowd", RC3 is driving the semi when he is forced out by a gang of bikers. "John Sherrod actually took the fall," says Peter Parros. "He was my first stunt double. It was great stunt work." However, Parros does not remain convinced about the scene which made it into the final cut. "It's not the best shot because you can see a lot of pads and I don't think the stunt guy looked like me." Despite that, Parros does remember this episode fondly. "It was a fun couple of days. The location was real remote and there were plenty of motorcycles to test ride!"

David Hasselhoff on set (Photo courtesy of Christopher Orlando)

Knight Knotes:

- Peter Parros on director Chuck Bail: "Chuck is a great guy and a terrific director. He was a stunt man so he's excellent with action. He had great stories about working on Westerns and was personally inspiring."
- NBC's comments on the script: "Adequate first draft received. Notes given to make the emotional base of the story more compelling. Second draft improved somewhat but cost cuts have scaled down this episode. There have been both good action and better than average performances. This episode starts fast but runs out of gas."

- TV Guide described this episode as follows: "Bikers hijack the Foundation's truck and use its advanced computers to go on a crime spree".
- The Ferret vehicle was initially built for the television series *Logan's Run*.
- This episode marked Scott Valentine's TV debut. Valentine would go on to become a regular on another NBC series, *Family Ties*.

K.I.T.T.'s Capabilities:

- Auto Cruise, Auto Phone, CO_2, Convertible Mode, Emergency Braking System , Medical Scan, Microlock, Passive Laser Restraint System, Police/Radio Frequency, Pursuit, Radar, Super Pursuit Mode , Thermo Dynamic Generator, Tinted Windows, Turbo Boost, Voice Projection

PROD. #60224

[EPISODE
   69]

Script History:

September 13, 1985 (F.R.)

KNIGHT STING

Written By: Herman Miller

Directed By: Sidney Hayers

Original Airdate: November 8, 1985 (Friday, 8:00 PM) (18.7%; 16,060,000)

NBC Rerun #1: May 2, 1986 (Friday, 8:00 PM) (15.9%; 13,660,000)

Filming Dates: September 27 – October 7, 1985

"I'm the Knight Industries Two Thousand, not a tomato on wheels."

-K.I.T.T.

Crew: Robert Foster (Executive Producer), Burton Armus (Supervising Producer), Bruce Lansbury (Supervising Producer), Gino Grimaldi (Producer), Glen A. Larson (Creator), Gregory S. Dinallo (Co-Producer), Robert Ewing (Coordinating Producer), Michael Eric Stein (Story Editor), Ron Martinez (Associate Producer/Unit Production Manager), Bruce Golin (Associate Producer), Stu Phillips (Theme), Don Peake (Music), H. John Penner (Director of Photography), Lou Montejano (Art Director), Edward Nassour (Editor), Louis Race (First Assistant Director), Bruce A. Humphrey (Second Assistant Director), Donna Dockstader (Casting), R. Lynn Smartt (Set Decorator), John Shouse (Sound Editor), Richard Lapham (Music Editor), Barry Downing (Costume Supervisor), Karen J. Braverman (Costume Supervisor), Jack Gill (2nd Unit Director/Stunt Coordinator), Pat Somerset (Sound), Jeremy Swan (Make-up), Allen Payne (Hairstylist)

Guest Cast: Walter Gotell (Simon Carascas), Kabir Bedi (Vascone), Pepe Serna (Lupo), Beth Miller (Gaye Hollenbeck), Larry Storch (Pascal), Tom Rosqui (August Hollenbeck), Marc Tubert (Antoun), Anthony Peck (Jorge), Frank Ronzio (Franco), James Ingersoll (Dr. Gottlieb), Richard Epcar (Guard), Branscombe Richmond (Hitman)

Michael goes undercover as a hit man in order to stop a diplomatically immune man from leaving the country with a canister of deadly poison.

A Look Back:

"Knight Sting" is partially remembered for the wild Lynx Imperial car that is featured throughout the episode. Peter Parros recalls, "I believe the car came from Jay Ohrberg, who provided most of the specialty cars for the show. I thought it was a pretty cool car.". Despite having that car on set, Parros had a soft spot in his heart for another vehicle on the show. "I got a kick out of driving the Mercedes 450SL convertible. At the time, it was my favorite car."

Parros likes to look back on this episode as the F.L.A.G. agents really working as a team to take down the bad guys. "'Knight Sting' was kind of a take on Mission Impossible. We really were a team! So, I liked this episode a lot because Michael, Bonnie and RC all had a lot to do. Even Devon got in on the act." Veteran actor Walter Gotell played the bad guy, Simon Carascas, and Parros remembers him well. "It was just great to have scenes with him. I had watched him as the bad guy in several James Bond movies, so working with him really made me feel that I had made it big. As I recall, Walter was personal friends with Sidney Hayers, who had previously directed him in a movie. They had some interesting stories."

Aside from working alongside such an astute actor, Parros confirms that he got to know someone much closer to home a bit better as well. "This was the first time that I had a chance to get to know Patricia McPherson, who was terrific in this episode."

"Knight Sting" will always have a special place in Parros' heart, as it coincided with a major event in his own life. "I got married to my wife, Jerri, on October 5th. At the time, I thought I would get the day before my wedding off (Friday), because I was getting married the next day. However, we had to shoot late. As I recall, we were at the hospital where I jump off the roof onto the bad guy."

Stunt coordinator Jack Gill recalls the Lynx Imperial and other specialized Knight Rider vehicles. "Some of the specialized vehicles ran, some of them didn't and some of them were just props that looked like supersonic vehicles. We had one that was supposed to be solar powered ["The Wrong Crowd"], much like what they have today, but that was just a prop it was never a realistic solar powered car. [The Lynx Imperial] was supposed to be a rocket car - that also was a prop. On occasion, we did get some interesting cars in like drag cars, but those two cars were just props that didn't do anything - they just provided something interesting to look at."

Producer Bruce Golin was intimately involved in the "look" of K.I.T.T. shedding his Lynx Imperial skin. He recalls, "Critical to the episode was how to 'believably' reveal K.I.T.T. shedding the red 'skin' and becoming himself again. There was much hand ringing in post as I tried several different solutions from our special effects team, finally finding a substance that would melt quickly enough in close up to sell the idea."

Knight Knotes:

- NBC's comments on the script: "First draft has some style, but still needs twists, turns and action. Revised script has more twists but still lacks scope. Dailies have been adequate although Mr. Gotell at times went too broad. This is a briskly paced episode that tells a better than average story quickly."
- TV Guide described this episode as follows: "Bonnie poses as a jetsetter to gain access to an embassy planning to ship a canister of deadly bacteria out of the country".
- Carascas' embassy can also be seen as the Helios estate in "Chariot of Gold" and as the home of Tanika in "Knight of the Rising Sun".
- The 1955 Lynx Imperial is, in reality, the famous Moon automotive "Moonliner". It was originally built by Jocko Johnson and later purchased by Dean Moon in 1964.
- The Mercedes convertible that RC3 drives in this episode is the same one that Devon drives in "Halloween Knight" – it even sports the same California license plate: 1BHO934.

Déjà Vu:

- Kabir Bedi returns in the *Team Knight Rider* episode "The Blonde Woman".

K.I.T.T.'s Capabilities:

- Audio/Video Playback, Audio/Video Record, Auto Cruise, Auto Phone, Medical Scan, Micro Jam, Super Pursuit Mode, Surveillance Mode, Turbo Boost, Vocal Synthesizer, Voice Projection, X-Ray Mode

PROD. #60203

{ EPISODE
70 }

Script History:

August 12, 1985 (F.R.)

MANY HAPPY RETURNS

Written By: Michael Halperin

Directed By: Georg Fenady

Original Airdate: November 15, 1985 (Friday, 8:00 PM) (20.1%; 17,270,000)

NBC Rerun #1: June 20, 1986 (Friday, 8:00 PM) (12.6%; 10,820,000)

Filming Dates: August 26 – September 4, 1985

"It's been four years since we've all been together. Four years ago, I was

reborn."

-Michael

Crew: Robert Foster (Executive Producer), Burton Armus (Supervising Producer), Bruce Lansbury (Supervising Producer), Gino Grimaldi (Producer), Glen A. Larson (Creator), Gregory S. Dinallo (Co-Producer), Robert Ewing (Coordinating Producer), Michael Eric Stein (Story Editor), Ron Martinez (Associate Producer/Unit Production Manager), Bruce Golin (Associate Producer), Stu Phillips (Theme), Don Peake (Music), H. John Penner (Director of Photography), Lou Montejano (Art Director), Lawrence J. Vallario (Editor), Roberto Villar (First Assistant Director), Bruce A. Humphrey (Second Assistant Director), Donna Dockstader (Casting), R. Lynn Smartt (Set Decorator), John Shouse (Sound Editor), Richard Lapham (Music Editor), Barry Downing (Costume Supervisor), Karen J. Braverman (Costume Supervisor), Jack Gill (2nd Unit Director/Stunt Coordinator), Pat Somerset (Sound), Jeremy Swan (Make-up), Allen Payne (Hairstylist)

Guest Cast: D.D. Howard (Amy Lowell), Nicholas Pryor (Vince Lewison), Arthur Batanides (Henry Quincy), Paul Brinegar (Chuck), Peter Mark Richman (Kleist), David Wells (Phil Miller)

Michael is enjoying his birthday when it is interrupted by a young executive who needs Michael's help when her prototype hovercraft is stolen.

A Look Back:

Peter Parros fondly remembers working with series co-star Edward Mulhare. "As a kid, I used to watch *The Ghost and Mrs. Muir*. It was like working with a childhood idol, somebody you really respect. He was such a pro and I learned a lot from him. For that time, it was like a little family. We had dinner together and things like that, but it was really a great pleasure to work with him. *Knight Rider* was my first series experience and he had so much experience, so he would give me little acting tips and whatnot. I wish he were here today."

David Hasselhoff eases K.I.T.T. into position (Photo courtesy of Tyler Ham)

Knight Knotes:

- NBC's comments on the script: "Script delivered in fair shape with third act problems. Notes given to make Michael and K.I.T.T. more active. Production cutbacks have scaled down the action. Dailies have been adequate. Although the hovercraft is promotable, this is an average, by the numbers episode."

Script to Screen:

- Vince's last name is revealed to be Lewison. He is the chief designer of the hovercraft. He is described as "plump" and "bald".
- The Twelve Palms Hotel is called the Carmel Pines Hotel.

- Instead of Michael being forced into the ocean, he instead jumps in K.I.T.T. and faces the killer car head-on. K.I.T.T. jumps over the car and the attacker and his car go into the ocean. He used a scuba tank stored in the car to escape.

- Michael chases the motorcycle carrying the man who killed Quincy. The chase leads to the L.A. riverbed where the cyclist disappears into a sewage tunnel. This scene sounds identical to the one we actually see in season three's "The Ice Bandits".

- Bonnie was able to jam the radio signal without Michael and K.I.T.T. travelling to the top of a mountain to act as a relay.

- The Lowell Industries guard's name is Tyler.

- In the room that Vince locks Michael and Amy in, he activates a halon gas used to extinguish fires. It sucks the air out of the room. Michael calls K.I.T.T. and he crashes into the building before opening the door.

- The Hovercraft rams K.I.T.T. in an attempt to get to the open sea, which disables K.I.T.T.'s Microlock. The Hovercraft then fires a "smart missile", but K.I.T.T. travels behind a sand dune to escape.

Featured Songs:

"Obsession" by Animotion

K.I.T.T.'s Capabilities:

- Auto Cruise, Auto Phone, Auto-Roof Left, Convertible Mode, Emergency Braking System, Grappling Hook, Medical Scan, Micro Jam, Super Pursuit Mode, Surveillance Lock, Surveillance Mode, Ultra Frequency Modulator, Ultrasonic Frequency, Winch

PROD. #60222

⎰ EPISODE ⎱
⎱   71   ⎰

Script History:

August 30, 1985 (F.R.)

September 4, 1985 (F.R.)

KNIGHT RACER

Written By: Paul Diamond

Directed By: Charles Watson Sanford

Original Airdate: November 29, 1985 (Friday, 8:00 PM) (17.2%; 14,770,000)

NBC Rerun #1: July 4, 1986 (Friday, 8:00 PM) (10.7%; 9,190,000)

Filming Dates: September 18-26, 1985

"If I keep feeling that beat, I won't just loosen up, I'll fall apart."

-K.I.T.T.

Crew: Robert Foster (Executive Producer), Burton Armus (Supervising Producer), Bruce Lansbury (Supervising Producer), Gino Grimaldi (Producer), Glen A. Larson (Creator), Gregory S. Dinallo (Co-Producer), Robert Ewing (Coordinating Producer), Michael Eric Stein (Story Editor), Ron Martinez (Associate Producer/Unit Production Manager), Bruce Golin (Associate Producer), Stu Phillips (Theme), Don Peake (Music), H. John Penner (Director of Photography), Lou Montejano (Art Director), Domenic G. DiMascio (Editor), Roberto Villar (First Assistant Director), Bruce A. Humphrey (Second Assistant Director), Donna Dockstader (Casting), R. Lynn Smartt (Set Decorator), John Shouse (Sound Editor), Richard Lapham (Music Editor), Barry Downing (Costume Supervisor), Karen J. Braverman (Costume Supervisor), Jack Gill (2nd Unit Director/Stunt Coordinator), Pat Somerset (Sound), Jeremy Swan (Make-up), Allen Payne (Hairstylist)

Guest Cast: Jourdan Fremin (Elena Thomas), William Windom (Wayne Altfield), John Crawford (Mac Thomas), Grainger Hines (Steve Cochran), Tom Williams (Lon), Cliff Carnel (Jonathan Tunkel), John Mahon (Alfie Girdler), Pamela Bach (Betty), Norbert Weisser (Fredo Lurani)

Bonnie's old friend needs the Foundation's help when her Indy car is destroyed during a racing accident.

A Look Back:

In 1985, television writer Paul Diamond was in demand. He had just wrote the *Miami Vice* episode "Evan", which to this day is regarded as one of the best episodes in the show's history. A few months later, he was hired to write an episode of *Knight Rider*.

"I turned in the first draft to the producers," says Diamond. "I had been working with Greg Dinallo and Bruce Lansbury. I was summoned to a meeting with them and supervising producer Burt Armus. I walked in the door and Burt, who I had never met, threw the script down in front of me and said, 'What is this? You made the car talk like a freakin' sissy!' Nice introduction. I said, 'The car is a freakin' sissy!", and the meeting went slightly uphill from there. K.I.T.T. always seemed a little prissy to me.. I'm sure this was remedied in my second and their subsequent drafts."

Diamond started his career with a piece he had written in college. "When I was 23, I sold a novel I'd written in college to Paramount called The Chicken Chronicles. It got me an agent who, in turn, started to get me work."

Diamond remembers that the studio would not give him all the details that he required in order to write the story. "Effects wise, all I knew was that this season was the debut of the new incarnation of K.I.T.T., so I had to use the super pursuit mode and the changing body surfaces. The outside writers were never given technical details for some reason. On a *Star Trek* show, for example, you would have a stack of paper a foot high. I had to learn all the new 'tricks' off a promotional postcard a friend had."

The original story for "Knight Racer" started as a completely different episode than what viewers see on screen. "I recall the original story was about an experimental racing engine that some foreign entity wanted to steal to use in a Humvee-style armored vehicle. At some point, this would have included a K.I.T.T. vs. race car chase through the streets of Long Beach and up and through the mothballed Queen Mary ocean liner at her mooring. It was a very elaborate story and it was replaced early on by what you see now."

Diamond recalls watching the episode when it originally aired. "I did see it. I thought it was adequate, nothing special. Remember, this was a story more or less by committee and a script that was out of my hands after the second draft. You don't get real proprietary with those."

Though Diamond did not meet David Hasselhoff at the time of writing the episode, he would years later. "David Hasselhoff's kids and my son went to the same school. I went over to him at an open house and jokingly thanked him for the ongoing royalty payments."

"Knight Racer" shows a classic example of the banter and humor shared between Devon and his newest employee, RC3. "Edward was a father figure to me," recalls Peter Parros. "We developed a very nice friendship. *Knight Rider* was my first big job - my 'big break'. Edward often gave me acting tips and was very gracious about the way he did it. He was fun, but in a very different way from David Hasselhoff. Very British, and I didn't always realize he was joking with me, until after." Parros confirms that the champagne opening at the very end was quite messy. "It sure looks like we got a good spray," jokes Parros.

Knight Knotes:

- NBC's comments on the script: "Predictable first draft received. Notes given to increase the suspense and credibility. Dailies have been disappointing as Mr. Sanford has covered the racing scenes awkwardly."
- Pamela Bach, who plays Betty in this episode, would go on to marry David Hasselhoff.
- The end credits feature a special note regarding the music video seen in the episode: "Music video courtesy of MCA Record. Kim Wilde – 'Go For It'"

Script to Screen:

- In the script, Steve Cochran was initially named Corky Batchelor, while Fredo Lurani was originally known as Paolo Lurani. Lurani's boat was named The Bullseye.

Featured Songs:

"Go For It" by Kim Wilde

K.I.T.T.'s Capabilities:

- Audio/Video Record, Auto Cruise, Auto Phone, Chemical Analyzer, Convertible Mode, Grappling Hook, Medical Scan, Metallurgical Stress Analyzer, Oxygen Vent, Passive Laser Restraint System, Printer, Self-Analyzing Probe, Signal, Super Pursuit Mode, Surveillance Mode, Trunk Lid, Ultrasonic Frequency, Video Playback, Voice Projection, Winch

PROD. #60202

{ EPISODE 72 }

Script History:

October 3, 1985 (F.R.)

October 10, 1985 (F.R.)

KNIGHT BEHIND BARS

Working Title: "Girls' Knight Out"

Written By: Richard Okie

Directed By: Bernard McEveety

Original Airdate: December 6, 1985 (Friday, 8:00 PM) (16.7%; 14,350,000)

NBC Rerun #1: July 18, 1986 (Friday, 8:00 PM) (13.3%; 11,600,000)

Filming Dates: October 22-30, 1985

"I've never seen a happy jogger."

-K.I.T.T.

Crew: Robert Foster (Executive Producer), Burton Armus (Supervising Producer), Bruce Lansbury (Supervising Producer), Gino Grimaldi (Producer), Glen A. Larson (Creator), Gregory S. Dinallo (Co-Producer), Robert Ewing (Coordinating Producer), Michael Eric Stein (Story Editor), Ron Martinez (Associate Producer/Unit Production Manager), Bruce Golin (Associate Producer), Stu Phillips (Theme), Don Peake (Music), H. John Penner (Director of Photography), Lou Montejano (Art Director), Grant Hoag (Editor), Louis Race (First Assistant Director), Bruce A. Humphrey (Second Assistant Director), Donna Dockstader (Casting), R. Lynn Smartt (Set Decorator), John Shouse (Sound Editor), Richard Lapham (Music Editor), Barry Downing (Costume Supervisor), Karen J. Braverman (Costume Supervisor), Jack Gill (2nd Unit Director/Stunt Coordinator), Pat Somerset (Sound), Jeremy Swan (Make-up), Allen Payne (Hairstylist)

Guest Cast: Julianne McNamara (Julie Rodgers), Peter Brown (Jason Nelson), Victoria Bass (Christine Brooks), Stephen Meadows (Matt Erickson), Rosalind Ingledew (Samantha Lawton), Bobb Hopkins (Officer Roark), Gloria Hayes (Dina Shelton), Bonnie Hellman (Woman Jogger), Dominick Brascia (Young Man), Stephen Anthony Henry (Guard), Elven Havard (Gate Guard), Faith Minton (Darleen), Douglas Lawrence (Walsh), Harold "Hal" Frizzell (Prison Guard)

The F.L.A.G. team investigates a team of women who break out of prison to commit robberies and then go back.

A Look Back:

Stephen Meadows was best known by television viewers as Peter Flint in *Santa Barbara* before landing the role of Matt Erikson in "Knight Behind Bars". "*Knight Rider* was one of my first roles after doing daytime soaps, so everything was very new and I was just trying to get the lay of the land. I got the job after I did a reading for April Webster, who I believe did the casting for the show. It was the standard audition process at the time."

Meadows remembers that by the fourth season, the *Knight Rider* cast and crew were used to getting scenes shot and done in the first take. "My impression of the show was that since it had been on the air for some time, the production crew was very efficient and there always seemed to be a feeling of 'get it done A.S.A.P.' Everyone was on their toes and the shooting days were finished on time and within budget. I noticed how this was very different from a feature film, where each scene had to be studied in detail and many of the crew are working together for the first time. The show by now was a very well-oiled machine when I worked on 'Knight Behind Bars'. As a result, there was little to no rehearsal and the 'factory-like' production of the show moved along quickly. David Hasselhoff and Patricia McPherson knew their characters and were very accustomed to working with guest actors. They were both very easy to work with."

Knight Knotes:

- NBC's comments on the script: "This is a re-worked script from last year that still has problems. Notes given to start faster, increase the jeopardy and add a time element to give the story some edge. Improved script delivered that still needs work in the middle. Dailies have been adequate."

- Producer Bruce Golin on guest star Julianne McNamara: "The episode with Olympian Ms. McNamara was memorable because I got to work with her on the scene where we eventually, in post, added the laser beams. She was incredibly gracious and seemed thrilled to be acting instead of competing."

- Peter Parros on Julianne McNamara. "Julianne was very nice. She was very soft spoken, just like her character."
- On December 8, 1985, K.I.T.T. made a cameo appearance in an *Amazing Stories* episode titled "Remote Control Man". The story revolved around a man named Walter who bought a special television that allowed the characters seen on the screen to appear in real life. Eventually, he conjured up such characters as Ed McMahon, Templeton Peck from *The A-Team*, and even *The Incredible Hulk*! Just as Walter started to crack with the dozens of characters in his living room, K.I.T.T. came crashing through the side of his house, scanner blazing, and asked if anyone had seen Michael! The car was not voiced by William Daniels, but another actor with a similar voice. Ed McMahon told Walter to start tuning out the television and pay attention to the people in real life. K.I.T.T. chimed in and said, "Don't be such a boob, Walter".
- Julianne McNamara was once a gold medalist in the 1984 Summer Olympics.
- Matt Erikson's car, which was stolen by Julie in the episode, wears the California license plate 2BLA672. This same plate is seen on the green Chevy that Michael hides behind while getting shot at in "Killer K.I.T.T."

Script to Screen:

- Many elements of this episode came from a third season script entitled "Girls' Knight Out". In it, Christine Brooks' last name is Briggs; she and Jason Nelson use inmates to commit crimes. Matt Erickson is seriously injured as the inmates flee the scene in his stolen Ferrari. The basic story stays the same, however many of the other elements are rewritten for this episode.

- Michael and Bonnie are taken in a prison bus to a remote part of the desert, but they escape with K.I.T.T.'s help and turbo boost through the side of the bus, stopping Nelson and Briggs.

Featured Songs:

"Walking on a Thin Line" by Huey Lewis and the News

K.I.T.T.'s Capabilities:

- Anharmonic Synthesizer, Audio/Video Record, Auto Cruise, Auto-Roof Left, Eject Left, Emergency Braking System, Medical Scan, Micro Jam, Passive Laser Restraint System, Polyphonic Synthesizer, Super Pursuit Mode, Surveillance Mode

PROD. #60230

$$\left[\begin{array}{c} \text{EPISODE} \\ 73 \end{array}\right]$$

Script History:

September 24, 1985 (F.R.)

October 2, 1985 (F.R.)

October 9, 1985 (F.R.)

October 10, 1985 (F.R.)

October 11, 1985 (F.R.)

KNIGHT SONG

Written By: Burton Armus

Directed By: Georg Fenady

Original Airdate: December 13, 1985 (Friday, 8:00 PM) (18.8%; 16,150,000)

NBC Rerun #1: July 25, 1986 (Friday, 8:00 PM) (13.0%; 11,170,000)

Filming Dates: October 11-21, 1985

"Likewise, Mr. K.I.T.T., likewise."

-Charley Conners

Crew: Robert Foster (Executive Producer), Burton Armus (Supervising Producer), Bruce Lansbury (Supervising Producer), Gino Grimaldi (Producer), Glen A. Larson (Creator), Gregory S. Dinallo (Co-Producer), Robert Ewing (Coordinating Producer), Michael Eric Stein (Story Editor), Ron Martinez (Associate Producer/Unit Production Manager), Bruce Golin (Associate Producer), Stu Phillips (Theme), Don Peake (Music), H. John Penner (Director of Photography), Lou Montejano (Art Director), Dayle Mustain (Editor), Lawrence J. Gleason (Editor), Roberto Villar (First Assistant Director), Bruce A. Humphrey (Second Assistant Director), Donna Dockstader (Casting), R. Lynn Smartt (Set Decorator), John Shouse (Sound Editor), Richard Lapham (Music Editor), Barry Downing (Costume Supervisor), Karen J. Braverman (Costume Supervisor), Jack Gill (Stunt Coordinator), Pat Somerset (Sound), Jeremy Swan (Make-up), Allen Payne (Hairstylist)

Guest Cast: Mark Venturini (Keith Lawson), Shelley Berman (Josh Bevins), Paul Carafotes (Velez), Sharon Acker (E.G. Sanford), The New Edition (The Kids), Tom Sullivan (Charley Conners), Hank Rolike (Bartender), Michael Masters (Cabby), Huck Liggett (Traffic Cop)

The opening of a new Chicago night club signals the rebirth of a troubled neighborhood, but pressure from a gang threatens to destroy it all.

A Look Back:

"Knight Song" was a unique episode in that it centered around RC3 and his roots back in Chicago. Peter Parros recalls, "It was very exciting to get a chance to delve into some of RC3's history and develop his character. Burt Armus introduced RC3 in 'Knight of the Juggernaut' and this episode brought out more of RC's values. 'Knight Song' is about not forgetting where you come from after you've 'made it'. Promoting positive American values, honor, community and making a difference were very much a part of *Knight Rider*. That's what the appeal of the show was."

Parros remembers some of the cast members from this episode. "Shelly Berman was a very funny guy. Tom Sullivan sang and played piano between takes. It was like a mini concert," jokes Parros. We also had the band New Edition who were very popular at the time. It really felt special to have them on 'my show'. Ricky Bell, Michael Bivins, Ronnie DeVoe and Ralph Tresvant were all very friendly and very humble. None of them had done much acting before, so they were all excited for the opportunity to work on *Knight Rider*."

One of the 'heavies' in "Knight Song" was played by Paul Carafotes. He recalls, "I auditioned for the part and I remember this big, tough looking guy who was very funny in the meeting. His name was Burt Armus. He remembered me from another show he was writing and producing called *Street Hawk*. I was penciled in for the second episode called "A Second Self", but the role ended up being played by George Clooney instead. Mr. Armus was instrumental in me getting that gig on *Knight Rider*".

Carafotes' character, Velez, is remembered for his hot temper, which included a one sided fight with RC3 (Peter Parros). "I'm Greek. My dad was very dramatic and a loving man but could get very hot very quick. Basically, I was playing one aspect of him. He was a bartender and I remember him breaking up the bar - so I just closed my eyes and let her rip. I loved James Cagney and he did things with such intensity. I come from the east coast and I saw a lot of brutality. It's acting and one of the great things about it is you can have these fantasies and act out all kinds of emotions and a lot of the time you don't even know you have this rage deep down inside you. You land a part and - bang - you get to work it out".

Carafotes' boss in "Knight Song" was played by the late Mark Venturini. Carafotes shared most of his scenes with Venturini and remembers him well. "He was good. I remembered him from the auditions and we talked beforehand. It is always interesting who they cast and when we got down there on the set it was like 'yeah, I knew you had it' and we had fun. I had no idea he was dead. I believe it was Mark's first job. We hung out a couple of times during the shoot. We shared a few drinks and stories. I think he was like all of us - young and impetus, chasing something, running after it thinking that if we catch it, it'll fix us".

Although the episode takes place in Chicago, nearly every scene was shot on Universal Studios' back lot. It's a prime example of the studio trying to cut costs for the show's final season. "We shot the episode on the good old lot", confirms Carafotes. "I loved working at the studios. There was something very magical about it. I suppose it's also ingrained in our minds as children, you know, the Hollywood dream machine. I was and still am excited to be on a lot. When I was shooting *Knots Landing* at MGM, one of the stages we shot was on stage 25 and there was still a piece of the Yellow Brick Road from *The Wizard of Oz.* I would tap dance on it every time. I mean how lucky was I? I was living the dream".

There always seemed room for negotiation on certain scenes and Carafotes would always try and add his own part to the script. "I always try to change things up a bit, but in television it's a producer/writer medium and no one likes to get their words changed. But I'm a bit of a nudge, so I was always trying this and that out. (David) Hasselhoff and (Peter) Parros were very generous and would engage. It's always best to get the star on your side so you can get away with a lot more".

One dramatic scene in *Knight Song* involved Michael Knight being chased by the bad guys through an office. With only the top floor window as a means of escape, Knight has no option but to jump out. "It was complicated, but they had some young and talented stunt men and they went for it. Mark and I were standing with them up on the 4th story set because we were trying to get the scene finished and do those stunts all at the same time. We were all together up there and I kept looking out the breakaway window they would jump through and land on a foam pad. Every actor wants to do his own stunts and we tried to talk the producers into that. But they just laughed at Mark and I and said you be good boys and let the professionals do their job. So we watched them crash and fall. They did it a few times and it was very exciting. We shot the episode in four days. Usually, for one hour television, you're looking at double that time".

Carafotes also got to spend some time with a certain talking car between filming. "They had several of those cars and some of them were called 'camera ready' with parts missing so that if they needed to shoot out from the right side, or from whichever point of view they needed, they could. They had the pristine K.I.T.T. which was the coolest. I did get to ride around the lot in one and it was fast. They also had someone who constantly kept feather dusting the car. You knew who the star was. The car had its own make-up department".

Carafotes has terrific memories of working with David Hasselhoff. "He was a guy's guy. He really liked to have fun. I think we shot that episode in late October or November and then I ran into him in a nightclub in Boston in December. We tore the town up. We were going on to another club and got into the limo and I was with my sister and he was trying to pull her into the car with us. I had to step in at that point and let it be known she was my sister and that she won't be coming on this adventure. Thankfully, she didn't. I met Hasselhoff at a bar for a few cocktails while I was on *Knots Landing*. This was a few years after *Knight Rider* ended but before *Baywatch*. He had bought several of the cars and took them on tours all over the world. He is a smart man".

Jack Gill fondly remembers another guest star in this episode, Tom Sullivan. "We did an episode with a blind man called 'Knight Song'. Originally, he was going to ride in the passenger side while I blind-drove the car from the driver's side. I suggested that we put him behind the wheel and I would drive from the passenger side. This guy got such a kick out of it, he literally said, 'I've been blind since I was a child and I've never sat in the driver's seat, held on to the steering wheel, and driven around town'".

Knight Knotes:

- This episode had problems from the start. The original draft was rejected by NBC and resulted in an extensive re-write. When NBC screened the episode on November 4, 1985, they described it as "erratic" and "weak". The quality of the script may be the reason why well-known artist Ray Charles pulled out of shooting the day before production was to begin. Charles was to play the role of blind pianist Charley Conners. He was replaced by Tom Sullivan.
- Tom Sullivan, who played Charley Conners, is blind in real-life.
- The character G. Sanford was named after the third season producer, Gerald Sanford.
- The New Edition song "Count Me Out" was released on their album *All For Love* three months before the airing of this episode. The song reached the Top 10 on the R&B singles charts.

Script to Screen:

- Charley Conners was to be singing a blues song at the start of the episode, not "Old Time Rock and Roll".
- The script refers to the kids at the Tenement Club as simply a "singing group". This was obviously before The New Edition were cast. The script says that the group is made up of four young African American kids named Ralph, Mick, Rick and Ronnie.

- During one of the passes that K.I.T.T. makes while Charley is behind the wheel, K.I.T.T. is in convertible mode.

Featured Songs:

"Old Time Rock and Roll" by Bob Seger

"Count Me Out" by The New Edition

K.I.T.T.'s Capabilities:

- Audio/Video Record, Auto Cruise, Auto-Roof Right, Infrared Tracking Scope, Polyphonic Synthesizer, Pursuit

PROD. #60212

$$\left[\begin{array}{c} \text{EPISODE} \\ 74 \end{array} \right]$$

Script History:

August 6, 1985 (F.R.)

August 28, 1985 (F.R.)

THE SCENT OF ROSES

Written By: E. Nick Alexander

Directed By: Sidney Hayers

Original Airdate: January 3, 1986 (Friday, 8:00 PM) (18.2%; 15,630,000)

NBC Rerun #1: May 16, 1986 (Friday, 8:00 PM) (14.7%; 12,630,000)

Filming Dates: November 8-18, 1985

"We're going home, K.I.T.T., to our family. We're going to the Foundation."

-Michael

Crew: Robert Foster (Executive Producer), Burton Armus (Supervising Producer), Bruce Lansbury (Supervising Producer), Gino Grimaldi (Producer), Glen A. Larson (Creator), Gregory S. Dinallo (Co-Producer), Robert Ewing (Coordinating Producer), Michael Eric Stein (Story Editor), Ron Martinez (Associate Producer/Unit Production Manager), Bruce Golin (Associate Producer), Stu Phillips (Theme), Don Peake (Music), H. John Penner (Director of Photography), Lou Montejano (Art Director), Edward Nassour (Editor) Louis Race (First Assistant Director), Bruce A. Humphrey (Second Assistant Director), Donna Dockstader (Casting), R. Lynn Smartt (Set Decorator), John Shouse (Sound Editor), Richard Lapham (Music Editor), Barry Downing (Costume Supervisor), Karen J. Braverman (Costume Supervisor), Jack Gill (2nd Unit Director/Stunt Coordinator), Pat Somerset (Sound), Jeremy Swan (Make-up), Allen Payne (Hairstylist)

Guest Cast: Catherine Hickland (Stevie Mason), Aharon Ipale (Durante/Kurt Rolands), Reid Smith (Stocker), Robert Feero (E. Martoni), Richard Partlow (Klus), Roy Jenson (Purdue), Michael John Meyer (Medic Driver), Craig Schaefer (Medic), Phyllis Applegate (Nurse Miller), William Knight (Head Surgeon), Tom McDonald (Guard), Henry Cutrona (Minister), Ellen Clark (Mildred)

Michael is shot and nearly killed while responding to a break-in at a government data center.

A Look Back:

Aharon Ipale played the notorious bad guy Durante in what fans remember as the true last episode of the series. Ipale's career up to the shooting of the episode had taken him half way around the world. "I was born in Morocco and in 1978 I moved to England and studied acting at the renowned LAMDA school. I remember my time well in London, starring in a production at the Haymarket theatre. In 1990, I permanently moved to America."

Ipale got the offer to star in "The Scent of Roses" fairly quickly. "Most of my work at that time was done through my agent. Getting the *Knight Rider* job was straight forward. I had the advantage in that I had starred in many films and television shows prior to the role."

"The Scent of Roses" is remembered as one of the most violent of the entire series and Ipale's character is surely remembered as one of Michael Knight's most evil nemesis. "I enjoyed the shoot a lot, it was great fun," says Ipale. "I had three different characters to play because of the disguises and I knew this was a big episode in the *Knight Rider* series."

The studio shot the episode as if it would be the last, although "The Scent of Roses" was moved to mid-season. "I had no idea at the time of filming that this would be intended to be the last episode, but you had the feeling on set that it was a major one, a very important one. That, there were no doubts."

Ipale had no qualms about playing the evil Durante. "You know, I am an actor so I can adapt very easily. I was in *The Shooting Party* prior to starring in *Knight Rider*, and in that I acted with John Gielgud playing an English Lord."

Although there was a lot of tension on the screen, off-screen, Ipale was good friends with the cast. "Sometimes when you shoot a film or television program, you do not get to meet the cast. You only meet the people that you starred with in a certain scene. Here I met everyone. David Hasselhoff was very friendly and professional and we became friends. I met him socially a few times after the episode wrapped."

Ipale's most famous scene and one of the most remembered throughout the *Knight Rider* series is the killing of Michael's wife, Stevie

Mason. Mason was played by Catherine Hickland, who was married to David Hasselhoff in real life at the time. "Yes, I remember that scene well," says Ipale. "I had to shoot Michael Knight's wife and they had just got married. I remember the crew driving me out early morning to a location for this one scene near the beach in California. It took several takes. In an episode where you shoot Michael Knight's wife dead, I realized that it would be a major story, not a run of the mill episode. Between takes, Catherine and I would have a lot of fun together. It was a relaxed atmosphere despite the importance of what we were filming."

Sidney Hayers directed "The Scent of Roses" and Ipale has nothing but good memories of him. "Sidney was a very good director, but it was a complex episode. I remember he would signal me over and whisper to me, 'You know, Aharon, can you stay on a few more hours?'. This could be after a 12 hour day, but we stayed on. The episode ran over its schedule by a few days, which is usually unheard of. When the show first aired, I watched it and I was happy with my performance. I enjoyed the episode a lot and thought we did a great job. The set was a good one and between takes, we would always have a laugh and joke. At one stage I even got to drive K.I.T.T.! I had a great experience on the show."

Producer Burton Armus also remembers his time working on this episode, and how it was the push of David Hasselhoff that made it possible. "I heard that David Hasselhoff was screaming since season 2 to shoot this story that he had called 'The Scent of Roses'. His wife at the time, Catherine Hickland, was lovely and very pleasant to be around. I looked her over and I knew instantly that we could cast her for the episode. The problem with the episode is that Hasselhoff wanted it to be the season ending episode. Back then, each November and February, the studio did something called a sweeps week, where the studio would study and analyze the Nielsen ratings of its competitors. November was the most important month, so those ratings had to be upped. 'The Scent of Roses' was a major story, so that came in mid-season. Hasselhoff was not pleased at all. But I had a job to do and I didn't work for David Hasselhoff, I worked for the studio."

RC3 was given the honor of being Michael's best man at his wedding to Stevie. Peter Parros recalls, "We shot the wedding in Malibu, right across the highway from where I lived as a kid. So, I loved the location. The estate had been used for the *Hardcastle and McCormick* TV series. It's on a bluff overlooking the ocean. You don't fully get a sense of just how beautiful it was. I liked that this episode showed a friendship building between Michael and RC." "The Scent of Roses" remains one of the most devastating episodes in the entire series, as Parros recalls. "At the time, David and Catherine were still together in real life. She is a beautiful person. I was recently married and the thought of losing your wife on your wedding day was horrible. There was a lot of emotion in this episode."

Knight Knotes:

- NBC's comments on the script: "Script delivered in workable shape. This is an unusual episode that is designed around the hook of the wedding. Dailies have been only adequate as the acting is at times heavy handed. This will be a very promotable, solid but very atypical episode."

- The Government Data Center is visited by Michael and K.I.T.T. again in "Knight of the Rising Sun" as Tanika's business complex.

- Michael and Stevie's wedding shadowed David Hasselhoff and Catherine Hickland's own wedding. In the episode, Devon gives the bride away while the ceremony is presided over by the Reverend Henry Cutrona. At Hasselhoff's wedding, Edward Mulhare and Reverend Cutrona performed the same duties two years earlier.

- The wedding dress worn by Stevie in this episode is the same one that Catherine Hickland wore when she married David Hasselhoff. Hasselhoff stated at the time, "I figured we've got to pay for her wedding dress. I said, 'Honey, you've worn that thing only once. It cost you a bundle. We're going to get it on the show and have *Knight Rider* buy it".
- Michael wears a black tux with a red handkerchief in the pocket, which matches K.I.T.T.'s color scheme.

Script to Screen:

- A scene found in the script but cut in the final episode has Michael testing the Emergency Braking System for Bonnie. The results reveal a two-degree pull to the right, but Michael wants to leave it alone because "it adds a little flair to the stops."
- The script also has Kurt Rolands' alias as The Falcon instead of Durante.
- A cut line has Stevie saying to Michael, "Devon told me you've always known where I was...every club I've worked...I always expected a call...." with Michael responding that "it would have just ended in another goodbye."
- The song that K.I.T.T. played when Michael and Stevie exited the restaurant was supposed to be "Let It Be Me" by David Hasselhoff and Catherine Hickland.
- Kurt Rolands initially disguised himself as the minister and killed Stevie before she and Michael got married.
- A dressmaker named Mildred helped Stevie with her dress. She is still given credit in the closing theme despite not appearing in the episode.

- Early scripts had K.I.T.T. connect to Rolands via a satellite relay chip that he implanted in the Government Data Center. The shooting script had Michael talk to him at Purdue Auto Parts.
- K.I.T.T. originally turbo boosts through the catwalk in the warehouse instead of driving through it.

Featured Songs:

"For All We Know" by The Carpenters

"As Time Goes By" by Rosemary Clooney

"White Bird" by It's a Beautiful Day

K.I.T.T.'s Capabilities:

- Audio Playback, Audio/Video Record, Audio/Video Transmit, Auto Cruise, Auto-Roof Left, Auto-Roof Right, Emergency Braking System, Medical Scan, Super Pursuit Mode, Turbo Boost

PROD. #60226

$$\left[\begin{array}{c} \text{EPISODE} \\ 75 \end{array}\right]$$

Script History:

October 21, 1985 (F.R.)

October 25, 1985 (F.R.)

October 30, 1985 (F.R.)

October 31, 1985 (F.R.)

October 31, 1985 (2nd rev.)

KILLER K.I.T.T.

Written By: Simon Rose

Directed By: Chuck Bail

Original Airdate: January 10, 1986 (Friday, 8:00 PM) (18.0%; 15,460,000)

NBC Rerun #1: May 30, 1986 (Friday, 8:00 PM) (11.7%; 10,050,000)

Filming Dates: October 30 – November 7, 1985

"Michael Knight sighted. Attack Mode engaged!"

-K.I.T.T.

Crew: Robert Foster (Executive Producer), Burton Armus (Supervising Producer), Bruce Lansbury (Supervising Producer), Gino Grimaldi (Producer), Glen A. Larson (Creator), Gregory S. Dinallo (Co-Producer), Robert Ewing (Coordinating Producer), Michael Eric Stein (Story Editor), Ron Martinez (Associate Producer/Unit Production Manager), Bruce Golin (Associate Producer), Stu Phillips (Theme), Don Peake (Music), H. John Penner (Director of Photography), Lou Montejano (Art Director), Domenic G. DiMascio (Editor) Roberto Villar (First Assistant Director), Bruce A. Humphrey (Second Assistant Director), Donna Dockstader (Casting), R. Lynn Smartt (Set Decorator), John Shouse (Sound Editor), Richard Lapham (Music Editor), Barry Downing (Costume Supervisor), Karen J. Braverman (Costume Supervisor), Jack Gill (2nd Unit Director/Stunt Coordinator), Pat Somerset (Sound), Jeremy Swan (Make-up), Allen Payne (Hairstylist)

Guest Cast: Harvey Jason (Marco Berio), Andrea Howard (Bronwyn Appleby), Anne Ramsey (Crossing Guard), Andy Epper (Gordon), Tony Epper (Nicholas Farrell)

K.I.T.T. is reprogrammed by a vengeful ex-Foundation employee to kill everyone in sight – including Michael Knight.

A Look Back:

Harvey Jason played Marco Berio, a former F.L.A.G. employee hell bent on reprogramming K.I.T.T. to seek revenge against the Foundation. Jason has been acting since 1961, starring in some of the most famous television shows in history including *Batman*, *Night Gallery* and *Colombo*. Because Jason was so well known, he did not have to audition for the role. "I had, of course, heard of the show before, but I had never seen it before," says Jason. "There wasn't an audition process for *Knight Rider*. Happily, I didn't have to. By then, my career was at the point where my agent would call with a firm offer to do whatever show there was and the script would be sent to me. I do remember Donna Dockstader though only by name." Jason also remembers K.I.T.T. very well. "The car was just fantastic. It was a great piece of artistry. Superb."

In the episode, Jason is seen sitting down in most of his scenes and this was because the actor was in pain. "I remember just prior to us shooting the show, my back had gone out and I was in pain. I could hardly walk." The director, Chuck Bail, did give Jason some advice on how to get over his pain. "I told Chuck and he gave me great advice. He said to brace myself, then break out on a huge run and the energy would cause the pain to abate. It worked! Chuck and I had worked before in a feature film for Warner Brothers called *Gumball Rally*. He was also a great stuntman and a very, very good action director who was a lot of fun to work with. I liked him enormously and still do."

With K.I.T.T. stolen and Michael needing a ride, he has no option but to borrow RC's motorcycle. "I did like motorcycles," says Peter Parros. "As a kid, I rode mini-bikes and small motorcycles, so I knew how to ride. After shooting the show, I bought a motorcycle and rode it for a while. It was fun, but I'm really more of a car man."

Like all *Knight Rider* episodes, "Killer K.I.T.T." involves a number of dangerous stunts which Peter Parros remembers well. "I remember Jack Gill very well. He was very nice to me and an amazing driver. In 'Killer K.I.T.T.', Jack had to drive K.I.T.T. through a set of convention center double glass doors. They replaced the real building doors with special breakaway ones. There was only a narrow clearance on each side of K.I.T.T. to the metal frame of the building that the doors were set in. I thought Jack was going to go half speed, because if he would have hit the metal door frame, not only would the car have been wrecked but the building would have been seriously damaged.

But Jack did the stunt at full speed, perfectly! That's when I was really impressed with his driving skills. Also, Jack coordinated a lot of the fights, so he helped make RC3 look good."

"Killer K.I.T.T." is a non-stop action episode that, among other things, features Michael Knight being plowed into a snack vendors building by a re-programmed K.I.T.T. "This was a scene that I did second unit on and also was blind driving the car," recalls Jack Gill. "I had Matt McComb doubling up for David Hasselhoff on the hood of the car and he's not cabled in because I had to bring him in fast, jump the curb and then go right into the building with him then falling off. Spike Silver is in the blue shirt and apron right in front of the snack building. We did a bunch of shots inside the car, looking at David from the hood. We had David cabled to the hood so he couldn't really go anywhere."

Knight Knotes:

- NBC's comments on the script:"Very straight forward and predictable first draft delivered. Good rough cut screened on 12/4. This episode is well paced and good fun."

- This is the first episode to feature RC3's dirt bike. His bike is again seen in "Knight of a Thousand Devils" and "Voo Doo Knight".

Script to Screen:

- A line cut from the shooting script has Michael explain to K.I.T.T. why he goes around a stalled truck during his initial chase of Farrell instead of jumping over it – "No turbo boost pal. There are cars on the other side."

- After Michael is ambushed at Farrell's place, Michael asks K.I.T.T. how he knew they were coming. This line does not make sense in the episode, and the reason is because David Hasselhoff misspoke it.

He was supposed to say "How did those two know we were coming?"

- K.I.T.T.'s evil voice is described as having "a malevolent tone with an *Exorcist* hiss."

- K.I.T.T. originally stopped so close to Devon and Dr. Albert in the Convention Center that his front bumper tapped the podium and knocked it over. Although that does not make it into the episode, a line at the end of the episode has K.I.T.T. saying, "To think, I introduced myself to the man who designed my systems by toppling his podium."

- Berio explains more of what his programming is doing to K.I.T.T.: "You see, at this very moment my analytical mode interceptor is breaking down each sub-set in the vehicle's program. It's already tapped into the audio matrix. Next it will trans-polarize the millions of command module permutations and devise an override which will give me total control. Within hours the Knight Two Thousand will be responding to my voice commands."

- The scene with Michael on K.I.T.T.'s hood didn't appear in early scripts. Instead, Michael hides under a pier and K.I.T.T. crashes into the support beams causing the pier to collapse on Michael.

Featured Songs:

"Finally Found a Home" By Huey Lewis and the News

K.I.T.T.'s Capabilities:

- Anharmonic Synthesizer, Anti-Theft System, Audio/Video Record, Audio Playback, Auto Cruise, Auto-Roof Left, Auto-Roof Right, Manual Override, Passive Laser Restraint System, Protect, Pursuit,

Signal, Super Pursuit Mode, Surveillance Mode, Tinted Windows, Video Analyzer, Voice Projection, Zoom-In

PROD. #60211

$$\left\{ \begin{array}{c} \text{EPISODE} \\ 76 \end{array} \right\}$$

Script History:

July 9, 1985 (F.R.)

July 11, 1985 (F.R.)

July 12, 1985 (F.R.)

July 15, 1985 (F.R.)

OUT OF THE WOODS

Written By: Gregory S. Dinallo

Directed By: Harvey Laidman

Original Airdate: January 17, 1986 (Friday, 8:00 PM) (18.4%; 15,810,000)

Filming Dates: July 17-25, 1985

"Hey Mickey, ya mind telling me where we're goin'?"

-K.I.T.T.

Crew: Robert Foster (Executive Producer), Burton Armus (Supervising Producer), Bruce Lansbury (Supervising Producer), Gino Grimaldi (Producer), Glen A. Larson (Creator), Gregory S. Dinallo (Co-Producer), Mark Jones (Co-Producer), Robert Ewing (Coordinating Producer), Michael Eric Stein (Story Editor), Ron Martinez (Associate Producer/Unit Production Manager), Bruce Golin (Associate Producer), Stu Phillips (Theme), Don Peake (Music), H. John Penner (Director of Photography), Lou Montejano (Art Director), Grant Hoag (Editor) Roberto Villar (First Assistant Director), Bruce A. Humphrey (Second Assistant Director), Donna Dockstader (Casting), R. Lynn Smartt (Set Decorator), John Shouse (Sound Editor), Richard Lapham (Music Editor), Barry Downing (Costume Supervisor), Karen J. Braverman (Costume Supervisor), Jack Gill (2nd Unit Director/Stunt Coordinator), Pat Somerset (Sound), Jeremy Swan (Make-up), Allen Payne (Hairstylist)

Guest Cast: Nancy Everhard (Samantha Dutton), Peter MacLean (Jonathan Dutton), P.J. Soles (Ellen Whitby), J. Eddie Peck (Erik Whitby), M.C. Gainey (Jerry Nash), Curtis Taylor (Dave Nash), Marty Arkelian (Log Grappler), Michael Grayson (Party Guest)

Michael investigates a couple's claim that a local logging company is cutting their timber illegally.

A Look Back:

Harvey Laidman was behind the lens for "Out of the Woods" - it was his sixth and final time directing on *Knight Rider*. "This is what I called another *Knight Rider* simulation show", recalls Laidman. "Like the circus show ("Circus Knights"), we couldn't duplicate the atmosphere, so, in this case, we were logging in Beverly Hills with surplus telephone poles."

The episode begins with Erik Whitby breaking into Jonathan Dutton's home and sawing up everything in sight with a chainsaw, including Dutton's piano. "When I was an assistant director around 1970, I worked on a film called *Sometimes a Great Notion*, which was from the novel by Ken Kesey about a logging family. In the film, Paul Newman walks into a finance company and saws a desk in half with a chainsaw. For "Out of the Woods", the prop guys purchased this cute black lacquer baby grand piano and took the insides out (the harp). After the episode was done, I asked if I could have the piano. I intended to glue it back together and put it in my living room. At first the studio said okay, but then the lawyers got into the act and said absolutely not, even if I paid what the studio paid. Their reasoning was that somehow I had manipulated the show into acquiring the piano and that I intended to have it all along. Oh my goodness, forget it! Years later, I was scouting locations on the Universal back lot and we passed a dump where I caught a glimpse of that black lacquer baby half buried in garbage."

While the final season of *Knight Rider* relied heavily on shooting on the Universal back lot, "Out of the Woods" went on location. "We shot the logging in Griffith Park smack in the center of Los Angeles," recalls Laidman. "That was right in the shadow of the Griffith Observatory where James Dean misbehaved in *Rebel Without a Cause*. There are a few acres of pines and some winding roads in Griffith Park. We also went out to Valencia to a farm that belonged to Lew Ayers. We used to shoot *The Dukes of Hazzard* there. There's a roadhouse set and a farmhouse that we burned. We used the same farmhouse on *The Dukes*."

In one scene, Michael and K.I.T.T. are buried beneath a mountain of trees. In a complex scene like this, miniatures had to be used. "I was not consulted with respect to miniatures, which was interesting because the coverage I shot had to meld with the miniatures. At that time, studios used to farm out the visual effect work to companies who would create these effects after the fact and after bidding a lower price. The miniatures are marginal and not good for more than a few frames."

Towards the end of the episode, Michael must rescue Erik and Ellen Whitby from a house fire. "We shot that scene in the all-purpose farmhouse at Lew Ayers ranch," explains Laidman. "We had great special effects people who totally controlled the fire using propane burners and long troughs. The troughs were placed beneath the view of the camera lens and were set for each camera angle and then rapidly extinguished. The fire department was present and usually fire scenes are very difficult to control. Being a practical house, not a set, all fire and camera angles were enclosed inside. We used a lot of fire between the camera and the actors, which made it look perilous. Everything went very quickly – quite unusual for scenes like this. It is a credit to a crew that worked together for years and was very professional."

If the house fire were not enough, Michael was then involved in a long fight sequence at the episode's climax. "The fight scenes were always choreographed on the spot. I would lay the scene out, and the stunt coordinator, I believe Bob Bralver or Jack Gill, would translate it into a flowing fight that I could break up into camera angles. Normally, we first used doubles and then replaced them for closer shots. I used multiple cameras and then a hand-held camera inside the fight action. We always had two cameras on *Knight Rider*. Mike Ferra, who operated the 'B' camera was a good friend and a spectacularly talented camera mechanic, but not much of an operator. It became a joke that after each shot, I would ask Mike how it was, and he would say 'Bits and Pieces'. Mike died last year and left behind a slew of patents and inventions. I miss him."

Laidman confirms that he had no idea that he was working on what would be the final season. "I was happy to be back and I had no idea about an impending cancellation - not a hint from David Hasselhoff. I hoped the show would go on forever. I really liked the cast and crew and the show was fun."

Knight Knotes:

- NBC's comments on the script: "While the script has plenty of action, notes given to make Michael more active and less re-active. Revised pages have improved Michael's motivation but script still relies on action to carry act four. Dailies have been adequate."
- RC3 does not appear in this episode.
- The Whitby's farm was previously used as the Dukes' homestead in *The Dukes of Hazzard*. The lumber mill was also featured in *The Dukes* as the Boar's Nest!

Script to Screen:

- The script describes Erik Whitby as "twenty-two, six feet three inches, 225 pounds of muscle, mackinaw, jeans and unbridled anger."
- Jerry Nash (spelled "Gerry" originally) is described as "thirty-four, a lumberjack-type with a *Deliverance* mentality."
- While Michael and K.I.T.T. are buried underneath the logs, K.I.T.T. comments that "there's enough lumber on top of us to make 10,658 hot tubs."

Featured Songs:

"Workin' Man Blues" by Merle Haggard

K.I.T.T.'s Capabilities:

- Audio/Video Record, Auto Cruise, Auto-Roof Left, Auto-Roof Right, Chemical Analyzer, CO_2, Convertible Mode, Emergency Braking System, Hydraulic Lift, Passive Laser Restraint System, Pursuit, Rapid

Cycle, Silent Mode, Speech Synthesis Module, Super Pursuit Mode, Surveillance Mode, Turbo Boost, Voice Synthesizer

PROD. #60229

| EPISODE 77 |

Script History:

November 18, 1985 (F.R.)

November 22, 1985 (F.R.)

November 27, 1985 (F.R.)

December 2, 1985 (F.R.)

December 4, 1985 (F.R.)

December 5, 1985 (F.R.)

DEADLY KNIGHTSHADE

Written By: Philip John Taylor

Directed By: Sidney Hayers

Original Airdate: January 24, 1986 (Friday, 8:00 PM) (17.9%; 15,380,000)

Filming Dates: December 3-11, 1985

"I'm definitely dark and handsome. I'm only tall when I'm climbing a steep

incline."

-K.I.T.T.

Crew: Robert Foster (Executive Producer), Burton Armus (Supervising Producer), Bruce Lansbury (Supervising Producer), Gino Grimaldi (Producer), Glen A. Larson (Creator), Gregory S. Dinallo (Co-Producer), Robert Ewing (Coordinating Producer), Michael Eric Stein (Story Editor), Ron Martinez (Associate Producer/Unit Production Manager), Bruce Golin (Associate Producer), Stu Phillips (Theme), Don Peake (Music), H. John Penner (Director of Photography), Lou Montejano (Art Director), Grant Hoag (Editor) Louis Race (First Assistant Director), Bruce A. Humphrey (Second Assistant Director), Donna Dockstader (Casting), R. Lynn Smartt (Set Decorator), John Shouse (Sound Editor), Richard Lapham (Music Editor), Barry Downing (Costume Supervisor), Karen J. Braverman (Costume Supervisor), Jack Gill (2nd Unit Director/Stunt Coordinator), Pat Somerset (Sound), Jeremy Swan (Make-up), Allen Payne (Hairstylist)

Guest Cast: Lance Burton (Austin Templeton), Mary Beth Evans (Nancy Marston), Hurd Hatfield (Ariel Marston), William Jordon (Dr. Ian Browning), Sally Julian (The Blond), William Utay (Harry), Mark Harris (Max Henderson), Roberta Haynes (Maid)

Michael and K.I.T.T. enter the spectacular world of magic when the prime suspect for the murder of a Foundation trustee is a magician who has a talent for being two places at one time - with deadly consequences!

A Look Back:

"Deadly Knightshade" is mostly remembered for guest star Lance Burton, a real-life magician and avid fan of the series. Burton recalls, "We shot 'Deadly Knightshade' in seven days. We worked long hours - sometimes 18 a day. I remember being tired and sleepy a lot of the time. Tired, but having a blast! I was a huge fan of *Knight Rider* long before I appeared on the show". Burton was a man in demand at the timing of the episode shoot but knew he had made the right decision to make his television acting show debut. "At the time I was performing my magic act in the Folies Bergere at the Tropicana Hotel in Las Vegas. I had performed several times on *The Tonight Show with Johnny Carson*, but had no experience working on TV dramas. My manager at the time, Marc Gurvitz, called me one day and said the producers of *Knight Rider* wanted to talk to me about playing the role of a magician on an upcoming episode. I flew to LA and met with Burt Armus and Bruce Lansbury. They were very nice and enthusiastic. We had lunch and they handed me a script to take home".

In one of the most memorable scenes from the episode, Burton was required to work with a live tiger, an experience he would rather forget. "That was my first and last time! I was terrified of the tiger. There was a professional animal handler with it at all times, but I gave that tiger plenty of space. There is one scene in the episode where the tiger is sitting in the car, and as I walk by him he reaches out for me with his paw. That was scary".

"Deadly Knightshade" was directed by the late Sidney Hayers and Burton reminisced that, on occasion, he was allowed to improvise during some of the magic acts. "Sidney was an outstanding director. He was very easy to work with. I tried to work as much magic as possible into the show. Of course, there were a lot of magic tricks that were written into the script, but I would always show Sidney what I had in mind to get his input. He was very open to suggestions. There was a scene where Templeton magically produced several red cloth hoods. This was an important plot point because it shot down Michael Knight's theory that Templeton was the killer. The script called for Templeton to pick up a shiny metal tube, show it empty, and produce the hoods from inside the tube. I felt this was not visual enough. So, I came up with the idea of producing the hoods bare-handed, snatching them out of thin air. I then followed that up by pulling more hoods out of Michael Knight's jacket. I showed the trick to Sidney and he approved, so that is what we wound up doing".

David Hasselhoff and Lance Burton on the set of "Deadly Knightshade" (Photo courtesy of Lance Burton)

The episode also required Burton's character Templeton to be romantically involved with Bonnie Barstow (Patricia McPherson). According to Burton, "Patricia was a joy to work with! She was very professional and very nice. I almost got to kiss her, but that Michael Knight interrupted us!" As for the other cast members, Burton's recollections are vivid. "I chained

Edward Mulhare up and tried to drown him in a tank of water. He was a good sport about it. As a kid, I remember seeing him in *The Ghost & Mrs. Muir*, so I was very excited to meet him. Sadly, I only had one scene with him. I did get to spend a good amount of time with David Hasselhoff. He is the consummate professional! He made everyone on the set feel comfortable. Everyone who worked on *Knight Rider* loved David. He was very nice to me and even gave me an autographed photo for my Mother. My mom was a big David Hasselhoff fan from his soap opera days, where he played a character called Snapper . He signed the photo 'To Hilma, Love, Snapper'.

While it was true that much of *Knight Rider's* final season was filmed at Universal Studios to save money, this particular episode still had some location shoots. "The Ambassador Hotel in Los Angeles was the primary location", recalls Burton. "Exteriors and many interiors were filmed there. The murder scene took place in the Presidential Suite".

The final scene in the episode features Michael Knight making a dove appear out of thin air. Even though Templeton was thrown in jail by this point, Burton was still around to assist. "They asked me to help David with this magic trick. I worked out a bit where David held up a handkerchief and the dove appeared fluttering and sits on the top edge of the hanky. That's what it looked like to the camera anyway. In actuality, I was hiding out of site behind K.I.T.T. holding the dove. When they shot a close-up of David and the top edge of the hanky, I slipped in underneath and released the dove. I just had to make sure I wasn't seen on camera, because Templeton was in prison by that time!"

For those fans of Austin Templeton, had the series been renewed for another year, you may have seen the deadly magician again. "After the show aired, I started to think of ways that Templeton could make a return appearance. He is a magician and could escape from prison! I was planning on calling Burt Armus and pitch him my idea. Templeton could be brought back the next season to take revenge on the man (and car) that put him away! Ahh...but no.... the show was canceled. Bummer!"

Since filming *Knight Rider,* Burton ran into David Hasselhoff a few more times. "We both appeared on a variety TV show in Spain in the late 80's. I even had his daughter on stage as a volunteer during a benefit show in Los Angeles in the mid 90's. She was 5 years old at the time. Appearing on the show was a big moment in my career, plus it was a lot of fun! I have been recognized many times from that appearance. Many years ago, I was doing a show in Japan. After the show, the cast was doing a meet-and-greet in the lobby of the theater. I was signing autographs when I felt someone tugging on my pants leg. I looked down and saw this five year old Japanese boy. He did not speak English, but he looked up at me and pointed and said 'Templeton!' Yes, *Knight Rider* aired in Japan, and I have a tape of my episode, all dubbed in Japanese!"

RC3, along with Bonnie, are tricked by the devious magician played by Burton. Peter Parros recalls, "Lance was great to work with. A mysterious kind of guy, but much nicer than his character. I also thought that he was a very good actor."

In "Deadly Knightshade", Parros spends some time in K.I.T.T.'s passenger seat with David Hasselhoff at the wheel. Parros rode with Hasselhoff and K.I.T.T. more than anyone and retains some wonderful memories of that experience. "David was a great joker. I'm sure, somewhere, there is an archive of him doing crazy slates before a scene starts. He could joke right before starting a serious scene. I need time to prepare. It was always a funny challenge to match our Super Pursuit Mode reactions to get the timing and the intensity. Though Jack Gill did the heavy stunt driving, I was surprised to learn that David was a very good driver. Sometimes, I would get a bit nervous when David would speed into a scene, but he would usually hit the mark and we'd jump out like it was no big deal. Unfortunately, RC never got the opportunity to drive K.I.T.T."

Knight Knotes:

- NBC's comments on the script:"Notes given to add more magic (and logic) to the story. Dailies have been adequate - plenty to cut from."
- This episode marks the final Ski Mode of the series.
- Ian Browning's car sports a license plate of CA 7FZF177. This is the same license plate as the Phantom's SUV a few episodes later in "Fright Knight".
- The hearse used by Templeton during his escape can be seen with two different license plates – CA 7WDV722 and CA 9WRB357.

Script to Screen:

- The woman who volunteers her car for Templeton's magic act at the start of the episode is named Pam. She is with her boyfriend, Gary Shaw. Templeton calls Gary by his name after swiping his wallet during the act.
- A description of the first time we see Harry and the blonde woman: "A luscious, busty Blonde is being escorted out the door by a burly, cigar-chomping Harry. She's the Judy Holliday type. He's the William Frawley type. He's grabbing her by the elbow as she reluctantly follows, leading her to his parked Buick Electra."

Featured Songs:

"Eine Kleine Nachtmusik" by Wolfgang Amadeus Mozart

K.I.T.T.'s Capabilities:

- Anharmonic Synthesizer, Audio Playback, Auto Cruise, Auto-Roof Left, Micro Jam, Ski Mode, Super Pursuit Mode, Ultrascan

PROD. #60227

$$\left[\begin{array}{c} \text{EPISODE} \\ 78 \end{array} \right]$$

Script History:

November 25, 1985 (F.R.)

December 3, 1985 (F.R.)

REDEMPTION OF A CHAMPION

Written By: E. Nick Alexander

Directed By: Chuck Bail

Original Airdate: January 31, 1986 (Friday, 8:00 PM) (18.9%; 16,240,000)

Rerun: August 8, 1986 (Friday, 8:00 PM) (13.6%; 11,680,000)

Filming Dates: December 13-23, 1985

"It talks? What'll they have in '88?"

-Ruth Keeler

Crew: Robert Foster (Executive Producer), Burton Armus (Supervising Producer), Bruce Lansbury (Supervising Producer), Gino Grimaldi (Producer), Glen A. Larson (Creator), Gregory S. Dinallo (Co-Producer), Robert Ewing (Coordinating Producer), Michael Eric Stein (Story Editor), Ron Martinez (Associate Producer/Unit Production Manager), Bruce Golin (Associate Producer), Stu Phillips (Theme), Don Peake (Music), H. John Penner (Director of Photography), Lou Montejano (Art Director), Domenic G. DiMascio (Editor) Roberto Villar (First Assistant Director), Richard Coad (Second Assistant Director), Donna Dockstader (Casting), R. Lynn Smartt (Set Decorator), John Shouse (Sound Editor), Richard Lapham (Music Editor), Barry Downing (Costume Supervisor), Karen J. Braverman (Costume Supervisor), Jack Gill (Stunt Coordinator), Pat Somerset (Sound), Jeremy Swan (Make-up), Allen Payne (Hairstylist)

Guest Cast: Terry Kiser (Lou "Royal" Davis), Kat Sawyer-Young (Jean Tremont), Tracy Reed (Ruth Keeler), John Snyder (Benson), Norman Burton (Damon Leyland), Ken Foree (Spiderman), Ken H. Norton (Bo Keeler), Don King (Himself), Jerry Quarry (Himself), Danny Lopez (Himself), Carlos Palomino (Himself), Donald Craig (Dr. Jack "Gil" Simmons), Ron Pinkard (Reporter #1), Pete Youngblood (Reporter #2), John Garwood (Guard), Monte Masters (Grant), Benjamin Jurand (Blue Lightning)

After finding a boxing reporter dead in his home, Michael goes undercover to get some answers.

A Look Back:

Producer Burton Armus has always loved boxing and saw this as an opportunity to get some greats from the sport on the show. "'Redemption of a Champion' was a fun episode because I am a huge fight fan. So, it was the opportunity to get in some boxing names. We got them all in and it was great. Don King, Jerry Quarry, Ken Norton, Danny Lopez and Carlos Palomino all appeared. They had all done this for a standard salary. They didn't need the money; they had made theirs already. But, they were fans of the show and *Knight Rider* was prime time and it was an opportunity for them to star in the show. I remember Don King was happy to be in this episode because we flew him in first class. The bottom line was they starred in the episode because they had done it for fun and they loved it."

Peter Parros fondly remembers this episode as the week he got to work with one of his idols. "I was a Ken Norton fan. He was a great fighter. One of the very few boxers to beat Muhammad Ali, and I got to meet him in this episode."

Knight Knotes:

- NBC's comments on the script:"Notes given to give the story some pace although this is an 'arena' episode which limits the story."
- The rerun of this episode was the last episode to ever be shown in its prime-time slot on NBC on August 8th, 1986.
- Terry Kiser is perhaps best remembered for his role as Bernie in *Weekend at Bernie's.*

Script to Screen:

- In the script, Don King's role is simply known as the "PR Man".
- The original script had Michael telling Ruth Keeler that K.I.T.T. was "an '86" – the episodes states "'87", since the episode aired in 1986.
- Damon Leland is said to live in the Brentwood Hills Motor Court.

K.I.T.T.'s Capabilities:

- Anharmonic Synthesizer, Audio/Video Record, Auto Cruise, Auto Phone, Chemical Analyzer, Medical Scan, Olfactory Scan, Printer, Pursuit, Smoke Release, Surveillance Mode, Trajectory Guide, Turbo Boost

PROD. #60228

$$\left[\begin{array}{c} \text{EPISODE} \\ 79 \end{array} \right]$$

Script History:

December 20, 1985 (F.R.)

December 27, 1985 (F.R.)

January 2, 1986 (F.R.)

January 3, 1986 (F.R.)

January 6, 1986 (F.R.)

KNIGHT OF A THOUSAND DEVILS

Written By: Peter Alan Fields

Directed By: Gino Grimaldi

Original Airdate: February 7, 1986 (Friday, 8:00 PM) (18.1%; 15,550,000)

NBC Rerun #1: August 1, 1986 (Friday, 8:00 PM) (12.9%; 11,080,000)

Filming Dates: January 6-15, 1986

"I'm fine, although I wouldn't rule out brain damage."

-Michael

Crew: Robert Foster (Executive Producer), Burton Armus (Supervising Producer), Bruce Lansbury (Supervising Producer), Gino Grimaldi (Producer), Glen A. Larson (Creator), Gregory S. Dinallo (Co-Producer), Robert Ewing (Coordinating Producer), Michael Eric Stein (Story Editor), Ron Martinez (Associate Producer/Unit Production Manager), Bruce Golin (Associate Producer), Stu Phillips (Theme), Don Peake (Music), H. John Penner (Director of Photography), Lou Montejano (Art Director), Edward Nassour (Editor) Louis Race (First Assistant Director), Richard Coad (Second Assistant Director), Donna Dockstader (Casting), R. Lynn Smartt (Set Decorator), John Shouse (Sound Editor), Richard Lapham (Music Editor), Barry Downing (Costume Supervisor), Karen J. Braverman (Costume Supervisor), Jack Gill (Stunt Coordinator), Pat Somerset (Sound), Jeremy Swan (Make-up), Allen Payne (Hairstylist)

Guest Cast: Jonathan Goldsmith (Ronald Becker), Kathy Shower (Claudia Torrell), Ada Maris (Ana Lucia Cortez), Henry Darrow (Roderigo De Lorca), Ted Grossman (Marcus), Bruce Neckels (Lew Jonas), Allen Gibbs (Hood #1), Gary McMillan (Driver), Donna Speir (Playmate #1), Marlene Slieter (Playmate #2), Venice Kong (Playmate #3)

Michael vows to find the man responsible when an FBI friend is murdered during a raid.

A Look Back:

Bruce Neckels played the role of federal agent Lew Jonas in "Knight of a Thousand Devils" thanks to a friendship with the episode's director. Neckels recalls, "I'd done a series pilot for Universal Studios in San Francisco in 1977 and Gino Grimaldi was one of the producers. When Gino told me he was going to direct a *Knight Rider* episode, I told him that I wanted to be in his very first show. "Knight of a Thousand Devils" was his directing debut. The cast and crew respected him. He knew the show very well as he was the producer from the very beginning. Gino was all business and very much in control. Gino and I are best friends to this day and we have just completed a screenplay together. Years ago, I became an ordained minister and when Gino found out about it, he asked me to perform his daughter's wedding ceremony"!

Neckels remembers his short time on the episode, and how friendly David Hasselhoff was. "My scenes were done in two hours. David was very professional. He knew his lines, showed up on time and never kept the cast or crew waiting. He was very friendly and very giving as an actor. There were no ego trips". Though Neckels had a cameo role in his friend's episode, he did return frequently to the series. "The casting directors liked my voice and brought me in for several other episodes to do voice-overs, which was a lot of fun".

Knight Knotes:

- NBC's comments on the script: "Notes given will pace script to give it more heart."

Script to Screen:

- This episode marks the only time that Michael lends his comlink to RC3. The script says that RC3 smiles at this "upgrade in status".
- A scene during the warehouse fire where K.I.T.T. says that his power plant cannot withstand the extreme heat is found in the script, but not the episode. The script then says that "K.I.T.T.'s engine hesitates; makes a sickly whine; then finally roars with authority."

K.I.T.T.'s Capabilities:

- Auto Cruise, Grappling Hook, Medical Scan, Pursuit, Silent Mode, Winch

PROD. #60220

$$\left[\begin{array}{c} \text{EPISODE} \\ 80 \end{array}\right]$$

Script History:

October 7, 1985 (F.R.)

October 29, 1985 (F.R.)

November 6, 1985 (F.R.)

November 7, 1985 (F.R.)

November 11, 1985 (F.R.)

November 18, 1985 (F.R.)

November 19, 1985 (F.R.)

November 25, 1985 (F.R.)

HILLS OF FIRE

Written By: Jackson Gillis

Directed By: Robert E. L. Bralver

Original Airdate: February 14, 1986 (Friday, 8:00 PM) (21.0%; 18,040,000)

Filming Dates: November 18-26, 1985

"It's always nice to give credit where credit is due."

-K.I.T.T.

Crew: Robert Foster (Executive Producer), Burton Armus (Supervising Producer), Bruce Lansbury (Supervising Producer), Gino Grimaldi (Producer), Glen A. Larson (Creator), Gregory S. Dinallo (Co-Producer), Robert Ewing (Coordinating Producer), Michael Eric Stein (Story Editor), Ron Martinez (Associate Producer/Unit Production Manager), Bruce Golin (Associate Producer), Stu Phillips (Theme), Don Peake (Music), H. John Penner (Director of Photography), Lou Montejano (Art Director), Dayle Mustain (Editor) Roberto Villar (First Assistant Director), Bruce A. Humphrey (Second Assistant Director), Donna Dockstader (Casting), R. Lynn Smartt (Set Decorator), John Shouse (Sound Editor), Richard Lapham (Music Editor), Barry Downing (Costume Supervisor), Karen J. Braverman (Costume Supervisor), Jack Gill (2nd Unit Director/Stunt Coordinator), Pat Somerset (Sound), Jeremy Swan (Make-up), Allen Payne (Hairstylist)

Guest Cast: David Raynr (Robert Wilson), Nana Visitor (Sandra Rusk), Zohra Lampert (Tess Hubbard), Tom Simcox (Deputy Bob Clark), Vernon Wells (Darryl Staples), Garret Pearson (Manuel Gomez), Jock Gaynor (Paxton), Jim Lefebyre (Bum), Tim Wise (Ted Flanders)

Devon asks Michael to investigate a mysterious forest fire at a national park.

A Look Back:

Jack Gill recalls working with the design team on the Super Pursuit K.I.T.T.: "My memories with George Barris and Dennis Braid for the Super Pursuit car are fairly complex. We had to sit down and figure out what we could actually do with the car. When all of these things started popping up and pushing out, we wondered if they were really going to be able to withstand the kind of speed I was doing? So we had to take them out to a dry lake bed and test them out. A lot of the time, when you did push the button and all the stuff started popping out and pushing up you got this high speed rattle in the car. That's when things started to break apart and fall off, but George fixed that after about a week of testing. He was able to fix that and stop the car from rattling itself to destruction."

Knight Knotes:

- NBC's comments on the script: "Average script delivered although there is some fun with the drone."
- Nana Visitor is perhaps best known for her role in *Star Trek: Deep Space Nine.*
- K.I.T.T. gains Traction Spikes in this episode.

Script to Screen:

- Wilson's first name is revealed as Robert, and Deputy Clark's first name is Bob.
- Darryl originally rescues a young fox, not a bunny.
- The location at F.L.A.G. where Bonnie unveils the Traction Spikes is known as the Foundation Workroom.
- The description of the first time S.I.D. is activated: "Tiny rods telescope out of S.I.D.'s equator and converge to form a gyrostablizing ring. Three metal probes pop up."
- The lady at the ATM is named Miss Lawrence.
- When Michael launches S.I.D., he imitates Devon and remarks, "Be careful, Sidney!"
- As Darryl is driving K.I.T.T. at the episode's conclusion, K.I.T.T. remarks that he could get used to this as Darryl is "lighter on the steering" and "gentler on the gas".

K.I.T.T.'s Capabilities:

- Audio/Video Record, Auto-Roof Right, CO_2, Infrared, Micro Jam, Passive Laser Restraint System, Police/Radio Frequency, Pursuit, Super Pursuit Mode, Traction Spikes, Voice Projection

PROD. #60232

Script History:

December 23, 1985 (F.R.)

January 14, 1986 (F.R.)

January 15, 1986 (F.R.)

January 15, 1986 (2nd rev.)

$$\left[\begin{array}{c} \text{EPISODE} \\ 81 \end{array}\right]$$

KNIGHT FLIGHT TO FREEDOM

Written By: Gregory S. Dinallo

Directed By: Winrich Kolbe

Original Airdate: February 21, 1986 (Friday, 8:00 PM) (18.1%; 15,550,000)

Filming Dates: January 16-27, 1986

"I never thought I'd see the day."

-K.I.T.T.

Crew: Robert Foster (Executive Producer), Burton Armus (Supervising Producer), Bruce Lansbury (Supervising Producer), Gino Grimaldi (Producer), Glen A. Larson (Creator), Gregory S. Dinallo (Co-Producer), Robert Ewing (Coordinating Producer), Michael Eric Stein (Story Editor), Ron Martinez (Associate Producer/Unit Production Manager), Bruce Golin (Associate Producer), Stu Phillips (Theme), Don Peake (Music), H. John Penner (Director of Photography), Lou Montejano (Art Director), Dayle Mustain (Editor) Roberto Villar (First Assistant Director), Richard Coad (Second Assistant Director), Donna Dockstader (Casting), R. Lynn Smartt (Set Decorator), John Shouse (Sound Editor), Richard Lapham (Music Editor), Barry Downing (Costume Supervisor), Karen J. Braverman (Costume Supervisor), Jack Gill (2nd Unit Director/Stunt Coordinator), Pat Somerset (Sound), Jeremy Swan (Make-up), Allen Payne (Hairstylist)

Guest Cast: Lina Raymond (Lisa Corrales), Miguel Fernandes (Colonel Peralta), Kip Niven (Tom Harrington), Eloy Casados (Raoul), William Marquez (President Sosa), Santos Morales (Martinez), Philip Morris (Soldier in Jail), Dino Rivera (Soldier), Cory Rand (Guard), Charron McBride (Laurette Harrington)

Michael and RC3 head to Mexico to rescue a political prisoner during a military takeover.

A Look Back:

Eloy Casados had been working in TV and movies for sixteen years before landing the role of Raoul in this episode. Casados was born in California but admits that his Latino looks were an advantage to landing some roles, including this one. "Back then, there were a lot of casting calls for

Latino bad guys and victims. I can look and sound Latino and the part of my character Raoul was a smart, covert, double agent type."

Casados recalls one incident in K.I.T.T. that was not part of the script. "The crew told David to drive K.I.T.T. about a quarter of a mile or more from the camera. David was alone in the car and he turned to me and said 'Eloy, have you ever done a one eighty?' I said 'no', and with that he said 'jump into K.I.T.T. and tighten your seatbelt'. I did and David sped K.I.T.T. down the road and then hit the brakes and spun us around in a cloud of dust and burning rubber. My first and only one eighty, with someone who knew how to do it, was a bonus thrill of acting with a crazy guy. You know, it wasn't in the script - David did it just for the fun of it."

"Knight Flight to Freedom" is most remembered for the scene where K.I.T.T. is driving through lava from the volcanic spill. "I have no formal training in acting so I don't remember what method I used to pretend we were driving K.I.T.T. through red hot lava", recalls Casados. "I had never seen *Knight Rider* previously and I do remember asking David how K.I.T.T. can drive through lava. David laughed and said, 'Don't think about it, K.I.T.T. can do anything - it's TV'. While driving through the lava I remember they used red lights that they flashed on us and Winrich Kolbe, the director, was looking at me to act more worried and scared but I started laughing. It was at that point that David and Lina laughed also. I screamed at K.I.T.T. to turn the air conditioner on. They had no choice but to cut the scene until David, Lina and I composed ourselves and stopped laughing. Sometimes acting is being serious between laughing."

Casados remembers one memorization technique that David Hasselhoff used while filming "Knight Flight to Freedom". "While David and I sat in K.I.T.T., I asked if we could rehearse some lines of the scene we were about to shoot. David turned to me and said that he didn't know his lines and then proceeded to tape pieces of paper with his lines on them to the dashboard and rear view mirror. He just read his lines off the dashboard and mirror when we shot that scene with us in the car. Some actors work like that and I am always cool with it. Some actors know their lines AND mine", jokes Casados.

The right hand blind drive car (#1198) (Photo courtesy of Christopher Orlando)

Casados only has the fondest memories of David Hasselhoff. "It was a pleasure working with David. We were not familiar with each other's work before filming, but during and after we became pals. I do remember David would always check and primp his hair in the mirror between takes. Jokingly, I asked him if he ever acts with his hair messed up and he replied that his 'do' stayed in place because it was an award-winning hairdo in Germany. David behaved like a very lucky regular guy with a great job."

During filming, Casados had the opportunity to give his neighbor an experience he would never forget. "My next door neighbor's kid was ten years old at the time and he loved *Knight Rider*. I invited him on the set and he met David. When he saw K.I.T.T., he was stone cold frozen. I think it made his day and his life."

Casados has been working as an actor for over forty years and has seen many changes in how TV is filmed. "Back then, the crews were mostly older grizzled men who smoked and drank a lot. Now the crews are younger with no smoking and everybody communicates with headsets and walkie-talkies. The bad guys and victims have gone from Latino types to Middle East types and computers have changed Hollywood and the world - wasn't K.I.T.T. a computer?"

There was one piece of final advice that David Hasselhoff passed on to Casados.

"I still have never heard him sing - he warned me not to ask. I thought that David had a healthy self-depreciating sense of humor about himself."

Lina Raymond starred as Lisa Corrales in "Knight Flight to Freedom", one of the series' final episodes. "My strongest recollection from doing this show was when we were back at the studio shooting and I was in the passenger seat of K.I.T.T. One of the stunt drivers was on the floor on the driver's side maneuvering the car and he was driving very fast. I think he was using his hands, just whipping around various buildings in the narrow thruways on the lot. If I appear terrified in that scene, I can tell you that wasn't acting."

This episode deals with a political coup with Raymond's character as both a news reporter and a guerrilla leader. "With all the uprisings in oppressed countries currently taking place, I find it quite interesting that we shot a political themed episode back in 1986. I'm glad children watched this, and I'm glad that my character helped the coup," says Raymond.

Ironically, Raymond had experienced a real life political coup that put Colonel Perata's plans in perspective. "I once did a mini-series (1985's *The Key to Rebecca*) where we were shooting in Tunisia. Libyan leader Gaddafi was literally next door to the hotel where the cast and crew were housed. Gaddafi was positioning to take over the country from the old and ailing leader. Men with machine guns were a common sight. It was nice that the *Knight Rider* episode was pretend."

Raymond has fond memories of David Hasselhoff. "I remember David as being very sweet and professional. He seemed to be enjoying starring in the show, and he was quite energetic and enthusiastic."

Raymond admits that there were frustrations being an actress in Hollywood at that time. "One aspect I found bizarre and unfortunate, and looking back now even more so, was how I was almost always cast as an exotic - someone who wasn't American. I'm your basic American of mixed ancestry (French, Irish, Native American, English), but since I was a brunette with exotic eyes, I was always cast as anything but American. This included roles as a robot, a genie, harem-girl, belly-dancer and even an extra-terrestrial alien (but it *was* kind of fun)," admits Raymond. "Fortunately, times have changed in the right direction and that is usually not the case anymore."

Raymond had starred in a whole host of TV shows in the 1970's and 80's including *The Incredible Hulk*, *Automan* and *Manimal*, but in 1992, Raymond quit the business. "I was a television actress during this period primarily to make a living in a manner that gave me plenty of opportunity to spend quality time raising my son. I have had several creative careers throughout my life, but I am basically an artist. Though a huge fan of fine films and good television, I was never truly comfortable using myself as the medium. I quit acting when my son left for college and then began my next endeavor." Raymond is now a successful artist and has exhibits of her work frequently.

Knight Knotes:

- Miguel Fernandes once again played the bad guy against David Hasselhoff in the 1996 television movie *Gridlock*.

- RC3 is whistling "The Star Spangled Banner" while mopping in the Mexican prison.

- This episode marks the 123rd, and final, turbo boost for the series. It is also the final time we see K.I.T.T. in convertible mode.

- Devon quotes *Mission: Impossible* here: "Should you or one of your people be caught or captured, the Foundation will disavow any knowledge of your activities."

- This episode marks one of the rare times that Michael is separated from his comlink. See "The Final Verdict", "Knightmares", and "Burial Ground" for others.

Script to Screen:

- Colonel Peralta was originally a General.

- The script mentions that Peralta's lieutenant should always be seen wearing a hat and dark glasses to conceal his identity. This is so RC3 can slip into that role in the episode's climax.

- A description of K.I.T.T. getting his disguise applied: "K.I.T.T. is being camouflaged by Martinez and his men who are tying battered suitcases and household items atop his roof and hood. One of them has a brush and bucket of muddy water and is "painting" K.I.T.T. Martinez lashes an old tire over his grille, then crosses, opens K.I.T.T.'s door, and gestures. As Michael (Levi jacket, T-shirt, worn jeans), Lisa and Raoul get in." K.I.T.T. comments that it's even worse than the time he went undercover in a junkyard as a crushed car.

- Lisa's undercover name that she gives to the guard at the checkpoint is Lizabetta Corazon.

K.I.T.T.'s Capabilities:

- Anharmonic Synthesizer, Auto Cruise, Convertible Mode, Passive Laser Restraint System, Printer, Pursuit, Pyroclastic Lamination, Trunk Lid, Turbo Boost, Voice Projection

PROD. #60223

$$\left[\begin{array}{c} \text{EPISODE} \\ 82 \end{array} \right]$$

Script History:

January 10, 1986 (F.R.)

January 16, 1986 (F.R.)

FRIGHT KNIGHT

Working Title: "Knight Fright"

Teleplay By: James Byrnes, Samm Smith, Leonard Kaufman

Story By: James Byrnes, Samm Smith

Directed By: Gilbert Shilton

Original Airdate: March 7, 1986 (Friday, 8:00 PM) (18.1%; 15,550,000)

Filming Dates: January 24 – February 3, 1986

"All this picture needs is one more jackrabbit-mobile."

-Buck

Crew: Robert Foster (Executive Producer), Burton Armus (Supervising Producer), Bruce Lansbury (Supervising Producer), Gino Grimaldi (Producer), Glen A. Larson (Creator), Gregory S. Dinallo (Co-Producer), Robert Ewing (Coordinating Producer), Michael Eric Stein (Story Editor), Ron Martinez (Associate Producer/Unit Production Manager), Bruce Golin (Associate Producer), Stu Phillips (Theme), Don Peake (Music), H. John Penner (Director of Photography), Lou Montejano (Art Director), Grant Hoag (Editor) Louis Race (First Assistant Director), Richard Coad (Second Assistant Director), Donna Dockstader (Casting), R. Lynn Smartt (Set Decorator), John Shouse (Sound Editor), Richard Lapham (Music Editor), Barry Downing (Costume Supervisor), Karen J. Braverman (Costume Supervisor), Jack Gill (2nd Unit Director/Stunt Coordinator), Pat Somerset (Sound), Jeremy Swan (Make-up), Allen Payne (Hairstylist)

Guest Cast: Michael Callan (Victor Gaven), Antony Ponzini (Mel Tobey), Lenore Kasdorf (Karen Bennett), Robert Englund (Edward Kent), Leann Hunley (Liz Preston), Richard X. Slattery (Sam Clifford), Pat Buttram (Buck), Hank Worden (Slim), Jerri Parros (Girl), Matt McColm (Clayton Travis), Harold "Hal" Frizzell (Studio Security Guard)

When reports of a Phantom begin to circulate on the set of the movie *Raging Sky* and one of the stuntmen is injured, Michael takes over as the movie's new stuntman while investigating the rumors.

A Look Back:

Actress Lenore Kasdorf re-appears in this episode as Karen Bennett, a movie producer trying to figure out who is sabotaging her picture, *Raging Sky*. Kasdorf previously appeared in season three's "Lost Knight". "I don't think I had to audition for this role. Much like my numerous guest appearances on *Murder, She Wrote*, once I had appeared on the show, I didn't have to audition again for subsequent appearances."

When Michael Knight first meets Karen, she is having an intense meeting in her office with the director over *Raging Sky*'s budget. Kasdorf recalls, "The office we used to film that scene was in the black Universal Studios tower. It was the office of *Knight Rider's* executive producer." Filming of this scene took place on January 28, 1986, the day of the space shuttle Challenger tragedy. "I remember that we took a break in filming to watch the shuttle launch and sat in horror as it blew apart....and then, had to continue shooting in total shock. It was awful."

"Fright Knight" was filmed entirely on the Universal Studios back lot, which meant that tourists on the back lot tour would get a glimpse of *Knight Rider's* filming. "It's so neat to see some of the old back lot attractions in this episode, such as *Jaws*. I remember that filming would halt any time a Tram tour came through the area. It was a huge moneymaker for Universal." Kasdorf also recalls how David Hasselhoff brought a very special fan to the set to see the filming. "David came through with a child suffering from cancer. The boy's dream came true through the Make-A-Wish Foundation. He just wanted to meet 'the *Knight Rider*' and David was so sweet to him. I asked David, 'How do you do it?' and he replied that it was just so worth it."

In fact, Kasdorf has nothing but fond memories of working with David Hasselhoff. "I met David when we were co-presenters at the 1981 Daytime Emmys. Years after *Knight Rider* ended, in the early 90's, I remember that I was dressed from an audition and walked into a Starbucks. Out of the blue, someone starts yelling for me! Instead of him saying something like, 'It's me, David', he starts yelling '*Knight Rider! Baywatch!*' instead of his name! It was quite funny."

In 2004, Kasdorf was paralyzed from a spinal infection. While she eventually regained the use of her legs, she decided to retire from acting. "As

I was recovering, my daughter and I attended a funeral for an acquaintance. I was still confined to a wheelchair and couldn't make it into the service, so my daughter and I waited outside, knowing that we were there in spirit. When the service let out, I watched the people leaving. Hardly anyone noticed me since I was in a wheelchair and below their line of sight. Then I heard a voice coming from the top of the stairs saying, 'Hey, what happened to you?'. It was David. He immediately came down the stairs to make sure I was okay. That's just the type of guy he is. I will never forget it."

Peter Parros recalls filming on a working studio lot. "The Universal lot is fun to shoot on. This was before the studio tour was as big as it is now, so it was very exciting to see the special effects. I think we shot here because the producers were trying to save on the budget for the last few episodes to see if we could get a fifth season. The show was doing great in the prime time rating, but they were trying to make a better financial deal for syndication. On the positive side, they had some great guest stars in the last few episodes.

"Fright Knight" is a horror themed episode but Parros likes to keep away from the genre. "I'm not a fan of horror movies, but my daughter, Petra, is. Still, I did enjoy meeting Robert Englund of *A Nightmare on Elm Street* fame. He's a very talented actor, even though he's mostly known for playing Freddy Krueger."

"Fright Knight" also contained a cameo from Parros' wife, Jerri. "I think the episode came up a few minutes short after editing," confirms Parros. "Burt Armus knew that my wife had done some acting and the scene was written specifically for her/us. In the scene, Jerri's character mistakes RC for OJ Simpson. Incidentally, my first national commercial was a Hertz commercial. In that commercial, they needed to recreate footage of OJ playing football in college at USC. I played OJ! It was great fun for both of us. It's the only opportunity we've had to work together."

There have been rumors for years that Stage 28 at Universal Studios is haunted with the Phantom of the Opera. "There was no phantom that I heard of at Universal," recalls producer Burton Armus. "That story was simply implied so we could stay on the Universal lot for the entire episode. You'll notice different buildings in that episode and that was all at Universal. I remember that we had Robert Englund starring in the episode. He was a very good actor and really professional. He had been on *V*, but he became a star later. Because of this, we could bring him in and pay him a normal salary. In fact, we hardly ever had to pay above the going rate to bring guest stars in. They were paid well but within industry standards."

Knight Knotes:

- NBC's comments on the script: "Uninspired first draft reflects a lower production budget. Better re-write delivered."
- The Phantom's gray SUV that Michael chases through the movie studio's lot appears to have some movie magic of its own: When the SUV first crashes through a fence before the chase starts, it has no front license plate. A few seconds later, it sports the California license plate 7FZF177. At the end of the chase, the plate is numbered 1H8A115. Also, the robotic motorcycle first has a license plate of CA 3W6810, but after it crashes, the plate reads CA 67Z345.
- Peter Parros' wife, Jerri, plays the girl that cannot get her motorized cart to start.
- As Michael and K.I.T.T. are cruising through the studio back lot, they pass Carrie Haver's show car from "Custom K.I.T.T."
- A sharp eye can spot the archway that leads to Devon's office set during the scene where Michael saves Liz from the falling light.
- This episode uses the Universal Studios back lot extensively throughout the story, especially during the climactic chase sequence.

During the chase, a quick eye can spot the remains of a Colonial Viper from *Battlestar Galactica*, the Monkey Bar from *Tales of the Gold Monkey*, and the rotating ice tunnel from *The Six Million Dollar Man*. During Michael's search for the phantom in the warehouse, a Cylon costume can be seen, also from *Battlestar Galactica*. Vocal references include *Ghostbusters* ("Just call us phantom busters!"), *Conan the Barbarian* ("There's enough stuff in here to make *Conan 3, 4 and 5*") and *Psycho* (Michael states "Hitchcock would've loved it... we've got a saboteur on our hands." Devon replies, "Let's hope it's not a psycho."). Other references include K.I.T.T. activating the shark from *Jaws* to use as a distraction, a chase scene through *The Ten Commandments* tour attraction and a movie marquee for 1954's *Cattle Queen of Montana*.

Script to Screen:

- Magee Studios was originally named Millennium Studios.
- The stuntman who is injured at the start of the story is named Clayton Travis; Sam Clifford's first name was originally Andy.
- The Phantom of Stage 28 was originally The Phantom of Stage 12.
- K.I.T.T. drives himself through the studio back lot, but since it's Hollywood, no one bats an eye to a car driving by itself.
- Instead of Liz being nearly flattened by a falling light, she instead suffers from a cut brake line while performing her stunt in the 4x4 (which takes place outdoors, not on a set). Michael pulls K.I.T.T. up next to her, jumps over to grab her and then jumps back to K.I.T.T. right before the 4x4 hits a concrete barrier and explodes.
- While investigating Stage 12, the Phantom traps Michael in an air duct and turns on a giant fan. The fan throws Michael against the

side and he's knocked unconscious. K.I.T.T. micro jams the fan controls and Michael exits the duct through a hatch.

- The Phantom crashes the set in a stunt car loaded with machine guns hidden in the grille.

- During the climatic chase scene through the back lot, K.I.T.T. turbo boosts over a parking lot to the dismay of the tourists watching below.

K.I.T.T.'s Capabilities:

- Auto Cruise, Auto-Roof Left, Medical Scan, Micro Jam, Polyphonic Synthesizer, Pursuit, Silent Mode, Tinted Windows

PROD. #60233

{ EPISODE
83 }

Script History:

January 27, 1986 (F.R.)

January 30, 1986 (F.R.)

February 3, 1986 (F.R.)

KNIGHT OF THE RISING SUN

Teleplay By: E. Nick Alexander

Story By: Burton Armus and Bruce Lansbury

Directed By: Winrich Kolbe

Original Airdate: March 14, 1986 (Friday, 8:00 PM) (19.4%; 16,660,000)

Filming Dates: February 5-13, 1986

"You gonna let me see this baby stuff its stuff?"

-Coy O'Brien

Crew: Robert Foster (Executive Producer), Burton Armus (Supervising Producer), Bruce Lansbury (Supervising Producer), Gino Grimaldi (Producer), Glen A. Larson (Creator), Gregory S. Dinallo (Co-Producer), Robert Ewing (Coordinating Producer), Michael Eric Stein (Story Editor), Ron Martinez (Associate Producer/Unit Production Manager), Bruce Golin (Associate Producer), Stu Phillips (Theme), Don Peake (Music), H. John Penner (Director of Photography), Lou Montejano (Art Director), Domenic G. DiMascio (Editor) Roberto Villar (First Assistant Director), Richard Coad (Second Assistant Director), Donna Dockstader (Casting), R. Lynn Smartt (Set Decorator), John Shouse (Sound Editor), Richard Lapham (Music Editor), Barry Downing (Costume Supervisor), Karen J. Braverman (Costume Supervisor), Jack Gill (Stunt Coordinator), Pat Somerset (Sound), Jeremy Swan (Make-up), Allen Payne (Hairstylist)

Guest Cast: Ken Swofford (Nick O'Brien), George Kee Cheung (Suki Tanika), Rummel Mor (Coy O'Brien), Bill Saito (Gobi), Michael Chong (Kumita), Seth Mitchell (Guard), Paul Tuerpe (Foreman), William Christopher Ford (Ninja), Tadashi Yamashita (Ninja)

Michael must stop a dangerous businessman from kidnapping a young boy who is part of a complex Japanese tradition.

A Look Back:

In order to keep K.I.T.T. looking pristine, even when criminals would beat on the car with a baseball bat, the stunt crew would sometimes place a shell over the Trans Am that could absorb all of the abuse from these stunts. Jack Gill recalls, "The shell is a hard and heavy polyurethane form that looks exactly like a car body with no windows or windshield. It took 4 guys to lift it onto the K.I.T.T. car and it stayed in place because it was molded to fit perfectly, so it did fit like the skin of an onion. We used to always say on the set, 'Let's peel the body off and put a fresh car underneath.' It was only a figure of speech. I guess it was cooler to say 'peel' the body off rather than 'lift' the body off. Either way, after an action scene, when the polyurethane body came off, K.I.T.T. was always dented and had to be repaired."

Knight Knotes:

- NBC's comments on the script: "First draft was confused. Slight improved re-write delivered. This episode is fairly well directed but suffers due to lack of action."

- The front gate to Tanika's house was also used in "Chariot of Gold" and "Knight Sting".

- Notice that Tanika's ninjas are all dressed in black outfits with a red stripe showing a parallel with Michael and K.I.T.T.

- When Michael and RC pull up to O'Brien's warehouse to stop the ninjas at the start of the episode, look in the far background of the scene and you will see a second K.I.T.T. car parked in front of a van.

- This is one of Peter Parros' favorite episodes.

K.I.T.T.'s Capabilities:

- Audio/Video Record, Auto Cruise, Auto Phone, Auto-Roof Left, Eject Left, Micro Jam, Passive Laser Restraint System, Pursuit, Super Pursuit Mode, Ultrasonic Frequency

PROD. #60225

[EPISODE
84]

Script History:

February 5, 1986 (F.R.)

February 6, 1986 (F.R.)

February 10, 1986 (F.R.)

February 12, 1986 (F.R.)

February 13, 1986 (F.R.)

February 18, 1986 (F.R.)

VOO DOO KNIGHT

Working Title: "Voodoo Knight"

Teleplay By: R. Timothy Kring and Deborah Dean Davis

Story By: R. Timothy Kring

Directed By: Georg Fenady

Original Airdate: April 4, 1986 (Friday, 8:00 PM) (18.6%; 15,980,000)

Filming Dates: February 18-25, 1986

"Sorry Harana, but a stolen crown never made a man a king nor woman a

princess."

-Michael

Crew: Robert Foster (Executive Producer), Burton Armus (Supervising Producer), Bruce Lansbury (Supervising Producer), Gino Grimaldi (Producer), Glen A. Larson (Creator), Gregory S. Dinallo (Co-Producer), Robert Ewing (Coordinating Producer), Michael Eric Stein (Story Editor), Ron Martinez (Associate Producer/Unit Production Manager), Bruce Golin (Associate Producer), Stu Phillips (Theme), Don Peake (Music), H. John Penner (Director of Photography), Lou Montejano (Art Director), Edward Nassour (Editor) Louis Race (First Assistant Director), Richard Coad (Second Assistant Director), Donna Dockstader (Casting), R. Lynn Smartt (Set Decorator), John Shouse (Sound Editor), Richard Lapham (Music Editor), Barry Downing (Costume Supervisor), Karen J. Braverman (Costume Supervisor), Jack Gill (Stunt Coordinator), Pat Somerset (Sound), Jeremy Swan (Make-up), Allen Payne (Hairstylist)

Guest Cast: Rosalind Cash (Harana/Bonita Vance), Christie Hauser (Elizabeth Wesley), Henry Gibson (Donald Crane), John Vernon (Claude Watkins), Chuck Lindsly (Guard), Dick Durock (Max), Allan Graf (Jarrett), Charles Davis (Jeremy Towers)

During Michael's investigation of a jeweler's suicide, he is hypnotized into driving into a condemned building marked for demolition.

A Look Back:

Producer Burton Armus recalls the show's cancellation. "When we wrapped the final episode, which was 'Voo Doo Knight', nobody knew that there would not be a season 5. No one knew that *Knight Rider* would end. Season 4 was within budget, the show was still successful and Universal was happy with the ratings. Season 5, up to then, was going to happen. The problem was selling the syndication rights. At that time, when a studio sold the rights, they would get $1.5 million for 110 episodes, which was seen as a complete package. *Knight Rider* had done 84 episodes, but if you count the doubles we had 90. We didn't get any offers for $1.5 million. To be honest, the studio would have accepted for $1 million. In the end, they received an offer for $100,000. This was embarrassing for them. Usually, the network can be responsible for canceling a show, but in *Knight Rider's* case, it was the studio. Universal canceled *Knight Rider*. It was a shame and I told them that we should film a season 5. I promised them that I would bring in each episode for under $900,000, but they were not interested. If they had received a good enough offer for syndication, there would definitely have been a season 5, no question. But in 1986, the market for such things had gone down."

Peter Parros never thought that "Voo Doo Knight" would be *Knight Rider's* curtain call. He even had an idea for RC if a fifth season had been given the green light. "*Knight Rider* was a hit, so I was sure there was going to be a season 5. When RC3's motorcycle was destroyed, I was sure that I'd be coming back the next year with something special. My hope was that the Foundation was going to build RC a hi-tech motorcycle... or something else."

Parros believes he was in "the perfect job" when the show ended. "I was totally bummed. At the time, it made no sense to me. The show was still extremely popular. We were winning our time slot. I loved the show and the character that I was playing and the people I was working with. For me, it was the perfect job. I was really upset that the show was cancelled and we couldn't keep going. NBC wanted to renew the show another year, but Universal wasn't getting the money they wanted for syndication. At that time, sitcoms were big, so *Knight Rider, Airwolf*, and all of those big action shows that Universal was doing - they were just shutting them down. So, they were trying to work out a deal and if you notice, the last few episodes, like 'Fright Knight' and 'Voo Doo Knight', they were shooting on the Universal lot trying to bring the cost down to convince Universal to go for another season and just shoot it for the licensing fee. We really had a lot of hope until the very end that we were going to get another year."

Knight Knotes:

- NBC's comments on the script: "By-the-numbers, low budget script delivered. Dailies have been weak. Weak, actionless rough cut screened on 3/6."
- Patricia McPherson is not in this episode due to a prior film commitment. "At the end of the '85-'86 season," recalls McPherson, "I was working on an action/adventure film where I played a diver. The dive knife came up out of the sheath in a running scene and cut my Achilles tendon in half and that took a year to heal."

Script to Screen:

- The script notes that to be sure that the director "establish that all three of them are wearing the same kind of ear clips that are used to discourage smoking, drinking and motion sickness."
- The script states that "Sharp Dressed Man" by ZZ Top was to be played during the opening act, not "Tush".

Featured Songs:

"Tush" by ZZ Top

K.I.T.T.'s Capabilities:

- Auto Cruise, Electronic Field Disruptor, Medical Scan, Pursuit, Signal, Surveillance Mode

About the Authors

Joe Huth IV has been actively involved with the *Knight Rider* community for the past 15 years. In 2002, he authored Knight Rider Legacy: The Unofficial Guide to the Knight Rider Universe, along with other specialized *Knight Rider* books. Joe lives in Pennsylvania with his wife and son.

David Bronstein has regularly written for online media in film, sports and music. He has lived in England, Australia and France and is an expert on American film and television. David resides near Paris, France.

Manufactured by Amazon.ca
Bolton, ON